A Casebook on Henry James

"The Turn of the Screw"

CROWELL LITERARY CASEBOOKS

Under the General Editorship of William Van O'Connor

PUBLISHED

A Casebook on Ezra Pound
Edited by William Van O'Connor and Edward Stone

A Casebook on Henry James's "The Turn of the Screw"
Edited by Gerald Willen

IN PREPARATION

A Casebook on Dylan Thomas
Edited by John Malcolm Brinnin

A Casebook on Othello
Edited by Leonard Dean

A Casebook on Henry James's

"The Turn of the Screw"

EDITED BY Gerald Willen

FAIRLEIGH DICKINSON UNIVERSITY

THOMAS Y. CROWELL COMPANY, NEW YORK · ESTABLISHED 1834

FIRST PRINTING, NOVEMBER, 1959
SECOND PRINTING, JANUARY, 1960

Library of Congress Catalog Card Number: 60-6066

Manufactured in the United States of America
By the Vail-Ballou Press, Inc., Binghamton, N.Y.

Contents

Introduction 1

HENRY JAMES
The Turn of the Screw 3

HENRY JAMES
From the Preface to *The Aspern Papers* 95

EDNA KENTON
Henry James to the Ruminant Reader: The Turn of the Screw 102

EDMUND WILSON
The Ambiguity of Henry James 115

NATHAN BRYLLION FAGIN
Another Reading of *The Turn of the Screw* 154

A RADIO SYMPOSIUM: KATHERINE ANNE PORTER, ALLEN TATE, MARK VAN DOREN
James: "The Turn of the Screw" 160

A. J. A. WALDOCK
Mr. Edmund Wilson and *The Turn of the Screw* 171

ROBERT HEILMAN
The Turn of the Screw as Poem 174

GLENN A. REED
Another Turn on James's "The Turn of the Screw" 189

OLIVER EVANS
James's Air of Evil: *The Turn of the Screw* 200

CHARLES G. HOFFMANN
Innocence and Evil in James's *The Turn of the Screw* 212

OSCAR CARGILL
Henry James as Freudian Pioneer 223

JOHN SILVER
A Note on the Freudian Reading of "The Turn of the Screw" 239

HAROLD C. GODDARD
A Pre-Freudian Reading of *The Turn of the Screw* 244

JOHN LYDENBERG
The Governess Turns the Screws 273

JOSEPH J. FIREBAUGH
Inadequacy in Eden: Knowledge and *The Turn of the Screw* 291

ALEXANDER E. JONES
Point of View in *The Turn of the Screw* 298

Bibliography 319

Exercises 323

A Casebook on Henry James's "The Turn of the Screw"

Introduction

In many ways "The Turn of the Screw" is a rewarding work to set before students. The reading of it demands close and serious attention; the critical problems it raises appear to be endless. Certainly it continues to arouse controversy in the critical and learned journals more than sixty years after its publication. As the subject, therefore, of a controlled research project, it affords students an opportunity to sharpen their reading, analytical, and critical abilities.

Whatever one may think of Edmund Wilson's reading of "The Turn of the Screw," the Freudian interpretation has triggered a great deal of discussion. Though there is a tendency now to discount Wilson's interpretation, students are inclined to accept it, at least until they have pondered some of the other analyses. Then, sooner or later, the more venturesome will attempt original readings, rising, as it were, to the challenge of the story. But even those who remain convinced by Wilson, or who accept, let us say, Heilman's reading, will defend their views with much conviction and, on occasion, passion.

In reading over the essays in this book, one may be struck by the fact that few, if any, critics take into account Douglas's role apart from that as reader of the manuscript entrusted to him. And he is worth pondering over. He is ten years younger than the governess whose manuscript he reads; Miles, in the story proper, "is scarce ten years old," the governess twenty. There is a corresponding parallel between Douglas's sister and Flora. Douglas says, before he begins reading the tale, that the governess had been in love. A member of the audience, a Mrs. Griffin, implies strongly that Douglas was in love with the governess.*

* Is it possible, then, that Douglas is Miles? That the governess, in love with Miles (Douglas), and unable to act in the situation, herself wrote a *story*,

Selecting the critical essays for this book posed the usual problems. Obviously everything written on "The Turn of the Screw" could not be included. And it was thought inadvisable to reprint excerpts, dealing with the story, from longer works on James or related subjects. The inclusion of fifteen complete essays, with "The Turn of the Screw" itself and James's remarks on it, will more than serve to awaken the reader to the possibilities of the subject. Moreover, books are more readily available in libraries than are periodicals. Instructors who desire their students to have some familiarity with the views of Joseph Warren Beach, Marius Bewley, Leon Edel, Philip Rahv, and others may have them read in the books that are starred in the bibliography.

With the exceptions noted below, the essays have been reprinted as they appeared originally. Footnotes have been left unchanged on the theory that students ought to simulate as closely as possible the techniques of original research. To have omitted the footnotes, or to have had them correspond to the pages in this book, would have had the undesirable effect of removing the student further from original research.

Only the Preface to *The Aspern Papers* is not reprinted in its entirety. The Charles Demuth drawings that accompanied Edna Kenton's article have been omitted. Edmund Wilson's third (1948) version of "The Ambiguity of Henry James" is reprinted in full, though it does not deal specifically with "The Turn of the Screw" for a greater part of its length. Mr. Wilson has furnished a postscript, dated 1959, for inclusion in this book.

---

a fiction? And, finally, that Douglas as a child, as well as a young man down from Trinity, was in love with the governess? These implications may be inferred from the story, although Douglas's precise relationship to the governess is not closely defined. But even if there is an understated connection between Douglas and the governess, the interpretations developed by various critics are not necessarily invalidated. For the essential fact remains that the story told by the governess needs to be read at varying levels. This is all the more true if we say that her story is, in effect, a fiction.

On the other hand, ruling out the possibility of an ulterior motive (involving Douglas) on the part of the governess, we may still maintain that her manuscript is not a true story at all, that it is a work of fiction she had already committed to paper before relating orally to Douglas. Or she may have made it up as she went along and then written it down. Whatever "The Turn of the Screw" is, however, a "true story" or a fiction, it still retains all its challenges.

The Turn of the Screw

Henry James

The story had held us, round the fire, sufficiently breathless, but except the obvious remark that it was gruesome, as, on Christmas eve in an old house, a strange tale should essentially be, I remember no comment uttered till somebody happened to say that it was the only case he had met in which such a visitation had fallen on a child. The case, I may mention, was that of an apparition in just such an old house as had gathered us for the occasion—an appearance, of a dreadful kind, to a little boy sleeping in the room with his mother and waking her up in the terror of it; waking her not to dissipate his dread and soothe him to sleep again, but to encounter also, herself, before she had succeeded in doing so, the same sight that had shaken him. It was this observation that drew from Douglas—not immediately, but later in the evening—a reply that had the interesting consequence to which I call attention. Someone else told a story not particularly effective, which I saw he was not following. This I took for a sign that he had himself something to produce and that we should only have to wait. We waited in fact till two nights later; but that same evening, before we scattered, he brought out what was in his mind.

"I quite agree—in regard to Griffin's ghost, or whatever it was—that its appearing first to the little boy, at so tender an age, adds a particular touch. But it's not the first occurrence of its charming

SOURCE: Appeared originally as a serial in *Collier's Weekly,* February 5–April 16, 1898. Published in book form in *The Two Magics: The Turn of the Screw, Covering End,* New York: The Macmillan Company, 1898. Revised, it was included in Volume XII of the New York Edition. The present text is that of 1898. Used by permission of Paul R. Reynolds & Sons.

kind that I know to have involved a child. If the child gives the effect another turn of the screw, what do you say to *two* children—?"

"We say, of course," somebody exclaimed, "that they give two turns! Also that we want to hear about them."

I can see Douglas there before the fire, to which he had got up to present his back, looking down at his interlocutor with his hands in his pockets. "Nobody but me, till now, has ever heard. It's quite too horrible." This, naturally, was declared by several voices to give the thing the utmost price, and our friend, with quiet art, prepared his triumph by turning his eyes over the rest of us and going on: "It's beyond everything. Nothing at all that I know touches it."

"For sheer terror?" I remember asking.

He seemed to say it was not so simple as that; to be really at a loss how to qualify it. He passed his hand over his eyes, made a little wincing grimace. "For dreadful—dreadfulness!"

"Oh, how delicious!" cried one of the women.

He took no notice of her; he looked at me, but as if, instead of me, he saw what he spoke of. "For general uncanny ugliness and horror and pain."

"Well then," I said, "just sit right down and begin."

He turned round to the fire, gave a kick to a log, watched it an instant. Then as he faced us again: "I can't begin. I shall have to send to town." There was a unanimous groan at this, and much reproach; after which, in his preoccupied way, he explained. "The story's written. It's in a locked drawer—it has not been out for years. I could write to my man and enclose the key; he could send down the packet as he finds it." It was to me in particular that he appeared to propound this—appeared almost to appeal for aid not to hesitate. He had broken a thickness of ice, the formation of many a winter; had had his reasons for a long silence. The others resented postponement, but it was just his scruples that charmed me. I adjured him to write by the first post and to agree with us for an early hearing; then I asked him if the experience in question had been his own. To this his answer was prompt. "Oh, thank God, no!"

"And is the record yours? You took the thing down?"

"Nothing but the impression. I took that *here*"—he tapped his heart. "I've never lost it."

"Then your manuscript—?"

"Is in old, faded ink, and in the most beautiful hand." He hung fire again. "A woman's. She has been dead these twenty years. She sent me the pages in question before she died." They were all listening now, and of course there was somebody to be arch, or at any rate to draw the inference. But if he put the inference by without a smile it was also without irritation. "She was a most charming person, but she was ten years older than I. She was my sister's governess," he quietly said. "She was the most agreeable woman I've ever known in her position; she would have been worthy of any whatever. It was long ago, and this episode was long before. I was at Trinity, and I found her at home on my coming down the second summer. I was much there that year—it was a beautiful one; and we had, in her off-hours, some strolls and talks in the garden—talks in which she struck me as awfully clever and nice. Oh yes; don't grin: I liked her extremely and am glad to this day to think she liked me too. If she hadn't she wouldn't have told me. She had never told anyone. It wasn't simply that she said so, but that I knew she hadn't. I was sure; I could see. You'll easily judge why when you hear."

"Because the thing had been such a scare?"

He continued to fix me. "You'll easily judge," he repeated: "*you* will."

I fixed him too. "I see. She was in love."

He laughed for the first time. "You *are* acute. Yes, she was in love. That is, she had been. That came out—she couldn't tell her story without its coming out. I saw it, and she saw I saw it; but neither of us spoke of it. I remember the time and the place—the corner of the lawn, the shade of the great beeches and the long, hot summer afternoon. It wasn't a scene for a shudder; but oh—!" He quitted the fire and dropped back into his chair.

"You'll receive the packet Thursday morning?" I inquired.

"Probably not till the second post."

"Well then; after dinner—"

"You'll all meet me here?" He looked us round again. "Isn't anybody going?" It was almost the tone of hope.

"Everybody will stay!"

"*I* will—and *I* will!" cried the ladies whose departure had been fixed. Mrs. Griffin, however, expressed the need for a little more light. "Who was it she was in love with?"

"The story will tell," I took upon myself to reply.

"Oh, I can't wait for the story!"

"The story *won't* tell," said Douglas; "not in any literal, vulgar way."

"More's the pity, then. That's the only way I ever understand."

"Won't *you* tell, Douglas?" somebody else inquired.

He sprang to his feet again. "Yes—tomorrow. Now I must go to bed. Good-night." And quickly catching up a candlestick, he left us slightly bewildered. From our end of the great brown hall we heard his step on the stair; whereupon Mrs. Griffin spoke. "Well, if I don't know who she was in love with, I know who *he* was."

"She was ten years older," said her husband.

"*Raison de plus*—at that age! But it's rather nice, his long reticence."

"Forty years!" Griffin put in.

"With this outbreak at last."

"The outbreak," I returned, "will make a tremendous occasion of Thursday night"; and everyone so agreed with me that, in the light of it, we lost all attention for everything else. The last story, however incomplete and like the mere opening of a serial, had been told; we handshook and "candlestuck," as somebody said, and went to bed.

I knew the next day that a letter containing the key had, by the first post, gone off to his London apartments; but in spite of—or perhaps just on account of—the eventual diffusion of this knowledge we quite let him alone till after dinner, till such an hour of the evening, in fact, as might best accord with the kind of emotion on which our hopes were fixed. Then he became as communicative as we could desire and indeed gave us his best reason for being so. We had it from him again before the fire in the hall, as we had had our mild wonders of the previous night. It appeared that the narrative he had promised to read us really required for a proper intelligence a few words of prologue. Let me say here distinctly, to have done with it, that this narrative, from an exact transcript of my own made much later, is what I shall presently give. Poor Douglas, before his death—when it was in sight—committed to me the manuscript that reached him on the third of these days and that, on the same spot, with immense effect, he began to read to our hushed little circle on the night of the fourth. The departing ladies who had said they would stay didn't, of course, thank heaven, stay: they departed, in consequence of arrangements made, in a rage of curiosity, as they professed, produced by the touches with which he had already worked us up. But that only made his little final auditory more compact and select, kept it, round the hearth, subject to a common thrill.

The first of these touches conveyed that the written statement took up the tale at a point after it had, in a manner, begun. The fact to be in possession of was therefore that his old friend, the youngest of several daughters of a poor country parson, had, at the age of twenty, on taking service for the first time in the schoolroom, come up to London, in trepidation, to answer in person an advertisement that had already placed her in brief correspondence with the advertiser. This person proved, on her presenting herself, for judgment, at a house in Harley Street, that impressed her as vast and imposing —this prospective patron proved a gentleman, a bachelor in the prime of life, such a figure as had never risen, save in a dream or an old novel, before a fluttered, anxious girl out of a Hampshire vicarage. One could easily fix his type; it never, happily, dies out. He was handsome and bold and pleasant, off-hand and gay and kind. He struck her, inevitably, as gallant and splendid, but what took her most of all and gave her the courage she afterwards showed was that he put the whole thing to her as a kind of favour, an obligation he should gratefully incur. She conceived him as rich, but as fearfully extravagant—saw him all in a glow of high fashion, of good looks, of expensive habits, of charming ways with women. He had for his own town residence a big house filled with the spoils of travel and the trophies of the chase; but it was to his country home, an old family place in Essex, that he wished her immediately to proceed.

He had been left, by the death of their parents in India, guardian to a small nephew and a small niece, children of a younger, a military brother, whom he had lost two years before. These children were, by the strangest of chances for a man in his position,—a lone man without the right sort of experience or a grain of patience,—very heavily on his hands. It had all been a great worry and, on his own part doubtless, a series of blunders, but he immensely pitied the poor chicks and had done all he could: had in particular sent them down to his other house, the proper place for them being of course the country, and kept them there, from the first, with the best people he could find to look after them, parting even with his own servants to wait on them and going down himself, whenever he might, to see how they were doing. The awkward thing was that they had practically no other relations and that his own affairs took up all his time. He had put them in possession of Bly, which was healthy and secure, and had placed at the head of their little establishment—but below stairs only—an excellent woman, Mrs. Grose, whom he was sure his visitor would like and who had formerly been maid to his mother. She was now housekeeper and was also acting for the time as superintendent to the little girl, of whom, without children of her own, she was, by good luck, extremely fond. There were plenty of people to help, but of course the young lady who should go down as governess would be in supreme authority. She would also have, in holidays, to look after the small boy, who had been for a term at school—young as he was to be sent, but what else could be done?—and who, as the holidays were about to begin, would be back from one day to the other. There had been for the two children at first a young lady whom they had had the misfortune to lose. She had done for them quite beautifully—she was a most respectable person—till her death, the great awkwardness of which had, precisely, left no alternative but the school for little Miles. Mrs. Grose, since then, in the way of manners and things, had done as she could for Flora; and there were, further, a cook, a housemaid, a dairywoman, an old pony, an old groom, and an old gardener, all likewise thoroughly respectable.

So far had Douglas presented his picture when someone put a question. "And what did the former governess die of?—of so much respectability?"

Our friend's answer was prompt. "That will come out. I don't anticipate."

"Excuse me—I thought that was just what you *are* doing."

"In her successor's place," I suggested, "I should have wished to learn if the office brought with it—"

"Necessary danger to life?" Douglas completed my thought. "She did wish to learn, and she did learn. You shall hear tomorrow what she learnt. Meanwhile, of course, the prospect struck her as slightly grim. She was young, untried, nervous: it was a vision of serious duties and little company, of really great loneliness. She hesitated—took a couple of days to consult and consider. But the salary offered much exceeded her modest measure, and on a second interview she faced the music, she engaged." And Douglas, with this, made a pause that, for the benefit of the company, moved me to throw in—

"The moral of which was of course the seduction exercised by the splendid young man. She succumbed to it."

He got up and, as he had done the night before, went to the fire, gave a stir to a log with his foot, then stood a moment with his back to us. "She saw him only twice."

"Yes, but that's just the beauty of her passion."

A little to my surprise, on this, Douglas turned round to me. "It *was* the beauty of it. There were others," he went on, "who hadn't succumbed. He told her frankly all his difficulty—that for several applicants the conditions had been prohibitive. They were, somehow, simply afraid. It sounded dull—it sounded strange; and all the more so because of his main condition."

"Which was—?"

"That she should never trouble him—but never, never: neither appeal nor complain nor write about anything; only meet all questions herself, receive all moneys from his solicitor, take the whole thing over and let him alone. She promised to do this, and she mentioned to me that when, for a moment, disburdened, delighted, he held her hand, thanking her for the sacrifice, she already felt rewarded."

"But was that all her reward?" one of the ladies asked.

"She never saw him again."

"Oh!" said the lady; which, as our friend immediately left us again, was the only other word of importance contributed to the subject till, the next night, by the corner of the hearth, in the best chair, he opened the faded red cover of a thin old-fashioned gilt-edged album. The whole thing took indeed more nights than one, but on the first occasion the same lady put another question. "What is your title?"

"I haven't one."

"Oh, *I* have!" I said. But Douglas, without heeding me, had begun to read with a fine clearness that was like a rendering to the ear of the beauty of his author's hand.

I

I remember the whole beginning as a succession of flights and drops, a little see-saw of the right throbs and the wrong. After rising, in town, to meet his appeal, I had at all events a couple of very bad days—found myself doubtful again, felt indeed sure I had made a mistake. In this state of mind I spent the long hours of bumping, swinging coach that carried me to the stopping-place at which I was to be met by a vehicle from the house. This convenience, I was told, had been ordered, and I found, toward the close of the June afternoon, a commodious fly in waiting for me. Driving at that hour, on a lovely day, through a country to which the summer sweetness seemed to offer me a friendly welcome, my fortitude mounted afresh and, as we turned into the avenue, encountered a reprieve that was probably but a proof of the point to which it had sunk. I suppose I had expected, or had dreaded, something so melancholy that what greeted me was a good surprise. I remember as a most pleasant impression the broad, clear front, its open windows and fresh curtains and the pair of maids looking out; I remember the lawn and the bright flowers and the crunch of my wheels on the gravel and the clustered treetops over which the rooks circled and cawed in the golden sky. The scene had a greatness that made it a different affair from my own scant home, and there immediately appeared at the door, with a little girl in her hand, a civil person who dropped me as decent a curtsey as if I had been the mistress or a distinguished visitor. I had received in Harley Street a narrower notion of the place, and that, as I recalled it, made me think the proprietor still more of a gentleman, suggested that what I was to enjoy might be something beyond his promise.

I had no drop again till the next day, for I was carried triumphantly through the following hours by my introduction to the younger of my pupils. The little girl who accompanied Mrs. Grose appeared to me on the spot a creature so charming as to make it a great fortune to have to do with her. She was the most beautiful child I had ever seen, and I afterwards wondered that my employer had not told me more of her. I slept little that night—I was too much excited; and this astonished me too, I recollect, remained with me, adding to my sense of the liberality with which I was treated. The large, impressive room, one of the best in the house, the great state bed, as I almost felt it, the full, figured draperies, the long glasses in which, for the first time, I could see myself from head to foot, all struck me—like the extraordinary charm of my small charge—as so many things thrown in. It was thrown in as well, from the first moment, that I should get on with Mrs. Grose in a relation over which, on my way, in the coach, I fear I had rather brooded. The only thing indeed that in this early outlook might have made me shrink again was the clear circumstance of her being so glad to see me. I perceived within half an hour that she was so glad—stout, simple, plain, clean, wholesome woman—as to be positively on her guard against showing it too much. I wondered even then a little why she should wish not to show it, and that, with reflection, with suspicion, might of course have made me uneasy.

But it was a comfort that there could be no uneasiness in a connection with anything so beatific as the radiant image of my little girl, the vision of whose angelic beauty had probably more than anything else to do with the restlessness that, before morning, made me several times rise and wander about my room to take in the whole picture and prospect; to watch, from my open window, the faint summer dawn, to look at such portions of the rest of the house as I could catch, and to listen, while, in the fading dusk, the first birds began to twitter, for the possible recurrence of a sound or two, less natural and not without, but within, that I had fancied I heard. There had been a moment when I believed I recognised, faint and far, the cry of a child; there had been another when I found myself just consciously starting as at the passage, before my door, of a light footstep. But these fancies were not marked enough not to be thrown off, and it is only in the light, or the gloom, I should rather say, of other and subsequent matters that they now come back to me. To watch, teach, "form" little Flora would too evidently be the making of a happy and useful life. It had been agreed between us downstairs that after this first occasion I should have her as a matter of course at night, her small white bed being already arranged, to that end, in my room. What I had undertaken was the whole care of her, and she had remained, just this last time, with Mrs. Grose only as an effect of our consideration for my inevitable strangeness and her natural timidity. In spite of this timidity —which the child herself, in the oddest way in the world, had been perfectly frank and brave about, allowing it, without a sign of uncomfortable consciousness, with the deep, sweet serenity indeed of one of Raphael's holy infants, to be discussed, to be imputed to her and to determine us—I felt quite sure she would presently like me. It was part of what I already liked Mrs. Grose herself for, the pleasure I could see her feel in my admiration and wonder as I sat at supper with four tall candles and with my pupil, in a high chair and a bib, brightly facing me, between them, over bread and milk. There were naturally things that in Flora's presence could pass between us only as prodigious and gratified looks, obscure and roundabout allusions.

"And the little boy—does he look like her? Is he too so very remarkable?"

One wouldn't flatter a child. "Oh, Miss, *most* remarkable. If you think well of this one!"—and she stood there with a plate in her hand, beaming at our companion, who looked from one of us to the other with placid heavenly eyes that contained nothing to check us.

"Yes; if I do—?"

"You *will* be carried away by the little gentleman!"

"Well, that, I think, is what I came for—to be carried away. I'm afraid, however," I remember feeling the impulse to add, "I'm rather easily carried away. I was carried away in London!"

I can still see Mrs. Grose's broad face as she took this in. "In Harley Street?"

"In Harley Street."

"Well, Miss, you're not the first—and you won't be the last."

"Oh, I've no pretension," I could laugh, "to being the only one. My other pupil, at any rate, as I understand, comes back tomorrow?"

"Not tomorrow—Friday, Miss. He arrives, as you did, by the coach, under care of the guard, and is to be met by the same carriage."

I forthwith expressed that the proper as well as the pleasant and friendly thing would be therefore that on the arrival of the public conveyance I should be in waiting for him with his little sister; an idea in which Mrs. Grose concurred so heartily that I somehow took her manner as a kind of comforting pledge—never falsified, thank heaven!—that we should on every question be quite at one. Oh, she was glad I was there!

What I felt the next day was, I suppose, nothing that could be fairly called a reaction from the cheer of my arrival; it was probably at the most only a slight oppression produced by a fuller measure of the scale, as I walked round them, gazed up at them, took them in, of my new circumstances. They had, as it were, an extent and mass for which I had not been prepared and in the presence of which I found myself, freshly, a little scared as well as a little proud. Lessons, in this agitation, certainly suffered some delay; I reflected that my first duty was, by the gentlest arts I could contrive, to win the child into the sense of knowing me. I spent the day with her out of doors; I arranged with her, to her great satisfaction, that it should be she, she only, who might show me the place. She showed it step by step and room by room and secret by secret, with droll, delightful, childish talk about it and with the result, in half an hour, of our becoming immense friends. Young as she was, I was struck, throughout our little tour, with her confidence and courage with the way, in empty chambers and dull corridors, on crooked staircases that made me pause and even on the summit of an old machicolated square tower that made me dizzy, her morning music, her disposition to tell me so many more things than she asked, rang out and led me on. I have not seen Bly since the day I left it, and I dare say that to my older and more informed eyes it would now appear sufficiently contracted. But as my little conductress, with her hair of gold and her frock of blue, danced before me round corners and pattered down passages, I had the view of a castle of romance inhabited by a rosy sprite, such a place as would somehow, for diversion of the young idea, take all colour out of storybooks and fairy-tales. Wasn't it just a storybook over which I had fallen a-doze and a-dream? No; it was a big, ugly, antique, but convenient house, embodying a few features of a building still older, half replaced and half utilised, in which I had the fancy of our being almost as lost as a handful of passengers in a great drifting ship. Well, I was, strangely, at the helm!

II

This came home to me when, two days later, I drove over with Flora to meet, as Mrs. Grose said, the little gentleman; and all the more for an incident that, presenting itself the second evening, had deeply disconcerted me. The first day had been, on the whole, as I have expressed, reassuring; but I was to see it wind up in keen apprehension. The postbag, that evening,—it came late,—contained a letter for me, which, however, in the hand of my employer, I found to be composed but of a few words enclosing another, addressed to himself, with a seal still unbroken. "This, I recognise, is from the head-master, and the head-master's an awful bore. Read him, please; deal with him; but mind you don't report. Not a word. I'm off!" I broke the seal with a great effort—so great a one that I was a long time coming to it; took the unopened missive at last up to my room and only attacked it just before going to bed. I had better have let it wait till morning, for it gave me a second sleepless night. With no counsel to take, the next day, I was full of distress; and it finally got so the better of me that I determined to open myself at least to Mrs. Grose.

"What does it mean? The child's dismissed his school."

She gave me a look that I remarked at the moment; then, visibly, with a quick blankness, seemed to try to take it back. "But aren't they all—?"

"Sent home—yes. But only for the holidays. Miles may never go back at all."

Consciously, under my attention, she reddened. "They won't take him?"

"They absolutely decline."

At this she raised her eyes, which she had turned from me; I saw them fill with good tears. "What has he done?"

I hesitated; then I judged best simply to hand her my letter—which, however, had the effect of making her, without taking it, simply put her hands behind her. She shook her head sadly. "Such things are not for me, Miss."

My counsellor couldn't read! I winced at my mistake, which I attenuated as I could, and opened my letter again to repeat it to her; then, faltering in the act and folding it up once more, I put it back in my pocket. "Is he really *bad?*"

The tears were still in her eyes. "Do the gentlemen say so?"

"They go into no particulars. They simply express their regret that it should be impossible to keep him. That can have only one meaning." Mrs. Grose listened with dumb emotion; she forebore to ask me what this meaning might be; so that, presently, to put the thing with some coherence and with the mere aid of her presence to my own mind, I went on: "That he's an injury to the others."

At this, with one of the quick turns of simple folk, she suddenly flamed up. "Master Miles! *him* an injury?"

There was such a flood of good faith in it that, though I had not yet seen the child, my very fears made me jump to the absurdity of the idea. I found myself, to meet my friend the better, offering it, on the spot, sarcastically. "To his poor little innocent mates!"

"It's too dreadful," cried Mrs. Grose, "to say such cruel things! Why, he's scarce ten years old."

"Yes, yes; it would be incredible."

She was evidently grateful for such a profession. "See him, Miss, first. *Then* believe it!" I felt forthwith a new impatience to see him; it was the beginning of a curiosity that, for all the next hours, was to deepen almost to pain. Mrs. Grose was aware, I could judge, of what she had produced in me, and she followed it up with assurance. "You might as well believe it of the little lady. Bless her," she added the next moment—"*look* at her!"

I turned and saw that Flora, whom, ten minutes before, I had established in the schoolroom with a sheet of white paper, a pencil, and a copy of nice "round O's," now presented herself to view at the open door. She expressed in her little way an extraordinary detachment from disagreeable duties, looking to me, however, with a great childish light that seemed to offer it as a mere result of the affection she had conceived for my person, which had rendered necessary that she should follow me. I needed nothing more than this to feel the full force of Mrs. Grose's comparison, and, catching my pupil in my arms, covered her with kisses in which there was a sob of atonement.

None the less, the rest of the day, I watched for further occasion to approach my colleague, especially as, toward evening, I began to fancy she rather sought to avoid me. I overtook her, I remember, on the staircase; we went down together, and at the bottom I detained her, holding her there with a hand on her arm. "I take what you said to me at noon as a declaration that *you've* never known him to be bad."

She threw back her head; she had clearly, by this time, and very honestly, adopted an attitude. "Oh, never known him—I don't pretend *that!*"

I was upset again. "Then you *have* known him—?"

"Yes indeed, Miss, thank God!"

On reflection I accepted this. "You mean that a boy who never is—?"

"Is no boy for *me!*"

I held her tighter. "You like them with the spirit to be naughty?" Then, keeping pace with her answer, "So do I!" I eagerly brought out. "But not to the degree to contaminate—"

"To contaminate?"—my big word left her at a loss. I explained it. "To corrupt."

She stared, taking my meaning in; but it produced in her an odd laugh. "Are you afraid he'll corrupt *you?*" She put the question with such a fine bold humour that, with a laugh, a little silly doubtless, to match her own, I gave way for the time to the apprehension of ridicule.

But the next day, as the hour for my drive approached, I cropped up in another place. "What was the lady who was here before?"

"The last governess? She was also young and pretty—almost as young and almost as pretty, Miss, even as you."

"Ah, then, I hope her youth and her beauty helped her!" I recollect throwing off. "He seems to like us young and pretty!"

"Oh, he *did,*" Mrs. Grose assented: "it was the way he liked everyone!" She had no sooner spoken indeed than she caught herself up. "I mean that's *his* way—the master's."

I was struck. "But of whom did you speak first?"

She looked blank, but she coloured. "Why, of *him.*"

"Of the master?"

"Of who else?"

There was so obviously no one else that the next moment I had lost my impression of her having accidentally said more than she meant; and I merely asked what I wanted to know. "Did *she* see anything in the boy—?"

"That wasn't right? She never told me."

I had a scruple, but I overcame it. "Was she careful—particular?"

Mrs. Grose appeared to try to be conscientious. "About some things—yes."

"But not about all?"

Again she considered. "Well, Miss—she's gone. I won't tell tales."

"I quite understand your feeling," I hastened to reply; but I thought it, after an instant, not opposed to this concession to pursue: "Did she die here?"

"No—she went off."

I don't know what there was in this brevity of Mrs. Grose's that struck me as ambiguous. "Went off to die?" Mrs. Grose looked straight out of the window, but I felt that, hypothetically, I had a right to know what young persons engaged for Bly were expected to do. "She was taken ill, you mean, and went home?"

"She was not taken ill, so far as appeared, in this house. She left it, at the end of the year, to go home, as she said, for a short holiday, to which the time she had put in had certainly given her a right. We had then a young woman—a nursemaid who had stayed on and who was a good girl and clever; and *she* took the children altogether for the interval. But our young lady never came back, and at the very moment I was expecting her I heard from the master that she was dead."

I turned this over. "But of what?"

"He never told me! But please, Miss," said Mrs. Grose, "I must get to my work."

III

Her thus turning her back on me was fortunately not, for my just preoccupations, a snub that could check the growth of our mutual esteem. We met, after I had brought home little Miles, more intimately than ever on the ground of my stupefaction, my general emotion: so monstrous was I then ready to pronounce it that such a child as had now been revealed to me should be under an interdict. I was a little late on the scene, and I felt, as he stood wistfully looking out for me before the door of the inn at which the coach had put him down, that I had seen him, on the instant, without and within, in the great glow of freshness, the same positive fragrance of purity, in which I had, from the first moment, seen his little sister. He was incredibly beautiful, and Mrs. Grose had put her finger on it: everything but a sort of passion of tenderness for him was swept away by his presence. What I then and there took him to my heart for was something divine that I have never found to the same degree in any child—his indescribable little air of knowing nothing in the world but love. It would have been impossible to carry a bad name with a greater sweetness of innocence, and by the time I had got back to Bly with him I remained merely bewildered—so far, that is, as I was not outraged—by the sense of the horrible letter locked up in my room, in a drawer. As soon as I could compass a private word with Mrs. Grose I declared to her that it was grotesque.

She promptly understood me. "You mean the cruel charge—?"

"It doesn't live an instant. My dear woman, *look* at him!"

She smiled at my pretension to have discovered his charm. "I assure you, Miss, I do nothing else! What will you say, then?" she immediately added.

"In answer to the letter?" I had made up my mind. "Nothing."

"And to his uncle?"

I was incisive. "Nothing."

"And to the boy himself?"

I was wonderful. "Nothing."

She gave with her apron a great wipe to her mouth. "Then I'll stand by you. We'll see it out."

"We'll see it out!" I ardently echoed, giving her my hand to make it a vow.

She held me there a moment, then whisked up her apron again with her detached hand. "Would you mind, Miss, if I used the freedom—"

"To kiss me? No!" I took the good creature in my arms and, after we had embraced like sisters, felt still more fortified and indignant.

This, at all events, was for the time: a time so full that, as I recall the way it went, it reminds me of all the art I now need to make it a little distinct. What I look back at with amazement is the situation I accepted. I had undertaken, with my companion, to see it out, and I was under a charm, apparently, that could smooth away the extent and the far and difficult connections of such an effort. I was lifted aloft on a great wave of infatuation and pity. I found it simple, in my ignorance, my confusion, and perhaps my conceit, to assume that I could deal with a boy whose education for the world was all on the point of beginning. I am unable even to remember at this day what proposal I framed for the end of his holidays and the resumption of his studies. Lessons with me, indeed, that charming summer, we all had a theory that he was to have; but I now feel that, for weeks, the lessons must have been rather my own. I learnt something—at first certainly—that had not been one of the teachings of my small, smothered life; learnt to be amused, and even amusing, and not to think for the morrow. It was the first time, in a manner, that I had known space and air and freedom, all the music of summer and all the mystery of nature. And then there was consideration—and consideration was sweet. Oh, it was a trap—not designed, but deep—to my imagination, to my delicacy, perhaps to my vanity; to whatever, in me, was most excitable. The best way to picture it all is to say that I was off my guard. They gave me so little trouble—they were of a gentleness so extraordinary. I used to speculate—but even this with a dim disconnectedness—as to how the rough future (for all futures are rough!) would handle them and might bruise them. They had the bloom of health and happiness; and yet, as if I had been in charge of a pair of little grandees, of princes of the blood, for whom everything, to be right, would have to be enclosed and protected, the only form that, in my fancy, the after-years could take for them was that of a romantic, a really royal extension of the garden and the park. It may be, of course, above all, that what suddenly broke into this gives the previous time a charm of stillness—that hush in which something gathers or crouches. The change was actually like the spring of a beast.

In the first weeks the days were long; they often, at their finest, gave me what I used to call my own hour, the hour when, for my pupils, tea-time and bed-time having come and gone, I had, before my final retirement, a small interval alone. Much as I liked my companions, this hour was the thing in the day I liked most; and I liked it best of all when, as the light faded—or rather, I should say, the day lingered and the last calls of the last birds sounded, in a flushed sky, from the old trees—I could take a turn into the grounds and enjoy, almost with a sense of property that amused and flattered me, the beauty and dignity of the place. It was a pleasure at these moments to feel myself tranquil and justified; doubtless, perhaps, also to reflect that by my discretion, my quiet good sense and general high propriety, I was giving pleasure—if he ever thought of it!—to the person to whose pressure I had responded. What I was doing was what he had earnestly hoped and directly asked of me, and that I *could*, after all, do it proved even a greater joy than I had expected. I dare say I fancied myself, in short, a remarkable young woman and took comfort in the faith that this would more publicly appear. Well, I needed to be remarkable to offer a front to the remarkable things that presently gave their first sign.

It was plump, one afternoon, in the middle of my very hour: the children were tucked away and I had come out for my stroll. One of the thoughts that, as I don't in the least shrink now from noting, used to be with me in these wanderings was that it would be as charming as a charming story suddenly to meet someone. Someone would appear there at the turn of a path and would stand before me and smile and approve. I didn't ask more than that—I only asked that he should *know;* and the only way to be sure he knew would be to see it, and the kind light of it, in his handsome face. That was exactly present to me—by which I mean the face was—when, on the first of these occasions, at the end of a long June day, I stopped short on emerging from one of the plantations and coming into view of the house. What arrested me on the spot—and with a shock much greater than any vision had allowed for—was the sense that my imagination had, in a flash, turned real. He did stand there!—but high up, beyond the lawn and at the very top of the tower to which, on that first morning, little Flora had conducted me. This tower was one of a pair—square, incongruous, crenelated structures—that were distinguished, for some reason, though I could see little difference, as the new and the old. They flanked opposite ends of the house and were probably architectural absurdities, redeemed in a measure indeed by not being wholly disengaged nor of a height too pretentious, dating, in their gingerbread antiquity, from a romantic revival that was already a respectable past. I admired them, had fancies about them, for we could all profit in a degree, especially when they loomed through the dusk, by the grandeur of their actual battlements; yet it was not at such an elevation that the figure I had so often invoked seemed most in place.

It produced in me, this figure, in the clear twilight, I remember, two distinct gasps of emotion, which were, sharply, the shock of my first and that of my second surprise. My second was a violent perception of the mistake of my first: the man who met my eyes was not the person I had precipitately supposed. There came to me thus a bewilderment of vision of which, after these years, there is no living view that I can hope to give. An unknown man in a lonely place is a permitted object of fear to a young woman privately bred; and the figure that faced me was—a few more seconds assured me—as little anyone else I knew as it was the image that had been in my mind. I had not seen it in Harley Street—I had not seen it anywhere. The place, moreover, in the strangest way in the world, had, on the instant, and by the very fact of its appearance, become a solitude. To me at least, making my statement here with a deliberation with which I have never made it, the whole feeling of the moment returns. It was as if, while I took in—what I did take in—all the rest of the scene had been stricken with death. I can hear again, as I write, the intense hush in which the sounds of evening dropped. The rooks stopped cawing in the golden sky and the friendly hour lost, for the minute, all its voice. But there was no other change in nature, unless indeed it were a change that I saw with a stranger sharpness. The gold was still in the sky, the clearness in the air, and the man who looked at me over the battlements was as definite as a picture in a frame. That's how I thought, with extraordinary quickness, of each person that he might have been and that he was not. We were confronted across our distance quite long enough for me to ask myself with intensity who then he was and to feel, as an effect of my inability to say, a wonder that in a few instants more became intense.

The great question, or one of these, is, afterwards, I know, with regard to certain matters, the question of how long they have lasted. Well, this matter of mine, think what you will of it, lasted while I caught at a dozen possibilities, none of which made a difference for the better, that I could see, in there having been in the house—and for how long, above all?—a person of whom I was in ignorance. It lasted while I just bridled a little with the sense that my office demanded that there should be no such ignorance and no such person. It lasted while this visitant, at all events,—and there was a touch of the strange freedom, as I remember, in the sign of familiarity of his wearing no hat,—seemed to fix me, from his position, with just the question, just the scrutiny through the fading light, that his own presence provoked. We were too far apart to call to each other, but there was a moment at which, at shorter range, some challenge between us, breaking the hush, would have been the right result of our straight mutual stare. He was in one of the angles, the one away from the house, very erect, as it struck me, and with both hands on the ledge. So I saw him as I see the letters I form on this page; then, exactly, after a minute, as if to add to the spectacle, he slowly changed his place—passed, looking at me hard all the while, to the opposite corner of the platform. Yes, I had the sharpest sense that during this transit he never took his eyes from me, and I can see at this moment the way his hand, as he went, passed from one of the crenelations to the next. He stopped at the other corner, but less long, and even as he turned away still markedly fixed me. He turned away; that was all I knew.

IV

It was not that I didn't wait, on this occasion, for more, for I was rooted as deeply as I was shaken. Was there a "secret" at Bly—a mystery of Udolpho or an insane, an unmentionable relative kept in unsuspected confinement? I can't say how long I turned it over, or how long, in a confusion of curiosity and dread, I remained where I had had my collision; I only recall that when I re-entered the house darkness had quite closed in. Agitation, in the interval, certainly had held me and driven me, for I must, in circling about the place, have walked three miles; but I was to be, later on, so much more overwhelmed that this mere dawn of alarm was a comparatively human chill. The most singular part of it in fact—singular as the rest had been—was the part I became, in the hall, aware of in meeting Mrs. Grose. This picture comes back to me in the general train—the impression, as I received it on my return, of the wide white panelled space, bright in the lamplight and with its portraits and red carpet, and of the good surprised look of my friend, which immediately told me she had missed me. It came to me straightway, under her contact, that, with plain heartiness, mere relieved anxiety at my appearance, she knew nothing whatever that could bear upon the incident I had there ready for her. I had not suspected in advance that her comfortable face would pull me up, and I somehow measured the importance of what I had seen by my thus finding myself hesitate to mention it. Scarce anything in the whole history seems to me so odd as this fact that my real beginning of fear was one, as I may say, with the instinct of sparing my companion. On the spot, accordingly, in the pleasant hall and with her eyes on me, I, for a reason that I couldn't then have phrased, achieved an inward revolution—offered a vague pretext for my lateness and, with the plea of the beauty of the night and of the heavy dew and wet feet, went as soon as possible to my room.

Here it was another affair; here, for many days after, it was a queer affair enough. There were hours, from day to day,—or at least there were moments, snatched even from clear duties,—when I had to shut myself up to think. It was not so much yet that I was more nervous than I could bear to be as that I was remarkably afraid of becoming so; for the truth I had now to turn over was, simply and clearly, the truth that I could arrive at no account whatever of the visitor with whom I had been so inexplicably and yet, as it seemed to me, so intimately concerned. It took little time to see that I could sound without forms of inquiry and without exciting remark any domestic complication. The shock I had suffered must have sharpened all my senses; I felt sure, at the end of three days and as the result of mere closer attention, that I had not been practised upon by the servants nor made the object of any "game." Of whatever it was that I knew nothing was known around me. There was but one sane inference: someone had taken a liberty rather gross. That was what, repeatedly, I dipped into my room and locked the door to say to myself. We had been, collectively, subject to an intrusion; some unscrupulous traveller, curious in old houses, had made his way in unobserved, enjoyed the prospect from the best point of view, and then stolen out as he came. If he had given me such a bold hard stare, that was but a part of his indiscretion. The good thing, after all, was that we should surely see no more of him.

This was not so good a thing, I admit, as not to leave me to judge that what, essentially, made nothing else much signify was simply my charming work. My charming work was just my life with Miles and Flora, and through nothing could I so like it as through feeling that I could throw myself into it in trouble. The attraction of my small charges was a constant joy, leading me to wonder afresh at the vanity of my original fears, the distaste I had begun by entertaining for the probable grey prose of my office. There was to be no grey prose, it appeared, and no long grind; so how could work not be charming that presented itself as daily beauty? It was all the romance of the nursery and the poetry of the schoolroom. I don't mean by this, of course, that we studied only fiction and verse; I mean I can express no otherwise the sort of interest my companions inspired. How can I describe that except by saying that instead of growing used to them—and it's a marvel for a governess: I call the sisterhood to witness!—I made constant fresh discoveries. There was one direction, assuredly, in which these discoveries stopped: deep obscurity continued to cover the region of the boy's conduct at school. It had been promptly given me, I have noted, to face that mystery without a pang. Perhaps even it would be nearer the truth to say that—without a word—he himself had cleared it up. He had made the whole charge absurd. My conclusion bloomed there with the real rose-flush of his innocence: he was only too fine and fair for the little horrid, unclean school-world, and he had paid a price for it. I reflected acutely that the sense of such differences, such superiorities of quality, always, on the part of the majority—which could include even stupid, sordid head-masters—turns infallibly to the vindictive.

Both the children had a gentleness (it was their only fault, and it never made Miles a muff) that kept them—how shall I express it?—almost impersonal and certainly quite unpunishable. They were like the cherubs of the anecdote, who had—morally, at any rate—nothing to whack! I remember feeling with Miles in especial as if he had had, as it were, no history. We expect of a small child a scant one, but there was in this beautiful little boy something extraordinarily sensitive, yet extraordinarily happy, that, more than in any creature of his age I have seen, struck me as beginning anew each day. He had never for a second suffered. I took this as a direct disproof of his having really been chastised. If he had been wicked he would have "caught" it, and I should have caught it by the rebound—I should have found the trace. I found nothing at all, and he was therefore angel. He never spoke of his school, never mentioned a comrade or a master; and I, for my part, was quite too much disgusted to allude to them. Of course I was under the spell, and the wonderful part is that, even at the time, I perfectly knew I was. But I gave myself up to it; it was an antidote to any pain, and I had more pains than one. I was in receipt in these days of disturbing letters from home, where things were not going well. But with my children, what things in the world mattered? That was the question I used to put to my scrappy retirements. I was dazzled by their loveliness.

There was a Sunday—to get on—when it rained with such force and for so many hours that there could be no procession to church; in consequence of which, as the day declined, I had arranged with Mrs. Grose that, should the evening show improvement, we would attend together the late service. The rain happily stopped, and I prepared for our walk, which, through the park and by the good road to the village, would be a matter of twenty minutes. Coming downstairs to meet my colleague in the hall, I remembered a pair of gloves that had required three stitches and that had received them—with a publicity perhaps not edifying—while I sat with the children at their tea, served on Sundays, by exception, in that cold, clean temple of mahogany and brass, the "grown-up" dining-room. The gloves had been dropped there, and I turned in to recover them. The day was grey enough, but the afternoon light still lingered, and it enabled me, on crossing the threshold, not only to recognise, on a chair near the wide window, then closed, the articles I wanted, but to become aware of a person on the other side of the window and looking straight in. One step into the room had sufficed; my vision was instantaneous; it was all there. The person looking straight in was the person who had already appeared to me. He appeared thus again with I won't say greater distinctness, for that was impossible, but with a nearness that represented a forward stride in our intercourse and made me, as I met him, catch my breath and turn cold. He was the same—he was the same, and seen, this time, as he had been seen before, from the waist up, the window, though the dining-room was on the ground-floor, not going down to the terrace on which he stood. His face was close to the glass, yet the effect of this better view was, strangely, only to show me how intense the former had been. He remained but a few seconds—long enough to convince me he also saw and recognised; but it was as if I had been looking at him for years and had known him always. Something, however, happened this time that had not happened before; his stare into my face, through the glass and across the room, was as deep and hard as then, but it quitted me for a moment during which I could still watch it, see it fix successively several other things. On the spot there came to me the added shock of a certitude that it was not for me he had come there. He had come for someone else.

The flash of this knowledge—for it was knowledge in the midst of dread—produced in me the most extraordinary effect, started, as I stood there, a sudden vibration of duty and courage. I say courage because I was beyond all doubt already far gone. I bounded straight out of the door again, reached that of the house, got, in an instant, upon the drive, and, passing along the terrace as fast as I could rush, turned a corner and came full in sight. But it was in sight of nothing now—my visitor had vanished. I stopped, I almost dropped, with the real relief of this; but I took in the whole scene—I gave him time to reappear. I call it time, but how long was it? I can't speak to the purpose today of the duration of these things. That kind of measure must have left me: they couldn't have lasted as they actually appeared to me to last. The terrace and the whole place, the lawn and the garden beyond it, all I could see of the park, were empty with a great emptiness. There were shrubberies and big trees, but I remember the clear assurance I felt that none of them concealed him. He was there or was not there: not there if I didn't see him. I got hold of this; then, instinctively, instead of returning as I had come, went to the window. It was confusedly present to me that I ought to place myself where he had stood. I did so; I applied my face to the pane and looked, as he had looked, into the room. As if, at this moment, to show me exactly what his range had been, Mrs. Grose, as I had done for himself just before, came in from the hall. With this I had the full image of a repetition of what had already occurred. She saw me as I had seen my own visitant; she pulled up short as I had done; I gave her something of the shock that I had received. She turned white, and this made me ask myself if I had blanched as much. She stared, in short, and retreated on just *my* lines, and I knew she had then passed out and come round to me and that I should presently meet her. I remained where I was, and while I waited I thought of more things than one. But there's only one I take space to mention. I wondered why *she* should be scared.

V

Oh, she let me know as soon as, round the corner of the house, she loomed again into view. "What in the name of goodness is the matter—?" She was now flushed and out of breath.

I said nothing till she came quite near. "With me?" I must have made a wonderful face. "Do I show it?"

"You're as white as a sheet. You look awful."

I considered; I could meet on this, without scruple, any innocence. My need to respect the bloom of Mrs. Grose's had dropped, without a rustle, from my shoulders, and if I wavered for the instant it was not with what I kept back. I put out my hand to her and she took it; I held her hard a little, liking to feel her close to me. There was a kind of support in the shy heave of her surprise. "You came for me for church, of course, but I can't go."

"Has anything happened?"

"Yes. You must know now. Did I look very queer?"

"Through this window? Dreadful!"

"Well," I said, "I've been frightened." Mrs. Grose's eyes expressed plainly that *she* had no wish to be, yet also that she knew too well her place not to be ready to share with me any marked inconvenience. Oh, it was quite settled that she *must* share! "Just what you saw from the dining-room a minute ago was the effect of that. What *I* saw—just before—was much worse."

Her hand tightened. "What was it?"

"An extraordinary man. Looking in."

"What extraordinary man?"

"I haven't the least idea."

Mrs. Grose gazed round us in vain. "Then where is he gone?"

"I know still less."

"Have you seen him before?"

"Yes—once. On the old tower."

She could only look at me harder. "Do you mean he's a stranger?"

"Oh, very much!"

"Yet you didn't tell me?"

"No—for reasons. But now that you've guessed—"

Mrs. Grose's round eyes encountered this charge. "Ah, I haven't guessed!" she said very simply. "How can I if *you* don't imagine?"

"I don't in the very least."

"You've seen him nowhere but on the tower?"

"And on this spot just now."

Mrs. Grose looked round again. "What was he doing on the tower?"

"Only standing there and looking down at me."

She thought a minute. "Was he a gentleman?"

I found I had no need to think. "No." She gazed in deeper wonder. "No."

"Then nobody about the place? Nobody from the village?"

"Nobody—nobody. I didn't tell you, but I made sure."

She breathed a vague relief: this was, oddly, so much to the good. It only went indeed a little way. "But if he isn't a gentleman—"

"What *is* he? He's a horror."

"A horror?"

"He's—God help me if I know *what* he is!"

Mrs. Grose looked round once more; she fixed her eyes on the duskier distance, then, pulling herself together, turned to me with abrupt inconsequence. "It's time we should be at church."

"Oh, I'm not fit for church!"

"Won't it do you good?"

"It won't do *them*—!" I nodded at the house.

"The children?"

"I can't leave them now."

"You're afraid—?"

I spoke boldly. "I'm afraid of *him*."

Mrs. Grose's large face showed me, at this, for the first time, the far-away faint glimmer of a consciousness more acute: I somehow made out in it the delayed dawn of an idea I myself had not given her and that was as yet quite obscure to me. It comes back to me that I thought instantly of this as something I could get from her; and I felt it to be connected with the desire she presently showed to know more. "When was it—on the tower?"

"About the middle of the month. At this same hour."

"Almost at dark?" said Mrs. Grose.

"Oh, no, not nearly. I saw him as I see you."

"Then how did he get in?"

"And how did he get out?" I laughed. "I had no opportunity to ask him! This evening, you see," I pursued, "he has not been able to get in."

"He only peeps?"

"I hope it will be confined to that!" She had now let go my hand; she turned away a little. I waited an instant; then I brought out: "Go to church. Good-bye. I must watch."

Slowly she faced me again. "Do you fear for them?"

We met in another long look. "Don't *you*?" Instead of answering she came nearer to the window and, for a minute, applied her face to the glass. "You see how he could see," I meanwhile went on.

She didn't move. "How long was he here?"

"Till I came out. I came to meet him."

Mrs. Grose at last turned round, and there was still more in her face. "*I* couldn't have come out."

"Neither could I!" I laughed again. "But I did come. I have my duty."

"So have I mine," she replied; after which she added: "What is he like?"

"I've been dying to tell you. But he's like nobody."

"Nobody?" she echoed.

"He has no hat." Then seeing in her face that she already, in this, with a deeper dismay, found a touch of picture, I quickly added stroke to stroke. "He has red hair, very red, close-curling, and a pale face, long in shape, with straight, good features and little, rather queer whiskers that are as red as his hair. His eyebrows are, somehow, darker; they look particularly arched and as if they might move a good deal. His eyes are sharp, strange—awfully; but I only know clearly that they're rather small and very fixed. His mouth's wide, and his lips are thin, and except for his little whiskers he's quite clean-shaven. He gives me a sort of sense of looking like an actor."

"An actor!" It was impossible to resemble one less, at least, than Mrs. Grose at that moment.

"I've never seen one, but so I suppose them. He's tall, active, erect," I continued, "but never—no, never!—a gentleman."

My companion's face had blanched as I went on; her round eyes started and her mild mouth gaped. "A gentleman?" she gasped, confounded, stupefied: "a gentleman *he*?"

"You know him then?"

She visibly tried to hold herself. "But he *is* handsome?"

I saw the way to help her. "Remarkably!"

"And dressed—?"

"In somebody's clothes. They're smart, but they're not his own."

She broke into a breathless affirmative groan. "They're the master's!"

I caught it up. "You *do* know him?"

She faltered but a second. "Quint!" she cried.

"Quint?"

"Peter Quint—his own man, his valet, when he was here!"

"When the master was?"

Gaping still, but meeting me, she pieced it all together. "He never wore his hat, but he did wear—well, there were waistcoats missed! They were both here—last year. Then the master went, and Quint was alone."

I followed, but halting a little. "Alone?"

"Alone with *us*." Then, as from a deeper depth, "In charge," she added.

"And what became of him?"

She hung fire so long that I was still more mystified. "He went too," she brought out at last.

"Went where?"

Her expression, at this, became extraordinary. "God knows where! He died."

"Died?" I almost shrieked.

She seemed fairly to square herself, plant herself more firmly to utter the wonder of it. "Yes. Mr. Quint is dead."

VI

It took of course more than that particular passage to place us together in presence of what we had now to live with as we could—my dreadful liability to impressions of the order so vividly exemplified, and my companion's knowledge, henceforth,—a knowledge half consternation and half compassion,—of that liability. There had been, this evening, after the revelation that left me, for an hour, so prostrate—there had been, for either of us, no attendance on any service but a little service of tears and vows, of prayers and promises, a climax to the series of mutual challenges and pledges that had straightway ensued on our retreating together to the schoolroom and shutting ourselves up there to have everything out. The result of our having everything out was simply to reduce our situation to the last rigour of its elements. She herself had seen nothing, not the shadow of a shadow, and nobody in the house but the governess was in the governess's plight; yet she accepted without directly impugning my sanity the truth as I gave it to her, and ended by showing me, on this ground, an awe-stricken tenderness, an expression of the sense of my more than questionable privilege, of which the very breath has remained with me as that of the sweetest of human charities.

What was settled between us, accordingly, that night, was that we thought we might bear things together; and I was not even sure that, in spite of her exemption, it was she who had the best of the burden. I knew at this hour, I think, as well as I knew later what I was capable of meeting to shelter my pupils; but it took me some time to be wholly sure of what my honest ally was prepared for to keep terms with so compromising a contract. I was queer company enough—quite as queer as the company I received; but as I trace over what we went through I see how much common ground we must have found in the one idea that, by good fortune, *could* steady us. It was the idea, the second movement, that led me straight out, as I may say, of the inner chamber of my dread. I could take the air in the court, at least, and there Mrs. Grose could join me. Perfectly can I recall now the particular way strength came to me before we separated for the night. We had gone over and over every feature of what I had seen.

"He was looking for someone else, you say—someone who was not you?"

"He was looking for little Miles." A portentous clearness now possessed me. "*That's* whom he was looking for."

"But how do you know?"

"I know, I know, I know!" My exaltation grew. "And *you* know, my dear!"

She didn't deny this, but I required, I felt, not even so much telling as that. She resumed in a moment, at any rate: "What if *he* should see him?"

"Little Miles? That's what he wants!"

She looked immensely scared again. "The child?"

"Heaven forbid! The man. He wants to appear to *them*." That he might was an awful conception, and yet, somehow, I could keep it at bay; which, moreover, as we lingered there, was what I succeeded in practically proving. I had an absolute certainty that I could see again what I had already seen, but something within me said that by offering myself bravely as the sole subject of such experience, by accepting, by inviting, by surmounting it all, I should serve as an expiatory victim and guard the tranquillity of my companions. The children, in especial, I should thus fence about and absolutely save. I recall one of the last things I said that night to Mrs. Grose.

"It does strike me that my pupils have never mentioned—"

She looked at me hard as I musingly pulled up. "His having been here and the time they were with him?"

"The time they were with him, and his name, his presence, his history, in any way."

"Oh, the little lady doesn't remember. She never heard or knew."

"The circumstances of his death?" I thought with some intensity. "Perhaps not. But Miles would remember—Miles would know."

"Ah, don't try him!" broke from Mrs. Grose.

I returned her the look she had given me. "Don't be afraid." I continued to think. "It *is* rather odd."

"That he has never spoken of him?"

"Never by the least allusion. And you tell me they were 'great friends'?"

"Oh, it wasn't *him!*" Mrs. Grose with emphasis declared. "It was

Quint's own fancy. To play with him, I mean—to spoil him." She paused a moment; then she added: "Quint was much too free."

This gave me, straight from my vision of his face—*such* a face—a sudden sickness of disgust. "Too free with *my* boy?"

"Too free with everyone!"

I forebore, for the moment, to analyse this description further than by the reflection that a part of it applied to several of the members of the household, of the half-dozen maids and men who were still of our small colony. But there was everything, for our apprehension, in the lucky fact that no discomfortable legend, no perturbation of scullions, had ever, within anyone's memory, attached to the kind old place. It had neither bad name nor ill fame, and Mrs. Grose, most apparently, only desired to cling to me and to quake in silence. I even put her, the very last thing of all, to the test. It was when, at midnight, she had her hand on the schoolroom door to take leave. "I have it from you then—for it's of great importance—that he was definitely and admittedly bad?"

"Oh, not admittedly. *I* knew it—but the master didn't."

"And you never told him?"

"Well, he didn't like tale-bearing—he hated complaints. He was terribly short with anything of that kind, and if people were all right to *him*—"

"He wouldn't be bothered with more?" This squared well enough with my impression of him: he was not a trouble-loving gentleman, nor so very particular perhaps about some of the company *he* kept. All the same, I pressed my interlocutress. "I promise you *I* would have told!"

She felt my discrimination. "I dare say I was wrong. But, really, I was afraid."

"Afraid of what?"

"Of things that man could do. Quint was so clever—he was so deep."

I took this in still more than, probably, I showed. "You weren't afraid of anything else? Not of his effect—?"

"His effect?" she repeated with a face of anguish and waiting while I faltered.

"On innocent little precious lives. They were in your charge."

"No, they were not in mine!" she roundly and distressfully returned. "The master believed in him and placed him here because he was supposed not to be well and the country air so good for him. So he had everything to say. Yes"—she let me have it—"even about *them*."

"Them—that creature?" I had to smother a kind of howl. "And you could bear it!"

"No. I couldn't—and I can't now!" And the poor woman burst into tears.

A rigid control, from the next day, was, as I have said, to follow them; yet how often and how passionately, for a week, we came back together to the subject! Much as we had discussed it that Sunday night, I was, in the immediate later hours in especial—for it may be imagined whether I slept—still haunted with the shadow of something she had not told me. I myself had kept back nothing, but there was a word Mrs. Grose had kept back. I was sure, moreover, by morning, that this was not from a failure of frankness, but because on every side there were fears. It seems to me indeed, in retrospect, that by the time the morrow's sun was high I had restlessly read into the facts before us almost all the meaning they were to receive from subsequent and more cruel occurrences. What they gave me above all was just the sinister figure of the living man —the dead one would keep awhile!—and of the months he had continuously passed at Bly, which, added up, made a formidable stretch. The limit of this evil time had arrived only when, on the dawn of a winter's morning, Peter Quint was found, by a labourer going to early work, stone dead on the road from the village: a catastrophe explained—superficially at least—by a visible wound to his head; such a wound as might have been produced—and as, on the final evidence, *had* been—by a fatal slip, in the dark and after leaving the public house, on the steepish icy slope, a wrong path, altogether, at the bottom of which he lay. The icy slope, the turn mistaken at night and in liquor, accounted for much—practically, in the end and after the inquest and boundless chatter, for everything; but there had been matters in his life—strange passages and perils, secret disorders, vices more than suspected—that would have accounted for a good deal more.

I scarce know how to put my story into words that shall be a credible picture of my state of mind; but I was in these days literally able to find a joy in the extraordinary flight of heroism the occasion demanded of me. I now saw that I had been asked for a service admirable and difficult; and there would be a greatness in letting it be seen—oh, in the right quarter!—that I could succeed where many another girl might have failed. It was an immense help to me—I confess I rather applaud myself as I look back!—that I saw my service so strongly and so simply. I was there to protect and defend the little creatures in the world the most bereaved and the most loveable, the appeal of whose helplessness had suddenly become only too explicit, a deep, constant ache of one's own committed heart. We were cut off, really, together; we were united in our danger. They had nothing but me, and I—well, I had *them.* It was in short a magnificent chance. This chance presented itself to me in an image richly material. I was a screen—I was to stand before them. The more I saw, the less they would. I began to watch them in a stifled suspense, a disguised excitement that might well, had it continued too long, have turned to something like madness. What saved me, as I now see, was that it turned to something else altogether. It didn't last as suspense—it was superseded by horrible proofs. Proofs, I say, yes—from the moment I really took hold.

This moment dated from an afternoon hour that I happened to spend in the grounds with the younger of my pupils alone. We had left Miles indoors, on the red cushion of a deep window-seat; he had wished to finish a book, and I had been glad to encourage a purpose so laudable in a young man whose only defect was an occasional excess of the restless. His sister, on the contrary, had been alert to come out, and I strolled with her half an hour, seeking the shade, for the sun was still high and the day exceptionally warm. I was aware afresh, with her, as we went, of how, like her brother, she contrived—it was the charming thing in both children—to let me alone without appearing to drop me and to accompany me without appearing to surround. They were never importunate and yet never listless. My attention to them all really went to seeing them amuse themselves immensely without me: this was a spectacle they seemed actively to prepare and that engaged me as an active admirer. I walked in a world of their invention—they had no occasion whatever to draw upon mine; so that my time was taken only with being, for them, some remarkable person or thing that the game of the moment required and that was merely, thanks to my superior, my exalted stamp, a happy and highly distinguished sinecure. I forget what I was on the present occasion; I only remember that I was something very important and very quiet and that Flora was playing very hard. We were on the edge of the lake, and, as we had lately begun geography, the lake was the Sea of Azof.

Suddenly, in these circumstances, I became aware that, on the other side of the Sea of Azof, we had an interested spectator. The way this knowledge gathered in me was the strangest thing in the world—the strangest, that is, except the very much stranger in which it quickly merged itself. I had sat down with a piece of work—for I was something or other that could sit—on the old stone bench which overlooked the pond; and in this position I began to take in with certitude, and yet without direct vision, the presence, at a distance, of a third person. The old trees, the thick shrubbery, made a great and pleasant shade, but it was all suffused with the brightness of the hot, still hour. There was no ambiguity in anything; none whatever, at least, in the conviction I from one moment to another found myself forming as to what I should see straight before me and across the lake as a consequence of raising my eyes. They were attached at this juncture to the stitching in which I was engaged, and I can feel once more the spasm of my effort not to move them till I should so have steadied myself as to be able to make up my mind what to do. There was an alien object in view—a figure whose right of presence I instantly, passionately questioned. I recollect counting over perfectly the possibilities, reminding myself that nothing was more natural, for instance, than the appearance of one of the men about the place, or even of a messenger, a postman or a tradesman's boy, from the village. That reminder had as little effect on my practical certitude as I was conscious—still even without looking—of its having upon the character and attitude of our visitor. Nothing was more natural than that these things should be the other things that they absolutely were not.

Of the positive identity of the apparition I would assure myself as soon as the small clock of my courage should have ticked out the right second; meanwhile, with an effort that was already sharp enough, I transferred my eyes straight to little Flora, who, at the moment, was about ten yards away. My heart had stood still for an instant with the wonder and terror of the question whether she too would see; and I held my breath while I waited for what a cry from her, what some sudden innocent sign either of interest or of alarm, would tell me. I waited, but nothing came; then, in the first place—and there is something more dire in this, I feel, than in anything I have to relate—I was determined by a sense that, within a minute, all sounds from her had previously dropped; and, in the second, by the circumstance that, also within the minute, she had, in her play, turned her back to the water. This was her attitude when I at last looked at her—looked with the confirmed conviction that we were still, together, under direct personal notice. She had picked up a small flat piece of wood, which happened to have in it a little hole that had evidently suggested to her the idea of sticking in another fragment that might figure as a mast and make the thing a boat. This second morsel, as I watched her, she was very markedly and intently attempting to tighten in its place. My apprehension of what she was doing sustained me so that after some seconds I felt I was ready for more. Then I again shifted my eyes—I faced what I had to face.

VII

I got hold of Mrs. Grose as soon after this as I could; and I can give no intelligible account of how I fought out the interval. Yet I still hear myself cry as I fairly threw myself into her arms: "They *know*—it's too monstrous: they know, they know!"

"And what on earth—?" I felt her incredulity as she held me.

"Why, all that *we* know—and heaven knows what else besides!" Then, as she released me, I made it out to her, made it out perhaps only now with full coherency even to myself. "Two hours ago, in the garden"—I could scarce articulate—"Flora *saw!*"

Mrs. Grose took it as she might have taken a blow in the stomach. "She has told you?" she panted.

"Not a word—that's the horror. She kept it to herself! The child of eight, *that* child!" Unutterable still, for me, was the stupefaction of it.

Mrs. Grose, of course, could only gape the wider. "Then how do you know?"

"I was there—I saw with my eyes: saw that she was perfectly aware."

"Do you mean aware of *him?*"

"No—of *her.*" I was conscious as I spoke that I looked prodigious things, for I got the slow reflection of them in my companion's face. "Another person—this time; but a figure of quite as unmistakeable horror and evil: a woman in black, pale and dreadful—with such an air also, and such a face!—on the other side of the lake. I was there with the child—quiet for the hour; and in the midst of it she came."

"Came how—from where?"

"From where they come from! She just appeared and stood there—but not so near."

"And without coming nearer?"

"Oh, for the effect and the feeling, she might have been as close as you!"

My friend, with an odd impulse, fell back a step. "Was she someone you've never seen?"

"Yes. But someone the child has. Someone *you* have." Then, to show how I had thought it all out: "My predecessor—the one who died."

"Miss Jessel?"

"Miss Jessel. You don't believe me?" I pressed.

She turned right and left in her distress. "How can you be sure?"

This drew from me, in the state of my nerves, a flash of impatience. "Then ask Flora—*she's* sure!" But I had no sooner spoken than I caught myself up. "No, for God's sake, *don't!* She'll say she isn't—she'll lie!"

Mrs. Grose was not too bewildered instinctively to protest. "Ah, how *can* you?"

"Because I'm clear. Flora doesn't want me to know."

"It's only then to spare you."

"No, no—there are depths, depths! The more I go over it, the more I see in it, and the more I see in it the more I fear. I don't know what I *don't* see—what I *don't* fear!"

Mrs. Grose tried to keep up with me. "You mean you're afraid of seeing her again?"

"Oh, no; that's nothing—now!" Then I explained. "It's of *not* seeing her."

But my companion only looked wan. "I don't understand you."

"Why, it's that the child may keep it up—and that the child assuredly *will*—without my knowing it."

At the image of this possibility Mrs. Grose for a moment collapsed, yet presently to pull herself together again, as if from the positive force of the sense of what, should we yield an inch, there would really be to give way to. "Dear, dear—we must keep our heads! And after all, if she doesn't mind it—!" She even tried a grim joke. "Perhaps she likes it!"

"Likes *such* things—a scrap of an infant!"

"Isn't it just a proof of her blessed innocence?" my friend bravely inquired.

She brought me, for the instant, almost round. "Oh, we must clutch at *that*—we must cling to it! If it isn't a proof of what you say, it's a proof of—God knows what! For the woman's a horror of horrors."

Mrs. Grose, at this, fixed her eyes a minute on the ground; then at last raising them, "Tell me how you know," she said.

"Then you admit it's what she was?" I cried.

"Tell me how you know," my friend simply repeated.

"Know! By seeing her! By the way she looked."

"At you, do you mean—so wickedly?"

"Dear me, no—I could have borne that. She gave me never a glance. She only fixed the child."

Mrs. Grose tried to see it. "Fixed her?"

"Ah, with such awful eyes!"

She stared at mine as if they might really have resembled them. "Do you mean of dislike?"

"God help us, no. Of something much worse."

"Worse than dislike?"—this left her indeed at a loss.

"With a determination—indescribable. With a kind of fury of intention."

I made her turn pale. "Intention?"

"To get hold of her." Mrs. Grose—her eyes just lingering on mine—gave a shudder and walked to the window; and while she stood there looking out I completed my statement. "*That's* what Flora knows."

After a little she turned round. "The person was in black, you say?"

"In mourning—rather poor, almost shabby. But—yes—with extraordinary beauty." I now recognised to what I had at last, stroke by stroke, brought the victim of my confidence, for she quite visibly weighed this. "Oh, handsome—very, very," I insisted; "wonderfully handsome. But infamous."

She slowly came back to me. "Miss Jessel—*was* infamous." She once more took my hand in both her own, holding it as tight as if to fortify me against the increase of alarm I might draw from this disclosure. "They were both infamous," she finally said.

So, for a little, we faced it once more together; and I found absolutely a degree of help in seeing it now so straight. "I appreciate," I said, "the great decency of your not having hitherto spoken; but the time has certainly come to give me the whole thing." She appeared to assent to this, but still only in silence; seeing which I went on: "I must have it now. Of what did she die? Come, there was something between them."

"There was everything."

"In spite of the difference—?"

"Oh, of their rank, their condition"—she brought it woefully out. "*She* was a lady."

I turned it over; I again saw. "Yes—she was a lady."

"And he so dreadfully below," said Mrs. Grose.

I felt that I doubtless needn't press too hard, in such company, on the place of a servant in the scale; but there was nothing to prevent an acceptance of my companion's own measure of my predecessor's abasement. There was a way to deal with that, and I dealt; the more readily for my full vision—on the evidence—of our employer's late clever, good-looking "own" man; impudent, assured, spoiled, depraved. "The fellow was a hound."

Mrs. Grose considered as if it were perhaps a little a case for a sense of shades. "I've never seen one like him. He did what he wished."

"With *her*?"

"With them all."

It was as if now in my friend's own eyes Miss Jessel had again appeared. I seemed at any rate, for an instant, to see their evocation of her as distinctly as I had seen her by the pond; and I brought out with decision: "It must have been also what *she* wished!"

Mrs. Grose's face signified that it had been indeed, but she said at the same time: "Poor woman—she paid for it!"

"Then you do know what she died of?" I asked.

"No—I know nothing. I wanted not to know; I was glad enough I didn't; and I thanked heaven she was well out of this!"

"Yet you had, then, your idea—"

"Of her real reason for leaving? Oh, yes—as to that. She couldn't have stayed. Fancy it here—for a governess! And afterwards I imagined—and I still imagine. And what I imagine is dreadful."

"Not so dreadful as what *I* do," I replied; on which I must have shown her—as I was indeed but too conscious—a front of miserable defeat. It brought out again all her compassion for me, and at the renewed touch of her kindness my power to resist broke down. I burst, as I had, the other time, made her burst, into tears; she took me to her motherly breast, and my lamentation overflowed. "I don't do it!" I sobbed in despair; "I don't save or shield them. It's far worse than I dreamed—they're lost!"

VIII

What I had said to Mrs. Grose was true enough: there were in the matter I had put before her depths and possibilities that I lacked resolution to sound; so that when we met once more in the wonder of it we were of a common mind about the duty of resistance to extravagant fancies. We were to keep our heads if we should keep nothing else—difficult indeed as that might be in the face of what, in our prodigious experience, was least to be questioned. Late that night, while the house slept, we had another talk in my room, when she went all the way with me as to its being beyond doubt that I had seen exactly what I had seen. To hold her perfectly in the pinch of that, I found I had only to ask her how, if I had "made it up," I came to be able to give, of each of the persons appearing to me, a picture disclosing, to the last detail, their special marks—a portrait on the exhibition of which she had instantly recognised and named them. She wished, of course,—small blame to her!—to sink the whole subject; and I was quick to assure her that my own interest in it had now violently taken the form of a search for the way to escape from it. I encountered her on the ground of a probability that with recurrence—for recurrence we took for granted—I should get used to my danger, distinctly professing that my personal exposure had suddenly become the least of my discomforts. It was my new suspicion that was intolerable; and yet even to this complication the later hours of the day had brought a little ease.

On leaving her, after my first outbreak, I had of course returned to my pupils, associating the right remedy for my dismay with that sense of their charm which I had already found to be a thing I could positively cultivate and which had never failed me yet. I had simply, in other words, plunged afresh into Flora's special society and there become aware—it was almost a luxury!—that she could put her little conscious hand straight upon the spot that ached. She had looked at me in sweet speculation and then had accused me to my face of having "cried." I had supposed I had brushed away the ugly signs: but I could literally—for the time, at all events—rejoice, under this fathomless charity, that they had not entirely disappeared. To gaze into the depths of blue of the child's eyes and pronounce their loveliness a trick of premature cunning was to be guilty of a cynicism in preference to which I naturally preferred to abjure my judgment and, so far as might be, my agitation. I couldn't abjure for merely wanting to, but I could repeat to Mrs. Grose—as I did there, over and over, in the small hours—that with their voices in the air, their pressure on one's heart and their fragrant faces against one's cheek, everything fell to the ground but their incapacity and their beauty. It was a pity that, somehow, to settle this once for all, I had equally to re-enumerate the signs of subtlety that, in the afternoon, by the lake, had made a miracle of my show of self-possession. It was a pity to be obliged to re-investigate the certitude of the moment itself and repeat how it had come to me as a revelation that the inconceivable communion I then surprised was a matter, for either party, of habit. It was a pity that I should have had to quaver out again the reasons for my not having, in my delusion, so much as questioned that the little girl saw our visitant even as I actually saw Mrs. Grose herself, and that she wanted, by just so much as she did thus see, to make me suppose she didn't, and at the same time, without showing anything, arrive at a guess as to whether I myself did! It was a pity that I needed once more to describe the portentous little activity by which she sought to divert my attention—the perceptible increase of movement, the greater intensity of play, the singing, the gabbling of nonsense, and the invitation to romp.

Yet if I had not indulged, to prove there was nothing in it, in this review, I should have missed the two or three dim elements of comfort that still remained to me. I should not for instance have been able to asseverate to my friend that I was certain—which was so much to the good—that I at least had not betrayed myself. I should not have been prompted, by stress of need, by desperation of mind,—I scarce know what to call it,—to invoke such further aid to intelligence as might spring from pushing my colleague fairly to the wall. She had told me, bit by bit, under pressure, a great deal; but a small shifty spot on the wrong side of it all still sometimes brushed my brow like the wing of a bat; and I remember how on this occasion—for the sleeping house and the concentration alike of our danger and our watch seemed to help—I felt the importance of giving the last jerk to the curtain. "I don't believe anything so horrible," I recollect saying; "no, let us put it definitely, my dear, that I don't. But if I did, you know, there's a thing I should require now, just without sparing you the least bit more—oh, not a scrap, come!—to get out of you. What was it you had in mind when, in our distress, before Miles came back, over the letter from his school, you said, under my insistence, that you didn't pretend for him that he had not literally *ever* been 'bad'? He has *not* literally 'ever,' in these weeks that I myself have lived with him and so closely watched him; he has been an imperturbable little prodigy of delightful, loveable goodness. Therefore you might perfectly have made the claim for him if you had not, as it happened, seen an exception to take. What was your exception, and to what passage in your personal observation of him did you refer?"

It was a dreadfully austere inquiry, but levity was not our note, and, at any rate, before the grey dawn admonished us to separate I had got my answer. What my friend had had in mind proved to be immensely to the purpose. It was neither more nor less than the circumstance that for a period of several months Quint and the boy had been perpetually together. It was in fact the very appropriate truth that she had ventured to criticise the propriety, to hint at the incongruity, of so close an alliance, and even to go so far on the subject as a frank overture to Miss Jessel. Miss Jessel had, with a most strange manner, requested her to mind her business, and the good woman had, on this, directly approached little Miles. What she had said to him, since I pressed, was that *she* liked to see young gentlemen not forget their station.

I pressed again, of course, at this. "You reminded him that Quint was only a base menial?"

"As you might say! And it was his answer, for one thing, that was bad."

"And for another thing?" I waited. "He repeated your words to Quint?"

"No, not that. It's just what he *wouldn't!*" she could still impress upon me. "I was sure, at any rate," she added, "that he didn't. But he denied certain occasions."

"What occasions?"

"When they had been about together quite as if Quint were his tutor—and a very grand one—and Miss Jessel only for the little lady. When he had gone off with the fellow, I mean, and spent hours with him."

"He then prevaricated about it—he said he hadn't?" Her assent was clear enough to cause me to add in a moment: "I see. He lied."

"Oh!" Mrs. Grose mumbled. This was a suggestion that it didn't matter; which indeed she backed up by a further remark. "You see, after all, Miss Jessel didn't mind. She didn't forbid him."

I considered. "Did he put that to you as a justification?"

At this she dropped again. "No, he never spoke of it."

"Never mentioned her in connection with Quint?"

She saw, visibly flushing, where I was coming out. "Well, he didn't show anything. He denied," she repeated; "he denied."

Lord, how I pressed her now! "So that you could see he knew what was between the two wretches?"

"I don't know—I don't know!" the poor woman groaned.

"You do know, you dear thing," I replied; "only you haven't my dreadful boldness of mind, and you keep back, out of timidity and modesty and delicacy, even the impression that, in the past, when you had, without my aid, to flounder about in silence, most of all made you miserable. But I shall get it out of you yet! There was something in the boy that suggested to you," I continued, "that he covered and concealed their relation."

"Oh, he couldn't prevent—"

"Your learning the truth? I dare say! But, heavens," I fell, with vehemence, a-thinking, "what it shows that they must, to that extent, have succeeded in making of him!"

"Ah nothing that's not nice *now!*" Mrs. Grose lugubriously pleaded.

"I don't wonder you looked queer," I persisted, "when I mentioned to you the letter from his school!"

"I doubt if I looked as queer as you!" she retorted with homely force. "And if he was so bad then as that comes to, how is he such an angel now?"

"Yes, indeed—and if he was a fiend at school! How, how, how? Well," I said in my torment, "you must put it to me again, but I shall not be able to tell you for some days. Only, put it to me again!" I cried in a way that made my friend stare. "There are directions in which I must not for the present let myself go." Meanwhile I returned to her first example—the one to which she had just previously referred—of the boy's happy capacity for an occasional slip. "If Quint—on your remonstrance at the time you speak of—was a base menial, one of the things Miles said to you, I find myself guessing, was that you were another." Again her admission was so adequate that I continued: "And you forgave him that?"

"Wouldn't *you?*"

"Oh, yes!" And we exchanged there, in the stillness, a sound of the oddest amusement. Then I went on: "At all events, while he was with the man—"

"Miss Flora was with the woman. It suited them all!"

It suited me too, I felt, only too well; by which I mean that it suited exactly the particularly deadly view I was in the very act of forbidding myself to entertain. But I so far succeeded in checking the expression of this view that I will throw, just here, no further light on it than may be offered by the mention of my final observation to Mrs. Grose. "His having lied and been impudent are, I confess, less engaging specimens than I had hoped to have from you of the outbreak in him of the little natural man. Still," I mused, "they must do, for they make me feel more than ever that I must watch."

It made me blush, the next minute, to see in my friend's face how much more unreservedly she had forgiven him than her anecdote struck me as presenting to my own tenderness an occasion for doing. This came out when, at the schoolroom door, she quitted me. "Surely you don't accuse *him*—"

"Of carrying on an intercourse that he conceals from me? Ah, remember that, until further evidence, I now accuse nobody." Then, before shutting her out to go, by another passage, to her own place, "I must just wait," I wound up.

IX

I waited and waited, and the days, as they elapsed, took something from my consternation. A very few of them, in fact, passing, in constant sight of my pupils, without a fresh incident, sufficed to give to grievous fancies and even to odious memories a kind of brush of the sponge. I have spoken of the surrender to their extraordinary childish grace as a thing I could actively cultivate, and it may be imagined if I neglected now to address myself to this source for whatever it would yield. Stranger than I can express, certainly, was the effort to struggle against my new lights; it would doubtless have been however, a greater tension still had it not been so frequently successful. I used to wonder how my little charges could help guessing that I thought strange things about them; and the circumstance that these things only made them more interesting was not by itself a direct aid to keeping them in the dark. I trembled lest they should see that they *were* so immensely more interesting. Putting things at the worst, at all events, as in meditation I so often did, any clouding of their innocence could only be—blameless and foredoomed as they were—a reason the more for taking risks. There were moments when, by an irresistible impulse, I found myself catching them up and pressing them to my heart. As soon as I had done so I used to say to myself: "What will they think of that? Doesn't it betray too much?" It would have been easy to get into a sad, wild tangle about how much I might betray; but the real account, I feel, of the hours of peace that I could still enjoy was that the immediate charm of my companions was a beguilement still effective even under the shadow of the possibility that it was studied. For if it occurred to me that I might occasionally excite suspicion by the little outbreaks of my sharper passion for them, so too I remember wondering if I mightn't see a queerness in the traceable increase of their own demonstrations.

They were at this period extravagantly and preternaturally fond of me; which, after all, I could reflect, was no more than a graceful response in children perpetually bowed over and hugged. The homage of which they were so lavish succeeded, in truth, for my nerves, quite as well as if I never appeared to myself, as I may say, literally to catch them at a purpose in it. They had never, I think, wanted to do so many things for their poor protectress; I mean—though they got their lessons better and better, which was naturally what would please her most—in the way of diverting, entertaining, surprising her; reading her passages, telling her stories, acting her charades, pouncing out at her, in disguises, as animals and historical characters, and above all astonishing her by the "pieces" they had secretly got by heart and could interminably recite. I should never get to the bottom—were I to let myself go even now—of the prodigious private commentary, all under still more private correction, with which, in these days, I overscored their full hours. They had shown me from the first a facility for everything, a general faculty which, taking a fresh start, achieved remarkable flights. They got their little tasks as if they loved them, and indulged, from the mere exuberance of the gift, in the most unimposed little miracles of memory. They not only popped out at me as tigers and as Romans, but as Shakespeareans, astronomers, and navigators. This was so singularly the case that it had presumably much to do with the fact as to which, at the present day, I am at a loss for a different explanation: I allude to my unnatural composure on the subject of another school for Miles. What I remember is that I was content not, for the time, to open the question, and that contentment must have sprung from the sense of his perpetually striking show of cleverness. He was too clever for a bad governess, for a parson's daughter, to spoil; and the strangest if not the brightest thread in the pensive embroidery I just spoke of was the impression I might have got, if I had dared to work it out, that he was under some influence operating in his small intellectual life as a tremendous incitement.

If it was easy to reflect, however, that such a boy could postpone school, it was at least as marked that for such a boy to have been "kicked out" by a school-master was a mystification without end. Let me add that in their company now—and I was careful almost never to be out of it—I could follow no scent very far. We lived in a cloud of music and love and success and private theatricals. The musical sense in each of the children was of the quickest, but the elder in especial had a marvellous knack of catching and repeating. The schoolroom piano broke into all gruesome fancies; and when that failed there were confabulations in corners, with a sequel of one of them going out in the highest spirits in order to "come in" as something new. I had had brothers myself, and it was no revelation to me that little girls could be slavish idolaters of little boys. What surpassed everything was that there was a little boy in the world who could have for the inferior age, sex, and intelligence so fine a consideration. They were extraordinarily at one, and to say that they never either quarrelled or complained is to make the note of praise coarse for their quality of sweetness. Sometimes, indeed, when I dropped into coarseness, I perhaps came across traces of little understandings between them by which one of them should keep me occupied while the other slipped away. There is a *naïf* side, I suppose, in all diplomacy; but if my pupils practised upon me, it was surely with the minimum of grossness. It was all in the other quarter that, after a lull, the grossness broke out.

I find that I really hang back; but I must take my plunge. In going on with the record of what was hideous at Bly, I not only challenge the most liberal faith—for which I little care; but—and this is another matter—I renew what I myself suffered, I again push my way through it to the end. There came suddenly an hour after which, as I look back, the affair seems to me to have been all pure suffering; but I have at least reached the heart of it, and the straightest road out is doubtless to advance. One evening—with nothing to lead up or to prepare it—I felt the cold touch of the impression that had breathed on me the night of my arrival and which, much lighter then, as I have mentioned, I should probably have made little of in memory had my subsequent sojourn been less agitated. I had not gone to bed; I sat reading by a couple of candles. There was a roomful of old books at Bly—last-century fiction, some of it, which, to the extent of a distinctly deprecated renown, but never to so much as that of a stray specimen, had reached the sequestered home and appealed to the unavowed curiosity of my youth. I remember that the book I had in my hand was Fielding's *Amelia;* also that I was wholly awake. I recall further both a general conviction that it was horribly late and a particular objection to looking at my watch. I figure, finally, that the white curtain draping, in the fashion of those days, the head of Flora's little bed, shrouded, as I had assured myself long before, the perfection of childish rest. I recollect in short that, though I was deeply interested in my author, I found myself, at the turn of a page and with his spell all scattered, looking straight up from him and hard at the door of my room. There was a moment during which I listened, reminded of the faint sense I had had, the first night, of there being something undefineably astir in the house, and noted the soft breath of the open casement just move the half-drawn blind. Then, with all the marks of a deliberation that must have seemed magnificent had there been anyone to admire it, I laid down my book, rose to my feet, and, taking a candle, went straight out of the room and, from the passage, on which my light made little impression, noiselessly closed and locked the door.

I can say now neither what determined nor what guided me, but I went straight along the lobby, holding my candle high, till I came within sight of the tall window that presided over the great turn of the staircase. At this point I precipitately found myself aware of three things. They were practically simultaneous, yet they had flashes of succession. My candle, under a bold flourish, went out, and I perceived, by the uncovered window, that the yielding dusk of earliest morning rendered it unnecessary. Without it, the next instant, I saw that there was someone on the stair. I speak of sequences, but I required no lapse of seconds to stiffen myself for a third encounter with Quint. The apparition had reached the landing halfway up and was therefore on the spot nearest the window, where at sight of me, it stopped short and fixed me exactly as it had fixed me from the tower and from the garden. He knew me as well as I knew him; and so, in the cold, faint twilight, with a glimmer in the high glass and another on the polish of the oak stair below, we faced each other in our common intensity. He was absolutely, on this occasion, a living, detestable, dangerous presence. But that was not the wonder of wonders; I reserve this distinction for quite another circumstance: the circumstance that dread had unmistakeably quitted me and that there was nothing in me there that didn't meet and measure him.

I had plenty of anguish after that extraordinary moment, but I had, thank God, no terror. And he knew I had not—I found myself at the end of an instant magnificently aware of this. I felt, in a fierce rigour of confidence, that if I stood my ground a minute I should cease—for the time, at least—to have him to reckon with; and during the minute, accordingly, the thing was as human and hideous as a real interview: hideous just because it *was* human, as human as to have met alone, in the small hours, in a sleeping house, some enemy, some adventurer, some criminal. It was the dead silence of our long gaze at such close quarters that gave the whole horror, huge as it was, its only note of the unnatural. If I had met a murderer in such a place and at such an hour, we still at least would have spoken. Something would have passed, in life, between us; if nothing had passed one of us would have moved. The moment was so prolonged that it would have taken but little more to make me doubt if even *I* were in life. I can't express what followed it save by saying that the silence itself—which was indeed in a manner an attestation of my strength—became the element into which I saw the figure disappear; in which I definitely saw it turn as I might have seen the low wretch to which it had once belonged turn on receipt of an order, and pass, with my eyes on the villainous back that no hunch could have more disfigured, straight down the staircase and into the darkness in which the next bend was lost.

X

I remained awhile at the top of the stair, but with the effect presently of understanding that when my visitor had gone, he had gone: then I returned to my room. The foremost thing I saw there by the light of the candle I had left burning was that Flora's little bed was empty; and on this I caught my breath with all the terror that, five minutes before, I had been able to resist. I dashed at the place in which I had left her lying and over which (for the small silk counterpane and the sheets were disarranged) the white curtains had been deceivingly pulled forward; then my step, to my unutterable relief, produced an answering sound: I perceived an agitation of the window-blind, and the child, ducking down, emerged rosily from the other side of it. She stood there in so much of her candour and so little of her nightgown, with her pink bare feet and the golden glow of her curls. She looked intensely grave, and I had never had such a sense of losing an advantage acquired (the thrill of which had just been so prodigious) as on my consciousness that she addressed me with a reproach. "You naughty: where *have* you been?"—instead of challenging her own irregularity I found myself arraigned and explaining. She herself explained, for that matter, with the loveliest, eagerest simplicity. She had known suddenly, as she lay there, that I was out of the room, and had jumped up to see what had become of me. I had dropped, with the joy of her reappearance, back into my chair—feeling then, and then only, a little faint; and she had pattered straight over to me, thrown herself upon my knee, given herself to be held with the flame of the candle full in the wonderful little face that was still flushed with sleep. I remember closing my eyes an instant, yieldingly, consciously, as before the excess of something beautiful that shone out of the blue of her own. "You were looking for me out of the window?" I said. "You thought I might be walking in the grounds?"

"Well, you know, I thought someone was"—she never blanched as she smiled out that at me.

Oh, how I looked at her now! "And did you see anyone?"

"Ah, *no!*" she returned, almost with the full privilege of childish inconsequence, resentfully, though with a long sweetness in her little drawl of the negative.

At that moment, in the state of my nerves, I absolutely believed she lied; and if I once more closed my eyes it was before the dazzle of the three or four possible ways in which I might take this up. One of these, for a moment, tempted me with such singular intensity that, to withstand it, I must have gripped my little girl with a spasm that, wonderfully, she submitted to without a cry or a sign of fright. Why not break out at her on the spot and have it all over?—give it to her straight in her lovely little lighted face? "You see, you see, you *know* that you do and that you already quite suspect I believe it; therefore why not frankly confess it to me, so that we may at least live with it together and learn perhaps, in the strangeness of our fate, where we are and what it means?" This solicitation dropped, alas, as it came: if I could immediately have succumbed to it I might have spared myself—well you'll see what. Instead of succumbing I sprang again to my feet, looked at her bed, and took a helpless middle way. "Why did you pull the curtain over the place to make me think you were still there?"

Flora luminously considered; after which, with her little divine smile: "Because I don't like to frighten you!"

"But if I had, by your idea, gone out—?"

She absolutely declined to be puzzled; she turned her eyes to the flame of the candle as if the question were as irrelevant, or at any rate as impersonal, as Mrs. Marcet or nine-times-nine. "Oh, but you know," she quite adequately answered, "that you might come back, you dear, and that you *have!*" And after a little, when she had got into bed, I had, for a long time, by amost sitting on her to hold her hand, to prove that I recognised the pertinence of my return.

You may imagine the general complexion, from that moment, of my nights. I repeatedly sat up till I didn't know when; I selected moments when my room-mate unmistakeably slept, and, stealing out, took noiseless turns in the passage and even pushed as far as to where I had last met Quint. But I never met him there again; and I may as well say at once that I on no other occasion saw him in the house. I just missed, on the staircase, on the other hand, a different adventure. Looking down it from the top I once recognised the presence of a woman seated on one of the lower steps with her back presented to me, her body half bowed and her head, in an attitude of woe, in her hands. I had been there but an instant, however, when she vanished without looking round at me. I knew, none the less, exactly what dreadful face she had to show; and I wondered whether, if instead of being above I had been below, I should have had, for going up, the same nerve I had lately shown Quint. Well, there continued to be plenty of chance for nerve. On the eleventh night after my latest encounter with that gentleman—they were all numbered now—I had an alarm that perilously skirted it and that indeed, from the particular quality of its unexpectedness, proved quite my sharpest shock. It was precisely the first night during this series that, weary with watching, I had felt that I might again without laxity lay myself down at my old hour. I slept immediately and, as I afterwards know, till about one o'clock; but when I woke it was to sit straight up, as completely roused as if a hand had shook me. I had left a light burning, but it was now out, and I felt an instant certainty that Flora had extinguished it. This brought me to my feet and straight, in the darkness, to her bed, which I found she had left. A glance at the window enlightened me further, and the striking of a match completed the picture.

The child had again got up—this time blowing out the taper, and had again, for some purpose of observation or response, squeezed in behind the blind and was peering out into the night. That she now saw—as she had not, I had satisfied myself, the previous time—was proved to me by the fact that she was disturbed neither by my re-illumination nor by the haste I made to get into slippers and into a wrap. Hidden, protected, absorbed, she evidently rested on the sill—the casement opened forward—and gave herself up. There was a great still moon to help her, and this fact had counted in my quick decision. She was face to face with the apparition we had met at the lake, and could now communicate with it as she had not then been able to do. What I, on my side, had to care for was, without disturbing her, to reach, from the corridor, some other window in the same quarter. I got to the door without her hearing me; I got out of it, closed it and listened, from the other side, for some sound from her. While I stood in the passage I had my eyes on her brother's door, which was but ten steps off and which, indescribably, produced in me a renewal of the strange impulse that I lately spoke of as my temptation. What if I should go straight in and march to *his* window?—what if, by risking to his boyish bewilderment a revelation of my motive, I should throw across the rest of the mystery the long halter of my boldness?

This thought held me sufficiently to make me cross to his threshold and pause again. I preternaturally listened; I figured to myself what might portentously be; I wondered if his bed were also empty and he too were secretly at watch. It was a deep, soundless minute, at the end of which my impulse failed. He was quiet; he might be innocent; the risk was hideous; I turned away. There was a figure in the grounds—a figure prowling for a sight, the visitor with whom Flora was engaged; but it was not the visitor most concerned with my boy. I hesitated afresh, but on other grounds and only a few seconds; then I had made my choice. There were empty rooms at Bly, and it was only a question of choosing the right one. The right one suddenly presented itself to me as the lower one—though high above the gardens—in the solid corner of the house that I have spoken of as the old tower. This was a large, square chamber, arranged with some state as a bedroom, the extravagant size of which made it so inconvenient that it had not for years, though kept by Mrs. Grose in exemplary order, been occupied. I had often admired it and I knew my way about in it; I had only after just faltering at the first chill gloom of its disuse, to pass across it and unbolt as quietly as I could one of the shutters. Achieving this transit, I uncovered the glass without a sound and, applying my face to the pane, was able, the darkness without being much less than within, to see that I commanded the right direction. Then I saw something more. The moon made the night extraordinarily penetrable and showed me on the lawn a person, diminished by distance, who stood there motionless and as if fascinated, looking up to where I had appeared—looking, that is, not so much straight at me as at something that was apparently above me. There was clearly another person above me—there was a person on the tower; but the presence on the lawn was not in the least what I had conceived and had confidently hurried to meet. The presence on the lawn—I felt sick as I made it out—was poor little Miles himself.

XI

It was not till late next day that I spoke to Mrs. Grose; the rigour with which I kept my pupils in sight making it often difficult to meet her privately, and the more as we each felt the importance of not provoking—on the part of the servants quite as much as on that of the children—any suspicion of a secret flurry or of a discussion of mysteries. I drew a great security in this particular from her mere smooth aspect. There was nothing in her fresh face to pass on to others my horrible confidences. She believed me, I was sure, absolutely: if she hadn't I don't know what would have become of me, for I couldn't have borne the business alone. But she was a magnificent monument to the blessing of a want of imagination, and if she could see in our little charges nothing but their beauty and amiability, their happiness and cleverness, she had no direct communication with the sources of my trouble. If they had been at all visibly blighted or battered, she would doubtless have grown, on tracing it back, haggard enough to match them; as matters stood, however, I could feel her, when she surveyed them, with her large white arms folded and the habit of serenity in all her look, thank the Lord's mercy that if they were ruined the pieces would still serve. Flights of fancy gave place, in her mind, to a steady fireside glow, and I had already begun to perceive how, with the development of the conviction that—as time went on without a public accident—our young things could, after all, look out for themselves, she addressed her greatest solicitude to the sad case presented by their instructress. That, for myself, was a sound simplification: I could engage that, to the world, my face should tell no tales, but it would have been, in the conditions, an immense added strain to find myself anxious about hers.

At the hour I now speak of she had joined me, under pressure, on the terrace, where, with the lapse of the season, the afternoon sun was now agreeable; and we sat there together while, before us, at a distance, but within call if we wished, the children strolled to and fro in one of their most manageable moods. They moved slowly, in unison, below us, over the lawn, the boy, as they went, reading aloud from a storybook and passing his arm round his sister to keep her quite in touch. Mrs. Grose watched them with positive placidity; then I caught the suppressed intellectual creak with which she conscientiously turned to take from me a view of the back of the tapestry. I had made her a receptacle of lurid things, but there was an odd recognition of my superiority—my accomplishments and my function—in her patience under my pain. She offered her mind to my disclosures as, had I wished to mix a witch's broth and proposed it with assurance, she would have held out a large clean saucepan. This had become thoroughly her attitude by the time that, in my recital of the events of the night, I reached the point of what Miles had said to me when, after seeing him, at such a monstrous hour, almost on the very spot where he happened now to be, I had gone down to bring him in; choosing then, at the window, with a concentrated need of not alarming the house, rather that method than a signal more resonant. I had left her meanwhile in little doubt of my small hope of representing with success even to her actual sympathy my sense of the real splendour of the little inspiration with which, after I had got him into the house, the boy met my final articulate challenge. As soon as I appeared in the moonlight on the terrace, he had come to me as straight as possible; on which I had taken his hand without a word and led him, through the dark spaces, up the staircase where Quint had so hungrily hovered for him, along the lobby where I had listened and trembled, and so to his forsaken room.

Not a sound, on the way, had passed between us, and I had wondered—oh, *how* I had wondered!—if he were groping about in his little mind for something plausible and not too grotesque. It would tax his invention, certainly, and I felt, this time, over his real embarrassment, a curious thrill of triumph. It was a sharp trap for the inscrutable! He couldn't play any longer at innocence; so how the deuce would he get out of it? There beat in me indeed, with the passionate throb of this question, an equal dumb appeal as to how the deuce *I* should. I was confronted at last, as never yet, with all the risk attached even now to sounding my own horrid note. I remember in fact that as we pushed into his little chamber, where the bed had not been slept in at all and the window, uncovered to the moonlight, made the place so clear that there was no need of striking a match—I remember how I suddenly dropped, sank upon the edge of the bed from the force of the idea that he must know how he really, as they say, "had" me. He could do what he liked, with all his cleverness to help him, so long as I should continue to defer to the old tradition of the criminality of those caretakers of the young who minister to superstitions and fears. He "had" me indeed, and in a cleft stick; for who would ever absolve me, who would consent that I should go unhung, if, by the faintest tremor of an overture, I were the first to introduce into our perfect intercourse an element so dire? No, no: it was useless to attempt to convey to Mrs. Grose, just as it is scarcely less so to attempt to suggest here, how, in our short, stiff brush in the dark, he fairly shook me with admiration. I was of course thoroughly kind and merciful; never, never yet had I placed on his little shoulders hands of such tenderness as those with which, while I rested against the bed, I held him there well under fire. I had no alternative but, in form at least, to put it to him.

"You must tell me now—and all the truth. What did you go out for? What were you doing there?"

I can still see his wonderful smile, the whites of his beautiful eyes, and the uncovering of his little teeth shine to me in the dusk. "If I tell you why, will you understand?" My heart, at this, leaped into my mouth. *Would* he tell me why? I found no sound on my lips to press it, and I was aware of replying only with a vague, repeated, grimacing nod. He was gentleness itself, and while I wagged my head at him he stood there more than ever a little fairy prince. It was his brightness indeed that gave me a respite. Would it be so great if he were really going to tell me? "Well," he said at last, "just exactly in order that you should do this."

"Do what?"

"Think me—for a change—*bad!*" I shall never forget the sweetness and gaiety with which he brought out the word, nor how, on top of it, he bent forward and kissed me. It was practically the end of everything. I met his kiss and I had to make, while I folded him for a minute in my arms, the most stupendous effort not to cry. He had given exactly the account of himself that permitted least of my going behind it, and it was only with the effect of confirming my acceptance of it that, as I presently glanced about the room, I could say—

"Then you didn't undress at all?"

He fairly glittered in the gloom. "Not at all. I sat up and read."

"And when did you go down?"

"At midnight. When I'm bad I *am* bad!"

"I see, I see—it's charming. But how could you be sure I would know it?"

"Oh, I arranged that with Flora." His answers rang out with a readiness! "She was to get up and look out."

"Which is what she did do." It was I who fell into the trap!

"So she disturbed you, and, to see what she was looking at, you also looked—you saw."

"While you," I concurred, "caught your death in the night air!"

He literally bloomed so from this exploit that he could afford radiantly to assent. "How otherwise should I have been bad enough?" he asked. Then, after another embrace, the incident and our interview closed on my recognition of all the reserves of goodness that, for his joke, he had been able to draw upon.

XII

The particular impression I had received proved in the morning light, I repeat, not quite successfully presentable to Mrs. Grose, though I reinforced it with the mention of still another remark that he had made before we separated. "It all lies in half-a-dozen words," I said to her, "words that really settle the matter. 'Think, you know, what I *might* do!' He threw that off to show me how good he is. He knows down to the ground what he 'might' do. That's what he gave them a taste of at school."

"Lord, you do change!" cried my friend.

"I don't change—I simply make it out. The four, depend upon it, perpetually meet. If on either of these last nights you had been with either child, you would clearly have understood. The more I've watched and waited the more I've felt that if there were nothing else to make it sure it would be made so by the systematic silence of each. *Never,* by a slip of the tongue, have they so much as alluded to either of their old friends, any more than Miles has alluded to his expulsion. Oh yes, we may sit here and look at them, and they may show off to us there to their fill; but even while they pretend to be lost in their fairy-tale they're steeped in their vision of the dead restored. He's not reading to her," I declared; "they're talking of *them*—they're talking horrors! I go on, I know, as if I were crazy; and it's a wonder I'm not. What I've seen would have made *you* so;

but it has only made me more lucid, made me get hold of still other things."

My lucidity must have seemed awful, but the charming creatures who were victims of it, passing and repassing in their interlocked sweetness, gave my colleague something to hold on by; and I felt how tight she held as, without stirring in the breath of my passion, she covered them still with her eyes. "Of what other things have you got hold?"

"Why, of the very things that have delighted, fascinated, and yet, at bottom, as I now so strangely see, mystified and troubled me. Their more than earthly beauty, their absolutely unnatural goodness. It's a game," I went on; "it's a policy and a fraud!"

"On the part of little darlings—?"

"As yet mere lovely babies? Yes, mad as that seems!" The very act of bringing it out really helped me to trace it—follow it all up and piece it all together. "They haven't been good—they've only been absent. It has been easy to live with them, because they're simply leading a life of their own. They're not mine—they're not ours. They're his and they're hers!"

"Quint's and that woman's?"

"Quint's and that woman's. They want to get to them."

Oh, how, at this, poor Mrs. Grose appeared to study them! "But for what?"

"For the love of all the evil that, in those dreadful days, the pair put into them. And to ply them with that evil still, to keep up the work of demons, is what brings the others back."

"Laws!" said my friend under her breath. The exclamation was homely, but it revealed a real acceptance of my further proof of what, in the bad time—for there had been a worse even than this! —must have occurred. There could have been no such justification for me as the plain assent of her experience to whatever depth of depravity I found credible in our brace of scoundrels. It was in obvious submission of memory that she brought out after a moment: "They *were* rascals! But what can they now do?" she pursued.

"Do?" I echoed so loud that Miles and Flora, as they passed at their distance, paused an instant in their walk and looked at us. "Don't they do enough?" I demanded in a lower tone, while the children, having smiled and nodded and kissed hands to us, resumed their exhibition. We were held by it a minute; then I answered: "They can destroy them!" At this my companion did turn, but the inquiry she launched was a silent one, the effect of which was to make me more explicit. "They don't know, as yet, quite how—but they're trying hard. They're seen only across, as it were, and beyond—in strange places and on high places, the top of towers, the roof of houses, the outside of windows, the further edge of pools; but there's a deep design, on either side, to shorten the distance and overcome the obstacle; and the success of the tempters is only a question of time. They've only to keep to their suggestions of danger."

"For the children to come?"

"And perish in the attempt!" Mrs. Grose slowly got up, and I scrupulously added: "Unless, of course, we can prevent!"

Standing there before me while I kept my seat, she visibly turned things over. "Their uncle must do the preventing. He must take them away."

"And who's to make him?"

She had been scanning the distance, but she now dropped on me a foolish face. "You, Miss."

"By writing to him that his house is poisoned and his little nephew and niece mad?"

"But if they *are,* Miss?"

"And if I am myself, you mean? That's charming news to be sent him by a governess whose prime undertaking was to give him no worry."

Mrs. Grose considered, following the children again. "Yes, he do hate worry. That was the great reason—"

"Why those fiends took him in so long? No doubt, though his indifference must have been awful. As I'm not a fiend, at any rate, I shouldn't take him in."

My companion, after an instant and for all answer, sat down again and grasped my arm. "Make him at any rate come to you."

I stared. "To *me?*" I had a sudden fear of what she might do. " 'Him'?"

"He ought to *be* here—he ought to help."

I quickly rose, and I think I must have shown her a queerer face than ever yet. "You see me asking him for a visit?" No, with her eyes on my face she evidently couldn't. Instead of it even—as a woman reads another—she could see what I myself saw: his derision, his amusement, his contempt for the break-down of my resignation at being left alone and for the fine machinery I had set in motion to attract his attention to my slighted charms. She didn't know—no one knew—how proud I had been to serve him and to stick to our terms; yet she none the less took the measure, I think, of the warning I now gave her. "If you should so lose your head as to appeal to him for me—"

She was really frightened. "Yes, Miss?"

"I would leave, on the spot, both him and you."

XIII

It was all very well to join them, but speaking to them proved quite as much as ever an effort beyond my strength—offered, in close quarters, difficulties as insurmountable as before. This situation continued a month, and with new aggravations and particular notes, the note above all, sharper and sharper, of the small ironic consciousness on the part of my pupils. It was not, I am as sure today as I was sure then, my mere infernal imagination: it was absolutely traceable that they were aware of my predicament and that this strange relation made, in a manner, for a long time, the air in which we moved. I don't mean that they had their tongues in their cheeks or did anything vulgar, for that was not one of their dangers: I do mean, on the other hand, that the element of the unnamed and untouched became, between us, greater than any other, and that so much avoidance could not have been so successfully effected without a great deal of tacit arrangement. It was as if, at moments, we were perpetually coming into sight of subjects before which we must stop short, turning suddenly out of alleys that we perceived to be blind, closing with a little bang that made us look at each other—for, like all bangs, it was something louder than we had intended—the doors we had indiscreetly opened. All roads lead to Rome, and there were times when it might have struck us that almost every branch of study or subject of conversation skirted forbidden ground. Forbidden ground was the question of the return of the dead in general and of whatever, in especial, might survive, in memory, of the friends little children had lost. There were days when I could have sworn that one of them had, with a small invisible nudge, said to the other: "She thinks she'll do it this time—but she *won't!*" To "do it" would have been to indulge for instance—and for once in a way—in some direct reference to the lady who had prepared them for my discipline. They had a delightful endless appetite for passages in my own history, to which I had again and again treated them; they were in possession of everything that had ever happened to me, had had, with every circumstance, the story of my smallest adventures and of those of my brothers and sisters and of the cat and the dog at home, as well as many particulars of the eccentric nature of my father, of the furniture and arrangement of our house, and of the conversation of the old women of our village. There were things enough, taking one with another, to chatter about, if one went very fast and knew by instinct when to go round. They pulled with an art of their own the strings of my invention and my memory; and nothing else perhaps, when I thought of such occasions afterwards, gave me so the suspicion of being watched from under cover. It was in any case over *my* life, *my* past, and *my* friends alone that we could take anything like our ease—a state of affairs that led them sometimes without the least pertinence to break out into sociable reminders. I was invited—with no visible connection—to repeat afresh Goody Gosling's celebrated *mot* or to confirm the details already supplied as to the cleverness of the vicarage pony.

It was partly at such junctures as these and partly at quite different ones that, with the turn my matters had now taken, my predicament, as I have called it, grew most sensible. The fact that the days passed for me without another encounter ought, it would have appeared, to have done something toward soothing my nerves. Since the light brush, that second night on the upper landing, of the presence of a woman at the foot of the stair, I had seen nothing, whether in or out of the house, that one had better not have seen. There was many a corner round which I expected to come upon Quint, and many a situation that, in a merely sinister way, would have favoured the appearance of Miss Jessel. The summer had turned, the summer had gone; the autumn had dropped upon Bly and had blown out half our lights. The place, with its grey sky and withered garlands, its bared spaces and scattered dead leaves, was like a theatre after the performance—all strewn with crumpled playbills. There were exactly states of the air, conditions of sound and of stillness, unspeakable impressions of the *kind* of ministering moment, that brought back to me, long enough to catch it, the feeling of the medium in which, that June evening out-of-doors, I had had my first sight of Quint, and in which, too, at those other instants, I had, after seeing him through the window, looked for him in vain in the circle of shrubbery. I recognised the signs, the portents—I recognised the moment, the spot. But they remained unaccompanied and empty, and I continued unmolested; if unmolested one could call a young woman whose sensibility had, in the most extraordinary fashion, not declined but deepened. I had said in my talk with Mrs. Grose on that horrid scene of Flora's by the lake—and had perplexed her by so saying—that it would from that moment distress me much more to lose my power than to keep it. I had then expressed what was vividly in my mind: the truth that, whether the children really saw or not—since, that is, it was not yet definitely proved—I greatly preferred, as a safeguard, the fulness of my own exposure. I was ready to know the very worst that was to be known. What I had then had an ugly glimpse of was that my eyes might be sealed just while theirs were most opened. Well, my eyes *were* sealed, it appeared, at present—a consummation for which it seemed blasphemous not to thank God. There was, alas, a difficulty about that: I would have thanked him with all my soul had I not had in a proportionate measure this conviction of the secret of my pupils.

How can I retrace today the strange steps of my obsession? There were times of our being together when I would have been ready to swear that, literally, in my presence, but with my direct sense of it closed, they had visitors who were known and were welcome. Then it was that, had I not been deterred by the very chance that such an injury might prove greater than the injury to be averted, my exultation would have broken out. "They're here, they're here, you little wretches," I would have cried, "and you can't deny it now!" The little wretches denied it with all the added volume of their sociability and their tenderness, in just the crystal depths of which—like the flash of a fish in a stream—the mockery of their advantage peeped up. The shock, in truth, had sunk into me still deeper than I knew on the night when, looking out to see either Quint or Miss Jessel under the stars, I had beheld the boy over whose rest I watched and who had immediately brought in with him—had straightway, there, turned it on me—the lovely upward look with which, from the battlements above me, the hideous apparition of Quint had played. If it was a question of a scare, my discovery on this occasion had scared me more than any other, and it was in the condition of nerves produced by it that I made my actual inductions. They harassed me so that sometimes, at odd moments, I shut myself up audibly to rehearse—it was at once a fantastic relief and a renewed despair—the manner in which I might come to the point. I approached it from one side and the other while, in my room, I flung myself about, but I always broke down in the monstrous utterance of names. As they died away on my lips, I said to myself that I should indeed help them to represent something infamous, if by pronouncing them, I should violate as rare a little case of instinctive delicacy as any schoolroom, probably, had ever known. When I said to myself: "*They* have the manners to be silent, and you, trusted as you are, the baseness to speak!" I felt myself crimson and I covered my face with my hands. After these secret scenes I chattered more than ever, going on volubly enough 'til one of our prodigious, palpable hushes occurred—I can call them nothing else—the strange, dizzy lift or swim (I try for terms!) into a stillness, a pause of all life, that had nothing to do with the more or less noise that at the moment we might be engaged in making and that I could hear through any deepened exhilaration or quickened recitation or louder strum of the piano. Then it was that the others, the outsiders, were there. Though they were not angels, they "passed," as the French say, causing me, while they stayed, to tremble with the fear of their addressing to their younger victims some yet more infernal message or more vivid image than they had thought good enough for myself.

What it was most impossible to get rid of was the cruel idea that, whatever I had seen, Miles and Flora saw *more*—things terrible and unguessable and that sprang from dreadful passages of intercourse in the past. Such things naturally left on the surface, for the time, a chill which we vociferously denied that we felt; and we had, all three, with repetition, got into such splendid training that we went, each time, almost automatically, to mark the close of the incident, through the very same movements. It was striking of the children, at all events, to kiss me inveterately with a kind of wild irrelevance and never to fail—one or the other—of the precious question that had helped us through many a peril. "When do you think he *will* come? Don't you think we *ought* to write?"—there was nothing like that inquiry, we found by experience, for carrying off an awkwardness. "He" of course was their uncle in Harley Street; and we lived in much profusion of theory that he might at any moment arrive to mingle in our circle. It was impossible to have given less encouragement than he had done to such a doctrine, but if we had not had the doctrine to fall back upon we should have deprived each other of some of our finest exhibitions. He never wrote to them—that may have been selfish, but it was a part of the flattery of his trust of me; for the way in which a man pays his highest tribute to a woman is apt to be but by the more festal celebration of one of the sacred laws of his comfort; and I held that I carried out the spirit of the pledge given not to appeal to him when I let my charges understand that their own letters were but charming literary exercises. They were too beautiful to be posted; I kept them myself; I have them all to this hour. This was a rule indeed which only added to the satiric effect of my being plied with the supposition that he might at any moment be among us. It was exactly as if my charges knew how almost more awkward than anything else that might be for me. There appears to me, moreover, as I look back, no note in all this more extraordinary than the mere fact that, in spite of my tension and of their triumph, I never lost patience with them. Adorable they must in truth have been, I now reflect, that I didn't in these days hate them! Would exasperation, however, if relief had longer been postponed, finally have betrayed me? It little matters, for relief arrived. I call it relief, though it was only the relief that a snap brings to a strain or the burst of a thunderstorm to a day of suffocation. It was at least change, and it came with a rush.

XIV

Walking to church a certain Sunday morning, I had little Miles at my side and his sister, in advance of us and at Mrs. Grose's, well in sight. It was a crisp, clear day, the first of its order for some time; the night had brought a touch of frost, and autumn air, bright and sharp, made the church-bells almost gay. It was an odd accident of thought that I should have happened at such a moment to be particularly and very gratefully struck with the obedience of my little charges. Why did they never resent my inexorable, my perpetual society? Something or other had brought nearer home to me that I had all but pinned the boy to my shawl and that, in the way our companions were marshalled before me, I might have appeared to provide against some danger of rebellion. I was like a gaoler with an eye to possible surprises and escapes. But all this belonged—I mean their magnificent little surrender—just to the special array of the facts that were most abysmal. Turned out for Sunday by his uncle's tailor, who had had a free hand and a notion of pretty waistcoats and of his grand little air, Miles's whole title to independence, the rights of his sex and situation, were so stamped upon him that if he had suddenly struck for freedom I should have had nothing to say. I was by the strangest of chances wondering how I should meet him when the revolution unmistakeably occurred. I call it a revolution because I now see how, with the word he spoke, the curtain rose on the last act of my dreadful drama and the catastrophe was precipitated. "Look here, my dear, you know," he charmingly said, "when in the world, please, am I going back to school?"

Transcribed here the speech sounds harmless enough, particularly as uttered in the sweet, high, casual pipe with which, at all interlocutors, but above all at his eternal governess, he threw off intonations as if he were tossing roses. There was something in them that always made one "catch," and I caught, at any rate, now so effectually that I stopped as short as if one of the trees of the park had fallen across the road. There was something new, on the spot, between us, and he was perfectly aware that I recognised it, though, to enable me to do so, he had no need to look a whit less candid and charming than usual. I could feel in him how he already, from my at first finding nothing to reply, perceived the advantage he had gained. I was so slow to find anything that he had plenty of time, after a minute, to continue with his suggestive but inconclusive smile: "You know, my dear, that for a fellow to be with a lady *always—!*" His "my dear" was constantly on his lips for me, and nothing could have expressed more the exact shade of the sentiment with which I desired to inspire my pupils than its fond familiarity. It was so respectfully easy.

But, oh, how I felt that at present I must pick my own phrases! I remember that, to gain time, I tried to laugh, and I seemed to see in the beautiful face with which he watched me how ugly and queer I looked. "And always with the same lady?" I returned.

He neither blenched nor winked. The whole thing was virtually out between us. "Ah, of course, she's a jolly, 'perfect' lady; but, after all, I'm a fellow, don't you see? that's—well, getting on."

I lingered there with him an instant ever so kindly. "Yes, you're getting on." Oh, but I felt helpless!

I have kept to this day the heartbreaking little idea of how he seemed to know that and to play with it. "And you can't say I've not been awfully good, can you?"

I laid my hand on his shoulder, for, though I felt how much better it would have been to walk on, I was not yet quite able. "No, I can't say that, Miles."

"Except just that one night, you know—!"

"That one night?" I couldn't look as straight as he.

"Why, when I went down—went out of the house."

"Oh, yes. But I forget what you did it for."

"You forget?"—he spoke with the sweet extravagance of childish reproach. "Why, it was to show you I could!"

"Oh, yes, you could."

"And I can again."

I felt that I might, perhaps, after all succeed in keeping my wits about me. "Certainly. But you won't."

"No, not *that* again. It was nothing."

"It was nothing," I said. "But we must go on."

He resumed our walk with me, passing his hand into my arm. "Then when *am* I going back?"

I wore, in turning it over, my most responsible air. "Were you very happy at school?"

He just considered. "Oh, I'm happy enough anywhere!"

"Well, then," I quavered, "if you're just as happy here—!"

"Ah, but that isn't everything! Of course *you* know a lot—"

"But you hint that you know almost as much?" I risked as he paused.

"Not half I want to!" Miles honestly professed. "But it isn't so much that."

"What is it, then?"

"Well—I want to see more life."

"I see; I see." We had arrived within sight of the church and of various persons, including several of the household of Bly, on their way to it and clustered about the door to see us go in. I quickened our step; I wanted to get there before the question between us opened up much further; I reflected hungrily that, for more than an hour, he would have to be silent; and I thought with envy of the comparative dusk of the pew and of the almost spiritual help of the hassock on which I might bend my knees. I seemed literally to be running a race with some confusion to which he was about to reduce me, but I felt that he had got in first when, before we had even entered the churchyard, he threw out—

"I want my own sort!"

It literally made me bound forward. "There are not many of your own sort, Miles!" I laughed. "Unless perhaps dear little Flora!"

"You really compare me to a baby girl?"

This found me singularly weak. "Don't you, then, *love* our sweet Flora?"

"If I didn't—and you too; if I didn't—!" he repeated as if retreating for a jump, yet leaving his thought so unfinished that, after we had come into the gate, another stop, which he imposed on me by the pressure of his arm, had become inevitable. Mrs. Grose and Flora had passed into the church, the other worshippers had followed, and we were, for the minute, alone among the old, thick graves. We had paused, on the path from the gate, by a low, oblong, table-like tomb.

"Yes. If you didn't—?"

He looked, while I waited, about at the graves. "Well, you know what!" But he didn't move, and he presently produced something that made me drop straight down on the stone slab, as if suddenly to rest. "Does my uncle think what *you* think?"

I markedly rested. "How do you know what I think?"

"Ah, well, of course I don't; for it strikes me you never tell me. But I mean does *he* know?"

"Know what, Miles?"

"Why, the way I'm going on."

I perceived quickly enough that I could make, to this inquiry, no answer that would not involve something of a sacrifice of my employer. Yet it appeared to me that we were all, at Bly, sufficiently sacrificed to make that venial. "I don't think your uncle much cares."

Miles, on this, stood looking at me. "Then don't you think he can be made to?"

"In what way?"

"Why, by his coming down."

"But who'll get him to come down?"

"*I* will!" the boy said with extraordinary brightness and emphasis. He gave me another look charged with that expression and then marched off alone into church.

XV

The business was practically settled from the moment I never followed him. It was a pitiful surrender to agitation, but my being aware of this had somehow no power to restore me. I only sat there on my tomb and read into what my little friend had said to me the fulness of its meaning; by the time I had grasped the whole of which I had also embraced, for absence, the pretext that I was ashamed to offer my pupils and the rest of the congregation such an example of delay. What I said to myself above all was that Miles had got something out of me and that the proof of it, for him, would be just this awkward collapse. He had got out of me that there was something I was much afraid of and that he should probably be able to make use of my fear to gain, for his own purpose, more freedom. My fear was of having to deal with the intolerable question of the grounds of his dismissal from school, for that was really but the question of the horrors gathered behind. That his uncle should arrive to treat with me of these things was a solution that, strictly speaking, I ought now to have desired to bring on; but I could so little face the ugliness and the pain of it that I simply procrastinated and lived from hand to mouth. The boy, to my deep discomposure, was immensely in the right, was in a position to say to me: "Either you clear up with my guardian the mystery of this interruption of my studies, or you cease to expect me to lead with you a life that's so unnatural for a boy." What was so unnatural for the particular boy I was concerned with was this sudden revelation of a consciousness and a plan.

That was what really overcame me, what prevented my going in. I walked round the church, hesitating, hovering; I reflected that I had already, with him, hurt myself beyond repair. Therefore I could patch up nothing, and it was too extreme an effort to squeeze beside him into the pew: he would be so much more sure than ever to pass his arm into mine and make me sit there for an hour in close, silent contact with his commentary on our talk. For the first minute since his arrival I wanted to get away from him. As I paused beneath the high east window and listened to the sounds of worship, I was taken with an impulse that might master me, I felt, completely should I give it the least encouragement. I might easily put an end to my predicament by getting away altogether. Here was my chance; there was no one to stop me; I could give the whole thing up—turn my back and retreat. It was only a question of hurrying again, for a few preparations, to the house which the attendance at church of so many of the servants would practically have left unoccupied. No one, in short, could blame me if I should just drive desperately off. What was it to get away if I got away only till dinner? That would be in a couple of hours, at the end of which—I had the acute prevision—my little pupils would play at innocent wonder about my non-appearance in their train.

"What *did* you do, you naughty, bad thing? Why in the world, to worry us so—and take our thoughts off too, don't you know?—did you desert us at the very door?" I couldn't meet such questions nor, as they asked them, their false little lovely eyes; yet it was all so exactly what I should have to meet that, as the prospect grew sharp to me, I at last let myself go.

I got, so far as the immediate moment was concerned, away; I came straight out of the churchyard and, thinking hard, retraced my steps through the park. It seemed to me that by the time I reached the house I had made up my mind I would fly. The Sunday stillness both of the approaches and of the interior, in which I met no one, fairly excited me with a sense of opportunity. Were I to get off quickly, this way, I should get off without a scene, without a word. My quickness would have to be remarkable, however, and the question of a conveyance was the great one to settle. Tormented, in the hall, with difficulties and obstacles, I remember sinking down at the foot of the staircase—suddenly collapsing there on the lowest step and then, with a revulsion, recalling that it was exactly where more than a month before, in the darkness of night and just so bowed with evil things, I had seen the spectre of the most horrible of women. At this I was able to straighten myself; I went the rest of the way up; I made, in my bewilderment, for the schoolroom, where there were objects belonging to me that I should have to take. But I opened the door to find again, in a flash, my eyes unsealed. In the presence of what I saw I reeled straight back upon my resistance.

Seated at my own table in clear noonday light I saw a person whom, without my previous experience, I should have taken at the first blush for some housemaid who might have stayed at home to look after the place and who, availing herself of rare relief from observation and of the schoolroom table and my pens, ink, and paper, had applied herself to the considerable effort of a letter to her sweetheart. There was an effort in the way that, while her arms rested on the table, her hands with evident weariness supported her head; but at the moment I took this in I had already become aware that, in spite of my entrance, her attitude strangely persisted. Then it was—with the very act of its announcing itself—that her identity flared up in a change of posture. She rose, not as if she had heard me, but with an indescribable grand melancholy of indifference and detachment, and, within a dozen feet of me, stood there as my vile predecessor. Dishonoured and tragic, she was all before me; but even as I fixed and, for memory, secured it, the awful image passed away. Dark as midnight in her black dress, her haggard beauty and her unutterable woe, she had looked at me long enough to appear to say that her right to sit at my table was as good as mine to sit at hers. While these instants lasted indeed I had the extraordinary chill of a feeling that it was I who was the intruder. It was as a wild protest against it that, actually addressing her—"You terrible, miserable woman!"—I heard myself break into a sound that, by the open door, rang through the long passage and the empty house. She looked at me as if she heard me, but I had recovered myself and cleared the air. There was nothing in the room the next minute but the sunshine and a sense that I must stay.

XVI

I had so perfectly expected that the return of my pupils would be marked by a demonstration that I was freshly upset at having to take into account that they were dumb about my absence. Instead of gaily denouncing and caressing me, they made no allusion to my having failed them, and I was left, for the time, on perceiving that she too said nothing, to study Mrs. Grose's odd face. I did this to such purpose that I made sure they had in some way bribed her to silence; a silence that, however, I would engage to break down on the first private opportunity. This opportunity came before tea: I secured five minutes with her in the housekeeper's room, where, in the twilight, amid a smell of lately-baked bread, but with the place all swept and garnished, I found her sitting in pained placidity before the fire. So I see her still, so I see her best: facing the flame from her straight chair in the dusky, shining room, a large clean image of the "put away"—of drawers closed and locked and rest without a remedy.

"Oh, yes, they asked me to say nothing; and to please them—so long as they were there—of course I promised. But what had happened to you?"

"I only went with you for the walk," I said. "I had then to come back to meet a friend."

She showed her surprise. "A friend—*you*?"

"Oh, yes, I have a couple!" I laughed. "But did the children give you a reason?"

"For not alluding to your leaving us? Yes; they said you would like it better. Do you like it better?"

My face had made her rueful. "No, I like it worse!" But after an instant I added: "Did they say why I should like it better?"

"No; Master Miles only said, 'We must do nothing but what she likes'!"

"I wish indeed he would! And what did Flora say?"

"Miss Flora was too sweet. She said, 'Oh, of course, of course!' —and I said the same."

I thought a moment. "You were too sweet too—I can hear you all. But none the less, between Miles and me, it's now all out."

"All out?" My companion stared. "But what, Miss?"

"Everything. It doesn't matter. I've made up my mind. I came home, my dear," I went on, "for a talk with Miss Jessel."

I had by this time formed the habit of having Mrs. Grose literally well in hand in advance of my sounding that note; so that even now, as she bravely blinked under the signal of my word, I could keep her comparatively firm. "A talk! Do you mean she spoke?"

"It came to that. I found her, on my return, in the schoolroom."

"And what did she say?" I can hear the good woman still, and the candour of her stupefaction.

"That she suffers the torments—!"

It was this, of a truth, that made her, as she filled out my picture, gape. "Do you mean," she faltered, "—of the lost?"

"Of the lost. Of the damned. And that's why, to share them—" I faltered myself with the horror of it.

But my companion, with less imagination, kept me up. "To share them—?"

"She wants Flora." Mrs. Grose might, as I gave it to her, fairly have fallen away from me had I not been prepared. I still held her there, to show I was. "As I've told you, however, it doesn't matter."

"Because you've made up your mind? But to what?"

"To everything."

"And what do you call 'everything'?"

"Why, sending for their uncle."

"Oh, Miss, in pity do," my friend broke out.

"Ah, but I will, I *will!* I see it's the only way. What's 'out,' as I told you, with Miles is that if he thinks I'm afraid to—and has ideas of what he gains by that—he shall see he's mistaken. Yes, yes; his uncle shall have it here from me on the spot (and before the boy himself if necessary) that if I'm to be reproached with having done nothing again about more school—"

"Yes, Miss—" my companion pressed me.

"Well, there's that awful reason."

There were now clearly so many of these for my poor colleague that she was excusable for being vague. "But—a—which?"

"Why, the letter from his old place."

"You'll show it to the master?"

"I ought to have done so on the instant."

"Oh, no!" said Mrs. Grose with decision.

"I'll put it before him," I went on inexorably, "that I can't undertake to work the question on behalf of a child who has been expelled—"

"For we've never in the least known what!" Mrs. Grose declared.

"For wickedness. For what else—when he's so clever and beautiful and perfect? Is he stupid? Is he untidy? Is he infirm? Is he ill-natured? He's exquisite—so it can be only *that;* and that would open up the whole thing. After all," I said, "it's their uncle's fault. If he left here such people—!"

"He didn't really in the least know them. The fault's mine." She had turned quite pale.

"Well, you shan't suffer," I answered.

"The children shan't!" she emphatically returned.

I was silent awhile; we looked at each other. "Then what am I to tell him?"

"You needn't tell him anything. *I'll* tell him."

I measured this. "Do you mean you'll write—?" Remembering she couldn't, I caught myself up. "How do you communicate?"

"I tell the bailiff. *He* writes."

"And should you like him to write our story?"

My question had a sarcastic force that I had not fully intended, and it made her, after a moment, inconsequently break down. The tears were again in her eyes. "Ah, Miss, *you* write!"

"Well—tonight," I at last answered; and on this we separated.

XVII

I went so far, in the evening, as to make a beginning. The weather had changed back, a great wind was abroad, and beneath the lamp, in my room, with Flora at peace beside me, I sat for a long time before a blank sheet of paper and listened to the lash of the rain and the batter of the gusts. Finally I went out, taking a candle; I crossed the passage and listened a minute at Miles's door. What, under my endless obsession, I had been impelled to listen for was some betrayal of his not being at rest, and I presently caught one, but not in the form I had expected. His voice tinkled out. "I say, you there—come in." It was a gaiety in the gloom!

I went in with my light and found him, in bed, very wide awake, but very much at his ease. "Well, what are *you* up to?" he asked with a grace of sociability in which it occurred to me that Mrs. Grose, had she been present, might have looked in vain for proof that anything was "out."

I stood over him with my candle. "How did you know I was there?"

"Why, of course I heard you. Did you fancy you made no noise? You're like a troop of cavalry!" he beautifully laughed.

"Then you weren't asleep?"

"Not much! I lie awake and think."

I had put my candle, designedly, a short way off, and then, as he held out his friendly old hand to me, had sat down on the edge of his bed. "What is it," I asked, "that you think of?"

"What in the world, my dear, but *you*?"

"Ah, the pride I take in your appreciation doesn't insist on that! I had so far rather you slept."

"Well, I think also, you know, of this queer business of ours."

I marked the coolness of his firm little hand. "Of what queer business, Miles?"

"Why, the way you bring me up. And all the rest!"

I fairly held my breath a minute, and even from my glimmering taper there was light enough to show how he smiled up at me from his pillow. "What do you mean by all the rest?"

"Oh, you know, you know!"

I could say nothing for a minute, though I felt, as I held his hand and our eyes continued to meet, that my silence had all the air of admitting his charge and that nothing in the whole world of reality was perhaps at that moment so fabulous as our actual relation. "Certainly you shall go back to school," I said, "if it be that that troubles you. But not to the old place—we must find another, a better. How could I know it did trouble you, this question, when you never told me so, never spoke of it at all?" His clear, listening face, framed in its smooth whiteness, made him for the minute as appealing as some wistful patient in a children's hospital; and I would have given, as the resemblance came to me, all I possessed on earth really to be the nurse or the sister of charity who might have helped to cure him. Well, even as it was, I perhaps might help! "Do you know you've never said a word to me about your school—I mean the old one; never mentioned it in any way?"

He seemed to wonder; he smiled with the same loveliness. But he clearly gained time; he waited, he called for guidance. "Haven't I?" It wasn't for me to help him—it was for the thing I had met!

Something in his tone and the expression of his face, as I got this from him, set my heart aching with such a pang as it had never yet known; so unutterably touching was it to see his little brain puzzled and his little resources taxed to play, under the spell laid on him, a part of innocence and consistency. "No, never—from the hour you came back. You've never mentioned to me one of your masters, one of your comrades, nor the least little thing that ever happened to you at school. Never, little Miles—no, never—have you given me an inkling of anything that *may* have happened there. Therefore you can fancy how much I'm in the dark. Until you came out, that way, this morning, you had, since the first hour I saw you, scarce even made a reference to anything in your previous life. You seemed so perfectly to accept the present." It was extraordinary how my absolute conviction of his secret precocity (or whatever I might call the poison of an influence that I dared but half to phrase) made him, in spite of the faint breath of his inward trouble, appear as accessible as an older person—imposed him almost as an intellectual equal. "I thought you wanted to go on as you are."

It struck me that at this he just faintly coloured. He gave, at any rate, like a convalescent slightly fatigued, a languid shake of his head. "I don't—I don't. I want to get away."

"You're tired of Bly?"

"Oh, no, I like Bly."

"Well, then—?"

"Oh, *you* know what a boy wants!"

I felt that I didn't know so well as Miles, and I took temporary refuge. "You want to go to your uncle?"

Again, at this, with his sweet ironic face, he made a movement on the pillow. "Ah, you can't get off with that!"

I was silent a little, and it was I, now, I think, who changed colour. "My dear, I don't want to get off!"

"You can't, even if you do. You can't, you can't!"—he lay beautifully staring. "My uncle must come down, and you must completely settle things."

"If we do," I returned with some spirit, "you may be sure it will be to take you quite away."

"Well, don't you understand that that's exactly what I'm working for? You'll have to tell him—about the way you've let it all drop: you'll have to tell him a tremendous lot!"

The exultation with which he uttered this helped me somehow, for the instant, to meet him rather more. "And how much will *you*, Miles, have to tell him? There are things he'll ask you!"

He turned it over. "Very likely. But what things?"

"The things you've never told me. To make up his mind what to do with you. He can't send you back—"

"Oh, I don't want to go back!" he broke in. "I want a new field."

He said it with admirable serenity, with positive unimpeachable gaiety; and doubtless it was that very note that most evoked for me the poignancy, the unnatural childish tragedy, of his probable reappearance at the end of three months with all this bravado and still more dishonour. It overwhelmed me now that I should never be able to bear that, and it made me let myself go. I threw myself upon him and in the tenderness of my pity I embraced him. "Dear little Miles, dear little Miles—!"

My face was close to his, and he let me kiss him, simply taking it with indulgent good-humour. "Well, old lady?"

"Is there nothing—nothing at all that you want to tell me?"

He turned off a little, facing round toward the wall and holding up his hand to look at as one had seen sick children look. "I've told you—I told you this morning."

Oh, I was sorry for him! "That you just want me not to worry you?"

He looked round at me now, as if in recognition of my understanding him; then ever so gently, "To let me alone," he replied.

There was even a singular little dignity in it, something that made me release him, yet, when I had slowly risen, linger beside him. God knows I never wished to harass him, but I felt that merely, at this, to turn my back on him was to abandon or, to put it more truly, to lose him. "I've just begun a letter to your uncle," I said.

"Well, then, finish it!"

I waited a minute. "What happened before?"

He gazed up at me again. "Before what?"

"Before you came back. And before you went away."

For some time he was silent, but he continued to meet my eyes. "What happened?"

It made me, the sound of the words, in which it seemed to me that I caught for the very first time a small faint quaver of consenting consciousness—it made me drop on my knees beside the bed and seize once more the chance of possessing him. "Dear little Miles, dear little Miles, if you *knew* how I want to help you! It's only that, it's nothing but that, and I'd rather die than give you a pain or do you a wrong—I'd rather die than hurt a hair of you. Dear little Miles"—oh, I brought it out now even if I *should* go too far—"I just want you to help me to save you!" But I knew in a moment after this that I had gone too far. The answer to my appeal was instantaneous, but it came in the form of an extraordinary blast and chill, a gust of frozen air and a shake of the room as great as if, in the wild wind, the casement had crashed in. The boy gave a loud, high shriek, which, lost in the rest of the shock of sound, might have seemed, indistinctly, though I was so close to him, a note either of jubilation or of terror. I jumped to my feet again and was conscious of darkness. So for a moment we remained, while I stared about me and saw that the drawn curtains were unstirred and the window tight. "Why, the candle's out!" I then cried.

"It was I who blew it, dear!" said Miles.

XVIII

The next day, after lessons, Mrs. Grose found a moment to say to me quietly: "Have you written, Miss?"

"Yes—I've written." But I didn't add—for the hour—that my letter, sealed and directed, was still in my pocket. There would be time enough to send it before the messenger should go to the village. Meanwhile there had been, on the part of my pupils, no more brilliant, more exemplary morning. It was exactly as if they had both had at heart to gloss over any recent little friction. They performed the dizziest feats of arithmetic, soaring quite out of *my* feeble range, and perpetrated, in higher spirits than ever, geographical and historical jokes. It was conspicuous of course in Miles in particular that he appeared to wish to show how easily he could let me down. This child, to my memory, really lives in a setting of beauty and misery that no words can translate; there was a distinction all his own in every impulse he revealed; never was a small natural creature, to the uninitiated eye all frankness and freedom, a more ingenious, a more extraordinary little gentleman. I had perpetually to guard against the wonder of contemplation into which my initiated view betrayed me; to check the irrelevant gaze and discouraged sigh in which I constantly both attacked and renounced the enigma of what such a little gentleman could have done that deserved a penalty. Say that, by the dark prodigy I knew, the imagination of all evil *had* been opened up to him: all the justice within me ached for the proof that it could ever have flowered into an act.

He had never, at any rate, been such a little gentleman as when, after our early dinner on this dreadful day, he came round to me and asked if I shouldn't like him, for half an hour, to play to me. David playing to Saul could never have shown a finer sense of the occasion. It was literally a charming exhibition of tact, of magnanimity, and quite tantamount to his saying outright: "The true knights we love to read about never push an advantage too far. I know what you mean now: you mean that—to be let alone yourself and not followed up—you'll cease to worry and spy upon me, won't keep me so close to you, will let me go and come. Well, I 'come,' you see—but I don't go! There'll be plenty of time for that. I do really delight in your society, and I only want to show you that I contended for a principle." It may be imagined whether I resisted this appeal or failed to accompany him again, hand in hand, to the schoolroom. He sat down at the old piano and played as he had never played, and if there are those who think he had better have been kicking a football I can only say that I wholly agree with them. For at the end of a time that under his influence I had quite ceased to measure I started up with a strange sense of having literally slept at my post. It was after luncheon, and by the schoolroom fire, and yet I hadn't really, in the least, slept: I had only done something much worse—I had forgotten. Where, all this time, was Flora? When I put the question to Miles he played on a minute before answering, and then could only say: "Why, my dear, how do I know?"—breaking moreover into a happy laugh which, immediately after, as if it were a vocal accompaniment, he prolonged into incoherent, extravagant song.

I went straight to my room, but his sister was not there; then, before going downstairs, I looked into several others. As she was nowhere about she would surely be with Mrs. Grose, whom, in the comfort of that theory, I accordingly proceeded in quest of. I found her where I had found her the evening before, but she met my quick challenge with blank, scared ignorance. She had only supposed that, after the repast, I had carried off both the children; as to which she was quite in her right, for it was the very first time I had allowed the little girl out of my sight without some special provision. Of course now indeed she might be with the maids, so that the immediate thing was to look for her without an air of alarm. This we promptly arranged between us; but when, ten minutes later and in pursuance of our arrangement, we met in the hall, it was only to report on either side that after guarded inquiries we had altogether failed to trace her. For a minute there, apart from observation, we exchanged mute alarms, and I could feel with what high interest my friend returned me all those I had from the first given her.

"She'll be above," she presently said—"in one of the rooms you haven't searched."

"No; she's at a distance." I had made up my mind. "She has gone out."

Mrs. Grose stared. "Without a hat?"

I naturally also looked volumes. "Isn't that woman always without one?"

"She's with *her?*"

"She's with *her!*" I declared. "We must find them."

My hand was on my friend's arm, but she failed for the moment, confronted with such an account of the matter, to respond to my pressure. She communed, on the contrary, on the spot, with her uneasiness. "And where's Master Miles?"

"Oh, *he's* with Quint. They're in the schoolroom."

"Lord, Miss!" My view, I was myself aware—and therefore I suppose my tone—had never yet reached so calm an assurance.

"The trick's played," I went on; "they've successfully worked their plan. He found the most divine little way to keep me quiet while she went off."

" 'Divine'?" Mrs. Grose bewilderedly echoed.

"Infernal, then!" I almost cheerfully rejoined. "He has provided for himself as well. But come!"

She had helplessly gloomed at the upper regions. "You leave him—?"

"So long with Quint? Yes—I don't mind that now."

She always ended, at these moments, by getting possession of my hand, and in this manner she could at present still stay me. But after gasping an instant at my sudden resignation, "Because of your letter?" she eagerly brought out.

I quickly, by way of answer, felt for my letter, drew it forth, held it up, and then, freeing myself, went and laid it on the great hall-table. "Luke will take it," I said as I came back. I reached the house-door and opened it; I was already on the steps.

My companion still demurred: the storm of the night and the early morning had dropped, but the afternoon was damp and grey. I came down to the drive while she stood in the doorway. "You go with nothing on?"

"What do I care when the child has nothing? I can't wait to dress," I cried, "and if you must do so, I leave you. Try meanwhile, yourself, upstairs."

"With *them?*" Oh, on this, the poor woman promptly joined me!

XIX

We went straight to the lake, as it was called at Bly, and I dare say rightly called, though I reflect that it may in fact have been a sheet of water less remarkable than it appeared to my untravelled eyes. My acquaintance with sheets of water was small, and the pool of Bly, at all events on the few occasions of my consenting, under the protection of my pupils, to affront its surface in the old flat-bottomed boat moored there for our use, had impressed me both with its extent and its agitation. The usual place of embarkation was half a mile from the house, but I had an intimate conviction that, wherever Flora might be, she was not near home. She had not given me the slip for any small adventure, and, since the day of the very great one that I had shared with her by the pond, I had been aware, in our walks, of the quarter to which she most inclined. This was why I had now given to Mrs. Grose's steps so marked a direction—a direction that made her, when she perceived it, oppose a resistance that showed me she was freshly mystified. "You're going to the water, Miss?—you think she's *in—?*"

"She may be, though the depth is, I believe, nowhere very great. But what I judge most likely is that she's on the spot from which, the other day, we saw together what I told you."

"When she pretended not to see—?"

"With that astounding self-possession! I've always been sure she wanted to go back alone. And now her brother has managed it for her."

Mrs. Grose still stood where she had stopped. "You suppose they really *talk* of them?"

I could meet this with a confidence! "They say things that, if we heard them, would simply appall us."

"And if she *is* there—?"

"Yes?"

"Then Miss Jessel is?"

"Beyond a doubt. You shall see."

"Oh, thank you!" my friend cried, planted so firm that, taking it in, I went straight on without her. By the time I reached the pool, however, she was close behind me, and I knew that, whatever, to her apprehension, might befall me, the exposure of my society struck her as her least danger. She exhaled a moan of relief as we at last came in sight of the greater part of the water without a sight of the child. There was no trace of Flora on that nearer side of the bank where my observation of her had been most startling, and none on the opposite edge, where, save for a margin of some twenty yards, a thick copse came down to the water. The pond, oblong in shape, had a width so scant compared to its length that, with its ends out of view, it might have been taken for a scant river. We looked at the empty expanse, and then I felt the suggestion of my friend's eyes. I knew what she meant and I replied with a negative headshake.

"No, no; wait! She has taken the boat."

My companion stared at the vacant mooring-place and then again across the lake. "Then where is it?"

"Our not seeing it is the strongest of proofs. She has used it to go over, and then has managed to hide it."

"All alone—that child?"

"She's not alone, and at such times she's not a child: she's an old, old woman." I scanned all the visible shore while Mrs. Grose took again, into the queer element I offered her, one of her plunges of submission; then I pointed out that the boat might perfectly be in a small refuge formed by one of the recesses of the pool, an indentation masked, for the hither side, by a projection of the bank and by a clump of trees growing close to the water.

"But if the boat's there, where on earth's *she?*" my colleague anxiously asked.

"That's exactly what we must learn." And I started to walk further.

"By going all the way around?"

"Certainly, far as it is. It will take us but ten minutes, but it's far enough to have made the child prefer not to walk. She went straight over."

"Laws!" cried my friend again; the chain of my logic was ever too much for her. It dragged her at my heels even now, and when we had got half-way round—a devious, tiresome process, on ground much broken and by a path choked with overgrowth—I paused to give her breath. I sustained her with a grateful arm, assuring her that she might hugely help me; and this started us afresh, so that in the course of but a few minutes more we reached a point from which we found the boat to be where I had supposed it. It had been intentionally left as much as possible out of sight and was tied to one of the stakes of a fence that came, just there, down to the brink and that had been an assistance to disembarking. I recognised, as I looked at the pair of short, thick oars, quite safely drawn up, the prodigious character of the feat for a little girl; but I had lived, by this time, too long among wonders and had panted to too many livelier measures. There was a gate in the fence, through which we passed, and that brought us, after a trifling interval, more into the open. Then, "There she is!" we both exclaimed at once.

Flora, a short way off, stood before us on the grass and smiled as if her performance was now complete. The next thing she did, however, was to stoop straight down and pluck—quite as if it were all she was there for—a big, ugly spray of withered fern. I instantly became sure she had just come out of the copse. She waited for us, not herself taking a step, and I was conscious of the rare solemnity with which we presently approached her. She smiled and smiled, and we met; but it was all done in a silence by this time flagrantly ominous. Mrs. Grose was the first to break the spell: she threw herself on her knees and, drawing the child to her breast, clasped in a long embrace the little tender, yielding body. While this dumb convulsion lasted I could only watch it—which I did the more intently when I saw Flora's face peep at me over our companion's shoulder. It was serious now—the flicker had left it; but it strengthened the pang with which I at that moment envied Mrs. Grose the simplicity of *her* relation. Still, all this while, nothing more passed between us save that Flora had let her foolish fern again drop to the ground. What she and I had virtually said to each other was that pretexts were useless now. When Mrs. Grose finally got up she kept the child's hand, so that the two were still before me; and the singular reticence of our communion was even more marked in the frank look she launched me. "I'll be hanged," it said, "if *I'll* speak!"

It was Flora who, gazing all over me in candid wonder, was the first. She was struck with our bareheaded aspect. "Why, where are your things?"

"Where yours are, my dear!" I promptly returned.

She had already got back her gaiety, and appeared to take this as an answer quite sufficient. "And where's Miles?" she went on.

There was something in the small valour of it that quite

finished me: these three words from her were, in a flash like the glitter of a drawn blade, the jostle of the cup that my hand, for weeks and weeks, had held high and full to the brim and that now, even before speaking, I felt overflow in a deluge. "I'll tell you if you'll tell *me*—" I heard myself say, then heard the tremor in which it broke.

"Well, what?"

Mrs. Grose's suspense blazed at me, but it was too late now, and I brought the thing out handsomely. "Where, my pet, is Miss Jessel?"

XX

Just as in the churchyard with Miles, the whole thing was upon us. Much as I had made of the fact that this name had never once, between us, been sounded, the quick, smitten glare with which the child's face now received it fairly likened my breach of the silence to the smash of a pane of glass. It added to the interposing cry, as if to stay the blow, that Mrs. Grose, at the same instant, uttered over my violence—the shriek of a creature scared, or rather wounded, which, in turn, within a few seconds, was completed by a gasp of my own. I seized my colleague's arm. "She's there, she's there!"

Miss Jessel stood before us on the opposite bank exactly as she had stood the other time, and I remember, strangely, as the first feeling now produced in me, my thrill of joy at having brought on a proof. She was there, and I was justified; she was there, and I was neither cruel nor mad. She was there for poor scared Mrs. Grose, but she was there most for Flora; and no moment of my monstrous time was perhaps so extraordinary as that in which I consciously threw out to her—with the sense that, pale and ravenous demon as she was, she would catch and understand it—an inarticulate message of gratitude. She rose erect on the spot my friend and I had lately quitted, and there was not, in all the long reach of her desire, an inch of her evil that fell short. This first vividness of vision and emotion were things of a few seconds, during which Mrs. Grose's dazed blink across to where I pointed struck me as a sovereign sign that she too at last saw, just as it carried my own eyes precipitately to the child. The revelation then of the manner in which Flora was affected startled me, in truth, far more than it would have done to find her also merely agitated, for direct dismay was of course not what I had expected. Prepared and on her guard as our pursuit had actually made her, she would repress every betrayal; and I was therefore shaken, on the spot, by my first glimpse of the particular one for which I had not allowed. To see her, without a convulsion of her small pink face, not even feign to glance in the direction of the prodigy I announced, but only, instead of that, turn at *me* an expression of hard, still gravity, an expression absolutely new and unprecedented and that appeared to read and accuse and judge me—this was a stroke that somehow converted the little girl herself into the very presence that could make me quail. I quailed even though my certitude that she thoroughly saw was never greater than at that instant, and in the immediate need to defend myself I called it passionately to witness. "She's there, you little unhappy thing—there, there, *there*, and you see her as well as you see me!" I had said shortly before to Mrs. Grose that she was not at these times a child, but an old, old woman, and that description of her could not have been more strikingly confirmed than in the way in which, for all answer to this, she simply showed me, without a concession, an admission, of her eyes, a countenance of deeper and deeper, of indeed suddenly quite fixed, reprobation. I was by this time—if I can put the whole thing at all together—more appalled at what I may properly call her manner than at anything else, though it was simultaneously with this that I became aware of having Mrs. Grose also, and very formidably, to reckon with. My elder companion, the next moment, at any rate, blotted out everything but her own flushed face and her loud, shocked protest, a burst of high disapproval. "What a dreadful turn, to be sure, Miss! Where on earth do you see anything?"

I could only grasp her more quickly yet, for even while she spoke the hideous plain presence stood undimmed and undaunted. It had already lasted a minute, and it lasted while I continued, seizing my colleague, quite thrusting her at it and presenting her to it, to insist with my pointing hand. "You don't see her exactly as *we* see?—you mean to say you don't now—*now?* She's as big as a blazing fire! Only look, dearest woman, *look—!*" She looked, even as I did, and gave me, with her deep groan of negation, repulsion, compassion—the mixture with her pity of her relief at her exemption —a sense, touching to me even then, that she would have backed me up if she could. I might well have needed that, for with this hard blow of the proof that her eyes were hopelessly sealed I felt my own situation horribly crumble, I felt—I saw—my livid predecessor press, from her position, on my defeat, and I was conscious, more than all, of what I should have from this instant to deal with in the astounding little attitude of Flora. Into this attitude Mrs. Grose immediately and violently entered, breaking, even while there pierced through my sense of ruin a prodigious private triumph, into breathless reassurance.

"She isn't there, little lady, and nobody's there—and you never see nothing, my sweet! How can poor Miss Jessel? when poor Miss Jessel's dead and buried? *We* know, don't we, love?"—and she appealed, blundering in, to the child. "It's all a mere mistake and a worry and a joke—and we'll go home as fast as we can!"

Our companion, on this, had responded with a strange, quick primness of propriety, and they were again, with Mrs. Grose on her feet, united, as it were, in pained opposition to me. Flora continued to fix me with her small mask of reprobation, and even at that minute I prayed God to forgive me for seeming to see that, as she stood there holding tight to our friend's dress, her incomparable childish beauty had suddenly failed, had quite vanished. I've said it already—she was literally, she was hideously, hard; she had turned common and almost ugly. "I don't know what you mean. I see nobody. I see nothing. I never *have*. I think you're cruel. I don't like you!" Then, after this deliverance, which might have been that of a vulgarly pert little girl in the street, she hugged Mrs. Grose more closely and buried in her skirts the dreadful little face. In this position she produced an almost furious wail. "Take me away, take me away—oh, take me away from *her!*"

"From *me?*" I panted.

"From you—from you!" she cried.

Even Mrs. Grose looked across at me dismayed, while I had nothing to do but communicate again with the figure that, on the opposite bank, without a movement, as rigidly still as if catching, beyond the interval, our voices, was as vividly there for my disaster as it was not there for my service. The wretched child had spoken exactly as if she had got from some outside source each of her stabbing little words, and I could therefore, in the full despair of all I had to accept, but sadly shake my head at her. "If I had ever doubted, all my doubt would at present have gone. I've been living with the miserable truth, and now it has only too much closed round me. Of course I've lost you: I've interfered, and you've seen—under *her* dictation"—with which I faced, over the pool again, our infernal witness—"the easy and perfect way to meet it. I've done my best, but I've lost you. Good-bye." For Mrs. Grose I had an imperative, an almost frantic "Go, go!" before which, in infinite distress, but mutely possessed of the little girl and clearly convinced, in spite of her blindness, that something awful had occurred and some collapse engulfed us, she retreated, by the way we had come, as fast as she could move.

Of what first happened when I was left alone I had no subsequent memory. I only knew that at the end of, I suppose, a quarter of an hour, an odorous dampness and roughness, chilling and piercing my trouble, had made me understand that I must have thrown myself, on my face, on the ground and given way to a wildness of grief. I must have lain there long and cried and sobbed, for when I raised my head the day was almost done. I got up and looked a moment, through the twilight, at the grey pool and its blank, haunted edge, and then I took, back to the house, my dreary and difficult course. When I reached the gate in the fence the boat, to my surprise, was gone, so that I had a fresh reflection to make on Flora's extraordinary command of the situation. She passed that night, by the most tacit, and I should add, were not the word so grotesque a false note, the happiest of arrangements, with Mrs. Grose. I saw neither of them on my return, but, on the other hand as by an ambiguous compensation, I saw a great deal of Miles. I saw—I can use no other phrase—so much of him that it was as if it were more than it had ever been. No evening I had passed at Bly had the portentous quality of this one; in spite of which—and in spite also of the deeper depths of consternation that had opened beneath my feet—there was literally, in the ebbing actual, an extraordinarily sweet sadness. On reaching the house I had never so much as looked for the boy; I had simply gone straight to my room to change what I was wearing and to take in, at a glance, much material testimony to Flora's rupture. Her little belongings had all been removed. When later, by the schoolroom fire, I was served with tea by the usual maid, I indulged, on the article of my other pupil, in no inquiry whatever. He had his freedom now—he might have it to the end! Well, he did have it; and it consisted—in part at least—of his coming in at about eight o'clock and sitting down with me in silence. On the removal of the tea-things I had blown out the candles and drawn my chair closer: I was conscious of a mortal coldness and felt as if I should never again be warm. So, when he appeared, I was sitting in the glow with my thoughts. He paused a moment by the door as if to look at me; then—as if to share them—came to the other side of the hearth and sank into a chair. We sat there in absolute stillness; yet he wanted, I felt, to be with me.

XXI

Before a new day, in my room, had fully broken, my eyes opened to Mrs. Grose, who had come to my bedside with worse news. Flora was so markedly feverish that an illness was perhaps at hand; she had passed a night of extreme unrest, a night agitated above all by fears that had for their subject not in the least her former, but wholly her present, governess. It was not against the possible re-entrance of Miss Jessel on the scene that she protested —it was conspicuously and passionately against mine. I was promptly on my feet of course, and with an immense deal to ask; the more that my friend had discernibly now girded her loins to meet me once more. This I felt as soon as I had put to her the question of her sense of the child's sincerity as against my own. "She persists in denying to you that she saw, or has ever seen, anything?"

My visitor's trouble, truly, was great. "Ah, Miss, it isn't a matter on which I can push her! Yet it isn't either, I must say, as if I much needed to. It has made her, every inch of her, quite old."

"Oh, I see her perfectly from here. She resents, for all the world like some high little personage, the imputation on her truthfulness and, as it were, her respectability. 'Miss Jessel indeed—*she!*' Ah, she's 'respectable,' the chit! The impression she gave me there yesterday was, I assure you, the very strangest of all; it was quite beyond any of the others. I *did* put my foot in it! She'll never speak to me again."

Hideous and obscure as it all was, it held Mrs. Grose briefly silent; then she granted my point with a frankness which, I made sure, had more behind it. "I think indeed, Miss, she never will. She do have a grand manner about it!"

"And that manner"—I summed it up—"is practically what's the matter with her now!"

Oh, that manner, I could see in my visitor's face, and not a little else besides! "She asks me every three minutes if I think you're coming in."

"I see—I see." I too, on my side, had so much more than worked it out. "Has she said to you since yesterday—except to repudiate her familiarity with anything so dreadful—a single other word about Miss Jessel?"

"Not one, Miss. And of course you know," my friend added, "I took it from her, by the lake, that, just then and there at least, there *was* nobody."

"Rather! And, naturally, you take it from her still."

"I don't contradict her. What else can I do?"

"Nothing in the world! You've the cleverest little person to deal with. They've made them—their two friends, I mean—still cleverer even than nature did; for it was wondrous material to play on! Flora has now her grievance, and she'll work it to the end."

"Yes, Miss; but to *what* end?"

"Why, that of dealing with me to her uncle. She'll make me out to him the lowest creature—!"

I winced at the fair show of the scene in Mrs. Grose's face; she looked for a minute as if she sharply saw them together. "And him who thinks so well of you!"

"He has an odd way—it comes over me now," I laughed, "—of proving it! But that doesn't matter. What Flora wants, of course, is to get rid of me."

My companion bravely concurred. "Never again to so much as look at you."

"So that what you've come to me now for," I asked, "is to speed me on my way?" Before she had time to reply, however, I had her in check. "I've a better idea—the result of my reflections. My going *would* seem the right thing, and on Sunday I was terribly near it. Yet that won't do. It's *you* who must go. You must take Flora."

My visitor, at this, did speculate. "But where in the world—?"

"Away from here. Away from *them*. Away, even most of all, now, from me. Straight to her uncle."

"Only to tell on you—?"

"No, not 'only'! To leave me, in addition, with my remedy."

She was still vague. "And what *is* your remedy?"

"Your loyalty, to begin with. And then Miles's."

She looked at me hard. "Do you think he—?"

"Won't if he has the chance, turn on me? Yes, I venture still to think it. At all events, I want to try. Get off with his sister as soon as possible and leave me with him alone." I was amazed, myself, at the spirit I had still in reserve, and therefore perhaps a trifle the more disconcerted at the way in which, in spite of this fine example of it, she hesitated. "There's one thing, of course," I went on: "they mustn't, before she goes, see each other for three seconds."

Then it came over me that, in spite of Flora's presumable sequestration from the instant of her return from the pool, it might already be too late. "Do you mean," I anxiously asked, "that they *have* met?"

At this she quite flushed. "Ah, Miss, I'm not such a fool as that! If I've been obliged to leave her three or four times, it has been each time with one of the maids, and at present, though she's alone, she's locked in safe. And yet—and yet!" There were too many things.

"And yet what?"

"Well, are you so sure of the little gentleman?"

"I'm not sure of anything but *you*. But I have, since last evening, a new hope. I think he wants to give me an opening. I do believe that—poor little exquisite wretch!—he wants to speak. Last evening, in the firelight and the silence, he sat with me for two hours as if it were just coming."

Mrs. Grose looked hard, through the window, at the grey, gathering day. "And did it come?"

"No, though I waited and waited, I confess it didn't, and it was without a breach of the silence or so much as a faint allusion to his sister's condition and absence that we at last kissed for good-night. All the same," I continued, "I can't, if her uncle sees her, consent to his seeing her brother without my having given the boy—and most of all because things have got so bad—a little more time."

My friend appeared on this ground more reluctant than I could quite understand. "What do you mean by more time?"

"Well, a day or two—really to bring it out. He'll then be on *my* side—of which you see the importance. If nothing comes, I shall only fail, and you will, at the worst, have helped me by doing, on your arrival in town, whatever you may have found possible." So I put it before her, but she continued for a little so inscrutably embarrassed that I came again to her aid. "Unless, indeed," I wound up, "you really want *not* to go."

I could see it, in her face, at last clear itself; she put out her hand to me as a pledge. "I'll go—I'll go. I'll go this morning."

I wanted to be very just. "If you *should* wish still to wait, I would engage she shouldn't see me."

"No, no: it's the place itself. She must leave it." She held me a moment with heavy eyes, then brought out the rest. "Your idea's the right one. I myself, Miss—"

"Well?"

"I can't stay."

The look she gave me with it made me jump at possibilities. "You mean that, since yesterday, you *have* seen—?"

She shook her head with dignity. "I've *heard—!*"

"Heard?"

"From that child—horrors! There!" she sighed with tragic relief. "On my honour, Miss, she says things—!" But at this evocation she broke down; she dropped, with a sudden sob, upon my sofa and, as I had seen her do before, gave way to all the grief of it.

It was quite in another manner that I, for my part, let myself go. "Oh, thank God!"

She sprang up again at this, drying her eyes with a groan. "'Thank God'?"

"It so justifies me!"

"It does that, Miss!"

I couldn't have desired more emphasis, but I just hesitated. "She's so horrible?"

I saw my colleague scarce knew how to put it. "Really shocking."

"And about me?"

"About you, Miss—since you must have it. It's beyond everything, for a young lady; and I can't think wherever she must have picked up—"

"The appalling language she applied to me? I can, then!" I broke in with a laugh that was doubtless significant enough.

It only, in truth, left my friend still more grave. "Well, perhaps I ought to also—since I've heard some of it before! Yet I can't bear it," the poor woman went on while, with the same movement, she glanced, on my dressing-table, at the face of my watch. "But I must go back."

I kept her, however. "Ah, if you can't bear it—!"

"How can I stop with her, you mean? Why, just *for* that: to get her away. Far from this," she pursued, "far from *them*—"

"She may be different? she may be free?" I seized her almost with joy. "Then, in spite of yesterday, you *believe*—"

"In such doings?" Her simple description of them required, in the light of her expression, to be carried no further, and she gave me the whole thing as she had never done. "I believe."

Yes, it was a joy, and we were still shoulder to shoulder: if I might continue sure of that I should care but little what else happened. My support in the presence of disaster would be the same as it had been in my early need of confidence, and if my friend would answer for my honesty, I would answer for all the rest. On the point of taking leave of her, none the less, I was to some extent embarrassed. "There's one thing of course—it occurs to me—to remember. My letter, giving the alarm, will have reached town before you."

I now perceived still more how she had been beating about the bush and how weary at last it had made her. "Your letter won't have got there. Your letter never went."

"What then became of it?"

"Goodness knows! Master Miles—"

"Do you mean *he* took it?" I gasped.

She hung fire, but she overcame her reluctance, "I mean that

I saw yesterday, when I came back with Miss Flora, that it wasn't where you had put it. Later in the evening I had the chance to question Luke, and he declared that he had neither noticed nor touched it." We could only exchange, on this, one of our deeper mutual soundings, and it was Mrs. Grose who first brought up the plumb with an almost elate "You see!"

"Yes, I see that if Miles took it instead he probably will have read it and destroyed it."

"And don't you see anything else?"

I faced her a moment with a sad smile. "It strikes me that by this time your eyes are open even wider than mine."

They proved to be so indeed, but she could still blush, almost, to show it. "I make out now what he must have done at school." And she gave, in her simple sharpness, an almost droll disillusioned nod. "He stole!"

I turned it over—I tried to be more judicial. "Well—perhaps."

She looked as if she found me unexpectedly calm. "He stole *letters!*"

She couldn't know my reasons for a calmness after all pretty shallow; so I showed them off as I might. "I hope then it was to more purpose than in this case! The note, at any rate, that I put on the table yesterday," I pursued, "will have given him so scant an advantage—for it contained only the bare demand for an interview—that he is already much ashamed of having gone so far for so little, and that what he had on his mind last evening was precisely the need of confession." I seemed to myself, for the instant, to have mastered it, to see it all. "Leave us, leave us"—I was already, at the door, hurrying her off. "I'll get it out of him. He'll meet me—he'll confess. If he confesses, he's saved. And if he's saved—"

"Then *you* are?" The dear woman kissed me on this, and I took her farewell. "I'll save you without him!" she cried as she went.

XXII

Yet it was when she had got off—and I missed her on the spot—that the great pinch really came. If I had counted on what it would give me to find myself alone with Miles, I speedily perceived, at least, that it would give me a measure. No hour of my stay in fact was so assailed with apprehensions as that of my coming down to learn that the carriage containing Mrs. Grose and my younger pupil had already rolled out of the gates. Now I *was*, I said to myself, face to face with the elements, and for much of the rest of the day, while I fought my weakness, I could consider that I had been supremely rash. It was a tighter place still than I had yet turned round in; all the more that, for the first time, I could see in the aspect of others a confused reflection of the crisis. What had happened naturally caused them all to stare; there was too little of the explained, throw out whatever we might, in the suddenness of my colleague's act. The maids and the men looked blank; the effect of which on my nerves was an aggravation until I saw the necessity of making it a positive aid. It was precisely, in short, by just clutching the helm that I avoided total wreck; and I dare say that, to bear up at all, I became, that morning, very grand and very dry. I welcomed the consciousness that I was charged with much to do, and I caused it to be known as well that, left thus to myself, I was quite remarkably firm. I wandered with that manner, for the next hour or two, all over the place and looked, I have no doubt, as if I were ready for any onset. So, for the benefit of whom it might concern, I paraded with a sick heart.

The person it appeared least to concern proved to be, till dinner, little Miles himself. My perambulations had given me meanwhile, no glimpse of him, but they had tended to make more public the change taking place in our relation as a consequence of his having at the piano, the day before, kept me, in Flora's interest, so beguiled and befooled. The stamp of publicity had of course been fully given by her confinement and departure, and the change itself was now ushered in by our non-observance of the regular custom of the schoolroom. He had already disappeared when, on my way down, I pushed open his door, and I learned below that he had breakfasted—in the presence of a couple of the maids—with Mrs. Grose and his sister. He had then gone out, as he said, for a stroll; than which nothing, I reflected, could better have expressed his frank view of the abrupt transformation of my office. What he would now permit this office to consist of was yet to be settled: there was a queer relief, at all events—I mean for myself in especial—in the renouncement of one pretension. If so much had sprung to the surface, I scarce put it too strongly in saying that what had perhaps sprung highest was the absurdity of our prolonging the fiction that I had anything more to teach him. It sufficiently stuck out that, by tacit little tricks in which even more than myself he carried out the care for my dignity, I had had to appeal to him to let me off straining to meet him on the ground of his true capacity. He had at any rate his freedom now; I was never to touch it again; as I had amply shown, moreover, when, on his joining me in the schoolroom the previous night, I had uttered, on the subject of the interval just concluded, neither challenge nor hint. I had too much, from this moment, my other ideas. Yet when he at last arrived the difficulty of applying them, the accumulations of my problem, were brought straight home to me by the beautiful little presence on which what had occurred had as yet, for the eye, dropped neither stain nor shadow.

To mark, for the house, the high state I cultivated I decreed that my meals with the boy should be served, as we called it, downstairs; so that I had been awaiting him in the ponderous pomp of the room outside of the window of which I had had from Mrs. Grose, that first scared Sunday, my flash of something it would scarce have done to call light. Here at present I felt afresh—for I had felt it again and again—how my equilibrium depended on the success of my rigid will, the will to shut my eyes as tight as possible to the truth that what I had to deal with was, revoltingly, against nature. I could only get on at all by taking "nature" into my confidence and my account, by treating my monstrous ordeal as a push in a direction unusual, of course, and unpleasant, but demanding, after all, for a fair front, only another turn of the screw of ordinary human virtue. No attempt, none the less, could well require more tact than just this attempt to supply, one's self, *all* the nature. How could I put even a little of that article into a suppression of reference to what had occurred? How, on the other hand, could I make a reference without a new plunge into the hideous obscure? Well, a sort of answer, after a time, had come to me, and it was so far confirmed as that I was met, incontestably, by the quickened vision of what was rare in my little companion. It was indeed as if he had found even now—as he had so often found at lessons—still some other delicate way to ease me off. Wasn't there light in the fact which, as we shared our solitude, broke out with a specious glitter it had never yet quite worn?—the fact that (opportunity aiding, precious opportunity which had now come) it would be preposterous, with a child so endowed, to forgo the help one might wrest from absolute intelligence? What had his intelligence been given him for but to save him? Mightn't one, to reach his mind, risk the stretch of an angular arm over his character? It was as if, when we were face to face in the dining-room, he had literally shown me the way. The roast mutton was on the table, and I had dispensed with attendance. Miles, before he sat down, stood a moment with his hands in his pockets and looked at the joint, on which he seemed on the point of passing some humorous judgment. But what he presently produced was: "I say, my dear, is she really very awfully ill?"

"Little Flora? Not so bad but that she'll presently be better. London will set her up. Bly had ceased to agree with her. Come here and take your mutton."

He alertly obeyed me, carried the plate carefully to his seat, and, when he was established, went on. "Did Bly disagree with her so terribly suddenly?"

"Not so suddenly as you might think. One had seen it coming on."

"Then why didn't you get her off before?"

"Before what?"

"Before she became too ill to travel."

I found myself prompt. "She's *not* too ill to travel: she only might have become so if she had stayed. This was just the moment to seize. The journey will dissipate the influence"—oh, I was grand!—"and carry it off."

"I see, I see"—Miles, for that matter, was grand too. He settled to his repast with the charming little "table manner" that, from the day of his arrival, had relieved me of all grossness of admonition. Whatever he had been driven from school for, it was not for ugly feeding. He was irreproachable, as always, today; but he was unmistakeably more conscious. He was discernibly trying to take for granted more things than he found, without assistance, quite easy; and he dropped into peaceful silence while he felt his situation. Our meal was of the briefest—mine a vain pretence, and I had the things immediately removed. While this was done Miles stood again with his hands in his little pockets and his back to me—stood and looked out of the wide window through which, that other day, I had seen what pulled me up. We continued silent while the maid was with us—as silent, it whimsically occurred to me, as some young couple who, on their wedding-journey, at the inn, feel shy in the presence of the waiter. He turned round only when the waiter had left us. "Well—so we're alone!"

XXIII

"Oh, more or less." I fancy my smile was pale. "Not absolutely. We shouldn't like that!" I went on.

"No—I suppose we shouldn't. Of course we have the others."

"We have the others—we have indeed the others," I concurred.

"Yet even though we have them," he returned, still with his hands in his pockets and planted there in front of me, "they don't much count, do they?"

I made the best of it, but I felt wan. "It depends on what you call 'much'!"

"Yes"—with all accommodation—"everything depends!" On this, however, he faced to the window again and presently reached it with his vague, restless, cogitating step. He remained there awhile, with his forehead against the glass, in contemplation of the stupid shrubs I knew and the dull things of November. I had always my hypocrisy of "work," behind which, now, I gained the sofa. Steadying myself with it there as I had repeatedly done at those moments of torment that I have described as the moments of my knowing the children to be given to something from which I was barred, I sufficiently obeyed my habit of being prepared for the worst. But an extraordinary impression dropped on me as I extracted a meaning from the boy's embarrassed back—none other than the impression that I was not barred now. This inference grew in a few minutes to sharp intensity and seemed bound up with the direct perception that it was positively *he* who was. The frames and squares of the great window were a kind of image, for him, of a kind of failure. I felt that I saw him, at any rate, shut in or shut out. He was admirable, but not comfortable: I took it in with a throb of hope. Wasn't he looking, through the haunted pane, for something he couldn't see?—and wasn't it the first time in the whole business that he had known such a lapse? The first, the very first: I found it a splendid portent. It made him anxious, though he watched himself; he had been anxious all day and, even while in his usual sweet little manner he sat at table, had needed all his small strange genius to give it a gloss. When he at last turned round to meet me, it was almost as if this genius had succumbed. "Well, I think I'm glad Bly agrees with *me!*"

"You would certainly seem to have seen, these twenty-four hours, a good deal more of it than for some time before. I hope," I went on bravely, "that you've been enjoying yourself."

"Oh, yes, I've been ever so far; all round about—miles and miles away. I've never been so free."

He had really a manner of his own, and I could only try to keep up with him. "Well, do you like it?"

He stood there smiling; then at last he put into two words—"Do *you?*"—more discrimination than I had ever heard two words contain. Before I had time to deal with that, however, he continued as if with the sense that this was an impertinence to be softened. "Nothing could be more charming than the way you take it, for of course if we're alone together now it's you that are alone most. But I hope," he threw in, "you don't particularly mind!"

"Having to do with you?" I asked. "My dear child, how can I help minding? Though I've renounced all claim to your company,—you're so beyond me,—I at least greatly enjoy it. What else should I stay on for?"

He looked at me more directly, and the expression of his face, graver now, struck me as the most beautiful I had ever found in it. "You stay on just for *that?*"

"Certainly. I stay on as your friend and from the tremendous interest I take in you till something can be done for you that may be more worth your while. That needn't surprise you." My voice trembled so that I felt it impossible to suppress the shake. "Don't you remember how I told you, when I came and sat on your bed the night of the storm, that there was nothing in the world I wouldn't do for you?"

"Yes, yes!" He, on his side, more and more visibly nervous, had a tone to master; but he was so much more successful than I that, laughing out through his gravity, he could pretend we were pleasantly jesting. "Only that, I think, was to get me to do something for *you!*"

"It was partly to get you to do something," I conceded. "But, you know, you didn't do it."

"Oh, yes," he said with the brightest superficial eagerness, "you wanted me to tell you something."

"That's it. Out, straight out. What you have on your mind, you know."

"Ah, then, is *that* what you've stayed over for?"

He spoke with a gaiety through which I could still catch the finest little quiver of resentful passion; but I can't begin to express the effect upon me of an implication of surrender even so faint. It was as if what I had yearned for had come at last only to astonish me. "Well, yes—I may as well make a clean breast of it. It was precisely for that."

He waited so long that I supposed it for the purpose of repudiating the assumption on which my action had been founded; but what he finally said was: "Do you mean now—here?"

"There couldn't be a better place or time." He looked round him uneasily, and I had the rare—oh, the queer!—impression of the very first symptom I had seen in him of the approach of immediate fear. It was as if he were suddenly afraid of me—which struck me indeed as perhaps the best thing to make him. Yet in the very pang of the effort I felt it vain to try sternness, and I heard myself the next instant so gentle as to be almost grotesque. "You want so to go out again?"

"Awfully!" He smiled at me heroically, and the touching little bravery of it was enhanced by his actually flushing with pain. He had picked up his hat, which he had brought in, and stood twirling it in a way that gave me, even as I was just nearly reaching port, a perverse horror of what I was doing. To do it in *any* way was an act of violence, for what did it consist of but the obtrusion of the idea of grossness and guilt on a small helpless creature who had been for me a revelation of the possibilities of beautiful intercourse? Wasn't it base to create for a being so exquisite a mere alien awkwardness? I suppose I now read into our situation a clearness it couldn't have had at the time, for I seem to see our poor eyes already lighted with some spark of a prevision of the anguish that was to come. So we circled about, with terrors and scruples, like fighters not daring to close. But it was for each other we feared! That kept us a little longer suspended and unbruised. "I'll tell you everything," Miles said—"I mean I'll tell you anything you like. You'll stay on with me, and we shall both be all right and I *will* tell you—I *will*. But not now."

"Why not now?"

My insistence turned him from me and kept him once more at his window in a silence during which, between us, you might have heard a pin drop. Then he was before me again with the air of a person for whom, outside, someone who had frankly to be reckoned with was waiting. "I have to see Luke."

I had not yet reduced him to quite so vulgar a lie, and I felt proportionately ashamed. But, horrible as it was, his lies made up my truth. I achieved thoughtfully a few loops of my knitting. "Well, then, go to Luke, and I'll wait for what you promise. Only, in return for that, satisfy, before you leave me, one very much smaller request."

He looked as if he felt he had succeeded enough to be able still a little to bargain. "Very much smaller—?"

"Yes, a mere fraction of the whole. Tell me"—oh, my work preoccupied me, and I was off-hand!—"if, yesterday afternoon, from the table in the hall, you took, you know, my letter."

XXIV

My sense of how he received this suffered for a minute from something that I can describe only as a fierce split of my attention—a stroke that at first, as I sprang straight up, reduced me to the mere blind movement of getting hold of him, drawing him close, and, while I just fell for support against the nearest piece of furniture, instinctively keeping him with his back to the window. The appearance was full upon us that I had already had to deal with here: Peter Quint had come into view like a sentinel before a prison. The next thing I saw was that, from outside, he had reached the window, and then I knew that, close to the glass and glaring in through it, he offered once more to the room his white face of damnation. It represents but grossly what took place within me at the sight to say that on the second my decision was made; yet I believe that no woman so overwhelmed ever in so short a time recovered her grasp of the *act.* It came to me in the very horror of the immediate presence that the act would be, seeing and facing what I saw and faced, to keep the boy himself unaware. The inspiration—I can call it by no other name—was that I felt how voluntarily, how transcendently, I *might.* It was like fighting with a demon for a human soul, and when I had fairly so appraised it I saw how the human soul—held out, in the tremor of my hands, at arm's length—had a perfect dew of sweat on a lovely childish forehead. The face that was close to mine was as white as the face against the glass, and out of it presently came a sound, not low nor weak, but as if from much further away, that I drank like a waft of fragrance.

"Yes—I took it."

At this, with a moan of joy, I enfolded, I drew him close; and while I held him to my breast, where I could feel in the sudden fever of his little body the tremendous pulse of his little heart, I kept my eyes on the thing at the window and saw it move and shift its posture. I have likened it to a sentinel, but its slow wheel, for a moment, was rather the prowl of a baffled beast. My present quickened courage, however, was such that, not too much to let it through, I had to shade, as it were, my flame. Meanwhile the glare of the face was again at the window, the scoundrel fixed as if to watch and wait. It was the very confidence that I might now defy him, as well as the positive certitude, by this time, of the child's unconsciousness, that made me go on. "What did you take it for?"

"To see what you said about me."

"You opened the letter?"

"I opened it."

My eyes were now, as I held him off a little again, on Miles's own face, in which the collapse of mockery showed me how complete was the ravage of uneasiness. What was prodigious was that at last, by my success, his sense was sealed and his communication stopped: he knew that he was in presence, but knew not of what, and knew still less that I also was and that I did know. And what did this strain of trouble matter when my eyes went back to the window only to see that the air was clear again and—by my personal triumph—the influence quenched? There was nothing there. I felt that the cause was mine and that I should surely get *all.* "And you found nothing!"—I let my elation out.

He gave the most mournful, thoughtful little headshake. "Nothing."

"Nothing, nothing!" I almost shouted in my joy.

"Nothing, nothing," he sadly repeated.

I kissed his forehead; it was drenched. "So what have you done with it?"

"I've burnt it."

"Burnt it?" It was now or never. "Is that what you did at school?"

Oh, what this brought up! "At school?"

"Did you take letters?—or other things?"

"Other things?" He appeared now to be thinking of something far off and that reached him only through the pressure of his anxiety. Yet it did reach him. "Did I *steal?*"

I felt myself redden to the roots of my hair as well as wonder if it were more strange to put to a gentleman such a question or to see him take it with allowances that gave the very distance of his fall in the world. "Was it for that you mightn't go back?"

The only thing he felt was rather a dreary little surprise. "Did you know I mightn't go back?"

"I know everything."

He gave me at this the longest and strangest look. "Everything?"

"Everything. Therefore *did* you—?" But I couldn't say it again.

Miles could, very simply. "No. I didn't steal."

My face must have shown him I believed him utterly; yet my hands—but it was for pure tenderness—shook him as if to ask him why, if it was all for nothing, he had condemned me to months of torment. "What then did you do?"

He looked in vague pain all round the top of the room and drew his breath, two or three times over, as if with difficulty. He might have been standing at the bottom of the sea and raising his eyes to some faint green twilight. "Well—I said things."

"Only that?"

"They thought it was enough!"

"To turn you out for?"

Never, truly, had a person "turned out" shown so little to explain it as this little person! He appeared to weigh my question, but in a manner quite detached and almost helpless. "Well, I suppose I oughtn't."

"But to whom did you say them?"

He evidently tried to remember, but it dropped—he had lost it. "I don't know!"

He almost smiled at me in the desolation of his surrender, which was indeed practically, by this time, so complete that I ought to have left it there. But I was infatuated—I was blind with victory, though even then the very effect that was to have brought him so much nearer was already that of added separation. "Was it to everyone?" I asked.

"No; it was only to—" But he gave a sick little headshake. "I don't remember their names."

"Were they then so many?"

"No—only a few. Those I liked."

Those he liked? I seemed to float not into clearness, but into a darker obscure, and within a minute there had come to me out of my very pity the appalling alarm of his being perhaps innocent. It was for the instant confounding and bottomless, for if he *were* innocent, what then on earth was *I*? Paralysed, while it lasted, by the mere brush of the question, I let him go a little, so that, with a deep-drawn sigh, he turned away from me again; which, as he faced toward the clear window, I suffered, feeling that I had nothing now there to keep him from. "And did they repeat what you said?" I went on after a moment.

He was soon at some distance from me, still breathing hard and again with the air, though now without anger for it, of being confined against his will. Once more, as he had done before, he looked up at the dim day as if, of what had hitherto sustained him, nothing was left but an unspeakable anxiety. "Oh, yes," he nevertheless replied—"they must have repeated them. To those *they* liked," he added.

There was, somehow, less of it than I had expected; but I turned it over. "And these things came round—?"

"To the masters? Oh, yes!" he answered very simply. "But I didn't know they'd tell."

"The masters? They didn't—they've never told. That's why I ask you."

He turned to me again his little beautiful fevered face. "Yes, it was too bad."

"Too bad?"

"What I suppose I sometimes said. To write home."

I can't name the exquisite pathos of the contradiction given to such a speech by such a speaker; I only know that the next instant I heard myself throw off with homely force: "Stuff and nonsense!" But the next after that I must have sounded stern enough. "What were these things?"

My sternness was all for his judge, his executioner; yet it made him avert himself again, and that movement made *me,* with a single bound and an irrepressible cry, spring straight upon him. For there again, against the glass, as if to blight his confession and stay his answer, was the hideous author of our woe—the white face of damnation. I felt a sick swim at the drop of my victory and all the return of my battle, so that the wildness of my veritable leap only served as a great betrayal. I saw him, from the midst of my act, meet it with a divination, and on the perception that even now he only guessed, and that the window was still to his own eyes free, I let the impulse flame up to convert the climax of his dismay into the very proof of his liberation. "No more, no more, no more!" I shrieked, as I tried to press him against me, to my visitant.

"Is she *here?*" Miles panted as he caught with his sealed eyes the direction of my words. Then as his strange "she" staggered me and, with a gasp, I echoed it, "Miss Jessel, Miss Jessel!" he with a sudden fury gave me back.

I seized, stupefied, his supposition—some sequel to what we had done to Flora, but this made me only want to show him that it was better still than that. "It's not Miss Jessel! But it's at the window—straight before us. It's *there*—the coward horror, there for the last time!"

At this, after a second in which his head made the movement of a baffled dog's on a scent and then gave a frantic little shake for air and light, he was at me in a white rage, bewildered, glaring vainly over the place and missing wholly, though it now, to my sense, filled the room like the taste of poison, the wide, overwhelming presence. "It's *he?*"

I was so determined to have all my proof that I flashed into ice to challenge him. "Whom do you mean by 'he'?"

"Peter Quint—you devil!" His face gave again, round the room, its convulsed supplication. "*Where?*"

They are in my ears still, his supreme surrender of the name and his tribute to my devotion. "What does he matter now, my own?—what will he *ever* matter? *I* have you," I launched at the beast, "but he has lost you for ever!" Then, for the demonstration of my work, "There, *there!*" I said to Miles.

But he had already jerked straight round, stared, glared again, and seen but the quiet day. With the stroke of the loss I was so proud of he uttered the cry of a creature hurled over an abyss, and the grasp with which I recovered him might have been that of catching him in his fall. I caught him, yes, I held him—it may be imagined with what a passion; but at the end of a minute I began to feel what it truly was that I held. We were alone with the quiet day, and his little heart, dispossessed, had stopped.

From the Preface to *The Aspern Papers*

Henry James

"The Turn of the Screw" . . . this perfectly independent and irresponsible little fiction rejoices, beyond any rival on a like ground, in a conscious provision of prompt retort to the sharpest question that may be addressed to it. For it has the small strength—if I shouldn't say rather the unattackable ease—of a perfect homogeneity, of being, to the very last grain of its virtue, all of a kind; the very kind, as happens, least apt to be baited by earnest criticism, the only sort of criticism of which account need be taken. To have handled again this so full-blown flower of high fancy is to be led back by it to easy and happy recognitions. Let the first of these be that of the starting-point itself—the sense, all charming again, of the circle, one winter afternoon, round the hall-fire of a grave old country-house where (for all the world as if to resolve itself promptly and obligingly into convertible, into "literary" stuff) the talk turned, on I forget what homely pretext, to apparitions and night-fears, to the marked and sad drop in the general supply, and still more in the general quality, of such commodities. The good, the really effective and heart-shaking ghost-stories (roughly so to term them) appeared all to have been told, and neither new crop nor new type in any quarter awaited us. The new type indeed, the mere modern "psychical" case, washed clean of all queerness as by exposure to a flowing laboratory tap, and equipped with credentials vouching for this—the new type clearly promised little, for the more

SOURCE: Copyright 1908 by Henry James; renewal copyright 1936. Reprinted from *The Art of the Novel,* Critical Prefaces by Henry James, with an Introduction by Richard P. Blackmur; pp. 169–177. Used by permission of Charles Scribner's Sons.

it was respectably certified the less it seemed of a nature to rouse the dear old sacred terror. Thus it was, I remember, that amid our lament for a beautiful lost form, our distinguished host expressed the wish that he might but have recovered for us one of the scantest of fragments of this form at its best. He had never forgotten the impression made on him as a young man by the withheld glimpse, as it were, of a dreadful matter that had been reported years before, and with as few particulars, to a lady with whom he had youthfully talked. The story would have been thrilling could she but have found herself in better possession of it, dealing as it did with a couple of small children in an out-of-the-way place, to whom the spirits of certain "bad" servants, dead in the employ of the house, were believed to have appeared with the design of "getting hold" of them. This was all, but there had been more, which my friend's old converser had lost the thread of: she could only assure him of the wonder of the allegations as she had anciently heard them made. He himself could give us but this shadow of a shadow—my own appreciation of which, I need scarcely say, was exactly wrapped up in that thinness. On the surface there wasn't much, but another grain, none the less, would have spoiled the precious pinch addressed to its end as neatly as some modicum extracted from an old silver snuffbox and held between finger and thumb. I was to remember the haunted children and the prowling servile spirits as a "value," of the disquieting sort, in all conscience sufficient; so that when, after an interval, I was asked for something seasonable by the promoters of a periodical dealing in the time-honoured Christmas-tide toy, I bethought myself at once of the vividest little note for sinister romance that I had ever jotted down.

Such was the private source of "The Turn of the Screw"; and I wondered, I confess, why so fine a germ, gleaming there in the wayside dust of life, had never been deftly picked up. The thing had for me the immense merit of allowing the imagination absolute freedom of hand, of inviting it to act on a perfectly clear field, with no "outside" control involved, no pattern of the usual or the true or the terrible "pleasant" (save always of course the high pleasantry of one's very form) to consort with. This makes in fact the charm of my second reference, that I find here a perfect example of an exercise of the imagination unassisted, unassociated—playing the game, making the score, in the phrase of our sporting day, off its own bat. To what degree the game was worth playing, I needn't attempt to say: the exercise I have noted strikes me now, I confess, as the interesting thing, the imaginative faculty acting with the *whole* of the case on its hands. The exhibition involved is in other words a fairy-tale pure and simple—save indeed as to its springing not from an artless and measureless, but from a conscious and cultivated credulity. Yet the fairy-tale belongs mainly to either of two classes, the short and sharp and single, charged more or less with the compactness of anecdote (as to which let the familiars of our childhood, Cinderella and Blue-Beard and Hop o' my Thumb and Little Red Riding Hood and many of the gems of the Brothers Grimm directly testify), or else the long and loose, the copious, the various, the endless, where, dramatically speaking, roundness is quite sacrificed—sacrificed to fulness, sacrificed to exuberance, if one will: witness at hazard almost any one of the Arabian Nights. The charm of all these things for the distracted modern mind is in the clear field of experience, as I call it, over which we are thus led to roam; an annexed but independent world in which nothing is right save as we rightly imagine it. We have to do *that,* and we do it happily for the short spurt and in the smaller piece, achieving so perhaps beauty and lucidity; we flounder, we lose breath, on the other hand—that is we fail, not of continuity, but of an agreeable unity, of the "roundness" in which beauty and lucidity largely reside—when we go in, as they say, for great lengths and breadths. And this, oddly enough, not because "keeping it up" isn't abundantly within the compass of the imagination appealed to in certain conditions, but because the finer interest depends just on *how* it is kept up.

Nothing is so easy as improvisation, the running on and on of invention; it is sadly compromised, however, from the moment its stream breaks bounds and gets into flood. Then the waters may spread indeed, gathering houses and herds and crops and cities into their arms and wrenching off, for our amusement, the whole face of the land—only violating by the same stroke our sense of the course and the channel, which is our sense of the uses of a stream and the virtue of a story. Improvisation, as in the Arabian Nights, may keep on terms with encountered objects by sweeping them in and floating them on its breast; but the great effect it so loses—that of keeping on terms with itself. This is ever, I intimate, the hard thing for the fairy-tale; but by just so much as it struck me as hard did it in "The Turn of the Screw" affect me as irresistibly prescribed. To improvise with extreme freedom and yet at the same time without the possibility of ravage, without the hint of flood; to keep the stream, in a word, on something like ideal terms with itself: that was here my definite business. The thing was to aim at absolute singleness, clearness and roundness, and yet to depend on an imagination working freely, working (call it) with extravagance; by which law it wouldn't be thinkable except as free and wouldn't be amusing except as controlled. The merit of the tale, as it stands, is accordingly, I judge, that it has struggled successfully with its dangers. It is an excursion into chaos while remaining, like Blue-Beard and Cinderella, but an anecdote—though an anecdote amplified and highly emphasised and returning upon itself; as, for that matter, Cinderella and Blue-Beard return. I need scarcely add after this that it is a piece of ingenuity pure and simple, of cold artistic calculation, an *amusette* to catch those not easily caught (the "fun" of the capture of the merely witless being ever but small), the jaded, the disillusioned, the fastidious. Otherwise expressed, the study is of a conceived "tone," the tone of suspected and felt trouble, of an inordinate and incalculable sort—the tone of tragic, yet of exquisite, mystification. To knead the subject of my young friend's, the suppositious narrator's, mystification thick, and yet strain the expression of it so clear and fine that beauty would result: no side of the matter so revives for me as that endeavour. Indeed if the artistic value of such an experiment be measured by the intellectual echoes it may again, long after, set in motion, the case would make in favour of this little firm fantasy—which I seem to see draw behind it to-day a train of associations. I ought doubtless to blush for thus confessing them so numerous that I can but pick among them for reference. I recall for instance a reproach made me by a reader capable evidently, for the time, of some attention, but not quite capable of enough, who complained that I hadn't sufficiently "characterised" my young woman engaged in her labyrinth; hadn't endowed her with signs and marks, features and humours, hadn't in a word invited her to deal with her own mystery as well as with that of Peter Quint, Miss Jessel and the hapless children. I remember well, whatever the absurdity of its now coming back to me, my reply to that criticism—under which one's artistic, one's ironic heart shook for the instant almost to breaking. "You indulge in that stricture at your ease, and I don't mind confiding to you that—strange as it may appear!—one has to choose ever so delicately among one's difficulties, attaching one's self to the greatest, bearing hard on those and intelligently neglecting the others. If one attempts to tackle them all one is certain to deal completely with none; whereas the effectual dealing with a few casts a blest golden haze under cover of which, like wanton mocking goddesses in clouds, the others find prudent to retire. It was 'déjà très-joli,' in 'The Turn of the Screw,' please believe, the general proposition of our young woman's keeping crystalline her record of so many intense anomalies and obscurities—by which I don't of course mean her explanation of them, a different matter; and I saw no way, I feebly grant (fighting, at the best too, periodically, for every grudged inch of my space) to exhibit her in relations other than those; one of which, precisely, would have been her relation to her own nature. We have surely as much of her own nature as we can swallow in watching it reflect her anxieties and inductions. It constitutes no little of a character indeed, in such conditions, for a young person, as she says, 'privately bred,' that she is able to make her particular credible statement of such strange matters. She has 'authority,' which is a good deal to have given her, and I couldn't have arrived at so much had I clumsily tried for more."

For which truth I claim part of the charm latent on occasion in the extracted reasons of beautiful things—putting for the beautiful always, in a work of art, the close, the curious, the deep. Let me place above all, however, under the protection of that presence the side by which this fiction appeals most to consideration: its choice of its way of meeting its gravest difficulty. There were difficulties not so grave: I had for instance simply to renounce all attempt to keep the kind and degree of impression I wished to produce on terms with the to-day so copious psychical record of cases of apparitions. Different signs and circumstances, in the reports, mark these cases; different things are done—though on the whole very little appears to be—by the persons appearing; the point is, however, that some things are never done at all: this negative quantity is large —certain reserves and properties and immobilities consistently impose themselves. Recorded and attested "ghosts" are in other words as little expressive, as little dramatic, above all as little continuous and conscious and responsive, as is consistent with their taking the trouble—and an immense trouble they find it, we gather—to appear at all. Wonderful and interesting therefore at a given moment, they are inconceivable figures in an *action*—and "The Turn of the Screw" was an action, desperately, or it was nothing. I had to decide in fine between having my apparitions correct and having my story "good"—that is producing my impression of the dreadful, my designed horror. Good ghosts, speaking by book, make poor subjects, and it was clear that from the first my hovering prowling blighting presences, my pair of abnormal agents, would have to depart altogether from the rules. They would be agents in fact; there would be laid on them the dire duty of causing the situation to reek with the air of Evil. Their desire and their ability to do so, visibly measuring meanwhile their effect, together with their observed and described success—this was exactly my central idea; so that, briefly, I cast my lot with pure romance, the appearances conforming to the true type being so little romantic.

This is to say, I recognise again, that Peter Quint and Miss Jessel are not "ghosts" at all, as we now know the ghost, but goblins, elves, imps, demons as loosely constructed as those of the old trials for witchcraft; if not, more pleasingly, fairies of the legendary order, wooing their victims forth to see them dance under the moon. Not indeed that I suggest their reducibility to any form of the pleasing pure and simple; they please at the best but through having helped me to express my subject all directly and intensely. Here it was—in the use made of them—that I felt a high degree of art really required; and here it is that, on reading the tale over, I find my precautions justified. The essence of the matter was the villainy of motive in the evoked predatory creatures; so that the result would be ignoble—by which I mean would be trivial—were this element of evil but feebly or inanely suggested. Thus arose on behalf of my idea the lively interest of a possible suggestion and process of *adumbration;* the question of how best to convey that sense of the depths of the sinister without which my fable would so woefully limp. Portentous evil—how was I to save that, as an intention on the part of my demon-spirits, from the drop, the comparative vulgarity, inevitably attending, throughout the whole range of possible brief illustration, the offered example, the imputed vice, the cited act, the limited deplorable presentable instance? To bring the bad dead back to life for a second round of badness is to warrant them as indeed prodigious, and to become hence as shy of specifications as of a waiting anti-climax. One had seen, in fiction, some grand form of wrong-doing, or better still of wrong-being, imputed, seen it promised and announced as by the hot breath of the Pit—and then, all lamentably, shrink to the compass of some particular brutality, some particular immorality, some particular infamy portrayed: with the result, alas, of the demonstration's falling sadly short. If *my* bad things, for "The Turn of the Screw," I felt, should succumb to this danger, if they shouldn't seem sufficiently bad, there would be nothing for me but to hang my artistic head lower than I had ever known occasion to do.

The view of that discomfort and the fear of that dishonour, it accordingly must have been, that struck the proper light for my right, though by no means easy, short cut. What, in the last analysis, had I to give the sense of? Of their being, the haunting pair, capable, as the phrase is, of everything—that is of exerting, in respect to the children, the very worst action small victims so conditioned might be conceived as subject to. What would *be* then, on reflection, this utmost conceivability?—a question to which the answer all admirably came. There is for such a case no eligible *absolute* of the wrong; it remains relative to fifty other elements, a matter of appreciation, speculation, imagination—these things moreover quite exactly in the light of the spectator's, the critic's, the reader's experience. Only make the reader's general vision of evil intense enough, I said to myself—and that already is a charming job—and his own experience, his own imagination, his own sympathy (with the children) and horror (of their false friends) will supply him quite sufficiently with all the particulars. Make him *think* the evil, make him think it for himself, and you are released from weak specifications. This ingenuity I took pains—as indeed great pains were required—to apply; and with a success apparently beyond my liveliest hope. Droll enough at the same time, I must add, some of the evidence—even when most convincing—of this success. How can I feel my calculation to have failed, my wrought suggestion not to have worked, that is, on my being assailed, as has befallen me, with the charge of a monstrous emphasis, the charge of all indecently expatiating? There is not only from beginning to end of the matter not an inch of expatiation, but my values are positively all blanks save so far as an excited horror, a promoted pity, a created expertness—on which punctual effects of strong causes no writer can ever fail to plume himself—proceed to read into them more or less fantastic figures. Of high interest to the author meanwhile—and by the same stroke a theme for the moralist—the artless resentful reaction of the entertained person who has abounded in the sense of the situation. He visits his abundance, morally, on the artist—who has but clung to an ideal of faultlessness. Such indeed, for this latter, are some of the observations by which the prolonged strain of that clinging may be enlivened!

. . . . .

Henry James to the Ruminant Reader: The Turn of the Screw

Edna Kenton

> "It is a piece of ingenuity pure and simple, of cold artistic calculation, an amusette to catch those not easily caught (the 'fun' of the capture of the merely witless being ever but small), the jaded, the disillusioned, the fastidious."—From the Preface to *The Turn of the Screw.*

Of his relation to his reader always, and particularly when working in the shadowy realm of the "supernatural," Henry James had somewhere, in the detached third person, a charming word to say: "He has revelled in the creation of alarm and suspense and surprise and relief, in all the arts that practise, with a scruple for nothing but any lapse of application, on the credulous soul of the candid or, immeasurably better, on the seasoned spirit of the cunning reader. He has built rejoicingly on that blest faculty of wonder . . . as on a strange passion planted in the heart of man for his benefit, a mysterious provision made for him in the scheme of nature. He has seen this particular sensibility, the need and the love of wondering, and the quick response to any pretext for it, as the beginning and the end of his affair." The rest is the reader's, and the novelist, he says, can hope for little more than the benefit involved in his having cast some spell upon the simpler, the very simplest forms of attention: any finer tribute coming as a result on the reader's part of any act of reflection or discrimination is only a gratuity thrown in. Nevertheless, of the reader's relation to him he says elsewhere, briefly and parenthetically: "Attention of perusal, I thus confess by

SOURCE: *The Arts,* VI (November, 1924), 245–255.

the way, is what I at every point, as well as here, absolutely invoke and take for granted."

But this meed of fond attention, so urgently, so almost despairingly invoked by a devoted author who rigidly took it for granted during the process of his work, persistently failed before the completed thing. From the 1880's on—from the appearance of The Portrait of a Lady—Henry James had to endure from his devotees the poor tribute of mere reverence. They all felt certain that Mr. James was "doing something about art"; that he was possessed by an "intention"; that the intention was indubitably "artistic"; and that, therefore, abiding mystery lurked behind his work. But there was abiding bewilderment before it. Only once in his career were his readers to react with unawed spontaneity to a recognized "intention." The Turn of the Screw caught every one in its trap. Bewilderment, in some cases reverence even, dropped before this nerve-shattering ghost story, this horrendous tale of children hounded by the evil spirits of Peter Quint and Miss Jessel. No befogged reader of the other novels and tales but knew what Henry James was writing about here; at last there was light on the dark path; at last there was clarity. But, with The Awkward Age and The Sacred Fount, darkness fell again, never to lighten. None the less the great author's admirers have liked to remember that for once at least, and during his lifetime, he was understandable and understood.

One of them, William Lyon Phelps, in a grieved and glowing appreciation published shortly after James's death in 1916, offered authentic confirmation to the prevalent impression that James himself was delighted with the reception accorded this his perhaps most "famous" story—an impression indeed which he himself sealed and stamped in his later Preface to The Turn of the Screw. Because this particular admirer sums up, in the story of his own private experience with this remarkable tale, the general trend of reactions of readers, ruminant and otherwise, to The Turn of the Screw, he is well worth quoting on it:

"This year (1898) was a notable year in our author's career; it saw the publication of The Turn of the Screw, which I found then and find again to be the most powerful, the most nerve-shattering ghost story I have ever read. The connoting strength of its author's reticence was never displayed to better advantage; had he spoken plainly the book might have been barred from the mails; yet it is a great work of art, profoundly ethical, and making to all those who are interested in the moral welfare of girls and boys an appeal terrific in its intensity. With none of the conventional machinery of melodrama, with no background of horrifying or threatening scenery, with no hysterical language, this story made my blood chill, my spine curl, and every individual hair to stand on end. When I told the author exactly how I felt while reading it, and thanked him for giving me sensations I thought no writer could give me at my age, he said he was made happy by my testimony.

"'For,' he said, 'I meant to scare the whole world with that story, and you had precisely the same emotion I hoped to rouse in every one. When I wrote it I was too ill to hold a pen. I therefore dictated the whole thing to a Scotch stenographer. I was glad to try this experiment, for I believed that I should be able to judge of its effect on the whole world by its effect on the man who should hear it first. Judge of my dismay when from the first page to the last this iron Scot betrayed not the slightest shade of feeling. I dictated to him sentences that I thought would make him leap from his chair; he shorthanded them as though they had been geometry; and whenever I paused to see him collapse, he would inquire in a dry voice, "What next?"'"

It is safe to say that this "iron Scot" is the only reader in the Jamesian world—and he happened to be not a reader—who has failed in the tribute of chilled blood, curling spine and hair erect in presence of this story so bathed in sunshine, so lighted from golden skies and so all suffused with mildness. Almost one wonders why such tribute to such beauty.

But it was the tribute paid, and it continues to be the tribute paid, notwithstanding the barren fact that the two marvelous years in the Jacobites' calendar are already fifteen years behind us.

For it was in 1908 and 1909 that Henry James broke once for all his silence on the why and the how of his thirty-four years of novel-writing, and offered his magnificent first aid to critics and readers in the long procession of Prefaces to his massive Definitive Edition. Nothing like these rich, leisurely ruminations on the Novel, the Novelist and the Critic-Reader has ever been done; but they were done in James's own terms which have remained, if not untranslatable, at least untranslated to this day. Old reactions to the novels and tales have not undergone re-evaluation; old criticism has not been re-written in the light of these terms; indeed, if anything at all has happened, which must be doubted, that which was to illumine has only served to obscure the more. The Princess Cassamassima lingers on as Mr. James's "unfortunate excursion into socialism and an alien world." The Tragic Muse still stands as his "only novel of the theatre." The Sacred Fount—but that had no Preface to help or hinder. And The Turn of the Screw remains today what it has been declared for a quarter of a century to be, "a relation of the imaginative—which is the moral and spiritual—defiling of two children by apparitional criminals"; "a romance of the English habit of leaving young children to the care of improper maids and salacious ostlers"; a brief on "the ugliness of corrupted childhood"; a tale in which "the hidden spectres of the dead Quint and his drab return to prey still further on the little children whom they had corrupted when alive"; a ghost story "the more ghostly because the apparitions of the valet and governess, appearing at the dangerous place, the top of the tower on the other side of the lake (sic), that they may tempt the children they corrupted in their lives to join them in their eternal torment, are seen by the clear eyes of the honorable and fearless lady who tells the tale."

There was a Preface, of course, to The Turn of the Screw—all of these quoted reactions to the story have appeared since 1908—a preface highly revelatory, highly amused, positively joyous in tone. The story was evidently "reader-proof," and in this all unconscious tribute of the higher criticism of his day to his own higher technic, Henry James permitted himself to take a tolerably serene satisfaction. No one was baffled by it; it held no secrets. It was simply a gorgeous ghost story, ethical, of course, profoundly moral, involving as it so evidently did, the problem of corrupted childhood. If to a few it seemed "immoral," to the many it was a riot of blood-curdling joy. And it is pleasant for the ironically-minded to feel that the firm surface of the story has remained "reader-proof"; that the traps and lures laid for the wary and unwary alike have caught their victims every time; that one of James's minor intentions in this tale—to make the reader do for once, even though all unconsciously, his half of the work—has survived the straight little tips offered in the Preface, has survived even his ironic warning flung out as he delightedly summed up "this irresponsible little fiction":

"It is a piece of ingenuity pure and simple, of cold artistic calculation, an *amusette* to catch those not easily caught (the 'fun' of the capture of the merely witless being ever but small), the jaded, the disillusioned, the fastidious." And then, having duly warned, he all gratuitously illustrated:

"I recall, for instance, a reproach made me by a reader capable evidently, for the time, of some attention, but not quite capable of enough, who complained that I hadn't sufficiently 'characterized' my young woman engaged in her labyrinth; hadn't endowed her with signs and marks, features and humours; hadn't in a word invited her to deal with her own mystery as well as with that of Peter

Quint and Miss Jessel and the hapless children. I remember well, whatever the absurdity of its coming back to me, my reply to that criticism—under which one's artistic, one's ironic heart shook for the instant almost to breaking. 'You indulge in that stricture at your ease, and I don't mind confiding to you that—strange as it may appear!—one has to choose ever so delicately among one's difficulties, attaching one's self to the greatest, bearing hard on those and intelligently neglecting the others. . . . It was *déjà très-joli* in "The Turn of the Screw," please believe, the general proposition of our young woman's keeping crystalline her record of so many intense anomalies and obscurities—by which I don't of course mean her explanation of them, a different matter; and I saw no way I feebly grant (fighting at the best too, periodically, for every grudged inch of my space) to exhibit her in relations other than those; one of which, precisely, would have been her relation to her own nature. We have surely as much of her own nature as we can swallow in watching it reflect her anxieties and inductions. It constitutes no little of a character, indeed, in such conditions, for a young person, as she says, "privately bred," that she is able to make her particular credible statement of such strange matters. She had "authority," which is a good deal to have given her, and I couldn't have arrived at so much had I clumsily tried for more.' "

Like many another charmed and mystified reader of The Turn of the Screw, I read it first "at night," in a "country house"—and in a long ago "first edition"—into and long past the midnight hour. The conditions were ideal, and all the admiring and admirable reactions to this "finest ghost story in the world" were mine; of all the thrills and spinal shudders born of the creeping ghosts and "haunted children" I had the full effect. But it was an effect differing in some inconsequential ways from many of the admiring and admirable reactions to this tale; even enhanced a little, I must now believe, by another kind of wondering that developed steadily alongside the prime inevitable wondering over "story" and "plot." There was the wondering over the portentous Evil that, from the first page to the last, floated through the great room of the story; but there was wondering also over the beauty no less portentous in the working of the evil spell. There were the "ghosts"; but there was also *the way they came*. There were the lovely "corrupted" children; but there was the exquisite little governess too, guarding her charges so explainingly—even she seemed a little infected by the sinister air she breathed in and out so pantingly. There was the thickly painted picture of horror—but where?—on the pages or in the mind? How had the magnificent trick of technic been turned; how in the name of the last fine stroke of elimination for the sake of effect had the whole been rounded out? Strange indeed, today, how this wondering over matters that few fictions generate blurred any serene certainty, at the end, of what the story was about; and so, in this particular instance, enhanced the first effect of The Turn of the Screw. Because here was a little oasis in the wordy desert of fiction; a spot inviting one to linger on a while and search about in all leisure for some possible buried treasure; a find, in short, worth any waste of curiosity in the hunt for the "fun" that might come out of it.

Now and then, in the amused, pondering search, one came upon some professional critic's appreciation of the story—appreciation, however, that fell somehow always short of any attempt at going behind. Critical appraisement of The Turn of the Screw has never, indeed, pressed beyond the outer circle of the story where the children and ghosts dance together, toward any discerned or discernible inner ring where another figure may be executing some frantic dance of terror, toward any possible story behind the "story," toward any character protected by its creator to the very top of his sardonic, ironic bent.

But any critical appraisement of James's work, let pass his technic, never gets far when it has neglected its precautions, one of which is never to fail to take into account his pure passion for "the protection of character," since, in his book of golden rules, no character is worth doing unless it is worth loving, and no lover is worthy of his love if he lacks the instinct to protect the beloved. Recall his small digression on Thackeray in The Lesson of Balzac, where he emphasizes the difference in point of view and feeling between Balzac's treatment of his Valerie Marneffe and Thackeray's dealings with his Blanche and his Becky. Balzac loved his Valerie; he did not expose her; his instinct was to cover her, to protect her, to leave her free, and so all of her story was "the long rope, for her acting herself out, that her creator's participation in her reality assures her." Thackeray, on the contrary, interfered, exposed, sacrificed; he hindered Becky from free progress through her Vanity Fair, and he gives us Blanche Amory "with the author's lash about her little bare white back from the first." It is a straight little tip that James is never so guileful, so suave and so honied as when he is busily engaged in "protecting." And it is only painting the gold of the lily to add that if one is making a collection of his agents of evil, they are not to be found among those endowed with the usual stripes and markings. He loves them even more than Balzac loved his Valerie, and protects them with far finer dexterity. In The Turn of the Screw the protection of character, by all the evidence, reached its apotheosis: not until he came to the writing of The Golden Bowl was James to lean quite so heavily on this strong arm of the novelist's finer technic.

It is as if, wearied of devoted readers who boasted of their "attention of perusal" and their consequent certainties of perception —certainties, by the way, which James was never wont to disturb— he determined to write, in The Turn of the Screw, a story for "the world." He would write it of course primarily for himself and for that reader for whom he must always write—the reader not content to have the author do all of the work—but he would make this particular work a supreme test, of attention and of inattention alike. He would have his own private "fun" in its writing, his own guarded intention, his own famous centre of interest. But he would put about this centre, not only traps set and baited for the least lapse of attention, but lures—delights and terrors mingled—calculated to distract or break off short any amount of alert intentness. Let some singularly astute reader avoid one and yet another of these—others would lie hidden or beckon invitingly ten steps ahead. It would be, as he said ten years later, "an *amusette* to catch those not easily caught." But to make the amusement more complete, he would see how far he might go, this single time, in catching not only the cunning but the casual reader, the latter too often not his prey, in the maze of an irresistible illusion. He would make a deliberate bid, not only for as much attention as possible, but for as little. Illusion, if it were based on some denominator common to mankind, could be irresistible, if the right emotional spring were only rightly touched. It would be amusing to see how far he might work on the cunning and the casual alike; it would be the very essence of irony if their reactions to the story were identical. As a little matter of critical history they were. And Henry James narrowly escaped writing a best seller.

In the submerged and disregarded foreword to the tale, in which the young governess and the children's uncle are set brightly before us—few readers of The Turn of the Screw remember this at all—lies a little painted portrait of the exquisite young creature who undertook the portentous task at Bly. The children and the ghosts have crowded forward to hide the only light thrown on her except for the irrepressible unconscious lights she casts on herself. It is never to be forgotten that it is she—not Henry James—who tells the story of Bly and its inhabitants, bound within confines of understanding as narrowly drawn as the circle which limited and defined, for instance, What Maisie Knew. But her freedom to tell her story, with no omniscient author at her elbow, is the "long rope, for acting herself out," that her creator, so fondly participating in her reality, tied so lightly to his foreword and then played out to her. The foreword is the only light we have on her present or her past—her whole concern is with the children and the ghosts. But of these we have only her story, and we have got nowhere near the "story of the story" until, pressing resolutely through her irresistibly credible recounting of the horrors at Bly, we come into closer quarters with the secret causes of her admirable *flair* for the evil she finds there.

She was twenty, so the submerged foreword tells us, a clergyman's daughter seeking her first position when she came up to London to answer an advertisement of the children's uncle. She found him "such a figure as had never risen, save in a dream or an old novel, before a fluttered, anxious girl out of a Hampstead vicarage." He was handsome and bold and pleasant, offhand and gay and kind, gallant and splendid. It was a difficult situation offered her, and it was put to her fairly; the condition of her taking it was that she should assume full responsibility for house, children and servants and leave him free to live his life in peace. She hesitated, but she was under a spell. "She succumbed to it . . . she saw him only twice . . . but that was the beauty of her passion . . . she never saw him again."

But she went to Bly. The master had come into her house and had gone out of it; she had only the house. She found it at first full of brightness, greatness, beauty and dignity and she began to enjoy it almost with a sense of property. Days passed, filled with dreams and dreamings. But there came a change which broke the hush of the first beautiful week at Bly; and the change, "actually like the spring of a beast," came at the close of a beautiful afternoon, at the end of a lonely stroll in which she walked, wrapped in day dreams. "One of the thoughts," wrote the little governess in her desperate diary, "that, as I don't in the least shrink from noting now, used to be with me in these wanderings was that it would be as charming as a charming story suddenly to meet some one. Some one would appear there at the turn of a path, and would stand before me and smile and approve. I didn't ask more than that—I only asked that he should know." And that evening, as she came within sight of the house, "he did stand there"—the figure that her dreamings had invoked.

It produced in me, this figure, in the clear twilight, I remember, two distinct gasps of emotion, which were, sharply, the shock of my first and that of my second surprise. My second was a violent perception of the mistake of my first: The man who met my eyes was not the person I had precipitately supposed. There came to me thus a bewilderment of vision which, after these years, there is no living view that I can hope to give. An unknown man in a lonely place is a permitted object of fear to a young woman privately bred; and the figure that faced me was—a few seconds more assured me—as little any one else I knew, as it was the image that had been in my mind. I had not seen it in Harley street—I had not seen it anywhere. The place, moreover, in the strangest way in the world, had, on the instant, and by the very fact of its appearance, become a solitude. To me, at least, making my statement here with a deliberation with which I have never made it, the whole feeling of the moment returns. It was as if, while I took in—what I did take in—all the rest of the scene had been stricken with death. I can hear again, as I write, the intense hush in which the sounds of evening dropped. The rooks stopped cawing in the golden sky and the friendly hour lost, for the minute, all its voice. But there was no other change in nature, unless indeed it were a change that I saw with a stranger sharpness. The gold was still in the sky, the clearness in the air, and the man who looked at me over the battlements was as definite as a picture in a frame. That's how I thought, with extraordinary quickness, of each person that he might have been and that he was not. We were confronted across our distance quite long enough for me to ask myself with intensity who then he was and to feel, as an effect of my inability to say, a wonder that in a few instants more became intense.

The great question, or one of these, is, afterwards, I know, with regard to certain matters, the question of how long they have lasted. Well, this matter of mine, think what you will of it, lasted while I caught at a dozen possibilities, none of which made a difference for the better, that I could see, in there having been in the house—and for how long, above all?—a person of whom I was in ignorance. It lasted just while I bridled a little with the sense that my office demanded that there should be no such ignorance and no such person. It lasted while this visitant at all events—and there was a touch of the strange freedom, as I remember, in the sign of familiarity of his wearing no hat—seemed to fix me, from his position, with just the question, just the scrutiny through the fading light, that his own presence provoked. We were too far apart to call to each other, but there was a moment at which, at shorter range, some challenge between us, breaking the hush, would have been the right result of our straight mutual stare. He was in one of the angles, the one away from the house, very erect, as it struck me and with both hands on the ledge. So I saw him as I see the letters I form on this page; then, exactly, after a minute, as if to add to the spectacle, he slowly changed his place—passed, looking at me hard all the while, to the opposite corner of the platform. Yes, I had the sharpest sense that during this transit he never took his eyes from me, and I can see at this moment the way his hand, as he went, passed from one of the crenelations to the next. He stopped at the other corner, but less long, and even as he turned away, still markedly fixed me. He turned away; that was all I knew.

This, no more, no less, is the first visitation of Peter Quint. There came another, as unexpectedly as the first, on a rainy Sunday afternoon. "He appeared thus again with I won't say greater distinctness, for that was impossible, but with a nearness that represented a forward stride in our intercourse and made me, as I met him, catch my breath and turn cold. He was the same—he was the same, and seen, this time, as he had been seen before, from the waist up. . . . He remained but a few seconds—long enough to convince me that he also saw and recognized; but it was as if I had been looking at him for years and had known him always. Something happened this time, however, that had not happened before; his stare into my face, through the glass and across the room, was as deep and hard as then, but it quitted me for a moment during which I could still watch it, see it fix successively several other things. On the spot there came to me the added shock of a certitude that it was not for me he had come there. He had come for some one else."

So the little governess says, and upon it she acts—both so convincingly as to sweep the reader, wary or unwary, headlong with her into her nightmare of horrors. Her way of escape is the reader's. And so subtlely [sic] does she build up the ring of fire about her house of life—as frightened women, in pioneer forests with their men away, lighted circles of flames about their homes to ward off the prowling beasts of night—that it is desperately difficult to catch her in the act.

The children hounded by the prowling ghosts—this is the hard and shining surface story of The Turn of the Screw; or, to put it more accurately, it is the traditional and accepted interpretation of the story as it has come down through a quarter of a century of readers' reactions resulting from "a cold, artistic calculation" on the part of its highly entertained author. As a tiny matter of literal fact, no reader has more to go on than the young governess's word for this rather momentous and sidetracking allegation. As a rather large matter of literal fact, we may know, with but a modicum of attention paid to her recital of these nerve-shattering affairs at Bly, that it is she—always she herself—who sees the lurking shapes and heralds them to her little world. Not to the charming little Flora, but behind Flora and facing the governess, the apparitional Miss Jessel first appeared. There are traps and lures in plenty, but just a little wariness will suffice to disprove, with a single survey of the ground, the traditional, we might almost call it lazy version of this tale. Not the children, but the little governess was hounded by the ghosts who, as James confides with such suave frankness in his Preface, merely "helped me to express my subject all directly and intensely." After her startling materializations of Peter Quint and Miss Jessel, Bly became a nest of lurking shapes, and she walked softly, in terror, expectantly. She came to know the moods that brought them: "There were states of the air, conditions of sound and stillness, unspeakable impressions of the *kind* of ministering moment, that brought back to me, long enough to catch it, the medium in which, that June evening out of doors, I had had my first sight of Quint. . . . I recognized the signs, the portents—I recognized the moment, the spot." So she made the shades of her recurring fevers dummy figures for the delirious terrifying of others, pathetically trying to harmonize her own disharmonies by creating discords outside herself.

"I meant to scare the whole world with that story," James has been quoted as saying—seemingly with serious solemnity. And indeed, in its exquisitely ironic Preface, he took up at length with its readers the turning, precisely, of just this little trick that has worked so well. He is more than confidential—he is explicit as to just how the screw was tightened, revelatory as to calculated causes of his calculated effects.

His problem here, he says gaily, was how *best* to convey that sense of the depths of the sinister which was essential for illusion. Portentous evil—how was that to be invoked; or, invoked, how saved from the comparative vulgarity of "the cited act, the limited, deplorable, presentable instance." "One had seen," he mused, "in fiction, some grand form of wrong-doing or, better still, of wrong being, imputed, seen it promised and announced as by the hot breath of the Pit—and then, all lamentably, shrink to the compass of some particular brutality, some particular immorality, some particular infamy portrayed; with the result, alas, of the demonstration's falling sadly short."

So, from the heap of aesthetic failures lying along fiction's path, he evolved, for the novel of evil, an aesthetic moral. Its sinister agent, he concluded, be it man or ghost, must be, in the last analysis, capable of *anything*, the very worst conceivable action. So far, very good; he had his sinister agent—his pair of them—in his two "ghosts." But still the question remained, of how best to convey to the reader the sense of this utmost capability without the author himself falling into the deadly trap of the "cited act." And this is his answer:

"Only make the reader's general vision of evil intense enough,

I said to myself—and that already is a charming job—and his own experience, his own imagination, his own sympathy (with the children) and horror (of their false friends) will supply him quite sufficiently with all the particulars. Make him *think* the evil, make him think it for himself, and you are released from weak specifications. This ingenuity I took pains—as indeed great pains were required—to apply; and with a success apparently beyond my liveliest hopes."

A success all the greater, incidentally, because he permitted his innocent young governess to write herself his novel of evil. She could not "specify," and readers of her tender, moving tale have of necessity had to think the evil for themselves. "Droll enough," adds James "some of the evidence—even when most convincing—of this success. How can I feel my calculation to have failed, my wrought suggestion not to have worked, that is, on my being assailed, as has befallen me, with the charge of a monstrous emphasis, the charge of all indecently expatiating. There is not only from beginning to end of the matter not an inch of expatiation, but my values are positively all blanks save only so far as an excited horror, a promoted pity, a created expertness—on which punctual effects of strong causes no writer can ever fail to plume himself—proceed to read into them more or less fantastic figures."

And the fantastic figures have been read into The Turn of the Screw; for once at least James succeeded in forcing his reader, however unconsciously, to do a share of the work left for him to do. Not all of it, however; the ironic beauty of his subtle device for best expressing the depths of evil is that it was at the same time the calculated trap of traps for the guarding of his heroine. The eager, thrilled, horrified reader, joined with her in her vivid hunt after hidden sins, has failed to think sufficiently of her; and has, all oddly, contrived to protect her quite as romantically as her creator permitted her to protect herself in her charming recital of the happenings at Bly. Her own story, so naively sympathetic, of the ghosts and children, has been her simple bulwark—even the cunning reader has been credulous.

So, on The Turn of the Screw, Henry James has won, hands down, all round; has won most of all when the reader, persistently baffled, but persistently wondering, comes face to face at last with the little governess, and realizes, with a conscious thrill greater than that of merely automatic nerve shudders before "horror," that the guarding ghosts and children—what they are and what they do—are only exquisite dramatizations of her little personal mystery, figures for the ebb and flow of troubled thought within her mind, acting out her story. If the reader has won for himself a blest sense of an extension of experience and consciousness in the recognition that her case, so delicate, so complicated, so critical and yet so transparent, has never in its whole treatment been cheapened or betrayed; if he has had, in the high modern sense, all of his "fun," he has none the less paid; he has worked for it all, and by that fruitful labor has verified James's earliest contention that there was a discoverable way to establish a relation of work shared between the writer and the reader sufficiently curious to follow through.

The Ambiguity of Henry James

Edmund Wilson

A discussion of Henry James's ambiguity may appropriately begin with *The Turn of the Screw*. This story, which seems to have proved more fascinating to the general reading public than anything else of James's except *Daisy Miller*, perhaps conceals another horror behind the ostensible one. I do not know who first suggested this idea, but I believe that Miss Edna Kenton, whose insight into James is profound, was the first to write about it,[*] and the water-colorist Charles Demuth did a set of illustrations for the tale that were evidently based on this interpretation.

The theory is, then, that the governess who is made to tell the story is a neurotic case of sex repression, and that the ghosts are not real ghosts but hallucinations of the governess.

Let us see how the narrative runs. This narrative is supposed to have been written by the governess herself, but it begins with an introduction in which we are told something about her by a man whose sister's governess she had been after the time of the story. The youngest daughter of a poor country parson, she struck him, he explains, as 'awfully clever and nice . . . the most agreeable woman I've ever known in her position' and 'worthy of any whatever.' (Now, it is a not infrequent trick of James's to introduce

SOURCE: Appeared originally in the Henry James issue of *Hound and Horn*, VII (April–June, 1934), 385–406. Revised for the first (1938) edition of Mr. Wilson's *The Triple Thinkers*. Further revised for *The Triple Thinkers*, Revised and Enlarged Edition, New York: Oxford University Press, 1948, pp. 88–132. The present text is that of the 1948 edition. It is used, along with a postscript dated 1959, by permission of the author.

[*] In *The Arts*, November, 1924. This issue contains also photographs of the Demuth illustrations.

sinister characters with descriptions that at first sound flattering, so this need not throw us off.) Needing work, she had come up to London to answer an advertisement and had found someone who wanted a governess for an orphaned nephew and niece. 'This prospective patron proved a gentleman, a bachelor in the prime of life, such a figure as had never risen, save in a dream or an old novel, before a fluttered, anxious girl out of a Hampshire vicarage.' It is made clear that the young woman has become thoroughly infatuated with her employer. He is charming to her and lets her have the job on condition that she will take all the responsibility and never bother him about the children; and she goes down to the house in the country where they have been left with a housekeeper and some other servants.

The boy, she finds, has been sent home from school for reasons into which she does not inquire but which she colors, on no evidence at all, with a significance somehow ominous. She learns that her predecessor left, and that the woman has since died, under circumstances which are not explained but which are made in the same way to seem queer. The new governess finds herself alone with the good but illiterate housekeeper and the children, who seem innocent and charming. As she wanders about the estate, she thinks often how delightful it would be if one should come suddenly round the corner and see the master just arrived from London: there he would stand, handsome, smiling, approving.

She is never to meet her employer again, but what she does meet are the apparitions. One day when his face has been vividly in her mind, she comes out in sight of the house and, looking up, sees the figure of a man on a tower, a figure which is not the master's. Not long afterwards, the figure appears again, toward the end of a rainy Sunday. She sees him at closer range and more clearly: he is wearing smart clothes but is obviously not a gentleman. The housekeeper, meeting the governess immediately afterwards, behaves as if the governess herself were a ghost: 'I wondered why she should be scared.' The governess tells her about the apparition and learns that it answers the description of one of the master's valets, who had stayed down there and who had sometimes stolen his clothes. The valet had been a bad character, had used 'to play with the boy . . . to spoil him'; he had finally been found dead, having apparently slipped on the ice coming out of a public house—though one couldn't say he hadn't been murdered. The governess cannot help believing that he has come back to haunt the children.

Not long afterwards, she and the little girl are out on the shore of a lake, the child playing, the governess sewing. The latter becomes aware of a third person on the opposite side of the lake. But she looks first at little Flora, who is turning her back in that direction and who, she notes, has 'picked up a small flat piece of wood, which happened to have in it a little hole that had evidently suggested to her the idea of sticking in another fragment that might figure as a mast and make the thing a boat. This second morsel, as I watched her, she was very markedly and intently attempting to tighten in its place.' This somehow 'sustains' the governess so that she is able to raise her eyes: she sees a woman 'in black, pale and dreadful.' She concludes that it is the former governess. The housekeeper, questioned, tells her that this woman, although a lady, had had an affair with the valet. The boy had used to go off with the valet and then lie about it afterwards. The governess concludes that the boy must have known about the valet and the woman—the boy and girl have been corrupted by them.

Observe that there is never any reason for supposing that anybody but the governess sees the ghosts. She believes that the children see them, but there is never any proof that they do. The housekeeper insists that she does not see them; it is apparently the governess who frightens her. The children, too, become hysterical; but this is evidently the governess' doing. Observe, also, from the Freudian point of view, the significance of the governess' interest in the little girl's pieces of wood and of the fact that the male apparition first takes shape on a tower and the female apparition on a lake. There seems here to be only a single circumstance which does not fit into the hypothesis that the ghosts are mere fancies of the governess: the fact that her description of the masculine ghost at a time when she knows nothing of the valet should be identifiable as the valet by the housekeeper. And when we look back, we see that even this has perhaps been left open to a double interpretation. The governess has never heard of the valet, but it has been suggested to her in a conversation with the housekeeper that there has been some other male about who 'liked everyone young and pretty,' and the idea of this other person has been ambiguously confused with the master and with the master's possible interest in her, the present governess. And may she not, in her subconscious imagination, taking her cue from this, have associated herself with her predecessor and conjured up an image who wears the master's clothes but who (the Freudian 'censor' intervening) looks debased, 'like an actor,' she says (would he not have to stoop to love her)? The apparition had 'straight, good features' and his appearance is described in detail. When we look back, we find that the master's appearance has never been described at all: we have merely been told that he was 'handsome,' and it comes out in the talk with the housekeeper that the valet was 'remarkably handsome.' It is impossible for us to know how much the phantom resembles the master—the governess, certainly, would never tell.

The new apparitions now begin to be seen at night, and the governess becomes convinced that the children get up to meet them, though they are able to give plausible explanations of the behavior that has seemed suspicious. The housekeeper now says to the governess that, if she is seriously worried about all this, she ought to report it to the master. The governess, who has promised not to bother him, is afraid he would think her insane; and she imagines 'his derision, his amusement, his contempt for the breakdown of my resignation at being left alone and for the fine machinery I had set in motion to attract his attention to my slighted charms.' The housekeeper, hearing this, threatens to send for the master herself; the governess threatens to leave if she does. After this, for a considerable period, the visions no longer appear.

But the children become uneasy: they wonder when their uncle is coming, and they try to communicate with him—but the governess suppresses their letters. The boy finally asks her frankly when she is going to send him to school, intimates that if he had not been so fond of her, he would have complained to his uncle long ago, declares that he will do so at once.

This upsets her: she thinks for a moment of leaving, but decides that this would be deserting them. She is now, it seems, in love with the boy. Entering the schoolroom, after her conversation with him, she finds the ghost of the other governess sitting with her head in her hands, looking 'dishonored and tragic,' full of 'unutterable woe.' At this point the new governess feels—the morbid half of her split personality is now getting the upper hand of the other—that it is she who is intruding upon the ghost: 'You terrible miserable woman!' she cries. The apparition disappears. She tells the housekeeper, who looks at her oddly, that the soul of the woman is damned and wants the little girl to share her damnation. She finally agrees to write to the master, but no sooner has she sat down to the paper than she gets up and goes to the boy's bedroom, where she finds him lying awake. When he demands to go back to school, she embraces him and begs him to tell her why he was sent away; appealing to him with what seems to her desperate tenderness but in a way that disquiets the child, she insists that all she wants is to save him. There is a sudden gust of wind—it is a stormy night outside—the casement rattles, the boy shrieks. She has been kneeling beside the bed: when she gets up, she finds the candle extinguished.

'It was I who blew it, dear!' says the boy. For her, it is the evil spirit disputing her domination. She cannot imagine that the boy may really have blown out the candle in order not to have to tell her with the light on about his disgrace at school. (Here, however, occurs a detail which is less easily susceptible of double explanation: the governess has *felt* a 'gust of frozen air' and yet sees that the window is 'tight.' Are we to suppose she merely fancied that she felt it?)

The next day, the little girl disappears. They find her beside the lake. The young woman for the first time now speaks openly to one of the children about the ghosts. 'Where, my pet, is Miss Jessel?' she demands—and immediately answers herself: 'She's there, she's there!' she cries, pointing across the lake. The housekeeper looks with a 'dazed blink' and asks where she sees anything; the little girl turns upon the governess 'an expression of hard, still gravity, an expression absolutely new and unprecedented and that appeared to read and accuse and judge me.' The governess feels her 'situation horribly crumble' now. The little girl breaks down, becomes feverish, begs to be taken away from the governess; the housekeeper sides with the child and hints that the governess had better go. But the young woman forces her, instead, to take the little girl away; and she tries to make it impossible, before their departure, for the children to see one another.

She is now left alone with the boy. A strange and dreadful scene ensues. 'We continued silent while the maid was with us—as silent, it whimsically occurred to me, as some young couple who, on their wedding-journey, at the inn, feel shy in the presence of the waiter.' When the maid has gone, and she presses him to tell her the reason for his expulsion from school, the boy seems suddenly afraid of her. He finally confesses that he 'said things'—to 'a few,' to 'those he liked.' It all sounds sufficiently harmless: there comes to her out of her 'very pity the appalling alarm of his being perhaps innocent. It was for the instant confounding and bottomless, for if he *were* innocent, what then on earth was I?' The valet appears at the window—it is 'the white face of damnation.' (But is it really the spirits who are damned or the governess who is slipping to damnation herself?) She is aware that the boy does not see it. 'No more, no more, no more!' she shrieks to the apparition. 'Is she *here?*' demands the boy in panic. (He has, in spite of the governess' efforts, succeeded in seeing his sister and has heard from her of the incident at the lake.) No, she says, it is not the woman: 'But it's at the window—straight before us. It's *there!*' . . . 'It's *he?*' then. Whom does he mean by 'he'? ' "Peter Quint—you devil!" His face gave again, round the room, its convulsed supplication. "Where?"' 'What does he matter now, my own?' she cries. 'What will he *ever* matter? *I* have you, but he has lost you forever!' Then she shows him that the figure has vanished: 'There, *there!*' she says, pointing toward the window. He looks and gives a cry; she feels that he is dead in her arms. From the governess' point of view, the final disappearance of the spirit has proved too terrible a shock for the child and 'his little heart, dispossessed, has stopped'; but if we study the dialogue from the other point of view, we see that he must have taken her 'There, *there!*' as an answer to his own 'Where?' Instead of persuading him that there is nothing to be frightened of, she has, on the contrary, finally convinced him either that he has actually seen or that he is just about to see some horror. He gives 'the cry of a creature hurled over an abyss.' She has literally frightened him to death.

When one has once got hold of the clue to this meaning of *The Turn of the Screw,* one wonders how one could ever have missed it. There is a very good reason, however, in the fact that nowhere does James unequivocally give the thing away: almost everything from beginning to end can be read equally in either of two senses. In the preface to the collected edition, however, as Miss Kenton has pointed out, James does seem to want to give a hint. He asserts that *The Turn of the Screw* is 'a fairy-tale pure and simple'—but adds that the apparitions are of the order of those involved in witchcraft cases rather than of those in cases of psychic research. And he goes on to tell of his reply to one of his readers who objected that he had not characterized the governess sufficiently. At this criticism, he says, 'One's artistic, one's ironic heart shook for the instant almost to breaking'; and he answered: 'It was "*déjà trés-joli*" . . . please believe, the general proposition of our young woman's keeping crystalline her record of so many intense anomalies and obscurities —*by which I don't of course mean her explanation of them, a different matter* . . . She has "authority," which is a good deal to have given her . . .' The italics above are mine: these words seem impossible to explain except on the hypothesis of hallucination (though this is hardly consistent with the intention of writing 'a fairy-tale pure and simple'). And note too, that in the collected edition James has not included *The Turn of the Screw* in the volume with his other ghost stories but with stories of another kind: between *The Aspern Papers* and *The Liar*—the first a study of a curiosity which becomes a mania and menace (to which we shall revert in a moment), the second a study of a pathological liar, whose wife protects his lies against the world, acting with very much the same sort of 'authority' as the governess in *The Turn of the Screw.*

When we look back in the light of these hints, we are inclined to conclude from analogy that the story is primarily intended as a characterization of the governess: her somber and guilty visions and the way she behaves about them seem to present, from the moment we examine them from the obverse side of her narrative, an accurate and distressing picture of the poor country parson's daughter, with her English middle-class class-consciousness, her inability to admit to herself her natural sexual impulses and the relentless English 'authority' which enables her to put over on inferiors even purposes which are totally deluded and not at all in the other people's best interests. Remember, also, in this connection, the peculiar psychology of governesses, who, by reason of their isolated position between the family and the servants, are likely to become ingrown and morbid. One has heard of actual cases of women who have frightened a household by opening doors or smashing mirrors and who have succeeded in torturing parents by mythical stories of kidnappers. The traditional 'poltergeist' who breaks crockery and upsets furniture has been for centuries a recurring phenomenon. First a figure of demonology, he later became an object of psychic research, and is now a recognized neurotic type.

Once we arrive at this conception of *The Turn of the Screw*, we can see in it a new significance in its relation to Henry James's other work. We find now that it is a variation on one of his familiar themes: the thwarted Anglo-Saxon spinster; and we remember unmistakable cases of women in James's fiction who deceive themselves and others about the origins of their aims and emotions. One of the most obvious examples is that remarkable and too little read novel, *The Bostonians*. The subject of *The Bostonians* is the struggle for the daughter of a poor evangelist between a young man from the South who wants to marry her and a well-to-do Boston lady with a Lesbian interest in her. The strong-minded and strong-willed spinster is herself apparently quite in the dark as to the real character of her feeling for the girl: she is convinced that her desire to dominate her, to have her always living with her, to teach her to make speeches on women's rights and to prevent the young Southerner from marrying her, is a disinterested ardor for the Feminist cause. But the reader is not left in doubt; and Olive Chancellor is shown us in a setting of other self-deluded New England idealists.

There is a theme of very much the same kind in the short story called *The Marriages*, which amused R. L. Stevenson so hugely. But here the treatment is frankly comic. A young and rather stupid girl, described as of the unmarriageable type, but much attached to her widower father and obsessed by the memory of her mother, undertakes to set up an obstacle to her father's proposed second marriage. Her project, which she carries out, is to go to his fiancée and tell this lady that her father is an impossible character who had made her late mother miserable. She thus breaks up the projected match; and when her brother calls her a raving maniac, she is not in the least disquieted in her conviction that, by frustrating her father, she has proved faithful in her duty to her mother.

James's world is full of these women. They are not always emotionally perverted. Sometimes they are apathetic—like the charming Francie Dosson of *The Reverberator,* who, though men are always falling in love with her, seems not really ever to have grasped what courtship and marriage mean and is apparently quite content to go on all the rest of her life eating *marrons glacés* with her family in a suite in a Paris hotel. Or they are longing, these women, for affection but too inhibited or passive to obtain it for themselves, like the pathetic Milly Theale of *The Wings of the Dove,* who wastes away in Venice and whose doctor recommends a lover.

II

James's men are not precisely neurotic; but they are the masculine counterparts of his women. They have a way of missing out on emotional experience, either through timidity or prudence or through heroic renunciation.

The extreme and fantastic example is the hero of *The Beast in the Jungle,* who is finally crushed by the realization that his fate is to be the man in the whole world to whom nothing at all is to happen. Some of these characters are presented ironically: Mr. Acton of *The Europeans,* so smug and secure in his clean-swept house, deciding not to marry the baroness who has proved such an upsetting element in his little New England community, is an amusing and accurate portrait of a certain kind of careful Bostonian. Others are made sympathetic, such as the starved Lambert Strether of *The Ambassadors,* who comes to Paris too late in life.

Sometimes, however, the effect is ambiguous. Though the element of irony in Henry James is often underestimated by his readers, there are stories which leave us in doubt as to whether or not the author could foresee how his heroes would strike the reader. Is the fishy Bernard Longueville, for example, of the early novel called *Confidence* really intended for a sensitive and interesting young man or is he a prig in the manner of Jane Austen? This is not due to a beginner's uncertainty, for some of James's later heroes make us uneasy in a similar way. The very late short story *Flickerbridge,* in which a young American painter decides not to marry a young newspaper woman (the men are always deciding *not* to marry the women in Henry James) because he fears that she will spoil by publicizing it a delightful old English house, the property of a cousin of hers, which she herself has not yet seen but at which he has enjoyed visiting—this story is even harder to swallow, since it is all too evident here that the author approves of his hero.

But what are we to think of *The Sacred Fount?* This short novel, surely James's most curious production, inspired when it first appeared a parody by Owen Seaman which had a certain historical significance because the book seemed to mark the point at which James, for the general public, had definitely become unassimilable, and therefore absurd or annoying. *The Sacred Fount* was written not long after *The Turn of the Screw* and is a sort of companion-piece to it. Here we have the same setting of an English country house, the same passages of a strange and sad beauty, the same furtive subversive happenings in an atmosphere of clarity and brightness, the same dubious central figure, the same almost inscrutable ambiguity. As in the case of *The Turn of the Screw,* the fundamental question presents itself and never seems to get properly answered: What is the reader to think of the protagonist?—who is here a man instead of a woman.

It would be tedious to analyze *The Sacred Fount* as I have done *The Turn of the Screw*—and it would prove, I think, somewhat more difficult. The book is not merely mystifying but maddening. Yet I believe that if one got to the bottom of it, a good deal of light would be thrown on the author. Rebecca West, in her little book on James, has given a burlesque account of this novel as the story of how 'a week-end visitor spends more intellectual force than Kant can have used on *The Critique of Pure Reason* in an unsuccessful attempt to discover whether there exists between certain of his fellow-guests a relationship not more interesting among these vacuous people than it is among sparrows.' This visitor, who himself tells the story, observes that, among the other guests, a man and a woman he knows, both of them middle-aged, appear to have taken a new lease on life, whereas a younger man and woman appear to have been depleted. He evolves a theory about them: he imagines that the married couples have been forming new combinations and that the younger man and woman have been feeding the older pair from the sacred fount of their youth at the price of getting used up themselves.

This theory seems rather academic—and does James really mean us to accept it? Do not the narrator's imaginings serve to characterize the narrator just as the governess' ghosts serve to characterize the governess? As this detached and rather eerie individual proceeds to spy on and question his friends in order to find out whether the facts fit his hypothesis, we decide, as we do with *The Turn of the Screw,* that there are two separate stories to be kept distinct: a romance which the narrator is spinning and a reality which we are supposed to divine from what he tells us about what actually happens. We remember the narrator of *The Aspern Papers,* another prying and importunate fellow, who is finally foiled and put to rout by the old lady whose private papers he is trying by fraud to get hold of. In the case of *The Aspern Papers,* there is no uncertainty whatever as to what we are to think of the narrator: the author is quite clear that the papers were none of the journalist's business and that the rebuff he received served him right. Now, the amateur detective of *The Sacred Fount* is also foiled and rebuffed, and in very much the same manner, by one of his recalcitrant victims. 'My poor dear, you *are* crazy, and I bid you good-night!' she says to him at the end of the story. 'Such a last word,' the narrator remarks, 'the word that put me altogether nowhere—was too inacceptable not to prescribe afresh that prompt test of escape to other air for which I had earlier in the evening seen so much reason. I *should* certainly never again, on the spot, quite hang together, even though it wasn't really that I hadn't three times her method. What I too fatally lacked was her tone.' But *why* did he lack her tone?—*why* would he not hang together? What view are we supposed to take of the whole exploit of this singular being?

Mr. Wilson Follett, the only writer, so far as I know, who has given special attention to *The Sacred Fount,** believes that the book is a parable—even a conscious parody—of James's own role as an artist. The narrator may or may not have been right as to the actual facts of the case. The point is that, in elaborating his theory, he has constructed a work of art, and that you cannot test the validity of works of art by checking them against actuality. The kind of reality that art achieves, made up of elements abstracted from experience and combined in a new way by the artist, would be destroyed by a collision with the actual, and the artist would find himself blocked.

Now it may very well be true that James has put himself into

* *Henry James's 'Portrait of Henry James'* in the *New York Times Book Review,* August 23, 1936. (Since my own essay was first written, Mr. Edward Sackville West, in the *New Statesman and Nation* of October 4, 1947, has taken issue with the views here expressed in the best defense of this book I have seen.)

The Sacred Fount—that he has intended some sort of fable about the brooding imaginative mind and the material with which it works. But it seems to me that Mr. Follett's theory assumes on James's part a conception of artistic truth which would hardly be worthy of him. After all, the novelist must pretend to know what people are actually up to, however much he may rearrange actuality; and it is not clear in *The Sacred Fount* whether the narrator really knows what he is talking about. If the book is, then, merely a parody, what is the point of the parody? Why should James have represented the artist as defeated by the breaking-in of life?

The truth is, I believe, that Henry James was not clear about the book in his own mind. Already, with *The Turn of the Screw,* he has carried his ambiguous procedure to a point where we almost feel that the author does not want the reader to get through to the hidden meaning. See his curious replies in his letters to correspondents who write him about the story: when they challenge him with leading questions, he seems to give evasive answers, dismissing the tale as a mere 'pot-boiler,' a mere *jeu d'esprit.* There was no doubt in *The Bostonians,* for example, as to what view the reader was intended to take of such a character as Olive Chancellor: Olive, though tragic perhaps, is definitely unhealthy and horrid, and she is vanquished by Basil Ransom. But James does leave his readers uncomfortable as to what they are to think of the governess. And now, in *The Sacred Fount,* we do not know whether the week-end guest, though he was unquestionably obnoxious to the other guests, is intended to be taken as one of the élite, a fastidious, highly civilized sensibility, or merely as a little bit cracked and a bore. The man who tried to get the Aspern papers was a fanatic, a cad and a nuisance; but many of James's inquisitive observers who never take part in the action are presented as superior people, and Henry James had confessed to being an inquisitive observer himself. Ambiguity was certainly growing on him. It was eventually to pass all bounds in those scenes in his later novels (of which the talks in *The Turn of the Screw* between the housekeeper and the governess are only comparatively mild examples) in which he compels his characters to carry on long conversations with each of the interlocutors always mistaking the other's meaning and neither ever yielding to the impulse to say one of the obvious things that would clear the situation up.

What if the hidden theme of *The Sacred Fount* is simply sex again? What if the real sacred fount, from which the narrator's acquaintances have been drawing their new vitality, is love, sexual love, instead of youth? They have something which he has not had, know something which he does not know; and, lacking the clue of experience, he can only misunderstand them and elaborate pedantic hypotheses; while they, having the forces of life on their side, are in a position to frighten him away. This theory may be dubious, also; but there is certainly involved in *The Sacred Fount,* whether or not Henry James quite meant to put it there, the conception of a man shut out from love, condemned to peep at other people's activities and to speculate about them rather barrenly, who will be shocked and put to rout when he touches the live current of human relations.

Hitherto, as I have said, it has usually been plain what James wanted us to think of his characters; but now there appears in his work a relatively morbid element which is not always handled objectively and which seems to have invaded the storyteller himself. It is as if at this point he had taken to dramatizing the frustrations of his own life without quite being willing to confess it, without fully admitting it even to himself.

But before we go further with this line of inquiry, let us look at Henry James in another connection.

III

Who *are* these characters of James's about whom we come to be less certain as to precisely what we ought to think?

The type of Henry James's observers and sometimes of his heroes is the cultivated American bourgeois, like Henry James himself, who lives on an income derived from some form of business activity, usually left rather vague, but who has rarely played any part in the efforts which have created the business. These men turn their backs on the commercial world; they disdain its vulgarity and dullness, and they attempt to enrich their experience through the society and art of Europe. But they bring to these the bourgeois qualities of timidity, prudence, primness, the habits of mind of a puritan morality, which, even when they wish to be men of the world, make it too easy for them to be disconcerted. They wince alike at the brutalities of the aristocracy and at the coarseness of the working class; they shrink most of all from the 'commonness' of the less polished bourgeoisie, who, having acquired their incomes more recently, are not so far advanced in self-improvement. The women have the corresponding qualities: they are innocent, conventional and rather cold—sometimes they suffer from Freudian complexes or a kind of arrested development, sometimes they are neglected or cruelly cheated by the men to whom they have given their hearts. And even when James's central characters are English, they assimilate themselves to these types.

It is enlightening in this connection to compare James's point of view with Flaubert's. The hero of *L'Education sentimentale* is a perfect Henry James character: he is sensitive, cautious, afraid of life; he lives on a little income and considers himself superior to the common run. But Flaubert's attitude toward Frédéric Moreau is devastatingly ironic. Frédéric has his aspects of pathos, his occasional flashes of spirit: but Flaubert is quite emphatic in his final judgment of Frédéric. He considers Frédéric a worm.

Now, James has his own kind of irony, but it is not Flaubert's kind. Frédéric Moreau, in a sense, is the hero of many of James's novels, and you can see how the American's relation to him usually differs from the Frenchman's if you compare certain kinds of scenes which tend to recur in Henry James with certain scenes in *L'Education sentimentale* of which they sometimes seem like an echo: those ominous situations in which we find the sensitive young man either immersed in some sort of gathering or otherwise meeting successively a number of supposed friends, more worldly and unscrupulous persons, who are obviously talking over his head, acting behind his back, without his being able, in his innocence, quite to make out what they are up to. You have this same situation, as I say, in James and in Flaubert; but the difference is that, whereas with James the young man is made wondering and wistful and is likely to turn out a pitiful victim, with Flaubert he is quietly and cruelly made to look like a fool and is as ready to double-cross these other people who seem to him so inferior to himself as they are to double-cross him.

In this contrast between Flaubert's treatment of Frédéric Moreau and James's treatment of, say, Hyacinth Robinson in *The Princess Casamassima* is to be found perhaps one of the reasons for James's resentment of Flaubert. James had known Flaubert, had read him when young, had obviously been impressed by his work; he had it in common with the older man that he wanted to give dignity and integrity to the novel of modern life by imposing on it rigorous esthetic form. Yet there is something about Flaubert that sticks in his crop, and he keeps up a sort of running quarrel with him, returning to the subject again and again in the course of his critical writing. But though it is plain that James cannot help admiring the author of *Madame Bovary,* he usually manages before he has done to give the impression of belittling him—and he is especially invidious on the subject of *L'Education sentimentale*. His great complaint is that Flaubert's characters are instrinsically so ignoble that they do not deserve to be treated at length or to have so much art expended on them and that there must have been something wrong with Flaubert for him ever to have supposed that they did. James does not seem to understand that Flaubert *intends* all his characters to be 'middling' and that the greatness of his work arises from the fact that it constitutes a criticism of something bigger than they are. James praises the portrait of Mme Arnoux: let us thank God, at least, he exclaims, that Flaubert was able here to command the good taste to deal delicately with a fine-grained woman! He does not seem to be aware that Mme Arnoux is treated as ironically as any of the other characters—that the virtuous bourgeois wife with her inhibitions and superstitions is pathetic only as a part of the failure of a civilization. Henry James mistakes Mme Arnoux for a refined American woman and he is worried because Frédéric isn't one of his own American heroes, quietly vibrating and scrupulously honorable. Yet it probably makes him uncomfortable to feel that Flaubert is flaying remorselessly the squeamish young man of this type; and it may be that Henry James's antagonism to Flaubert has something to do with the fact that the latter's all-permeating criticism of the pusillanimity of the bourgeois soul has touched Henry James himself. The protagonists of the later James are always regretting having lived too meagerly; and James distills from these non-participants all the sad self-effacing nobility, all the fine wan beauty, they are good for. Flaubert extracts something quite different from Frédéric Moreau—a kind of acrid insecticide: when Frédéric and his friend, both middle-aged by now, recall at the end of the book their first clumsy and frightened visit to a brothel as the best that life has had to offer them, it is a damnation of their whole society.

But there was another kind of modern society which Gustave Flaubert did not know and which Henry James did. Henry James was himself that new anomalous thing, an American. He had, to be sure, lived a good deal in Europe both in childhood and early manhood, and he had to a considerable extent become imbued with the European point of view—so that the monuments of antiquity and feudalism, the duchesses and princesses and princes who seem to carry on the feudal tradition, are still capable of having the effect for him of making modern life look undistinguished. But the past, in the case of James, does not completely dwarf the present, as the vigil of Flaubert's Saint Anthony and the impacts of his pagan armies diminish Frédéric Moreau. The American in Henry James asserts himself insistently against Europe. After all, Frédéric Moreau and the respectable Mme Arnoux are the best people of Albany and Boston!—but in America they are not characters in Flaubert. Their scruples and renunciations have a real moral value here—for Frédéric Moreau at home possesses a real integrity; and when these best people come over to Europe, they judge the whole thing in a quite new way. James speaks somewhere of his indignation at an Englishwoman's saying to him in England, in connection with something they were discussing: 'That is true of the aristocracy, but in one's own class it is quite different.' As an American and the grandson of a millionaire, it had never occurred to James that anyone could consider him a middle-class person. When Edith Wharton accused him in his later years of no longer appreciating Flaubert and demanded of him why Emma Bovary, the choice of whom as a heroine he had always deplored, was not just as good a subject for fiction as Tolstoy's Anna Karenina, he replied: 'Ah, but one paints the fierce passions of a luxurious aristocracy; the other deals with the petty miseries of a little bourgeoise in a provincial town!' But if Emma Bovary is small potatoes, what about Daisy Miller? Why, Daisy Miller is an American girl! Emma Bovary has her longings and her debts and her adulteries, but she is otherwise a conventional person, she remains in her place in the social scheme even when she dreams of rising out of it. So great is the prestige for her of the local nobility that when she goes to the château for the ball, the very sugar in the sugar bowl seems to her whiter and finer than the sugar she has at home; whereas a girl like Daisy Miller as well as one like Isabel Archer represents a human species that had been bred outside of Europe and that cannot be accommodated or judged inside the European frame. When this species comes back to Europe, it tends to disregard the social system. Europe is too much for Daisy Miller: she catches cold in the Coliseum, where according to European conventions she oughtn't to have been at that hour. But the great popularity of her story was certainly due to the fact that her creator had somehow conveyed the impression that her spirit went marching on.

There evidently went on in the mind of James a debate that was never settled between the European and the American points of view; and this conflict may have had something to do with his inability sometimes to be clear as to what he wants us to think of a certain sort of person. It is quite mistaken to talk as if James had uprooted himself from America in order to live in England. He had traveled so much from his earliest years that he had never had real roots anywhere. His father had himself been a wandering intellectual, who had oscillated back and forth between Europe and the United States; and even in America the Jameses were always oscillating between New York and Boston. They were not New Englanders even by ancestry, but New Yorkers of Irish and Scotch-Irish stock, and they had none of the tight New England local ties—they always came to Boston from a larger outside world and their point of view about it was objective and often rather ironical. To this critical attitude on Henry's part was probably partly due the failure of *The Bostonians;* and this failure seems to mark the moment of his abandonment of his original ambition of becoming the American Balzac, as it does that of his taking up his residence in England and turning, for the subjects of his fiction, from the Americans to the English. He had been staying for some time in London, and he found he liked living in London better than in New York or New England, better than in Paris or Rome. His parents in the States had just died, and his sister came over to join him.

IV

And this brings us to what seems to have been the principal crisis in Henry James's life and work. We know so little about his personal life from any other source than himself, and even in his memoirs and letters he tells us so little about his emotions, that it is impossible to give any account of it save as it reflects itself in his writings.

Up to the period of his playwriting, his fiction has been pretty plain sailing. He has aimed to be a social historian, and, in a limited field, he has succeeded. His three long novels of the later eighties—*The Bostonians, The Princess Casamassima* and *The Tragic Muse*—are, indeed, as social history, his most ambitious undertakings, and from the conventional point of view—that of the reporting of the surface of life—by far his most successful. The first hundred pages of *The Bostonians,* with the arrival of the young Southerner in Boston and his first contacts with the Boston reformers, is, in its way, one of the most masterly things that Henry James ever did. *The Princess Casamassima,* with its opening in the prison and its revolutionary exiles in London, deals with issues and social contrasts of a kind that James had never before attempted. The familiar criticism of Henry James—the criticism made by H. G. Wells: that he had no grasp of politics or economics—does not, in fact, hold true of these books. Here his people do have larger interests and functions aside from their personal relations: they have professions, missions, practical aims; and they also engage in more drastic action than in his novels of any other period. Basil Ransom pursues Verena Tarrant and rescues her from the terrible Olive Chancellor; Hyacinth Robinson pledges himself to carry out a political assassination, then commits suicide instead; Miriam Rooth makes her career as a great actress. One finds in all three of these novels a will to participate in life, to play a responsible role, quite different from the passive ones of the traveler who merely observes or the victim who merely suffers, that had seemed characteristic of James's fiction. Up to a point these books are brilliant.

But there is a point—usually about half way through—at which every one of these novels begins strangely to run into the sands; the excitement of the story lapses at the same time as the treatment becomes more abstract and the color fades from the picture. The ends are never up to the beginnings. This is most obvious—even startling—in *The Tragic Muse,* the first volume of which, as we read it, makes us think that it must be James's best novel, so solid and alive does it seem. Here are areas of experience and types of a kind that James has never before given us: a delicately comic portrait of a retired parliamentarian, which constitutes, by implication, a criticism of British Liberal politics; a really charged and convincing scene between a man and a woman (Nick Dormer and Julia Dallow) in place of the mild battledore-and-shuttlecock that we are accustomed to getting from James; and, in Miriam Rooth, the Muse, a character who comes nearer to carrying the author out of the bounds of puritan scruples and prim prejudices on to the larger and more dangerous stage of human creative effort than any other he has hitherto drawn. Here at last we are among complete people, who have the appetites and ambitions that we recognize—and in comparison, the characters of his earlier works only seem real in a certain convention. Then suddenly the story stops short: after the arrival of Miriam in London, *The Tragic Muse* is almost a blank. Of the two young men who have been preoccupied with Miriam, one renounces her because she will not leave the stage and the other doesn't, apparently, fall in love with her. Miriam herself, to be sure, makes a great success as an actress, but we are never taken into her life, we know nothing at first hand of her emotions. The only decisions that are looming are negative ones, and the author himself seems to lose interest.

These earlier chapters of *The Tragic Muse* are the high point of the first part of James's career, after which something snaps. He announces that he will write no more long novels, but only fiction of shorter length; and it may be that he has become aware of his failure in his longer novels to contrive the mounting-up to a climax of intensity and revelation which, in order to be effective, this kind of full-length fiction demands. At any rate, he applied himself to writing plays, and for five years he produced little else; but one wonders when one reads these plays—in the two volumes he called *Theatricals*—why James should have sacrificed not only his time but also all the strength of his genius for work that was worse than mediocre. He had had reason to complain at this period that he had difficulty in selling his fiction, and he confessed that his plays were written in the hope of a popular success, and that they were intended merely as entertainment and were not to be taken too seriously—seeking to excuse that which 'would otherwise be inexplicable' by invoking 'the uttermost regions of dramatic amiability, the bland air of the little domestic fairy-tale.' Yet the need for money and even for fame is surely an insufficient explanation for the phenomenon of a novelist of James's gifts almost entirely abandoning the art in which he has perfected himself to write plays that are admittedly trivial.

That there was something insufficient and unexplained about James's emotional life seems to appear unmistakably from his novels. I believe that it may be said that there have not been up to this point any consummated love affairs in his fiction—that is, none among the principal characters and while the action of the story is going on; and this deficiency must certainly have contributed to his increasing loss of hold on his readers. It is not merely that he gave in *The Bostonians* an unpleasant picture of Boston, and in *The Tragic Muse*, on the whole, a discouraging picture of the English; it is not merely that *The Princess Casamassima* treated a social-revolutionary subject from a point of view that was non-political and left neither side a moral advantage. It was not merely that he was thus at this period rather lost between America and England. It was also that you cannot enchant an audience with stories about men wooing women in which the parties either never get together or are never seen functioning as lovers. And you will particularly dampen your readers with a story—*The Tragic Muse*—which deals with two men and a girl but in which neither man ever gets her. There is, as I have said, in *The Tragic Muse*, one of his more convincing man-and-woman relationships. Julia Dallow is really female and she behaves like a woman with Nick Dormer; but here the woman's political ambitions get between Nick and her, so that this, too, never comes to anything: here the man, again, must renounce. (In Henry James's later novels, these healthily female women—Kate Croy and Charlotte Stant—are to take on a character frankly sinister.) Years later, Henry James explained in his preface to *The Tragic Muse* that the prudery, in the eighties, of the American magazines had made it impossible for Miriam Rooth to follow the natural course of becoming Nick Dormer's mistress; and certainly the skittishness of a public that was scandalized by *Jude the Obscure* is not to be underestimated. But, after all, Hardy did write about Jude, and Meredith about Lord Ormont and his Aminta, and let the public howl; and it might well have enhanced Henry James's reputation—to which he was by no means indifferent—if he had done the same thing himself. Problems of sexual passion in conflict with convention and law were beginning to be subjects of burning interest. But it is probable that James had by this time—not consciously, perhaps, but instinctively—come to recognize his unfittedness for dealing with them and was far too honest to fake.

One feels about the episode of his playwriting that it was an effort to put himself over, an effort to make himself felt, as he had never succeeded in doing. His brother William James wrote home in the summer of 1889, at the beginning of this playwriting period, that Henry, beneath the 'rich sea-weeds and rigid barnacles and things' of 'strange heavy alien manners and customs' with which he had covered himself like a 'marine crustacean,' remained the 'same dear old, good, innocent and at bottom very powerless-feeling Harry.' He had seriously injured his back in an accident in his boyhood, and it was necessary for him still, in his forties, to lie down for regular rests. And now it is as if he were trying to put this 'broken back,' as he once called it, into making an impression through the drama as he had never been able to put it into a passion. His heroine Miriam Rooth has just turned away from the Philistine English world which rejects her and taken into the theater the artist's will with which she is to conquer that world; and her creator is now to imitate her.

But his plays were either not produced or not well received. At the first night of *Guy Domville* (January 5, 1895), he ran foul of a gallery of hooligans, who booed and hissed him when he came before the curtain. Their displeasure had evidently been partly due to a feeling of having been let down by one of James's inevitable scenes of abdication of the lover's role: the hero, at the end of the play, had rejected a woman who adored him and an estate he had just inherited in order to enter the Church. These five years of unsuccessful playwriting had put Henry James under a strain, and this was the final blow. When he recovers from his disappointment, he is seen to have passed through a crisis.

Now he enters upon a new phase, of which the most obvious feature is a subsidence back into himself. And now sex *does* appear in his work—even becoming a kind of obsession—in a queer and left-handed way. We have *The Turn of the Screw* and *The Sacred*

Fount; What Maisie Knew and *In the Cage*. There are plenty of love affairs now and plenty of irregular relationships, but there are always thick screens between them and us; illicit appetites, maleficent passions, now provide the chief interest, but they are invariably seen from a distance.

For the Jamesian central observer who has become a special feature of his fiction—the reflector by whose consciousness is registered all that we know of events—has undergone a diminution. This observer is less actively involved and is rarely a complete and a full-grown person: we have a small child who watches her elders, a female telegraph operator who watches the senders of telegrams and lives vicariously through them, a week-end guest who seems not to exist in any other capacity whatever except that of week-end guest and who lives vicariously through his fellow guests. The people who surround this observer tend to take on the diabolic values of the specters of *The Turn of the Screw*, and these diabolic values are almost invariably connected with sexual relations that are always concealed and at which we are compelled to guess. The innocent Nanda Brookenham of *The Awkward Age*, a work of the same period and group, is hemmed in by a whole host of goblins who beckon and hint and whisper and exhale a creepy atmosphere of scandal. It has for the time become difficult for James to sustain his old objectivity: he has relapsed into a dreamy interior world, where values are often uncertain and where it is not even possible any longer for him to judge his effect on his audience—on the audience which by this time has shrunk to a relatively small band of initiated readers. One is dismayed, in reading his comments on *The Awkward Age*, which he regarded as a technical triumph, to see that he was quite unaware of the inhuman aspect of the book which makes it a little repellent. The central figure of *The Sacred Fount* may perhaps have been presented ironically; but James evidently never suspected how the ordinary reader would feel about this disemboweled gibbering crew who hover around Nanda Brookenham with their shadowy sordid designs.

This phase of Henry James's development is also distinguished by a kind of expansion of the gas of the psychological atmosphere—an atmosphere which has now a special flavor. With *What Maisie Knew*, James's style, as Ford Madox Ford says, first becomes a little gamey. He gets rid of some of his old formality and softens his mechanical hardness; and, in spite of the element of abstraction which somewhat dilutes and dims his writing at all periods, his language becomes progressively poetic.

With all this, his experience of playwriting has affected his fiction in a way which does not always seem quite to the good. He had taken as models for his dramatic work the conventional 'well made' French plays of the kind that Bernard Shaw was ridiculing as 'clock-work mice'; and when he took to turning his plays into novels (*Covering End* and *The Outcry*), their frivolity and artificiality became even more apparent (it was only in *The Other House*, which he also made into a novel, that he had dared to be at all himself, and had produced a psychological thriller that had something in common with *The Turn of the Screw; Guy Domville,* too, was evidently more serious, but the text has never been published). Even after he had given up the theater, he went on casting his novels in dramatic form—with the result that *The Awkward Age,* his supreme effort in this direction, combines a lifeless trickery of logic with the equivocal subjectivity of a nightmare.

In this period also originates a tendency on James's part to exploit his sleight-of-hand technique for the purpose of diverting attention from the inadequacies of his imagination. This has imposed on some of James's critics and must of course have imposed on James himself. One can see from his comments at various periods how a method like that of Tolstoy became more and more distasteful to him. Tolstoy, he insisted, was all over the shop, never keeping to a single point of view but entering the minds of all his characters and failing to exercise sufficiently the principle of selection, and James was even reckless enough, in his preface to *The Tragic Muse,* to class *War and Peace* with *Les Trois Mousquetaires* and *The Newcomes,* as 'large loose baggy monsters, with . . . queer elements of the accidental and the arbitrary'—though the truth was, of course, that Tolstoy had spent six years on his novel, had reduced it by a third of its original length and made of every little scene a masterpiece of economy and relevance. He speaks in the same preface of the difficulty he has found himself in handling a complex subject—though it is only a problem here of going into the minds of two of the characters. The truth is, of course, that the question of whether or not the novelist enters into a variety of points of view has nothing necessarily to do with his technical mastery of his materials or even with his effect of concentration. Precisely one trouble with *The Tragic Muse* is that James does not get inside Miriam Rooth; and if he fails even to try to do so, it is because, in his experience of the world and his insight into human beings, he is inferior to a man like Tolstoy. So, in *The Wings of the Dove,* the 'messengering,' as the drama courses say, of Kate Croy's final scene with Merton Densher is probably due to James's increasing incapacity for dealing directly with scenes of emotion rather than to the motives he alleges. And so his recurring complaint that he is unable to do certain things because he can no longer find space within his prescribed limits has the look of another excuse. Henry James never seems aware of the amount of space he is wasting through the long abstract formulations that do duty for concrete details, the unnecessary circumlocutions and the gratuitous meaningless verbiage—the *as it were's* and *as we may say's* and all the rest—all the words with which he pads out his sentences and which themselves are probably symptomatic of a tendency to stave off his main problems, since they are a part of the swathing process with which he makes his embarrassing subjects always seem to present smooth contours.

V

But after this a new process sets in. In *The Ambassadors, The Wings of the Dove* and *The Golden Bowl,* the psychological atmosphere thickens and fills up the structure of the novel, so carefully designed and contrived, with the fumes of the Jamesian gas; and the characters, though apprehended as recognizable human entities, loom obscurely through a phantasmagoria of dream-like similes and metaphors that seem sometimes, as Miss West has said, more vivid and solid than the settings.

But a positive element reappears. The novels of *The Awkward Age* period were written not merely from an international limbo between Europe and the United States but in the shadow of defeat and self-doubt. Yet in these queer and neurotic stories (some of them, of course—*The Turn of the Screw* and *What Maisie Knew*—among James's masterpieces) moral values begin to reassert themselves. These present themselves first in an infantile form, in Maisie Farrange and in Nanda Brookenham, whose innocence is a touchstone for the other characters. Then, in the longer novels that follow, embodied in figures of a more mature innocence, they come completely to dominate the field. These figures are now always Americans. We have returned to the pattern of his earlier work, in which the typical dramatic conflict took place between glamorous people who were worldly and likely to be wicked, and people of superior scruples who were likely to be more or less homely, and in which the glamorous characters usually represented Europe and the more honorable ones the United States. In those earlier novels of James, it had not been always—as in *The Portrait of a Lady*—the Americans who were left with the moral advantage; the Europeans—as in the story with that title—had been sometimes made the more sympathetic. But in these later ones it is always the Americans who command admiration and respect—where they are pitted against a fascinating Italian prince, a charming and appealing French lady, and a formidable group of rapacious English. Yes: there *was* a beauty and there was also a power in the goodness of these naïve but sensitive people—there *were* qualities which did not figure in Flaubert's or Thackeray's picture. This *was* something new in the world which did not fit into the formulas of Europe. What if poor Lambert Strether *had* missed in Woollett, Mass., many things he would have enoyed in Paris: he had brought to Paris something it lacked. And the burden of James's biography of William Wetmore Story, which came out at the same time as these novels, the early years of the century—rather different from that of his study of Hawthorne, published in 1880—is that artists like Story who left Boston for Europe eventually found themselves in a void and might better have stayed at home.

And now Henry James revisits America, writes *The American Scene,* and, for the first time since the rejected *Bostonians,* lays the scene of a novel—*The Ivory Tower,* which he dropped and did not live to finish—entirely in the United States.

In another unfinished novel, the fantasia called *The Sense of the Past,* he makes a young contemporary American go back into eighteenth-century England. Here the Jamesian ambiguity serves an admirable artistic purpose. Is it the English of the past who are ghosts or the American himself who is only a dream?—will the moment come when *they* will vanish or will he himself cease to exist? And, as before, there is a question of James's own asking at the bottom of the ambiguity: Which is real—America or Europe?—a question which was apparently to be answered by the obstinate survival of the American in the teeth of the specters who would drag him back. (It is curious, by the way, to compare *The Sense of the Past* with Mark Twain's *Connecticut Yankee:* the two books have a good deal in common.)

Yes: in spite of the popular assumption, founded on his expatriation and on his finally becoming a British citizen, it is the ideals of the United States which triumph in James's work. His warmest tributes to American genius come out of these later years. Though he could not, in *Notes of a Son and Brother,* resist the impulse to remove references to Lincoln as 'old Abe' from William James's early letters of the wartime, this autobiographical novel contains pages on Lincoln's death of a touching appreciation and pride. 'It was vain to say,' he writes of Andrew Johnson, of whom he declares that the American people felt him unworthy to represent them, 'that we had deliberately invoked the "common" in authority and must drink the wine we had drawn. No countenance, no salience of aspect nor composed symbol, could superficially have referred itself less than Lincoln's mold-smashing mask to any mere matter-of-course type of propriety; but his admirable unrelated head had itself revealed a type—as if by the very fact that what made in it for roughness of kind looked out only less than what made in it for splendid final stamp; in other words for commanding Style.' And of the day when the news reached Boston: 'I was fairly to go in shame of its being my birthday. These would have been the hours of the streets if none others had been—when the huge general gasp filled them like a great earth-shudder and people's eyes met people's eyes without the vulgarity of speech. Even this was, all so strangely, part of the lift and the swell, as tragedy has but to be of a pure enough strain and a high enough connection to sow with its dark hand the seed of greater life. The collective sense of what had occurred was of a sadness too noble not somehow to inspire, and it was truly in the air that, whatever we had as a nation produced or failed to produce, we could at least gather round this perfection of classic woe.' In *The American Scene,* he writes of Concord: 'We may smile a little as we "drag in" Weimar, but I confess myself, for my part, much more satisfied than not by our happy equivalent, "in American money," for Goethe and Schiller. The money is a potful in the second case as in the first, and if Goethe, in the one, represents the gold and Schiller the silver, I find (and quite putting aside any bimetallic prejudice) the same good relation in the other between Emerson and Thoreau. I open Emerson for the same benefit for which I open Goethe, the sense of moving in large intellectual space, and that of the gush, here and there, out of the rock, of the crystalline cupful, in wisdom and poetry, in *Wahrheit* and *Dichtung;* and whatever I open Thoreau for (I needn't take space here for the good reasons) I open him oftener than I open Schiller.' Edith Wharton says that he used to read Walt Whitman aloud 'in a mood of subdued ecstasy' and with tremendous effect on his hearers.

James's visit to the United States in 1904–05, after nearly a quarter of a century's absence, had been immensely exciting to him. He had plunged into his sensations with a gusto, explored everything accessible with a voracity and delivered himself of positive ideas (the presence and the opinions of William must have stimulated this, as a passage in Henry's note-books suggests) at a rate that seems almost to transform the personality of the modest recluse of Lamb House, with his addiction to the crepuscular and the dubious. One realizes now for the first time, as he was realizing for the first time himself, how little of America he had seen before. He had never been West or South. He had known only New York, Boston and Newport. But he now traveled all the way south to Florida and all the way west to California, apparently almost drunk with new discoveries and revelations. His account of his trip in *The American Scene,* published in 1907, has a magnificent solidity and brilliance quite different from the vagueness of impressionism which had been making the backgrounds of his novels a little unsatisfactory; and the criticism of the national life shows an incisiveness, a comprehensiveness, a sureness in knowing his way about, a grasp of political and economic factors, that one might not have expected of Henry James returning to Big Business America. It is probably true that James—as W. H. Auden has suggested—had never approached Europe with anything like the same boldness. In Italy, France, or England, he had been always a 'passionate pilgrim' looking for the picturesque. But with long residence abroad, as he tells us, the romance and the mystery had evaporated, and America, of which he had been hearing such sensational if sometimes dismaying news, had in its turn been coming to seem romantic. What is exhilarating and most surprising is the old-fashioned American patriotism which whether he is admiring or indignant—throbs in every pulse of *The American Scene.* It would be difficult to understand why James should have been credited in the United States with being an immoderate Anglophile—even if the implications of *The Wings of the Dove* had been missed—after *The American Scene* had appeared, if one did not have to allow for the shallowness of professional criticism and the stupid indifference of the public that marked that whole period in the United States. The truth is that he returns to America with something like an overmastering homesickness that makes him desire to give it the benefit of every doubt, to hope for the best from what shocks or repels him. He is not at the mercy of his wincings from the elements that are alien and vulgar. The flooding-in of the new foreign population, though he has to make an effort to accept it, does not horrify him or provoke him to sneers, as it did that professional explorer but professional Anglo-Saxon, Kipling—after all, the James family themselves had not been long in the United States and were so nearly pure Irish that Henry speaks of their feeling a special interest in the only set of their relatives that represented the dominant English blood. He thinks it a pity that the immigrants should be standardized by barren New York, but he is gratified at the evidence that America has been able to give them better food and clothing. The popular consumption of candy, in contrast to the luxury and privilege that sweets have always been in Europe, seems to please him when he attends the Yiddish theater. He is angry over the ravages of commercialism—the exploitation of real-estate values and the destruction of old buildings and landmarks that followed the Civil War—but he is optimistic enough to hope that the time is approaching when the national taste will have improved sufficiently to check this process. And in the meantime at Mount Vernon he feels awe at the memory of Washington, invokes in the Capitol the American eagle as a symbol of the republican idealism, and writes one of the most eloquent and most moving pages to be found in the whole range of his work in celebration of the Concord bridge and the shot heard round the world. It is as if, after the many books which James had written in countries not native to him, under the strain of maintaining an attitude that should be rigorously international, yet addressing himself to an audience that rarely understood what he was trying to do and in general paid little attention to him—it is as if, after a couple of decades of this, his emotions had suddenly been given scope, his genius for expression liberated, as if his insight had been confronted with a field on which it could play without diffidence; and he produced in *The American Scene,* one of the very best books about modern America.

The point is that James's career—given his early experience of Europe—had inevitably been affected by the shift in American ambitions which occurred after the Civil War. It has been shown by Mr. Van Wyck Brooks in his literary history of the United States how the post-Revolutionary American had been stimulated—much like the Russian of the first years of the Soviet regime—to lay the foundations for a new humanity, set free from the caste-barriers and the poverties of Europe, which should return to the mother-continent only to plunder her for elements of culture that might be made to serve the new aim; but how, with the growth of industry, the ascendancy of business ideals, the artists and the other intellectuals found it difficult to function at home and discouraged with the United States, more and more took refuge in Europe. James explains, in *The American Scene,* that the residence abroad of Americans like himself, of small incomes and non-acquisitive tastes, had by this time become merely a matter of having found oneself excreted by a society with whose standards of expenditure one was not in a position to keep up, at the same time that one could not help feeling humiliated at being thrust by it below the salt. But though his maturity belonged to this second phase, he had grown up during the first—the brothers of his grandmother James had fought in the Revolution and been friends of Lafayette and Washington, and his James grandfather had come to America from Ireland and made a fortune of three million dollars—and he had never lost the democratic idealism, the conviction of having scored a triumph and shown the old world a wonder, that were characteristic of it. This appears at the beginning of James's career in the name of 'the American,' Newman, and at the end in his magnificent phrase about Lincoln's 'mold-smashing mask.'

VI

But Henry James is a reporter, not a prophet. With less politics even than Flaubert, he can but chronicle the world as it passes, and in his picture the elements are mixed. In the Americans of Henry James's later novels (those written before his return)—the Milly Theales, the Lambert Strethers, the Maggie Ververs—he shows us all that was magnanimous, reviving and warm in the Americans at the beginning of the new century along with all that was frustrated, sterile, excessively refined, depressing—all that they had in common with the Frédéric Moreaus and with the daughters of poor English parsons. Here they are with their ideals and their blights: Milly Theale, for example, quite real at the core of her cloudy integument, probably the best portrait in fiction of a rich New Yorker of the period. It is the period of the heyday of Sargent; but compare such figures of James's with the fashionable paintings of Sargent, truthful though these are in their way, and see with what profounder insight as well as with what superior delicacy Henry James has caught the monied distinction of the Americans of this race.

But between the first blooming and the second something tragic has happened to these characters. What has become of Christopher Newman? What has become of Isabel Archer? They are Lambert Strether and Milly Theale—the one worn out by Woollett, Mass., the other overburdened with money and dying for lack of love. Neither finds any fulfillment in Europe, neither ever gets his money's worth. Maggie Verver has her triumph in the end, but she, too, is much too rich for comfort. These people look wan and they are more at sea than the people of the earlier novels. They have been tumbled along or been ground in the sand by the surf of commercial success that has been running in the later part of the century, and in either case are very much the worse for it. It seems to me foolish to reproach Henry James for having neglected the industrial background. Like sex, we never get very close to it, but its effects are a part of his picture. James's tone is more often old-maidish than his sense of reality is feeble; and the changes in

American life that have been going on during his absence are implied in these later books.

When he revisits the States at last, he is aroused to a new effort in fiction as well as to the reporting of *The American Scene*. The expatriate New Yorker of *The Jolly Corner* comes back to the old house on Fifth Avenue to confront the apparition of himself as he would have been if he had stayed and worked 'downtown.' 'Rigid and conscious, spectral yet human, a man of his own substance and stature waited there to measure himself with his power to dismay.' At first this *alter ego* covers its face with its hands; then it advances 'as for aggression, and he knew himself give ground. Then harder pressed still, sick with the force of his shock, and falling back as under the hot breath and the sensed passion of a life larger than his own, a rage of personality before which his own collapsed, he felt the whole vision turn to darkness and his very feet give way.' He faints.

Yet at contact with this new America which is extravagant at the same time as ugly, the old Balzac in James revives. I do not know why more has not been made in the recent discussion of James—especially by the critics of the Left, who are so certain that there is nothing in him—of the unfinished novel called *The Ivory Tower*. The work of James's all but final period has been 'poetic' rather than 'realistic'; but now he passes into a further phase in which the poetic treatment is applied to what is for James a new kind of realism. The fiction of his latest period is occupied in a special way with the forgotten, the poor and the old, even—what has been rare in James—with the uncouth, the grotesque. It is perhaps the reflection of his own old age, his own lack of worldly success, the strange creature that he himself has become. This new vein had already appeared in the long short story *The Papers*, with its fantastically amusing picture of the sordid lives of journalists in London; and he later wrote *Fordham Castle*, in which he said he had tried to do something for the parents of the Daisy Millers whose children had left them behind—a curious if not very successful glimpse of the America of Sinclair Lewis; and *The Bench of Desolation*, the last story but one that he published, surely one of the most beautifully written and wonderfully developed short pieces in the whole range of James's work: a sort of prose poem of loneliness and poverty among the nondescript small shopkeepers and retired governesses of an English seaside resort.

But in the meantime the revelation of Newport, as it presented itself in the nineteen hundreds—so different from the Newport which James had described years ago in *An International Episode*

—stimulates him to something quite new: a kind of nightmare of the American *nouveaux riches.* Here his appetite for the varied forms of life, his old interest in social phenomena, seem brusquely to wake him up from revery. The appearances of things become vivid again. To our amazement, there starts into color and relief the America of the millionaries, at its crudest, corruptest and phoniest: the immense amorphous mansions, complicated by queer equipment which seems neither to have been purchased by personal choice nor humanized by personal use; the old men of the Rockefeller-Frick generation, landed, with no tastes and no interests, amidst a limitless magnificence which dwarfs them; the silly or clumsy young people of the second generation with their dubious relationships, their enormous and meaningless parties, their touching longings and resolute strivings for an elegance and cultivation which they have no one to guide them in acquiring. The specter of *The Jolly Corner* appeared to the expatriate American 'quite as one of those expanding fantastic images projected by the magic lantern of childhood'; and in somewhat the same way, for the reader of James, with the opening of *The Ivory Tower,* there emerges the picture of old Abner Gaw, a kind of monster from outside the known Jamesian world, sitting and rocking his foot and looking out on the sparkling Atlantic while he waits for his business partner to die. *The Ivory Tower,* in dealing with the newest rich, is comic and even homely; but it is also, like all this later work of Henry James, poetic in that highest sense that its characters and scenes and images shine out with the incandescence which shows them as symbols of phases through which the human soul has passed. The moral of the novel —which seems quite plain from the scenario left by James—is also of particular interest. The ivory tower itself, a fine piece of Chinese carving, is to represent, for the young American who has just returned from Europe and inherited his uncle's fortune, that independence of spirit, that private cultivation of sensations and that leisure for literary work, which the money is to make possible for him; but it fatally contains, also, the letter in which Abner Gaw, out of vindictiveness toward the partner who has double-crossed him, has revealed all the swindles and perfidies by which the fortune has been created. So that the cosmopolitan nephew (he has always had a *little* money) is finally to be only too glad to give up the independence with the fortune.

Henry James dropped *The Ivory Tower* when the war broke out in 1914, because he felt it was too remote from the terrible contemporary happenings. These events seem to have presented themselves to James as simply a critical struggle between, on the one hand, French and English civilization and, on the other, German barbarity. He had believed in and had invoked rather vaguely the possible salutary effect for the world of an influential group of international élite made up of the kind of people with whom he associated and whom he liked to depict in his novels; but now he spoke of the past as 'the age of the mistake,' the period when people had thought that the affairs of the world were sufficiently settled for such an élite to flourish. He was furiously nationalistic, or at least furiously pro-Ally. He railed against Woodrow Wilson for his delay in declaring war, and he applied in 1915, in a gesture of rejection and allegiance, to become a British subject. 'However British you may be, I am more British still!' he is said to have exclaimed to Edmund Gosse, when the process had been completed—something which, Gosse is supposed to have remarked, 'nobody wanted him to be.' He had hitherto refrained from this step, feeling, as we gather from *The American Scene*, some pride and some advantage in his status as a citizen of the United States. But he had been thrown off his balance again, had been swung from his poise of detachment, always a delicate thing to maintain and requiring special conditions. It never occurred to James that he had been, in *The Ivory Tower*, much closer to contemporary realities than he was when he threw up his hat and enlisted in a holy war on Germany; that the partnership of Betterman and Gaw was not typical merely of the United States but had its European counterparts—any more than it was present to him now that the class antagonisms of *The Princess Casamassima*, his response to the depression of the eighties, must inevitably appear again and that the events he was witnessing in Europe were partly due to that social system whose corruption he had been consciously chronicling, and were expediting the final collapse which he had earlier half-predicted.

But as Hyacinth Robinson had died of the class struggle, so Henry James died of the war. He was cremated, and a funeral service was held—on March 3, 1916—at Chelsea Old Church in London; but his ashes, as he had directed, were brought to the United States and buried in the Cambridge cemetery beside his parents and sister and brother. One occasionally, however, finds references to him which assume that he was buried in England—just as one sometimes also finds references which assume that he was born in New England—so that even Henry James's death has been not without a suggestion of the equivocal.

The English had done him the honor, not long before he died, of awarding him the Order of Merit. But I do not think that anybody has yet done full justice to his genius as an international critic of manners, esthetic values and morals. The strength of that impartial intelligence of which his hesitating and teasing ambiguity sometimes represented a weakness had prompted him to find his bearings among social gravitational fields which must at the time have seemed almost as bewildering as the astronomical ones with which the physics of relativity were just beginning to deal. It had fortified him to meet and weather the indifference or ridicule of both the two English-speaking peoples to whom he had addressed himself and whose historian he had trained himself to be; and it had stimulated him, through more than half a hundred books, a long life of unwearying labor, to keep recreating himself as an artist and even to break new ground at seventy.

For Henry James *is* a first-rank writer in spite of certain obvious deficiencies. His work is incomplete as his experience was; but it is in no respect second-rate, and he can be judged only in company with the greatest. I have been occupied here with the elements that travail or contend or glow beneath the surface of his even fiction, and my argument has not given me occasion to insist, as ought to be done in any 'literary' discussion of James, on his classical equanimity in dealing with diverse forces, on his combination, equally classical, of hard realism with formal harmony. These are qualities—I have tried to describe them in writing about Pushkin—which have always been rather rare in American and English literature and of which the fiction of James is one of the truest examples.

•

1948. I have left my description of *The Turn of the Screw* mainly as I originally wrote it. In going over it again, however, it has struck me that I forced a point in trying to explain away the passage in which the housekeeper identifies, from the governess' description, the male apparition with Peter Quint. The recent publication of Henry James's note-books seems, besides, to make it quite plain that James's conscious intention, in *The Turn of the Screw,* was to write a *bona fide* ghost story; and it also becomes clear that the theme of youth feeding age was to have been the real subject of *The Sacred Fount.* I should today restate my thesis as follows:

At the time that James wrote these stories, his faith in himself had been somewhat shaken. Though he had summoned the whole force of his will and brought his whole mind to bear on writing plays, he had not made connections with the theater. The disastrous opening night of *Guy Domville* had occurred on January 5, 1895.

On the evening of January 10, we learn from an entry in the note-books, James had heard from Archbishop Benson the story that suggested *The Turn of the Screw.* On January 23, he writes: 'I take up my *own* old pen again—the pen of all my old unforgettable efforts and sacred struggles. To myself—today—I need say no more. Large and full and high the future still opens. It is now indeed that I may do the work of my life. And I will . . . I have only to face my problems.' *The Turn of the Screw* was begun in the fall of 1897 (*The Spoils of Poynton* and *What Maisie Knew* had been written in between). Now, to fail as James had just done is to be made to doubt one's grasp of reality; and the doubts that some readers feel as to the soundness of the governess' story are, I believe, the reflection of James's doubts, communicated unconsciously by James himself (in sketching out his stories in his note-books—as for *The Friends of the Friends,* described below—he sometimes shifts over without a break from a first person which refers to himself to a first person which refers to the imaginary teller). An earlier story, *The Path of Duty,* published in 1884, is perhaps the most obvious example of James's interest in cases of self-deception and his trick of presenting them from their own points of view; and it is given a special relevance to the problem of *The Turn of the Screw* by the entry about it in the note-books. This entry is simply a notation of a curious piece of gossip which James had heard in London, with a discussion of the various ways in which it could be treated in fiction; but the story that James afterwards wrote depends for its effectiveness on an element which James does not mention there. The original anecdote is used, but it here gets another dimension from the attitude of the woman who is supposed to be telling it. This American lady in London is enamored of an attractive nobleman in line for a desirable baronetcy, with whom she is on fairly close terms but who takes no serious interest in her. She therefore intervenes in a mischievous way, under the pretense of keeping him to the 'path of duty,' to prevent him from marrying the woman he loves and induce him to marry one he doesn't—a situation in which everybody else is to be left as dissatisfied as she is. She has never admitted to herself her real motives for what she is doing, and they gradually dawn on the reader in the form of intermittent suspicions like the suspicions that arise in one's mind in reading *The Turn of the Screw.* But in the case of *The Path of Duty,* we are quite clear as we finish the story, as to what role the narrator has actually played. She has written her account, we realize, though ostensibly to satisfy a friend who has been asking her about the episode, really as a veiled confession; and then she has decided to withhold it, ostensibly to shield the main actors, but really to shield herself. Here James, having noted down an anecdote, as he was also to do for *The Turn of the Screw* and had already done with the notion that was to be used in *The Sacred Fount,* has produced a psychological study for which the anecdote is only a pretext. Another story, *The Friends of the Friends,* the idea for which James first noted in the December of 1895 and which he immediately afterwards wrote, also offers a clue to the process which I believe was at work in *The Turn of the Screw. The Friends of the Friends* is a ghost story, which involves, like *The Marriages* and *The Path of Duty,* a mischievous intervention prompted by interested motives on the part of a woman narrator; and the ghost is presumably a product of this narrator's neurotic jealousy. *Maud-Evelyn,* a story written later and first published in 1900, though the first suggestion of it seems also to occur in the note-books of 1895, presents a young man who from interested motives lends himself to the spiritualistic self-deceptions of parents who have lost their daughter. One is led to conclude that, in *The Turn of the Screw,* not merely is the governess self-deceived, but that James is self-deceived about her.

A curious feature of these note-books is the tone that Henry James takes in collecting his materials and outlining his plots. It is not, as with the notes of most writers, as if James were sitting in the workshop of his mind, alone and with no consciousness of an audience, but exactly as if he were addressing a letter to a friend who took a keen interest in his work but with whom he is not sufficiently intimate to discuss his personal affairs. He calls himself *mon bon* and *caro mio*—'Causons, causons, mon bon,' he will write —and speaks to himself with polite depreciation—referring to 'the narrator of the tale, as I may in courtesy call it.' But, though he talks to himself a good deal—and sometimes very excitedly and touchingly—about his relation to his work, his 'muse,' he never notes down personal emotions in relation to anything else as possible subjects for fiction. One comes to the conclusion that Henry James, in a special and unusual way, was what is nowadays called an 'extrovert'—that is, he did not brood on himself and analyze his own reactions, as Stendhal, for example, did, but always dramatized his experience immediately in terms of imaginary people. One gets the impression here that James was not introspective. Nor are his characters really so. They register, as James himself registered, a certain order of perceptions and sensations; but they justify to some degree the objection of critics like Wells that his psychology is superficial—though it would be more correct to put it that, while his insight is not necessarily superficial, his 'psychologizing' tends to be so. What we are told is going on in the characters' heads is a sensitive reaction to surfaces which itself seems to take place on the surface. We do not often see them grappling with their problems in terms of concrete ambitions or of intimate relationships. What we see when we are supposed to look into their minds is something as much arranged by James to conceal, to mislead and to create suspense as the actual events presented. These people, so far as the 'psychologizing' goes, are not intimate even with themselves. They talk to themselves about what they are doing and what is happening to them even a good deal less frankly than James talks to himself about them, and that is already with the perfect discretion of an after-dinner conversation between two gentlemanly diners-out. As Henry James gets further away—beginning with *What Maisie Knew*—from the realism of his earlier phases, his work—as Stephen Spender has said in connection with *The Golden Bowl*—becomes all a sort of ruminative poem, which gives us not really a direct account of the internal workings of his characters, but rather James's reflective feelings, the flow of images set off in his mind, as he peeps not impolitely inside them. Not, however, that his sense of life—of personal developments and impacts—is not often profound and sure. The point is merely that it is not always so, and that the floor of the layer of consciousness that we are usually allowed to explore sometimes rings rather hollow. Where motivations are rarely revealed, we cannot always tell how much the author knows; and it is on this account that arguments occur—and not only in the case of *The Turn of the Screw* but also in that of *The Golden Bowl*—as to what is supposed to be happening in a given situation or as to what kind of personalities the characters are supposed to be. Carefully though, from one point of view, the point of view of technical machinery, Henry James always planned his novels, he seems sometimes to falter and grope in dealing with their human problems. The habits he imposed on himself in his attempt to write workable plays was unfortunate in this connection. The unperformed comedies that he published in the two volumes of *Theatricals*, which are almost the only things he wrote that can really be called bad, show a truly appalling self-discipline in sterile and stale devices and artificial motivations. In the stage world of Henry James, young men are always prepared to marry, regardless of personal taste or even of close acquaintance, from an interest in a property or an inheritance, or because they have been told that they have compromised girls or simply because women have proposed to them; and an element of this false psychology was afterwards carried by James through the whole of his later fiction along with his stage technique. It is true that in this later fiction there is a good deal of illicit passion, as had not been the case in his plays; but his adulteries seem sometimes as arbitrary as the ridiculous engagements of *Theatricals.* They are not always really explained, we cannot always be sure they are really there, that the people have been to bed together. But, on the other hand, we sometimes feel the presence, lurking like 'the beast in the jungle,' of other emotional factors with which the author himself does not always appear to have reckoned.

I once gave *The Turn of the Screw* to the Austrian novelist Franz Höllering to see what impression he would get of it. It did not occur to him that it was not a real ghost story, but he said to me, after he had read it: 'The man who wrote that was a *Kinderschänder*'; and I remembered that in all James's work of this period —which extends from *The Other House* through *The Sacred Fount* —the favorite theme is the violation of innocence, with the victim in every case (though you have in *The Turn of the Screw* a boy as well as a girl) a young or a little girl. In *The Other House* a child is murdered; in *What Maisie Knew* and *The Awkward Age,* a child and a young virgin are played upon by forces of corruption which, though they do not destroy the girls' innocence, somewhat harm them or dislocate their emotions by creating abnormal relationships; in *The Turn of the Screw,* whichever way you take it, the little girl is either hurt or corrupted. (The candid and loyal young heroines of *The Spoils of Poynton* and *In the Cage,* though they can hardly be said to be violated, are both, in their respective ways, represented as shut out from something.) This, of course, in a sense, is an old theme for James: *Washington Square* and *The Portrait of a Lady* were studies in innocence betrayed. But there is something rather peculiar, during this relatively neurotic phase, in his interest in and handling of this subject. The real effectiveness of all these stories derives, not from the conventional pathos of a victim with whom we sympathize but from the excitement of the violation; and if we look back to Henry James's first novel, *Watch and Ward,* serialized when he was twenty-eight, we find a very queer little tale about a young man of twenty-six who becomes the guardian of a girl of ten and gradually falls in love with her but is for a long time debarred from marrying her, when she comes of age to marry, by a complication of scruples and misunderstandings. The relationship clearly connects itself with the relationship, in *The Awkward Age,* between Nanda and Mr. Langdon, in which, also, the attitude of the pseudo-father is given a flavor of unavowed sex. We are not in a position to explain, on any basis of early experience, this preoccupation of James with immature girls who are objects of desire or defilement; but it seems clear what symbolic role they played from time to time in his work. He seems early to have 'polarized' with his brother William in an opposition of feminine and masculine. This appears in a significant anecdote which he tells in his autobiography about William's having left him once to go to play, as he said, with 'boys that curse and swear'; and in his description of his feeling from the first that William was "occupying a place in the world to which I couldn't at all aspire—to any approach to which in truth I seem to myself ever conscious of having signally forfeited a title'; and one finds it in their correspondence and in everything one has heard of their relations. There was always in Henry James an innocent little girl whom he cherished and loved and protected and yet whom he later tried to violate, whom he even tried to kill. He must have felt particularly helpless, particularly unsuited for the battle with the world, particularly exposed to rude insult, after the failure of his dramatic career, when he retreated into his celibate solitude. The maiden innocent of his early novels comes to life again; but he now does not merely pity her, he does not merely adore her: in his impotence, his impatience with himself, he would like to destroy or rape her. The real dramatic and esthetic values of the stories that he writes at this period are involved with an equivocal blending of this impulse and an instinct of self-pity. (The conception of *innocence excluded* is a reaction to the same situation: Fleda Vetch, in *The Spoils of Poynton,* misses marrying the man she loves and misses inheriting the spoils, which in any case go up in flames; the girl in the telegraph office finds that it is not she who is 'in the cage' but the dashing young captain whose amours she has fascinatedly watched from afar—just as James must have had to decide that the worldly success he had tried for was, after all, not worth having. So the innocents in certain of the other stories, too, are left with a moral advantage.) This is not in the least, on the critic's part, to pretend to reduce the dignity of these stories by reading into them the embarrassments of the author. They do contain, I believe, a certain subjective element which hardly appears to the same degree elsewhere in James's mature work; but he has expressed what he had to express—disappointments and dissatisfactions that were poignantly and not ignobly felt—with dramatic intensity and poetic color. These are fairy-stories, but fairy-stories that trouble, that get a clear and luminous music out of chords very queerly combined. They are unique in literature, and their admirable style and form are not quite like anything else even in the work of James. In *The Wings* *of the Dove,* of course, which follows *The Awkward Age,* he is still occupied with violated innocence, but now his world is firm again on its base, and we are back on the international stage of *The Portrait of a Lady.* Milly Theale, though languishing and fatally ill, is a real and full-grown woman dealing with a practical conspiracy, not a tender little girl or *jeune fille* jeopardized by an ambiguous dream.*

* The immaturity of the heroines in James serves sometimes to provide one of his many pretexts for making it impossible for the heroes to marry them. The whole question of the motif of impotence in James has been discussed very suggestively and interestingly—though on the basis of an incomplete acquaintance with Henry James's work—in a paper called *The Ghost of Henry James: A Study in Thematic Apperception* by Dr. Saul Rosenzweig (*Character and Personality,* December 1943). Dr. Rosenzweig suggests that the accident in which Henry James sprained his back at eighteen—'a horrid even if an obscure hurt,' as James himself calls it—and from which he suffered, sometimes acutely, all the rest of his life, may have been partly neurotic not only in its results but even in its origin—since it offers a strangely close parallel with the accident in which the elder Henry James had lost his leg—also in extinguishing a fire—at the age of thirteen. The son's accident had occurred, as he tells us himself, at the beginning of the Civil War and put it out of the question for him to answer Lincoln's first call for volunteers. Dr. Rosenzweig has brought to light a very early story of James, the first he ever published: *The Story of a Year,* which appeared in the *Atlantic Monthly* in March 1865. Here you have a young man of the North who, just before going off to the war, becomes engaged to a girl but makes her promise that, if he should die, she will forget him and marry someone else. She dreams, when he has gone, that she is walking in a wood with a man who calls her wife and that they find a dead man covered with wounds. They lift the corpse up to bury it, and it opens its eye and says 'Amen'; they stamp down the dirt of the grave. The lover is actually wounded, lingers for some time between life and death, and then dies, leaving the fiancée to marry another man. Another factor in the story is the young man's mother, who comes between him and the girl, being unwilling to have him marry her and trying to prevent her seeing him after he has been brought home wounded—Henry James, it seems, was his mother's favorite child. Dr. Rosenzweig might also have cited another early short story. *An Extraordinary Case* (1868), in which another returned soldier, suffering from an unspecified ailment, loses his girl to another man and dies.

One can agree with Dr. Rosenzweig that a castration theme appears here —one recognizes it as the same that figures through the whole of James's work; but that work does not bear out the contention put forward by Dr. Rosenzweig that James was to suffer all his life from unallayed feelings of guilt for not having taken part in the war. The only real pieces of evidence that Dr. Rosenzweig is able to produce are the short story, *Owen Wingrave,* which deals with the deliberate pacifism of a young man from a military family and leaves the moral advantage all with the pacifist, who dies in the cause of peace; and Henry James's excitement at the beginning of World War I and his memories at this time of the Civil War. He must certainly be right, however, in assuming that well before the age when *The Story of a Year* was written, a state of mind in which 'aggression and sexuality were repressed' had been

It is of course no longer true, as is implied in the above essay, that the stature and merits of James are not fully appreciated in the English-speaking world. Since the centenary of James's birth in 1943, he has been celebrated, interpreted, reprinted, on a scale which, I believe, is unprecedented for a classical American writer. There have contributed to this frantic enthusiasm perhaps a few rather doubtful elements. A novelist whose typical hero invariably decides not to act, who remains merely an intelligent onlooker, appeals for obvious reasons to a period when many intellectuals, formerly romantic egoists or partisans of the political Left, have been resigning themselves to the role of observer or of passive participant in activities which cannot command their whole allegiance. The stock of Henry James has gone up in the same market as that of Kafka, and the recent apotheosis of him has sometimes been conducted as uncritically as the prayers and contemplations of the Kafka cult. At the same time, in a quite different way, he has profited from—or, at any rate, been publicized by—the national propaganda movement which has been advertising American civilization under stimulus of our needs in the war and our emergence into the international world. The assumption seems to be that Henry James is our counterpart to Yeats, Proust and Joyce, and he has been tacitly assigned to high place in the official American Dream along with 'Mr. Jefferson,' the *Gettysburg Address,* Paul Bunyan, the Covered Wagon, and Mom's Huckleberry Pie. He will doubtless be translated for the Japanese, who were fascinated before the war by the refinements of Paul Valéry and Proust.*

Yet we do well to be proud of him, and there are very good reasons for young people to read him straight through, as—incredible though it would have sounded at the time he was still alive—they seem more and more to be doing. Henry James stands out today as unique among our fiction writers of the nineteenth century in having devoted wholeheartedly to literature the full span of a long life and brought to it first-rate abilities. Beside James's half century of achievement, with its energy, continuity and variety, the production of Hawthorne looks furtive and meager and the work of Poe's brief years fragmentary. Alone among our novelists

'established as a *modus vivendi.*' One of James's most curious symbols for his chronic inhibition occurs in a very early story called first *Théolinde,* then *Rose-Agathe,* in which a man falls in love with a dummy in a Parisian hairdresser's window and finally buys her and takes her home to live with. The wax dummy is cut off at the waist.

* Since writing this, I have found in a book catalogue—along with a Japanese translation of *Ulysses*—a volume of James's short stories translated into Japanese (1924), and a Japanese book about James (1934).

of the past, Henry James managed to master his art and to practice it on an impressive scale, to stand up to popular pressures so as not to break down or peter out, and to build up what the French call an *oeuvre.*

•

1959. Since writing the above, I have become convinced that James knew exactly what he was doing and that he intended the governess to be suffering from delusions. The story, in the New York Edition, is placed, as I have mentioned above, not among the ghost stories but between *The Aspern Papers* and *The Liar.* My description above of *The Liar,* which I had not reread in years, really misses the point of the title, which, as has been noted by Mr. Marius Bewley, is that the liar is not the harmless romancer who is adored and protected by his wife, but the painter who is telling the story. This narrator has been in love with the wife and is still unable to forgive her for having married someone else, so, in painting a portrait of the husband, he falsifies the latter's personality by representing him as more false than he is. The parallel with the governess is thus complete. In both cases, the mind of the narrator is warped, and the story he tells untrue. The narrator of *The Aspern Papers,* in a somewhat similar way, is presenting his impudent activities in quite a different light from that in which they appear to his victims. As for the explanation of the governess's describing correctly the person of Peter Quint, it is so clear that—though slily contrived—one wonders how one could ever have missed it; yet it had never, so far as I know, been brought out before the publication, in *American Literature* of May, 1957, of a paper by John Silver called *A Note on the Freudian Reading of "The Turn of the Screw."* The governess, Mr. Silver suggests, had learned about Quint's appearance from the people in the village with whom we know she had talked and who had presumably also told her of the manner of Quint's death.

Another Reading of *The Turn of the Screw*

Nathan Bryllion Fagin

Henry James himself claimed for *The Turn of the Screw* only the right to be considered "a piece of ingenuity pure and simple, of cold artistic calculation, an *amusette* to catch those not easily caught . . . , the jaded, the disillusioned, the fastidious."[1] Yet those not easily caught have been unable to shake off the impression that there is in this story much more than an amusing novelette. Students of James know, of course, that his interest in any series of incidents was confined neither to their dramatic value nor to their realistic impact, but rather to their potentialities as artistic pattern, and that, for him, a story lay not in mere physical plot, but in the undercurrent of suggestion and implication. Like Edmund Wilson, most of us cannot remember that James ever wrote a story "which did not have a more or less serious point,"[2] and, like Wilson, we feel that *The Turn of the Screw* is more than a ghost story. What, however, that "more" is constitutes a problem of interpretation. Is *The Turn of the Screw*, as Mr. Wilson believes, "a study in morbid psychology" and are the ghosts "merely the governess's hallucinations?"

I

The danger in the psychoanalytic method of criticism lies in the apparent plausibility. To Mr. Wilson, for instance, the young

SOURCE: *Modern Language Notes,* LVI (March, 1941), 196–202. Reprinted by permission of the editors.

[1] *The Novels and Tales of Henry James* (New York, 1917), Preface, XII, xviii.

[2] "The Ambiguity of Henry James," *Hound and Horn,* VII (April: June, 1934), 391.

governess who narrates the story of *The Turn of the Screw* is "a neurotic case of sex repression." And that, from a psychoanalytic point of view, is a plausible hypothesis. The daughter of a poor country parson, she has fallen in love with the children's guardian, "a bachelor in the prime of life," eligible and charming. Alone with her young charges, she wanders about the estate thinking of its master and thus comes upon the ghost of Quint, the valet, who is wearing the master's smart clothes. Quint, in Wilson's theory, "has been ambiguously confused"—in the governess's mind—"with the master and with the master's interest in her."[3]

Mr. Wilson is less clear about the symbolism of Miss Jessel's ghost. The former governess had apparently had an affair with Quint and had been an accomplice in corrupting the children. "Observe," says Wilson, "from the Freudian point of view, the significance of the governess's interest in the little girl's pieces of wood and of the fact that the male apparition first appears on a tower and the female apparition on a lake."[4] These hints, however, fail to explain Miss Jessel's symbolic necessity in James's Freudian pattern, and Wilson wisely drops her completely and devotes himself to Quint and his influence on little Miles.

The trouble with Wilson's interpretation—and Miss Edna Kenton's (to whose theory Mr. Wilson acknowledges indebtedness)—is that, although it may carry an air of plausibility, it clearly has no relation to James's intention. Mr. Wilson is, presumably, aware of the fact that Freudian psychology was something Henry James could not have been conscious of dealing with; he therefore places *The Turn of the Screw,* along with *Moby Dick* and the *Alice* books, among the "small group of fairy tales whose symbols exert a peculiar power by reason of the fact that they have behind them, *whether or not the authors are aware of it,* a profound grasp of subconscious processes."[5] But by the same method it is possible to build up an excellent case for a Freudian interpretation of *Hamlet,* and surely that would not be reflective of Shakespeare's intention. Although it might be an interesting disclosure of the workings of the psychoanalyst's mind, it would tell us little or nothing about Shakespeare's. *The Turn of the Screw,* if read as Edmund Wilson reads it, becomes orthodox James Joyce or D. H. Lawrence; it ceases to be Henry

[3] *Ibid.,* p. 388.

[4] *Ibid.,* p. 387. Apropos the implied interpretation of the last "fact," some irreverent wag in Washington, D.C., has observed that the monuments to George Washington and Abraham Lincoln, in our National capital, suggest, in Freudian symbolism, that Washington was the father and Lincoln the mother of our country.

[5] *Ibid.,* pp. 390–391. The italics are mine.

James. Wilson fails to take advantage of much that we know of James's life, personality, and concepts and methods of art. In the light of this knowledge it is possible to read *The Turn of the Screw* more simply and, it seems to this writer, more convincingly.

II

In a consideration of James's "Ethics," Professor Joseph Warren Beach came to the conclusion that James "may not be American as Mark Twain or Benjamin Franklin or Edgar Lee Masters are American, but he is American as Emerson and Thoreau and Hawthorne are."[6] James's Americanism is, just now, not our concern, but any one who has read James carefully, especially his *Hawthorne,* cannot help feeling that his kinship with the Puritan and transcendental traditions is, at least as it affected his artistic attitude, much closer than it might appear on the surface. Rebecca West[7] and Cornelia Pulsifer Kelley[8] have shown the influence of Hawthorne on James's artistic development. James admired Hawthorne and thought him "the most valuable example of the American genius."[9] One of the things in Hawthorne he singled out for special praise was his preoccupation with sin, which, James noted, "seems to exist" in Hawthorne's mind "merely for an artistic purpose. . . . He played with it and used it as a pigment; he treated it, as the metaphysicians say, objectively. . . . It was a necessary condition for a man of Hawthorne's stock that if his imagination should take license to amuse itself, it should at least select this grim precinct of the Puritan morality for its playground." Another thing he approved of was the formative influence on Hawthorne of *Pilgrim's Progress* and the *Faery Queen.* "A boy," he writes, "may have worse company than Bunyan and Spenser. . . ."[10]

Why then inject Freud into the interpretation of a story by James when it is obvious that the tradition represented by Hawthorne furnishes a more likely clue? *The Turn of the Screw* is a simple allegory of the type which fascinated Hawthorne. To be sure, James considered allegory as "one of the lighter exercises of the imagination." He admitted that "Many excellent judges have a great stomach for it; they delight in symbols and correspondences,

[6] *The Method of Henry James* (New Haven and London, 1918), p. 144.
[7] *Henry James* (New York, 1916), p. 250.
[8] *The Early Development of Henry James* (Urbana, 1930), See especially pp. 18, 22, 251–5.
[9] *Hawthorne* (London, 1879), p. 2.
[10] *Ibid.,* p. 17.

in seeing a story told as if it were another and a very different story." For himself, however, he confessed deriving "but little enjoyment of it," not being able to consider it "a first rate literary form." Yet he was willing to grant that "It has produced assuredly some first-rate works; and," he added, "Hawthorne in his younger years had been a great reader and devotee of Bunyan and Spenser, the great masters of allegory." He singled out for approval the kind of allegory which is "extremely spontaneous, when the analogy presents itself with eager promptitude."[11] Two things are important to add in this connection. One is that James never valued *The Turn of the Screw* higher than as "one of the lighter exercises of the imagination."[12] The other is that the analogy in the tale "presents itself with eager promptitude."

III

In simple terms, *The Turn of the Screw* is an allegory which dramatizes the conflict between Good and Evil. The apparitions are the personifications of evil; they are the Emerson's dead men's thoughts by which we permit ourselves to be guided, and like Ibsen's ghosts which come to haunt Mrs. Alving. The governess, the parson's daughter, is a sort of Guardian Angel, hovering protectingly over the two innocent children placed in her charge.

Read this way, the numerous hints throughout the story become significant and fall into the pattern. Perhaps even the names of the characters may have been selected with conscious aptness: Miles, the little show-off, who seizes every opportunity to flaunt the "badness" that is within him; Flora, part lovely flower and part wanton weed; Mrs. Grose, a simple, illiterate, undiscerning person. But it is not important to stress this point.[13] The governess herself has no name: she's merely a point of view, that of a clergyman's daughter, for whom Evil would have strong and sinister power. Both children are outwardly angelically beautiful. How could they be corrupt? Yet Quint dominates the tower of their home, Quint who has red hair and red whiskers, the conventional guise of the Devil.

[11] *Ibid.*, pp. 62–63.

[12] See his letter to F. W. H. Myers: "The *T of the S.* is a very mechanical matter, I honestly think—an inferior, a merely pictorial, subject and rather a shameless pot-boiler." *The Letters of Henry James,* ed. Percy Lubbock (New York, 1920), I, 300.

[13] It is interesting to note, however, that in a later article, Edmund Wilson remarks that James's idealism "appears in the name of the hero of *The American: Newman.*" "The Last Phase of Henry James," *Partisan Review,* IV (February, 1938), 5.

The children want to get to the two horrors. "But for what?" asks the good and simple Mrs. Grose. "For the love of all the evil that . . . the pair put into them," says the governess. "And to ply them with that evil still, to keep up the work of demons, is what brings the others back."

All this is reminiscent of Hawthorne, of "Young Goodman Brown" and "Rappaccini's Daughter." And, indeed, these two stories were pronounced by James as "little masterpieces"; they were, in his opinion, representative of "the highest point that Hawthorne reached" in the field of fantasy and allegory.[14] The purposes for which Quint seeks to meet little Miles are the same old purposes for which the Devil met young Goodman Brown in the woods near Salem. And little Flora is another Beatrice Rappaccini, outwardly marvelously beautiful, but inwardly corrupted by the poison of evil. Miss Jessel's rôle in the story is, of course, the same as that of Quint, although her inclusion at all is probably due to James's sense of artistic balance.[15] Miss Jessel is to Flora what Quint is to Miles; each is a corrupting influence: and each helps to complicate and thicken the texture of a capital story—which is what *The Turn of the Screw* set out primarily to be; it is an allegory only secondarily. The rôles of the uncle and Mrs. Grose have less significance; primarily they help the physical story; secondarily, they represent lack of vigilance, nay, indifference (especially the uncle) to the possibilities of evil.

It is logical for the governess to be tempted to run away from it all, but Duty keeps her on the spot, fighting for the souls of her charges. It is almost as if Hawthorne's Salem ancestors were writing about little Flora: "She was not at these times a child, but an old, old woman." Evil *is* old. After Mrs. Grose finally takes Flora away, the governess remains with Miles to extract his confession. "If he confesses," she says, "he's saved." But he doesn't confess—entirely. For just then Quint appears to make his last stand against the governess. As soon as Miles admits that he took the letter Quint disappears and "the air is clear again." Just as Miles is about to confess what things he had said at school Quint reappears, "as if to blight his [Miles's] confession and stay his answer." In the end the Agent of Good is almost successful, but little Miles is dead, like Beatrice Rappaccini, exhausted by the ordeal. "Frightened to death," says Edmund Wilson. More likely too corrupted to live

[14] *Hawthorne*, p. 56.

[15] Note, for example, "The Private Life," the story of Clare Vawdrey, a person who has no creative public life. This fictive thread is complicated and balanced by another, relating to Lord Mellifont, who exists only in public.

without evil, like the beautiful wife in Hawthorne's "The Birthmark," whose husband, a surgeon, removed the one blemish to her perfect beauty, only to find that it was imbedded in her heart.

IV

It is possible, of course, that we have read into this novelette more than its author intended it to convey. Perhaps it is really nothing but "a shameless pot-boiler" and our readings of it are merely fanciful? "I am only afraid," wrote James to Dr. Louis Waldstein, "that my conscious intention strikes you as having been larger than I deserve it should be thought." And yet, a little later, "*But,* of course, where there *is* life, there's truth, and the truth was at the back of my head."[16] What was at the back of James's head is worth surmising, in the light of what we know of his ideas, his preoccupations, his methods, and, above all, the literary influences he acknowledged. This is not the same thing as surmising "subconscious processes" in the light of Freud.

[16] *Letters*, I, 297.

James: "The Turn of the Screw"

A Radio Symposium:

Katherine Anne Porter, Allen Tate, Mark Van Doren

VAN DOREN: This great and famous story is told by a governess, who lets us know how she saw two children under her charge, a little boy and a little girl, in an English house of indeterminate antiquity and solitude, corrupted by the ghosts of two evil servants, recently dead. Now the first question we shall be expected to settle, if we can, is the question whether all that happens, all that is seen, is in the mind of the governess, or whether—or to what extent—there are objective existences here over which she has no control.

TATE: Mr. Van Doren, if you mean by "objective existences" only those existences which can be seen visually, I would say no, except in so far as the governess sees them; but I think there are objective existences which don't manifest themselves visually. Again, I think that these apparitions, in so far as they become agents in the action affecting human lives, are just as real as if they were people in the sense that we are people around a table. I don't want to quibble about it, but I think that a discussion along that line is the way to get at it.

VAN DOREN: Is that true for you, Miss Porter? Does it seem to you a false problem if I state it by asking whether everything happens in the mind of the governess or nothing does?

PORTER: When I first read this story, I accepted the governess's visions as real, that is, the ghosts were real in themselves, and not only the governess, perhaps, but others might have seen them; they

SOURCE: *The New Invitation to Learning,* edited by Mark Van Doren, pp. 223–235. Copyright 1942 by The Columbia Broadcasting System, Inc. Reprinted by permission of Random House, Inc. Broadcast May 3, 1942, on "Invitation to Learning."

had a life of their own. But as I went on reading the story and studying it through the years, and I read Henry James's notes on it, I decided that the ghosts were a projection of the governess's imagination and were part of her plot.

TATE: It is evident, Miss Porter, isn't it, that nobody actually sees these people but the governess?

PORTER: Nobody.

TATE: James is very adroit in convincing the readers that perhaps they can be seen by other people, or have been, but if you look closely it is perfectly evident that nobody sees them as physical existences but the governess. I don't say that that destroys their reality.

PORTER: Not at all.

VAN DOREN: And, of course, there's no possible doubt that she does see them. The statement "the governess sees the ghosts" is a true statement.

TATE: Oh, there's no question of that.

VAN DOREN: Not only does she have no doubt herself, but it never occurs to her that anyone else could question their presence.

TATE: She has a momentary doubt of a certain kind, Mr. Van Doren. Doesn't she say toward the end that if Flora goes out into the world and people come in from outside—for example, her employer, the uncle of the children—and look at the situation and find that the apparitions don't visually exist, then she will have to say: "Where am I?" Those are her exact words.

VAN DOREN: Yes, and there is one moment when Mrs. Grose, the housekeeper, the plain and simple woman of the story, fails to see Miss Jessel, the evil governess who has died.

TATE: That is one of the most interesting moments in the whole story.

VAN DOREN: The present governess even then, as you say, seems to understand that she may be lost if she can't make Mrs. Grose see this woman who is "as big as a blazing fire," for then she has no case. She does seem, at that moment, to think of herself as one having a case.

TATE: She has been so hard-pressed that she feels she must build the case herself even at the expense of the children. That is the sinister note which enters the second half of the story.

PORTER: In her attempt to vindicate herself she's doing the whole thing really at the expense of the children—I have always believed for the sake of destroying them, of putting them out of the way in some manner or other in order to clear a road to the master.

TATE: I agree with Miss Porter. But does the governess realize that consciously?

PORTER: No, never.

VAN DOREN: Well, this is the question then that frames itself in my mind: are we to take the story as a piece of psychology, as an exploration of a peculiar temperament, namely, the governess', suffering under illusions and hallucinations? I prefer not to take it that way. It seems to me that the story would shrink a great deal in power and significance if it were merely a story which psychoanalyzed an old maid.

TATE: I think we've got to take it that way and the other way, too—both at once—and perhaps if we take it both ways, we've got to take it in a third way which will explain the fact that the story is a unified thing, a single thing which is neither psychological wholly nor a mere naive attempt on the part of this governess to protect her children.

VAN DOREN: You see, I am interested in Miss Porter's statement that the first time she read the story she believed the governess. This is certainly true for me.

TATE: And for me, too.

VAN DOREN: And it still is. The first time Miss Porter read the story, it never occurred to her that the evil personified in these two persons—at least these two, because Miss Porter would add a third, or . . .

PORTER: Even a fourth, perhaps—

VAN DOREN: . . . all right, that the evil somehow was there. Now, I think we must take that as a fact. If the story were merely —I'm agreeing with you, Mr. Tate—if the story were merely a clever piece of psychology, no reader, even a child, would feel in it the powerful presence of evil.

TATE: That's absolutely right. It seems to me that given the time in which James lived and the growing interest then in the processes of the mind, we have to see James as taking that peculiar interest as a medium through which to set forth the reality of evil; because the reality of evil in this story is not destroyed, or made a false issue, by explaining it psychologically. In James's time the psychological basis was necessary. In the past, treatment of ghosts, the material projection of evil in earlier literature, didn't follow a psychological bent; it wasn't done psychologically; the evil creatures were presented in their full physical body and the public accepted them at their face value. We have become more sophisticated, and perhaps a little more decadent in our literature—certainly more critical. Don't we demand that all of these allegorical effects, all of these realities of evil, be set forth on some level that will also satisfy the critical point of view?

PORTER: Yes, that is important. James himself confessed that he wished to catch those not easily caught.

VAN DOREN: Exactly.

PORTER: And he made in effect booby-traps of a very high order, with a great deal of wit and a great deal of good humor. But I was thinking that one of the really interesting levels of analysis in this story is theological, admitting the existence of original sin, of the fact that we really are conceived in sin, brought forth in iniquity. I think that is a very interesting point in the study of this story.

TATE: Wasn't James always preoccupied with evil?

PORTER: Yes.

VAN DOREN: That is one reason we call him a great writer.

TATE: But wasn't his problem then to make that evil as dramatically convincing as possible?

VAN DOREN: Yes, but I think of him as suffering under the limitations which modern literature and the critical mind imposed upon him. He wasn't able to ask us to believe that anything like Furies or devils existed. Aeschylus could put the Furies on his stage, and even Shakespeare could put on a ghost. All James was able to do was to ask us to believe in the return—somehow—of two very evil individuals. They are not devils; they don't represent evil; they simply *are* evil. A very bad man, Peter Quint.

PORTER: Known to have been bad, yes. And the woman, known to have been bad.

VAN DOREN: A very tragic and dishonored woman, Miss Jessel.

TATE: Now, are they described as necessarily evil during their lives? My feeling is that they were merely "bad." Couldn't we make this distinction: that this story is not about good and bad, but about good and evil? The question of the way in which James makes evil dramatic and convincing has always fascinated me in this book. If you will remember, Quint first appears dressed in the master's clothes; it is the first thing the governess notices about him. Then she notices that he has red hair, and strange pointed eyebrows, and . . .

PORTER: All the physical attributes of the legendary devil.

TATE: Exactly.

PORTER: The evil eye.

TATE: Precisely. And I think James is playing with us a little there—bringing in an additional dimension of the imagination. But when she tells Mrs. Grose about Quint, it seems to me that

James's dramatic powers, his powers as a writer of fiction, are at their very highest, because his job is to insert Quint into the scene and make him an actor in it, and that is very difficult. In order to do that, he must have the governess get some objective verification for her vision, and the way in which the governess makes the simple Mrs. Grose identify Quint establishes him in the scene. Well, that is—if you wish—a trick of fiction. It is the novelist's technique. Actually, at the same time, it doesn't invalidate Quint as an evil person. That's the ambivalent thing in the story.

VAN DOREN: And of course there are some wonderful strokes as Quint is painted. Remember, his first two appearances do not reveal anything except the upper half of him. Once he is standing behind a sort of balustrade on top of the tower; another time he is merely looking in a window, but the lower half of him is not there—it is as if he were in some ghastly way truncated. I am also interested in the fact that he is pale—that he has a pale face with light hair. If he is the devil, at least he is a very special sort of devil; he's not swarthy or grimacing; his face is rigid. He has a thin face and light curly red hair.

TATE: He never changes his expression. I recall something that James says in his preface to this book about the presentation of supernatural creatures in fiction. We must remember that neither Quint nor Miss Jessel ever does much of anything; they just appear; they just stand there and look—and their mere appearance is enough to set all this machinery of horror into motion.

VAN DOREN: That's enough, incidentally.

TATE: Yes. He says supernatural creatures should do as little as possible, as little as is "consistent with their consenting to appear at all."

VAN DOREN: Exactly. The awful thing is that they should appear.

PORTER: The one thing we haven't talked about yet is the role of the children in this story. This, I think, is terribly important, because the governess persistently tries to fix upon the children evil motives and base actions, and takes seriously an accusation made against the little boy by the head-master of the school when he is sent home with a note saying that he had been an immoral influence. She was using this accusation as a weapon against the little boy—a kind of moral blackmail. The girl, who was in some ways a simpler nature, I think, and of a more positive mind than the little boy, was uncomplicated by the fact that she had had no sad experiences. Well, their simplest and most natural acts are interpreted by the governess as being of a suspicious nature, even when they got up in the night and went out to look at the moonlight, and that sort of thing. The governess constantly attempts to draw the children into her orbit of evil and force them to share it and prove them guilty. She transfers her guilty motives to them, making them accomplices to justify herself. But it seems to me that their conduct is perfectly simple and intuitive. They surmise the purpose and the enormous threat to them . . .

TATE: But the threat was real, wasn't it, Miss Porter?

PORTER: Very real. The children were frightened for good reasons, though they did not understand anything; they acted with the curious reserved defensiveness of children who don't know what is happening to them. They surmised evil, surmised the threat and were trying to escape. They even tried to get together to confide in each other, but the governess made constant efforts to keep them separate so that they would never be able to work up a common defense against her.

VAN DOREN: She assumes that when they are together they talk unspeakably evil things.

PORTER: Yes.

VAN DOREN: But I wonder if we're not a bit misleading about the governess. I quite agree that the children are in some sense innocent, beautiful and clear. But so is the governess. We are suggesting that she is more sinister than she ever, at any rate, knows herself as being.

TATE: She never knows herself as being sinister.

VAN DOREN: We almost have imputed to her a plot to corrupt the children herself. Now I'm willing to believe that it is she who corrupts the children and brings about the death of the little boy. Nevertheless, that is precisely my way of understanding how potent the evil in this story is. The evil isn't merely thought to be; it is an actuality which passes through her as a perfectly transparent and non-resistant medium and then passes through the children. The evil is somehow there.

PORTER: And finally it is projected to an immense distance.

VAN DOREN: Yes, for she has great power. If it were merely a story of what she thought, of what she could fool herself into seeing, she wouldn't have the power she has over us as readers; she wouldn't be able, as you say, to project Quint and Miss Jessel to great distances, across lakes; to the tops of towers, and so on.

TATE: Mr. Van Doren, couldn't we put it this way? The governess doesn't invent these apparitions; they merely use her as a medium. Because, obviously, the monstrous proportions of the evil are so great that they are beyond the power of any individual imagination to invent. There is something much stronger than the governess operating through her. She has her own innocent later existence, as is proved, I think, by the prologue of the story, where we learn that after this terrible incident had passed, she went on to other posts and nothing like it occurred again. It was some peculiar conjunction of forces which permitted this evil to emerge through her here.

VAN DOREN: That is extremely interesting, Mr. Tate. You suggest to me another reason why James is a great writer. Living as he did in our time, which usually does not take stock in either good or evil, he was able to construct in the governess a creature almost like Cassandra, through whom evil tears its way without any instigation on her part at all—without, so to speak, her permission.

TATE: Don't you feel then that the governess, at the end of the story, in spite of the fact that you see what she's done, has a certain dignity of her own, that she is a person of great proportions? She is not in the least an insignificant creature.

VAN DOREN: She is no such creature as a story-teller makes his victim when he wants to deal in mere delusion. She is not ridiculous or trivial. As a matter of fact, she becomes tragic.

TATE: Exactly. It's her tragedy.

VAN DOREN: Of course, individual creatures can be the vehicles or channels of great good also. Just as Cassandra is a person through whom evil tears, so a saint may be a person through whom good pours in floods.

PORTER: An illuminant is not always an illuminant for good. The most dangerous people in the world are the illuminated ones through whom forces act when they themselves are unconscious of their own motives. And yet, no force has ever acted through either a saint or an evil person that wasn't somehow directed to further the ends and the ambitions and the hopes of that person, which makes me feel that the instrument is not altogether so innocent and so helpless as we have been saying. Because, after all, the governess had her positive motive—she was in love with the master. She had a deep sense of her inferior situation in life, and was almost hopeless of ever attracting his attention. And I do think that this love, which was quite hopeless, which was an ingrown thing, took this form; she herself, in her imagination—yes, unconscious of her motives—designed all this drama to make the desired situation possible—that she would arrive somewhere at a level with the man she loved and create some sort of communication with him.

TATE: I agree with you, Miss Porter, but it has always seemed to me that that level of the governess's experience—that is, her personal motivation, what she expected to get out of it and all that

—has a perfectly naturalistic basis. Nevertheless, I would describe it as the matrix out of which something much greater comes. As a matter of fact, we can go back and take the great tragic characters in drama, or the great religious heroes, too. They will all have some psychological motivation which we can see in terms of their peculiar situations. At the same time, are we agreed that in the case of the true saints, of the great tragic heroes, possibly in the case of the governess here, the psychological basis doesn't explain it all?

PORTER: The popular psychological explanation is too superficial.

VAN DOREN: Otherwise we should be aware that an explanation is ready and easy as we read along, whereas the truth is—we all grant this—that as we read along we're not explaining anything to ourselves at all. We're not saying: Well, a dreadful, dreadful thing is happening, yet we know the reason. In a very important sense we don't know the reason. Something is loose here in the world, if only in the mind of a woman. Something is loose in the world which is very powerful and beyond the control of any human being.

PORTER: I would say quite beyond the Freudian explanation.

VAN DOREN: Oh, decidedly.

PORTER: Here is one place where I find Freud completely defeated.

TATE: James knew substantially all that Freud knew before Freud came on the scene.

PORTER: All major artists do.

VAN DOREN: Any great story-teller has to, because a great story-teller has for his subject good and evil.

TATE: There is an aspect of this story which has always interested me very much. It is what we might call the technical aspects. I should think readers of the story would be very much interested in how James established the realities of these things which would otherwise be incredible. Consider the fact that the story is told by a governess and the fact that, as Mr. Van Doren said some time ago, in reading it we tend to forget that the governess is telling it; we think we are actually participating. That is due, I think, to the great art of James. Isn't it true that one trouble with the first-person narrative, the story told by somebody in the story, is that the authority of that person is usually not quite established? We say usually of such a person: she is participating in it, you can't expect her to give us an unbiased version of it; she's not sufficiently detached; she's not disinterested. But, while that's a liability in most first-person narratives, it seems to me that James's triumph consists in the fact that he has been able to take the defect of the method and use it for a positive purpose. The very fact that the governess is biased becomes a dramatic factor. The bias becomes a part of the story.

PORTER: Yes, and because she has no understanding at all of her real motive, she gives herself away completely and constantly.

TATE: Constantly. There are two levels: the level at which she sees the action and the level at which the reader can see it, and this creates an irony of which the governess is not aware.

VAN DOREN: She is not aware, for instance, of how much it is against her own nature and her own desire to plague the little boy at the end, to make him tell more and more and more about the bad things he had done. They turn out to be rather slight things, don't you think? No reader assumes that the little boy has done anything very bad.

TATE: Nothing bad at all.

PORTER: Some vague little offense against Victorian morality, no doubt.

VAN DOREN: Yet the governess all along has wanted to spare the children. Indeed, her declared intention was to protect, to shield them. Here she is forced by the irony of her character and fate to torture this little boy into confessions which he doesn't want to make, which he doesn't even know how to make because he has nothing to confess.

TATE: Isn't that a wonderful scene in Miles's room at night? The governess comes—it bears out just what you were saying, Mr. Van Doren—she comes to have a talk with him, as you will remember, and to try to get out of him what he did at school. It's a general stock-taking of Miles's situation. It is one of the most powerful pieces of irony I've ever read, because the governess is actually making love to the little boy and she doesn't know it. But he knows it in a curious instinctive way; he blows the candle out to get rid of her.

PORTER: And the scene is wonderfully written—his terror at this visit in the night, with what for him was ghost or devil, all evil in fact, everything he had reason to be terrified of, coming into his room with that unpardonable invasion of his privacy—this is all projected with such admirable simplicity and directness that the reader forgets the words and shares the impression.

VAN DOREN: His very childish understanding of the fact that she is in love with him comes out, it seems to me, in the conversation in which he suggests that he should be going back to school now, because, after all, he's just a "fellow," and has no right to spend all of his time with a lady.

TATE: He shows something perfectly wonderful there. It is so simple that the implications are sometimes lost on the reader. He is sitting with her and there's a silence. The governess says, "Well, here we are." And Miles says, "Yes, we're here." Just like that.

VAN DOREN: That's right. But again it seems to me that the fame of this story among all of James's stories is justified by the fact that the evil in it somehow remains pure and general, remains undefined. All of the attempts on the part of the governess to find out what it is, after all, are frustrated. There is never any danger that evil will shrink here into vice, into misdemeanor.

TATE: James says that evil is never credible in fiction if it is presented in "weak specifications."

VAN DOREN: We have all had the experience of reading a story about some villain whom we can believe to be unspeakable—we like to believe in unspeakable villains—and then of being shocked by the discovery that all he did was murder his grandmother. That never is enough.

PORTER: Yes, nearly always the specific act, the crime, does seem inadequate compared to the great force of evil which produces it.

VAN DOREN: I am reminded of Iago, whose evil is never explained by the specific motives he is said to have, and even himself thinks he has. Iago thinks that he is jealous of Othello, but it isn't jealousy, it isn't ambition, it isn't anything you can name at all. That is why Iago is a force. He is one of these figures who are being used.

TATE: But he's an evil figure, not merely a bad one. There's a fundamental difference between the evil and the bad.

VAN DOREN: Good and evil is the distinction. I wonder if everyone agrees with us that the great theme is good and evil. We keep saying so.

PORTER: Yes, or rather the conflict between them in the minds of men.

VAN DOREN: Do you suppose anyone doubts us?

TATE: Otherwise we get merely social literature, the literature of social problems, political and economic literature.

PORTER: I think that during the nineteenth century, when the perfectability of man was an accepted doctrine, James was one of the few who had this genuine knowledge of good and evil, and the courage to take it as his theme.

TATE: I would like to read the very last paragraph of this story. It is the moment after Miles has died. He is lying there dead and the governess is looking at him.

"But he had already jerked straight round, stared, glared again and seen but the quiet day. With the stroke of the loss I was so proud of, he uttered a cry of a creature hurled over an abyss, and the grasp with which I recovered him might have been that of catching him in his fall. I caught him; yes, I held him, it may be imagined with what a passion. But at the end of a minute I began to feel what it truly was that I held. We were alone with the quiet day and his little heart, dispossessed, had stopped."

Mr. Edmund Wilson and *The Turn of the Screw*

A. J. A. Waldock

Some years ago Mr. Edmund Wilson wrote an essay—which has since become famous, or not far short of it—on "The Ambiguity of Henry James."[1] In it he propounded a theory of *The Turn of the Screw*. The theory, in brief, is that the story is not a proper ghost-story at all, but a study in the psychology of a frustrated Anglo-Saxon spinster. The governess, who sees the ghosts, is neurotic and "repressed," and the ghosts are merely symptoms of her state—not "real" ghosts, but only hallucinations. No one, as far as I know, has troubled to point out that the theory is quite untenable, that—apart from general considerations—there are details within the story itself that decisively negative it.

The apparition of the man is first seen by the governess at a distance: he is on the tower. She sees him clearly enough to realize that he is unknown to her. She is strangely affected, but does not report the occurrence. The next time she sees him it is at close quarters. She takes in every detail of his appearance, and *does* report the occurrence. She describes the man she saw to Mrs. Grose, the housekeeper; and before she is half-way through her description Mrs. Grose has identified the person being described: the late Peter Quint, the valet. Two points are to be observed. (1) The identification is absolute. Mrs. Grose is not merely reminded of Peter Quint by the description: she recognizes him positively in it. The man

SOURCE: *Modern Language Notes,* LXII (May, 1947), 331–334. Reprinted by permission of the editors.

[1] Published originally in *Hound and Horn,* VII (April–June, 1934), 385–406. The essay, slightly modified, was republished in Mr. Wilson's *The Triple Thinkers,* and, more recently, in *American Harvest.*

the governess saw *was* Peter Quint, or his absolute double: this is a fact of the story. (2) Up to this moment the governess has never heard of Peter Quint.

Here are two stubborn facts of the story, and *they must be accounted* for. There are others, but these two will do, for unless they are accounted for Mr. Wilson's whole case collapses like a house of cards. "Almost everything from beginning to end," he declares, "can be read equally in either of two senses."[2] "Almost everything"! But what if there is one thing, one little thing, that cannot be read in either of two senses, that can be read only in one sense? What then? How strange that Mr. Wilson does not see that any such fact, however insignificant, could be the sharp little rock on which his whole theory must split.

I suggest that it does split on the fact just noted. Mr. Wilson, it is true, makes a brave attempt to steer round it.

> When we look back [he says] we see that even this has been left open to a double interpretation. The governess has never heard of the valet, but it has been suggested to her in conversation with the housekeeper that there has been some other male somewhere about who "liked everyone young and pretty," and the idea of this other person has been ambiguously confused with the master and with the master's possible interest in her, the present governess. And has she not, in her subconscious imagination, taking her cue from this, identified herself with her predecessor and conjured up an image who wears the master's clothes but who (the Freudian "censor" coming into play) looks debased, "like an actor," she says (would he not have to stoop to love her!)? The apparition had "straight good features" and his appearance is described in detail. When we look back we find that the master's appearance has never been described at all: we have merely been told that he was "handsome." It is impossible for us to know how much the ghost resembles the master—certainly the governess would never tell us.[3]

I will not attempt to comment on the psychology of this. Let us still stick—amid the giddy swirl of these subconscious identifications, transferences and projections—to the facts. (1) "An image who wears the master's clothes." Peter Quint was the valet, and made free with his master's clothes: Mrs. Grose tells us this. So there is no reason why his ghost should not have been seen wearing them: Mrs. Grose expected that he *would* be wearing them. (2) "The

[2] Quoted from the version of the essay as it appeared in *The Triple Thinkers* (Oxford, 1938), 130. Argumentatively, it would have been better for Mr. Wilson to have stuck to his original flat assertion: "*everything* from beginning to end" etc.

[3] Quoted again from *The Triple Thinkers,* 125–126.

apparition . . . is described in detail." He emphatically is. The man had red hair, close-curling; queer little red whiskers; eyebrows somewhat darker than the hair and the whiskers, and particularly arched; wide mouth, thin lips. He was clean-shaven except for the little whiskers, and he wore no hat.[4]

What does Mr. Wilson really mean? Is he suggesting that the master was so like Quint—queer little red whiskers and all—that the governess was capable of experiencing an hallucination of the master and of describing him in such detail to Mrs. Grose that Mrs. Grose recognized him instantly as the valet? Has Mr. Wilson (one wonders) ever really tried to make quite clear to himself what he means by that concluding sentence about the possible likeness between the master and the ghost?

Once more let us face the critical question. Let us grant, for the sake of the argument, the governess neurotic; let us concede all the "identifications" Mr. Wilson wishes. How did the governess succeed in projecting on vacancy, out of her own subconscious mind, a perfectly precise, point-by-point image of a man, then dead, whom she had never seen in her life and never heard of? What psychology, normal or abnormal, will explain that? And what is the right word for such a vision but "ghost"?

[4] *The Aspern Papers* etc. (London: Macmillan and Co., 1922), 167.

The Turn of the Screw as Poem

Robert Heilman

There is probably no other short work of fiction which has been the center, during the first fifty years of its life, of such regular attention and speculation as have been called forth by Henry James's *The Turn of the Screw.* The more obvious reasons for this phenomenon—those summarized, for instance, in Heywood Broun's rather uncomplex description of *The Turn* as "the thriller of thrillers, the last word in creeping horror stories"—actually explain almost nothing. For thrillers that exert a "hideous thralldom" are incontinently begotten and die, like movies, each year; and the continuing devotion to *The Turn* has hardly been that of the multitudes in search of hashish. That devotion is significant, indeed, because it has been critical; *The Turn* has elicited special comment from such writers as Edmund Wilson, Philip Rahv, F. O. Matthiessen, Katherine Anne Porter, Mark Van Doren, Allen Tate. Since the book first appeared, there has been a series of interpretations; as these come forth periodically, and as the alterations in them show the different decades endeavoring to adjust James's materials to new interpretative methods, what is unmistakable is that James has hit upon some fundamental truth of experience that no generation can ignore and that each generation wishes to restate in its own terms. For half a century sensitive readers have felt the story exert a pull that far transcends any effects springing from the cool manipulations of mystery-mongers. Mr. Matthiessen's remark that the story exhibits James's "extraordinary command of . . . the darkness of moral evil"

SOURCE: *The University of Kansas City Review,* XIV (Summer, 1948), 277–289. Published also in *Forms of Modern Fiction,* William Van O'Connor, editor, Minneapolis: University of Minnesota Press, 1948, pp. 211–228. Reprinted by permission of *The University of Kansas City Review* and of the author.

suggests the nature of the almost unique reality with which the story is infused. For critical readers the problem has been the definition of the evil, and the identification of the methods by which the awareness of evil is brought to disturbing intensity.

It is probably safe to say that the Freudian interpretation of the story, of which the best known exponent is Edmund Wilson, no longer enjoys wide critical acceptance.[1] If, then, we cannot account for the evil by treating the governess as pathological, we must seek elsewhere an explanation of the story's hold. I am convinced that, at the level of action, the story means exactly what it says: that at Bly there are apparitions which the governess sees, which Mrs. Grose does not see but comes to believe in because they are consistent with her own independent experience, and of which the children have a knowledge which they endeavor to conceal. These dramatic circumstances have a symbolic import which seems not too difficult to get hold of: the ghosts are evil, evil which comes subtly, conquering before it is wholly seen; the governess, Cassandra-like in the intuitions which are inaccessible to others, is the guardian whose function it is to detect and attempt to ward off evil; Mrs. Grose—whose name, like the narrator's title, has virtually allegorical significance—is the commonplace mortal, well intentioned, but perceiving only the obvious; the children are the victims of evil, victims who, ironically, practice concealment—who doubtless must conceal—when not to conceal is essential to salvation. If this reading of the symbolism be tenable, we can understand in part the imaginative power of the story, for, beneath the strange and startling action-surface, we have the oldest of themes—the struggle of evil to possess the human soul. And if this struggle appears to resolve itself into a Christian form, that impulse, as it were, of the materials need not be surprising.

II

But the compelling theme and the extraordinarily vivid plot-form are not the entirety of *The Turn of the Screw;* there are other

[1] Philip Rahv calls attempts to explain away the ghosts "a fallacy of rationalism," and asserts, I think correctly, that the Freudian view narrows and conventionalizes the story in a way that contradicts both James's intentions and artistic habits, and, I might add, our own sense that large matters are at stake. In their symposium in *Invitation to Learning,* Katherine Anne Porter, Mark Van Doren, and Allen Tate have all specifically denied the validity of the Freudian reading of the story. I have attempted, in some detail, to show how Wilson's account of *The Turn* runs afoul of both the story and James's preface (*Modern Language Notes,* 1947, pp. 433–45).

methods by which James extends and intensifies his meaning and strikes more deeply into the reader's consciousness. Chief of these is a highly suggestive and even symbolic language which permeates the entire story. After I had become aware of and begun to investigate this phenomenon, I found Mr. Matthiessen, in quite fortuitous corroboration of my own critical method, commenting on the same technical aspect of James's later works—his ability to "bind together his imaginative effects by subtly recurrent images of a thematic kind" and to "extend a metaphor into a symbol," and the fact that later in his career "realistic details had become merely the covering for a content that was far from realistic." In *The Turn* there is a great deal of recurrent imagery which powerfully influences the tone and the meaning of the story; the story becomes, indeed, a dramatic poem, and to read it properly one must assess the role of the language precisely as one would if public form of the work were poetic. For by his iterative imagery and by the very unobtrusive management of symbols, which in the organic work co-function with the language, James has severely qualified the bare narrative; and, if he has not defined the evil which, as he specified, was to come to the reader as something monstrous and unidentified, he has at least set forth the mode and the terms of its operation with unrecognized fullness.

For a mature reader it is hardly necessary to insist that the center of horror is not the apparitions themselves, though their appearances are worked out with fine uniqueness, but is the children, and our sense of what is happening to them. What is happening to them is Quint and Jessel; the governess's awareness of the apparitions is her awareness of a change within the children; the shock of ghostly appearances is the shock of evil perceived unexpectedly, suddenly, after it has secretly made inroads. Matthiessen and R. P. Blackmur both refer, as a matter of course, to the corruption of the children; E. M. W. Tillyard, in a volume on Shakespeare, remarks incidentally that James "owes so much of the power with which evil is conveyed to showing it in the minds of children; where it should least be found." Perhaps two modern phenomena, the sentimentalizing of children and the disinclination to concede to evil any status more profound than the melodramatic, account for a frequent unwillingness to accept what the story says. James is not disposed to make things easier; he emphasizes that it is the incorruptible who have taken on corruption. He introduces no mere pathos of childhood catastrophe; his are not ordinary children. He is at pains to give them a special quality—by repetition which in so careful an artist can hardly have been a clumsy accident. As the repeated words achieve a cumulative tonal force, we can see the working of the poetic imagination.

Flora has "extraordinary charm," is "most beautiful." Miles is "incredibly beautiful." Both have "the bloom of health and happiness." Miles is "too fine and fair" for the world; he is a "beautiful little boy." The governess is "dazzled by their loveliness." They are "most loveable" in their "helplessness." Touching their "fragrant faces" one could believe only "their incapacity and their beauty." Miles is a "prodigy of delightful, loveable goodness." In midstory Flora still emerges from concealment "rosily," and one is caught by "the golden glow of her curls," by her "loveliest, eagerest simplicity," by "the excess of something beautiful that shone out of the blue" of her eyes, by "the lovely little lighted face." In both, "beauty and amiability, happiness and cleverness" are still paramount. Miles has still the "wonderful smile" and the "beautiful eye" of "a little fairy prince." Both write letters "too beautiful to be posted." On the final Sunday the governess sees still Miles's "beautiful face" and talks of him as "beautiful and perfect"; he smiles at her "with the same loveliness" and spars verbally with "serenity" and "unimpeachable gaiety." Even after Flora is gone, Miles is "the beautiful little presence" as yet with "neither stain nor shadow"; his expression is "the most beautiful" the governess has ever known.

James devotes an almost prodigal care to creating an impression of special beauty in the children, an impression upon which depends the extraordinary effectiveness of the change which takes place in them. In such children the appearance of any imperfection is a shock. The shock is emphasized when the governess wonders whether she must "pronounce their loveliness a trick of premature cunning" and reflects upon the possibility that "the immediate charm . . . was studied"; when Miles's "sweet face" must be described as a "sweet ironic face"; when his "happy laugh" goes off into "incoherent, extravagant song"; and when, above all, the governess must declare with conviction that their "more than earthly beauty, their absolutely unnatural goodness [is] a game, . . . a policy and a fraud."

Is James, then, laboriously overusing the principle of contrast, clothing the children with an astonishing fascination merely to accentuate the shock of their being stripped bare? Obviously not. Beneath the superficial clash we can already sense a deeper paradox. When James speaks of Miles's "beautiful fevered face" and says that he "lives in a setting of beauty and misery," he puts into words what the reader has already come to feel—that his real subject is the dual nature of man, who is a little lower than the angels, and who yet can become a slave in the realm of evil. The children's beauty, we have come to feel, is a symbol of the spiritual perfection of which man is capable. Thus the battle between the governess and the demons becomes the old struggle of the morality play in new dress.

III

But that statement of the struggle is much more general and abstract than the formulation of it made by the story itself. When James speaks of "any clouding of their innocence," he reminds us again of a special quality in their beauty which he has quietly stressed with almost thematic fullness. The *clouding* suggests a *change* in a characteristic brightness of theirs, a brightness of which we are made aware by a recurrent imagery of light. Flora, at the start, "brightly" faces the new governess; hers is a "radiant" image; the children "dazzle" the governess; Flora has "a lovely little lighted face," and she considers "luminously"; in his "brightness" Miles "fairly glittered"; he speaks "radiantly"; at his "revolution" he speaks with "extraordinary brightness." This light-giving quality of theirs is more than a mere amplification of a charm shockingly to be destroyed; it is difficult not to read it as a symbol of their being, as it were, at the dawn of existence. For they are children, and their radiance suggests the primal and the universal. This provisional interpretation is supported by another verbal pattern which James uses to describe the children. Miles has a "great glow of freshness," a "positive fragrance of purity," a "sweetness of innocence"; the governess comments again on the "rose-flush of his innocence"; in him she finds something "extraordinarily happy, that, . . . struck me as beginning anew each day"; he could draw upon "reserves of goodness." Then, as things change, the governess remarks, on one occasion, that "He couldn't play any longer at innocence," and mentions, on another, his pathetic struggles to "play . . . a part of innocence." To the emphasis upon beauty, then, is added this emphasis upon brightness and freshness and innocence. What must come across to us, from such a context, is echoes of the Garden of Eden; we have the morality play story, as we have said, but altered, complemented, and given unique poignance by being told of mankind at its first radical crisis, in consequence of which all other morality stories are; Miles and Flora become the childhood of the race. They are symbolic children as the ghosts are symbolic ghosts. Even the names themselves have a representative quality as those of James's characters often do:

Miles—the soldier, the archetypal male; Flora—the flower, the essential female. Man and woman are caught even before the first hint of maturity, dissected, and shown to have within them all the seeds—possible of full growth even now—of their own destruction.

James's management of the setting and of other ingredients in the drama deepens one's sense of a story at once primeval and eternal, lurking beneath the surface of the action. Bly itself is almost an Eden with its "lawn and bright flowers"; the governess comments, "The scene had a greatness . . ." Three times James writes of the "golden" sky, and one unconsciously recalls that Flora was a "rosy sprite" with "hair of gold." Miss Jessel first appears "in the garden," where "the old trees, the thick shrubbery, made a great and pleasant shade. . . ." Here, for a time, the three "lived in a cloud of music and love . . ."; the children are "extraordinarily at one" in "their quality of sweetness." Now it is significant that James uses even the seasons to heighten his drama: the pastoral idyl begins in June, when spring is at the full, and then is gradually altered until we reach the dark ending of a November whose coldness and deadness are unobtrusively but unmistakably stressed: ". . . the autumn had dropped . . . and blown out half our lights" (a variation of the light-pattern); the governess now notices "grey sky and withered garlands," "bared spaces and scattered dead leaves." What might elsewhere be Gothic trimming is here disciplined by the pattern. When, on the final Sunday night, the governess tries hard to "reach" Miles, there is "a great wind"; she hears "the lash of the rain and the batter of the gusts"; at the climax there is "an extraordinary blast and chill," and then darkness. The next afternoon is "damp and grey." After Flora's final escapade at the pond, James stresses the governess's feelings at the end of the day; the evening is "portentous" without precedent; she blows out the candles and feels a "mortal coldness." On the final day with Miles she notices "the stupid shrubs," "the dull things of November," "the dim day." So it is not merely the end of a year but the end of a cycle: the spring of gay, bright human innocence has given way to the dark autumn—or rather, as we might pun, to the dark *fall.*

And in the darkness of the latter end of things we might note the special development of the light which, to the sensitive governess, the children seem actually to give off. It is, I think, more than a coincidence that, when the governess mentions Miss Jessel, Flora's face shows a "quick, smitten glare," and that, in the final scene, Miles is twice said to be "glaring"—the same verb which has been used to describe Quint's look. All three characters, of course, look with malevolence; yet *glare* must suggest, also, a hard, powerful, ugly light—an especially effective transformation of the apparently benign luminousness of the spring.

The same movement of human experience James portrays in still another symbolic form. As the light changes and the season changes and the children's beauty becomes ambiguous, another alteration takes place in them. Their youth, of course, is the prime datum of the story, and of it we are ever conscious; and at the same time we are aware of a strange maturity in them—in, for instance, their poise, their controlled utilization of their unusual talents to give pleasure. Our sense of something that transcends their youth is first defined overtly late in the story when the governess speaks of her feeling that Miles is "accessible as an older person." Though she does not speak of change, there is subtly called forth in us a conviction that years have been added to Miles. So we are not surprised when the governess assures Mrs. Grose, and goes out of her way, a little later, to remind her of the assurance, that, at meetings with Miss Jessel, Flora is "not a child" but "an old, old woman"—an insight that receives a measure of authentication, perhaps, by its reminiscence of the Duessa motif. The suggestion that Flora has become older is skillfully conveyed, in the pond scene, by her silence (and silence itself has an almost symbolic value throughout the story), by her quick recovery of her poised gaiety, and especially by the picture of her peeping at the governess over the shoulder of Mrs. Grose, who is embracing her—the first intimation of a cold adult calculatingness which appears in all her remaining actions. The governess says, ". . . her incomparable childish beauty had suddenly failed, had quite vanished . . . she was literally . . . hideously, hard; she had turned common and almost ugly." Mrs. Grose sums up, "It has made her, every inch of her, quite old." More effective, however, than any of this direct presentation of vital change is a delicate symbol which may pass almost unnoticed: when she is discovered at the pond, Flora picks up, and drops a moment later, "a big, ugly spray of withered fern"—a quiet commentary on the passage of symbolic spring, on the spiritual withering that is the story's center. When, at the end of the scene, the governess looks "at the grey pool and its blank, haunted edge," we automatically recall, "The sedge has withered from the lake"—the imagery used by Keats in his account of an ailing knight-at-arms in another bitter autumn.

Besides the drying of foliage and the coming of storms and darkness there is one other set of elements, loosely working together and heavy with implications, which suggest that this is a story of the decay of Eden. At Quint's first appearance Bly "had been stricken with death." After Miles's nocturnal exploit the governess utters a cliché that, under the influence of the context, becomes vigorously meaningful: ". . . you . . . caught your death in the night air!" There are, further, some arresting details in the description of Quint: "His eyes are sharp, strange—awfully; . . . rather small and very fixed. His mouth's wide, and his lips are thin, . . ." These are unmistakably the characteristics of a snake. James is too fine an artist to allegorize the point, but, as he has shaped the story, the coming of Quint is the coming of the serpent into the little Eden that is Bly (both Miss Porter and Mr. Tate have noted other physical characteristics of Quint which traditionally belong to the devil). Quint's handsomeness and his borrowed finery, by which he apes the gentleman, suggest, perhaps, the specious plausibleness of the visitor in the Garden. As for the "fixed eyes": later we learn that Miss Jessel "only fixed the child" and that the apparition of Quint "fixed me exactly as it had fixed me from the tower and from the garden." Of Quint's position at Bly Mrs. Grose says, "The master believed in him and placed him here because he was supposed not to be well and the country air so good for him." The master, in other words, has nourished a viper in his bosom. The secret influence upon Miles the governess describes as "poison," and at the very end she says that the demonic presence "filled the room like the taste of poison." In the first passage the governess equates "poison" with "secret precocity"; toward the end she emphasizes Miles's freedom and sorrowfully gives up "the fiction that I had anything more to teach him." Why is it a fiction? Because he already knew too much, because he had eaten of the fruit of the tree of knowledge? We have already been told of the "dark prodigy" by which "the imagination of all evil *had* been opened up to him," and of his being "under some influence operating in his small intellectual life as a tremendous incitement."

IV

We should not press such analogies too hard, or construct inflexible parables. Our business is rather to trace all the imaginative emanations that enrich the narrative, the associations and intimations by which it transcends the mere horror story and achieves its own kind of greatness. But by now it must be clear from the antipodal emphases of the story that James has an almost religious sense of the duality of man, and, as if to manifest an intention, he makes that sense explicit in terms broadly religious and even Christian. The image of Flora's "angelic beauty" is "beatific"; she has "the deep, sweet serenity . . . of one of Raphael's holy infants"; she has "placid heavenly eyes." In Miles there is "something divine that I have never found to the same degree in any child." In a mildly humorous context the children are called "cherubs." Seeing no signs of suffering from his school experience, the governess regards Miles as an "angel." Mrs. Grose imputes to Flora a "blessed innocence," and the governess surrenders to the children's "extraordinary childish grace"—a noun which in this patterned structure can hardly help being ambivalent. In mid-story Flora has still a "divine smile"; both children remain "adorable." This verbal pattern, which is too consistent to be coincidental, irresistibly makes us think of the divine in man, of his capability of salvation. Now what is tragic and terrifying in man is that to be capable of salvation is to be capable also of damnation—an equivocal potentiality suggested early by the alternation of moods in the newly arrived governess, who senses immediately a kind of wavering, a waiting for determination, at Bly. And James, to present the spiritual decline of the children, finds terms which exactly balance those that connote their spiritual capabilities.

We are never permitted to see the apparitions except as moral realities. Miss Jessel is a figure of "unmistakeable horror and evil . . . in black, pale and dreadful." She is a "horror of horrors," with "awful eyes," "with a kind of fury of intention," and yet "with extraordinary beauty." Again she is described as "Dark as midnight in her black dress, her haggard beauty, and her unutterable woe. . . ." It is brilliant to give her beauty, which not only identifies her with Flora and thus underscores the dual possibilities that lie ahead of Flora, but also enriches the theme with its reminder of Milton's fallen angels who retain something of their original splendor—"the excess / Of glory obscured." So, with the repeated stress upon her woe, we almost expect the passage which tells us that she "suffers the torments . . . of the damned": she is both damned and an agent of damnation—another reminiscence of the Miltonic myth. She is called later a "pale and ravenous demon," not "an inch of whose evil . . . fell short"—which reminds us of James's prefatory insistence that the apparitions were to be thought of as demons. Again, she is "our infernal witness"; she and Quint are "those fiends"; "they were not angels," and they could be bringing "some yet more infernal message." "And to ply them with that evil still, to keep up the work of demons, is what brings the others back." They are "tempters," who work subtly by holding out fascinating "suggestions of danger." In the last scene Quint presents—the phrase is used twice—"his white face of damnation."

By this series of words, dispersed throughout the story yet combining in a general statement, James defines as diabolic the forces attacking the children of whose angelic part we are often reminded. Now these attacking forces, as often in Elizabethan drama, are seen in two aspects. Dr. Faustus has to meet an enemy which has an inner and an outer reality—his own thoughts, and Mephistopheles; James presents evil both as agent (the demons) and as effect (the transformation in the once fresh and beautiful and innocent children). The dualistic concept of reality appears most explicitly when Mrs. Grose asks, "And if he was so bad there as that comes to, how is he such an angel now?" and the governess replies, "Yes, indeed—and if he was a fiend at school!" By the *angel-fiend* antithesis James underscores what he sees as a central human contradiction, which he emphasizes throughout the book by his chosen verbal pattern. The governess speaks of the children's "love of evil" gained from Quint and Miss Jessel, of Miles's "wickedness" at school. In such a context the use of the word *revolution* to describe Miles's final taking matters up with the governess—a move by which, we should remember, he becomes completely "free"—cannot help calling to mind the Paradise and Eden revolutions of Judæo-Christian mythology. The revolutionary change in character is nicely set forth by the verbal counterpoint in one passage. "He found the most divine little way," the governess says, "to keep me quiet while she went off." "'Divine'?" Mrs. Grose asks, and the governess replies, "Infernal then!" The divine has paradoxically passed into the infernal. Then we see rapidly the completed transition in Flora: she turns upon the governess an expression of "hard, fixed gravity" and ignores the "hideous plain presence" of Miss Jessel—"a stroke that somehow converted the little girl herself into the very presence that could make me quail." In Miles, by contrast, we see a protracted struggle, poignantly conveyed by a recurrent metaphor of illness. Early in the story Miles is in "the bloom of health and happiness," but near the end he seems like a "wistful patient in a children's hospital," "like a convalescent slightly fatigued." At the end he shows "bravery" while "flushing with pain"; he gives "a sick little headshake"; his is a "beautiful fevered face." But the beauty goes, the fever gains; Miles gives "a frantic little shake for air and light"; he is in a "white rage." The climax of his disease, the binding together of all the strands we have been tracing, is his malevolent cry to the governess—"you devil!" It is his final transvaluation of values: she who would be his savior has become for him a demon. His face gives a "convulsive supplication"—that is, actually, a prayer, for and to Quint, the demon who has become his total deity. But the god isn't there, and Miles despairs and dies. We need not labor the dependence of this brilliant climax upon the host of associations and evocations by which, as this outline endeavors to show, James prepares us for the ultimate resolution of the children's being.

There are glimmerings of other imaginative kinships, such as that already mentioned, the Faustian. Miles's "You devil" is in one way almost identical with Faustus's savage attack, in Marlowe's play, upon the Old Man who has been trying to save him; indeed James's story, in its central combat, is not unlike the Faustus story as it might be told by the Good Angel. But whereas Dr. Faustus is a late intellectualist version of Everyman, James, as we have said, weaves in persuasive hints, one after another, of mankind undergoing, in his Golden Age, an elemental conflict: thus we have the morality play, but in a complicated, enriched, and intensified version. When the governess first sees Quint, she is aware of "some challenge between us"; the next time it seems "as if I had been looking at him for years and had known him always"; near the end she says, "I *was* . . . face to face with the elements," and, of the final scene, "It was like fighting with a demon for a human soul."

V

What, then, does the story say about the role of the governess, and how does this contribute to the complex of the impressions built up in part by James's language? From the start the words used by the governess suggest that James is attaching to her the quality of savior, not only in a general sense, but with certain Christian associations. She uses words like "atonement"; she speaks of herself as an "expiatory victim," of her "pure suffering," and at various times—twice in the final scene—of her "torment." Very early she plans to "shelter my pupils," to "absolutely save" them; she speaks variously of her "service," "to protect and defend the little creatures . . . bereaved . . . loveable." When she fears that she cannot "save or shield them" and that "they're lost," she is a "poor protectress." At another time she is a "sister of Charity" attempting to "cure" Miles. But by now what we cannot mistake is the relation of pastor and flock, a relationship which becomes overt when the governess tells Miles, "I just want you to help me to save you." It is in this sense that the governess "loves" Miles—a loving which must not be confused, as it is confused by some critics, with "making love to" or "being in love with" him. Without such pastoral love no guardian would consider his flock worth the sacrifice. The governess's priestly function is made still more explicit by the fact that she comes ultimately to act as confessor and to use every possible means to bring Miles to confession; the long final scene really takes place in the confessional, with the governess as priest endeavoring, by both word and gesture, to protect her charge against the evil force whose invasion has, with consummate irony, carried even there. In one sense the governess must elicit confession because, in her need for objective reassurance, she will not take the lead as accuser; but securing the confession is, more importantly, a mitigation of Miles's own pride, his self-will; it could soften him, make him accessible to grace. The experience has a clear sacramental quality: the governess says that Miles senses "the need of confession . . . he'll confess. If he confesses, he's saved." It is when he begins to break and confess that "the white face of damnation" becomes baffled and at a vital moment retreats; but it returns "as if to blight his confession," and it is in part through the ineptitude of the governess-confessor-savior, we are led to understand, that Miles is lost.

It is possible that there are even faint traces of theological speculation to give additional substance to the theme of salvation and damnation which finally achieves specific form in the sacramentalism of the closing scenes. Less than halfway through the story the governess refers to the children thus: "blameless and foredoomed as they were." By *blameless* she can only mean that she does not have direct, tangible evidence of voluntary evil-doing on their part; they still look charming and beautiful; she does not have grounds for a positive placing of blame. Why, then, "foredoomed"? May this not be a suggestion of original sin (which Miss Porter has already seen as an ingredient in the story), an interpretation consistent with the view of Bly as a kind of Eden? Three-quarters of the way through the story the governess again turns to speculation: ". . . I constantly both attacked and renounced the enigma of what such a little gentleman could have done that deserved a penalty." *Enigma* is perhaps just the word to be applied to a situation, of which one technical explication is the doctrine of original sin, by an inquiring lay mind with a religious sense but without precise theological tools. What is significant is that the governess does not revolt against the penalty as if it betokened a cosmic injustice. And original sin, whether it be natural depravity or a revolt in a heavenly or earthly paradise, fits exactly into the machinery of this story of two beautiful children who in a lovely springtime of existence already suffer, not unwillingly, hidden injuries which will eventually destroy them.

VI

This summary of the imaginative overtones in *The Turn of the Screw* has taken us rather deeply into a view of the book as strongly religious in cast. Yet this very moving impression is produced by agencies that quietly penetrate the story, not by devices that stick out of it, so to speak, and become commanding guideposts. There are no old familiar signs announcing a religious orientation of experience. There is nothing of the Bible overtly; there are no texts, no clergymen; there are no conventional indices of religious feeling—no invocations or prayers or meditations; all there is is a certain amount of church-going of a very matter-of-fact sort, and otherwise the context is ostensibly secular. Thus the story becomes no bland preachment; it simply "has life"—to use James's criterion of excellence—and it is left to us to define the boundaries and extensions and reverberations of that life. Right where we might expect the most positive assistance, perhaps, in seeking that definition, we find least. Yet even in a few dry and casual ecclesiastical mementoes we sense some ever-so-mild symbolic pressures, as of a not-very-articulate wispish presence that quietly makes itself felt. These intimations of a presence would not be magnified into a solid "character" who demands our attention. But in their small way they collaborate with other intimations. The reading of the story, for instance, takes place during the Christmas season; the framework action begins on Christmas Eve. Quint appears for the second time on a Sunday, a grey, rainy Sunday, just before the governess is about to go to the late church service with Mrs. Grose; after that she is, she says, "not fit for church"; and their only service is then "a little service of tears and vows, of prayers and promises, . . ." This is the important occasion on which Mrs. Grose identifies the apparition with Quint. As the governess reflects on the situation, she speaks of the "inconceivable communion" of which she has learned—a Black Mass, as it were. The event next in importance to the identification of Quint also occurs on a Sunday—Miles's "revolution." Miles and the governess are "within sight of the church"; she thinks "with envy" of the "almost spiritual help of the hassock." After they enter the churchyard gate, Miles detains her "by a low, oblong, table-like tomb"—a reminder that Bly was "stricken with death" on the first appearance of Quint. Then Miles threatens to bring his uncle down, and it is he, with fine irony, who "marched off alone into church," while the governess can only walk "round the church" and listen "to the sounds of worship." Here, for once, what we may call the

Christian apparatus is out in the open, with a clear enough ironic function. From this we go on to the most tantalizing body of suggestion in the whole book, less a body than a wraith, indeed, and yet the more urgent for its not falling within the every-day commonplaces of fictional method. Miles's revolution introduces a straight-line action which continues with remarkably increasing tension to the end of the story. James allots forty percent of his total space to this action, which—and here is the notable point—takes only three days. Thus he puts the heaviest emphasis on those three days—Sunday, Monday, and Tuesday. During those three days the governess, the clergyman's daughter, undertakes her quasi-priestly function with a new intensity and aggressiveness. On Sunday night she enters upon a newly determined, if still cautious, effort to bring Miles to confession; she openly asserts her role as savior. On Monday she tries to shock Flora into spiritual pliability—and fails. All her will to redeem, she now turns upon Miles; in the final scene she fights the adversary directly. She succeeds to an extent: Miles cannot see Quint. But the end of the climactic triduum of her ordeal as savior is failure: Quint comes again, as if to "blight" Miles's confession; Miles still cannot see him—and dies. The would-be redeemer of the living is called "devil"; in Quint we see one who has risen again to tempt the living to destruction—that is, the resurrection and the death. Here, Sunday does not triumphantly end a symbolic ordeal that had begun in apparent failure on Friday; rather it hopefully initiates a struggle which is to end, on the third day, in bitter loss. We have, then, a modern late-fall defeat patterned on the ancient springtide victory. To transmit its quality and to embrace all of its associations, may we not call it a Black Easter?

VII

If this interpretation will hold up, it will crown the remarkable associational edifice which is both a part of and an extension of the dramatic structure of the story, an edifice which figures forth man's quality, his living, so to speak, as a potentiality which may be fulfilled or may paradoxically be transformed into its radical opposite. This we are told, by implication, through the beauty which can become ugliness, the brightness which becomes darkness, the innocence which can become sophistication, the spring which becomes fall, the youth which becomes age, the Eden which can be stricken with death, the angelic which becomes diabolic; and through the pictured capacity, whether it be understood as original sin or otherwise, for revolt, for transvaluation of values, for denial of the agency of salvation. And this truth comes to us with peculiar shock because we see enacted, not that imperceptible movement by which man's advance in age and in corruption becomes endurable, but the transformation from one extreme to the other in pure state, in essence, in symbolic immediacy. In this poem about evil, youth is age.

James deliberately chose to omit certain matters from his narrative statement. But in his poetic statement he has elaborated upon his story and given adequate clues to the metaphysical foundations of his plot. The universality which has stimulated many critics is the Christian dualism of good and evil; this substance James has projected by poetic methods into numerous details of symbolic language and action of which the implications may, in their subtlety, almost be missed. For, like all poetic statements, James's is not direct; even in prose medium it eschews a conventional prose logic; it endows his tale with an atmosphere in which we sense the pressure of so much more imaginative force than meets the casual fiction-reading eye. In attempting to state schematically the origins of that pressure, we fall into much more blunt statements than we ought to make. We say, too forthrightly, that Bly "becomes" a Garden of Eden. As in studying all good poetry, we must resist the impulse to line up, on a secondary level of meaning, exact equivalents for the narrative elements, for such a procedure stems from the rude assumption that every part of the story is a precision-tooled cog in an allegorical machine. But we must be sensitive to parallels, analogies, intimations; thus, while preserving the fullness and flexibility of the work, we can investigate its extraordinarily moving tonal richness. And in accounting for tone we necessarily move toward a definition of structure. The verbal and imagistic patterns which have been described do not have the structural finality that they would have in lyric verse. Yet these patterns, which overlap and interfuse in a way badly obscured by the clumsy analytical process, are unquestionably important in the formation of the story and the qualifying of its meaning; they are one of the ways in which the esemplastic imagination, as Coleridge called it, works; and they collaborate closely with the larger structural units—the parts of the narrative as such—in defining this version of the struggle between good and evil.

Another Turn on James's "The Turn of the Screw"

Glenn A. Reed

In his Preface to the New York Edition of "The Turn of the Screw" (1908), Henry James confidently asserted this was the kind of story "least apt to be baited by earnest criticism."[1] Yet from the date the story was published in 1898 it has continued to agitate the pens of commentators and critics. Early commentary was content with epithetically patting and praising the work: it has variously been called "indescribably hellish,"[2] "the most monstrous and incredible ghost-story,"[3] "the most eerie and harrowing"[4] story ever written, yet "the finest work he has ever done."[5] More recent criticism, however, has been occupied almost exclusively with the question of interpretation. There are two schools of thought: the more traditional interpretation holds that the dead servants, in a preternatural flair of evil, actually returned to haunt the children; the more recent psychological theory is based on the belief that the governess alone was possessed of these demons, that her sexually frustrated mind generated the ghosts and the atmosphere of corruption surrounding the innocent children. Although many critics have disagreed with this latter interpretation, none, so far as I have been able to ascertain,

SOURCE: *American Literature*, XX (January, 1949), 413–423. Reprinted by permission of the Duke University Press.

[1] Preface, p. xiv. All quotations from the Preface and from "The Turn of the Screw" refer to the New York Edition of *The Novels and Tales of Henry James* (New York, 1908), Vol. XII.

[2] *American Monthly Review of Reviews*, XVIII, 732 (Dec., 1898).

[3] *Critic*, XXXIII, 524 (Dec., 1898).

[4] F. M. Hueffer, *Henry James: A Critical Study* (London: Martin Secker, 1913), p. 151.

[5] *American Monthly*, XVIII, 733.

have attempted a refutation of the specific arguments presented.[6] It is the purpose of this paper to present briefly the conclusions of the psychological interpretation, and by re-examining them in the light of internal evidence and of James's critical comments on the story to show how little basis there is for such a theory.

The psychological theory did not gain prominence until a number of years after James's death in 1916, although one of the earliest reviewers suggests the ground later disputed.

> The subject-matter of "The Turning [sic] of the Screw" is also made up of feminine intuitions, but the heroine—this time a governess—has nothing in the least substantial upon which to base her deep and startling cognitions. She perceives what is beyond perception, and the reader who begins by questioning whether she is supposed to be sane ends by accepting her conclusions and thrilling over the horrors they involve.[7]

It remained for later critics to study more carefully the possibility of the governess's insanity and to arrive at a conclusion quite different from that presented in the above passage. Edna Kenton suggested that the ghosts and children, the pictorial isolation are "only the exquisite dramatizations of her [the governess's] little personal mystery, figures for the ebb and flow of the troubled thought within her mind, acting out her story." [8] According to Miss Kenton, to interpret the story in any other way is to fall into the trap James set for unwary readers.

> The children hounded by the prowling ghosts—this is the hard and shining surface story of The Turn of the Screw. . . . As a tiny matter of literal fact, no reader has more to go on than the young governess's word for this rather momentous and sidetracking allegation. As a rather large matter of literal fact, we know, with but a modicum of attention paid to her recital of these nerve-shattering affairs at Bly, that it is she —always she herself—who sees the lurking shapes and heralds them to her little world. . . . There are traps and lures in plenty, but just a little wariness will suffice to disprove, with a single survey of the ground, the traditional, we might almost call it lazy version of this tale. Not the children, but the little governess was hounded by the ghosts who,

[6] Since this article was written, three refutations of the psychological interpretation have appeared: A. J. A. Waldock, "Mr. Edmund Wilson and 'The Turn of the Screw,'" *Modern Language Notes,* LXII, 331 ff. (May, 1947); R. B. Heilman, "The Freudian Reading of 'The Turn of the Screw,'" *ibid.,* LXII, 433 ff. (Nov., 1947); and E. E. Stoll, "Symbolism in Coleridge," *PMLA,* LXIII, 214–233 (March, 1948).

[7] *Critic, loc. cit.*

[8] "Henry James to the Ruminant Reader: The Turn of the Screw," *Arts,* VI, 255 (Nov., 1924).

as James confides with such suave frankness in his Preface, merely "help me to express my subject all directly and intensely." [9]

Edmund Wilson followed this lead with a more detailed analysis of this psychological interpretation.

> According to this theory, the young governess who tells the story is a neurotic case of sex repression, and the ghosts are not real ghosts at all but merely the hallucinations of the governess.[10]

Mr. Wilson proceeds to retell the story in the light of this theory. The evils in the story are all in the mind of the governess and are accounted for in two ways: the governess reads sinister significance into trivial events which, in themselves, are quite innocent (thus the expelling of Miles from school is, according to Mr. Wilson, an event "which she colors, on no evidence at all, with a significance somehow sinister"); or the overwrought mind of the sexually frustrated governess is visited by apparitions, so that she perceives what is beyond all perception—ghosts, sexual symbolism, corrupted children. Mr. Wilson concludes his analysis:

> When one has once been given this clue to "The Turn of the Screw," one wonders how one could ever have missed it. There is a very good reason, however, in the fact that nowhere does James unequivocally give the thing away: almost everything from beginning to end can be read equally in either of two senses.[11]
>
> When we look back in the light of these hints, we become convinced that the whole story has been primarily intended as a characterization of the governess: her visions and the way she behaves about them, as soon as we look at them from the obverse side, present a solid and unmistakable picture of the poor country parson's daughter, with her English middle-class class-consciousness, her inability to admit to herself her sexual impulses and the relentless English "authority" which enables her to put over on inferiors even purposes which are totally deluded. . . .[12]

From the above passages it would seem that Miss Kenton and Mr. Wilson are in agreement at least on three points: (1) the story is a psychological case study of neurotic sex repression; (2) the characterization of the governess is James's main concern; (3) the evils in the story exist only in the mind of the governess. There are other issues upon which they do not agree. Miss Kenton believes

[9] *Ibid.*, VI, 254.
[10] "The Ambiguity of Henry James," *The Triple Thinkers* (New York, 1938), p. 122.
[11] *Ibid.*, p. 130.
[12] *Ibid.*, p. 131.

James intended the story as a trap for unwary readers, but any intelligent reader would see through the shining surface to the true meaning of the tale. Mr. Wilson, however, argues that the meaning is ambiguous, that the story may be read equally in either of two senses. Whether James consciously or unconsciously created this ambiguity is not clearly stated.

Before attempting to point out some of the weaknesses of this psychological theory, I should admit that some critics might argue that any interpretation not specifically opposed by the facts in the story is possible. But such an attitude, it seems to me, offers but feeble justification for not probing the author's intentions and techniques. It is my conviction that the psychological interpretation is based on intuitive judgments and cognitions even less substantial than those the governess is accused of making. My thesis obviously admits of no startling imaginary discoveries, but it does have the virtue of returning the story from the arid atmosphere of a psychic case to its proper province as a haunted and haunting ghost story replete with all imaginable intangible horrors.

First of all let us consider James's avowed intention in writing the story. He tells us the germ of "The Turn of the Screw" was in a little story told by Archbishop Benson in January, 1895, "dealing as it did with a couple of small children in an out-of-the-way place, to whom the spirits of certain 'bad' servants, dead in the employ of the house, were believed to have appeared with the design of 'getting hold' of them."[13] In *The Notebooks of Henry James* an even clearer statement of intent may be found. "The servants, wicked and depraved, corrupt and deprave the children; the children are bad, full of evil, to a sinister degree. The servants *die* . . . and their apparitions, figures, return to haunt the house *and* children. . . ."[14] This germ, as James explains in the Preface to the story, became his central idea.

> They [the ghosts] would be agents in fact; there would be laid on them the dire duty of causing the situation to reek with the air of Evil. Their desire and their ability to do so, visibly measuring meanwhile their effect, together with their observed and described success—this was exactly my central idea. . . .[15]

[13] Preface, p. xv. For a detailed discussion of the origin, see F. X. Roellinger, Jr., "Psychical Research and 'The Turn of the Screw,'" published in this issue of *American Literature*.

[14] Ed. F. O. Matthiessen and Kenneth B. Murdock (New York, 1947), p. 178.

[15] Preface, p. xx.

Whom were these abnormal "agents in fact" intended to haunt—the governess or the children?

What, in the last analysis, had I to give the sense of? Of their being, the haunting pair, capable, as the phrase is, of everything—that is of exerting, in respect to the children, the very worst action small victims so conditioned might be conceived as subject to.[16]

It seems clear from these passages that James conceived of the central idea of the story as the relationship between corrupt servants and the children. There is no indication here, or in any other critical remarks on the story, that James intended the governess to be a third, in fact dominant factor in this relationship. In the light of James's expressed plan for having the ghosts carry the burden of creating an atmosphere of horror and of exerting the worst possible action on the children there would be a decided deterioration of his haunting matrix if the evils and the ghosts are able to escape as mere hallucinations of the governess. In fact, if we treat the story as a psychological study in sexual frustration, as Mr. Wilson suggests, then James is guilty of attempting to write the very type of modern "psychical" case he scorned.

The new type [of ghost story] indeed, the mere modern "psychical" case, washed clean of all queerness as by exposure to a flowing laboratory tap, and equipped with credentials vouching for this—the new type clearly promised little, for the more it was respectably certified the less it seemed of a nature to rouse the dear old sacred terror.[17]

How does James classify his story? Without any hedging or ambiguity he identifies it as a "fairy-tale pure and simple," which he compares to the classic stories of the Brothers Grimm. There is the same objective horror with no attempt to explain it away. "Peter Quint and Miss Jessel are not 'ghosts' at all, as we now know the ghost, but goblins, elves, imps, demons as loosely constructed as those of the old trials for witchcraft; if not, more pleasingly, fairies of the legendary order, wooing their victims forth to see them dance under the moon." [18]

In view of this evidence, can we not say that in so far as James's intentions were concerned there is no ambiguity, no obvious intent to fool the reader, but merely a conscious and cultivated attempt to "catch those not easily caught" in his vise of horror and mystifica-

[16] *Ibid.*, p. xxi.
[17] *Ibid.*, p. xv.
[18] *Ibid.*, p. xx.

tion? Let us now turn our attention to an analysis of the story itself.

What role does the governess play in the story? Mr. Wilson and Miss Kenton would have her take the center of the stage—a woman "emotionally perverted," "a variation on one of James's familiar themes: the frustrated Anglo-Saxon spinster." [19] There are several difficulties with this interpretation. In the first place, it has been noted that James does not even mention the governess when he discusses the central idea of his story. In the second place, it is difficult to see how a girl of twenty, with little knowledge of the world since she comes to her first job of governess fresh from a country parsonage, could be a version of the frustrated Anglo-Saxon spinster, particularly when her relationship with the Master is developed no further than a schoolgirlish crush and is inserted into the story, it seems to me, partly to motivate her acceptance of a position peculiarly encumbered and partly to explain her reluctance to consult the Master when she is hard pressed. In the third place, the character of the governess is not sufficiently particularized to hold the spotlight. When H. G. Wells blamed James for not sufficiently characterizing the governess, James replied:

> Of course I had, about my young woman, to take a very sharp line. The grotesque business I had to make her picture and the childish psychology I had to make her trace and present, were . . . a very difficult job, in which absolute lucidity and logic, a singleness of effect, were imperative. Therefore I had to rule out subjective complications of her own—play of tone etc; and keep her impersonal save for the most obvious and indispensable little note of neatness, firmness and courage—without which she wouldn't have had her data.[20]

If James had intended to dramatize the governess's personal mystery, he certainly would have further delineated these subjective complications instead of keeping her as impersonal as possible in order to give her the authority to tell the story.

References to the governess in the Preface and in his letters indicate that James intended her as the narrator or revealer of the horrors. In one place he speaks of the necessity of kneading "the subject of my young friend's, the suppositious narrator's, mystification thick, and yet strain the expression of it so clear and fine that beauty would result." [21] In *The Notebooks* he ends his January 12, 1895, entry with the statement: "The story to be told—tolerably

[19] *The Triple Thinkers, passim.*

[20] *The Letters of Henry James,* ed. Percy Lubbock (New York, 1920), I, 298–299.

[21] Preface, p. xviii.

obviously—by an outside spectator, observer."[22] In the Preface to the story he even specifies her exact limitations as a narrator. He sees himself faced with the "general proposition of our young woman's keeping crystalline her record of so many intense anomalies and obscurities—by which I don't of course mean her explanation of them, a different matter."[23] Thus we see her job is to keep a clear record of these strange happenings at Bly, but she is not to explain them away because by so doing she would remove the atmosphere of thick mystification so essential to the tone of horror and evil James is trying to sustain. And to the degree that the governess observed and records, yet is mystified, so is the reader held to the very end in the vise of expectant disclosure, always straining to penetrate the atmospheric haze of mystification.

The revealing of action through a character who is at the same time in the place of action (thus able to observe and report more directly) yet not involved too personally in the action (thus able to analyze and interpret objectively) is one of James's most frequently employed methods of story telling.

Throughout the story there are hints intended to convince the reader that the governess is a thoroughly trustworthy witness. In the introductory framework James is careful to give her the proper credentials to speak authoritatively on the strange events she is to record. Douglas, who possesses her document on the events at Bly, admits he was half in love with her, "a most charming person, . . . most agreeable woman I've ever known . . . she'd have been worthy of any whatever . . . awfully clever and nice." Douglas knew her after the events of the story. Thus James is making sure she is sufficiently accredited by presenting her as a charming person of good breeding with no obvious signs of mental instability either before or after the events of the story. Young, sensitive, inexperienced, she is indeed the type of person who would vibrate intensely to manifestations of evil around her. We note how impersonal James keeps her by giving her no name, by describing her appearance in the sketchiest fashion, and by having her tell the story from the grave. We observe that by having the story recorded after the events had happened he gives the governess a chance to weigh her evidence objectively and at the same time removes the possibility that the data were the product of emotional hysteria. The clarity and logic of her record should convince any reader that at least at the time of the writing the governess was not suffering from an emotionally overburdened mind.

[22] P. 179.

[23] Preface, p. xix.

More persuasive still are other devices James employed to make the reader accept the conclusions of the governess. There are times when the governess herself questions her sanity, but in every case she is faced with what James considered irrefutable proof that she is on the right track. In a manner of speaking Mrs. Grose is the testing ground for just how far the reader may be expected to go in accepting the tenuous evidence of the governess. To the degree that Mrs. Grose accepts the evidence, so are we as readers to accept it. When she balks, as she does on several occasions, the governess faces her, and us, with one undeniable fact:

I found that to keep her thoroughly in the grip . . . I had only to ask her how, if I had "made it up," I came to be able to give, of each of the persons appearing to me, a picture disclosing, to the last detail, their special marks—a portrait on the exhibition of which she had instantly recognized and named them [the ghosts].[24]

Mr. Wilson takes cognizance of this objection to his thesis:

There seems here to be only a single circumstance which does not fit into the hypothesis that the ghosts are hallucinations of the governess: the fact that the governess's description of the first ghost at a time when she has never heard of the valet should be identifiable as the valet by the housekeeper.[25]

Yet even here he finds a way open for his interpretation on the assumption that there might have been a physical resemblance between the Master and Quint. Thus unconsciously she gives the ghost of Quint the features of the Master. This explanation is not only pure conjecture but conjecture which violates the facts presented. It will be remembered that the governess is thinking of the Master at the time she sees the ghost for the first time. Even at a considerable distance she immediately realizes it is not the Master, is not in fact anyone she has ever seen before. Added to this is the fact that there is no hesitation in Mrs. Grose's identification of the description as Quint. If there had been any possibility of confusing the two, Mrs. Grose would certainly have thought of the Master, whose presence would not have been supernatural, rather than of Quint, who had to return from the dead. Even so, such a theory as Mr. Wilson proposes does not explain the description the governess is able to give of Miss Jessel with no foreknowledge at all.

Undoubtedly these arguments could be extended; but sufficient

[24] P. 209.
[25] *Op. cit.*, p. 125.

evidence has been presented, it seems to me, to show that James intended the governess as a narrator character and used a variety of techniques to convince the reader of the authenticity of her story. Let us now turn our attention to the last main contention of the critics of the psychological theory: the evils in the story exist only in the mind of the governess.

Both Miss Kenton and Mr. Wilson seem to agree that there is no horror or evil in the story except that which exists in the governess's mind. But this is palpably untrue since it is Mrs. Grose, not the governess, who reluctantly discloses the machinations of the Quint-Jessel regime. It will be remembered that Mrs. Grose was inordinately glad to see the new governess. She attempts to hide all irregularities of the former occupants for fear of frightening the governess away, but under pressure she admits the diabolical deeds and mysterious deaths of the corrupt pair. That evil had existed and that the children had been exposed to it can hardly be questioned, unless we are also to discredit the entire testimony of the unlettered housekeeper.

From the standpoint of the governess it is bad enough to know that the children have been exposed to evil; but when it becomes evident that the evil is still active, that the children are conspiring with these demons and know far more than the governess or Mrs. Grose will ever know about the evil of this pair, then the governess realizes how desperate is the battle to save their little souls. Why do the children deny seeing the ghosts? Such denial, according to the governess, shows the extent to which the children have been corrupted. If there had been no sense of guilt, matters and personalities of the past would have been discussed quite openly. But the children are doing their best to throw the governess off the scent of their perversions by apparently innocent diversions and silences. Mrs. Grose confirms that such a technique had been used before. She says that under highly irregular circumstances "for a period of several months Quint and the boy had been perpetually together." When she remonstrated with Miles, "he denied certain occasions. . . . When he had gone off with the fellow, I mean, and spent hours with him." It will be noted that throughout the story the intuitive cognitions of the governess are verified by Mrs. Grose.

Near the end of the story the housekeeper declares she can remain no longer at Bly. Why? Not for fear of the governess but, as she says, because of the things she has "heard . . . From that child —horrors! . . . On my honour, Miss, she says things—! . . . Really shocking . . . I can't think wherever she must have picked up—." These broken phrases show that Mrs. Grose, although she has not seen the ghosts, agrees with the governess as to their corrupting influence.

Such corroborating testimony is not all. The governess has been so shaken by the events of the story that she demands positive proof that her deductions are sound. When, in the tension of the final scene, Miles utters the corrupting servant's name, which he has so long withheld, the governess has her conclusive proof that demons did exist for the boy—either visually or mentally—since otherwise he certainly would not have had the slightest inkling of the meaning of her pressing insinuations. We might, of course, disagree violently with the governess's technique for dispossessing her young charge of the devil, but we can hardly deny that the devils (and other objective horrors) exist in the story quite apart from the mind of the governess.

Perhaps the most surprising part of this controversy over interpretation is the unwillingness of critics to accept James's own classification of the story as a fairy tale pure and simple. There is hardly a fairy story that does not contain objective, pictorial evil—evil that is in the world for no good reason and that lures innocent victims to their doom. This interpretation makes it as unnecessary to explain the demons as psychological phenomena as it would be to explain in psychological terms how a wolf could dress up in woman's clothing and talk to Little Red Ridinghood. In fact, when critics probe what they term the sexual symbolism in "The Turn of the Screw," it might be questioned whether they are psychoanalyzing the governess or James, and what he consciously or subconsciously brought to the story.

There are, as in fairy stories, many questions left unanswered. James uses the technique of the fairy tale in leading the reader on step by step to accept impossible happenings without ever attempting a rational explanation of them. Thus if there is little possibility of ambiguity of interpretation regarding the governess, there is intentional and calculated lack of explicitness in identifying the evils that pervade the story. To James this obscurity was of the utmost importance in allowing the reader's imagination fertile ground in which to pullulate.

> Portentous evil—how was I to save that . . . from the drop . . . inevitably attending . . . the offered example, the imputed vice, the cited act, the limited deplorable presentable instance? To bring the bad dead back to life for a second round of badness is to warrant them as indeed prodigious, and to become hence as shy of specifications as of a waiting anti-climax.[26]

[26] Preface, pp. xx–xxi.

Only make the reader's general vision of evil intense enough, . . . his own experience, his own imagination, his own sympathy (with the children) and horror (of their false friends) will supply him quite sufficiently with all the particulars. Make him *think* the evil, make him think it for himself, and you are released from weak specifications.[27]

Unspecified, unidentified evils presented against an isolated background haunted by demons and spirits and unexplainable actions—these are the ingredients of James's pictorial fairy story, his pot-boiler of horror. And he stirs these ingredients in his witches' brew with a careful pen, never allowing the curious observer a chance to specify the particulars but pushing him ever deeper into the thick vapors arising from the brew—vapors compounded of evils, horror, and mystification.

[27] *Ibid.*, pp. xxi–xxii.

James's Air of Evil: *The Turn of the Screw*

Oliver Evans

It is exactly half a century since *The Turn of the Screw* first appeared on the literary scene. Its commercial success, which it is very likely that James himself did not foresee, was instantaneous; it soon proved, after *Daisy Miller,* to be his most popular book. Reading contemporary reviews of the new Jamesian "thriller," one becomes convinced that it was the sensational character of the subject which, more than anything else, appealed to most readers, and that this sensationalism, in turn, derived from the two most immediately obvious elements in the story: the author's preoccupation, first, with the theme of the supernatural; and, second, with that of perverse sexuality. The first of these themes was new with James; the second had previously (in such stories as "The Pupil" and "The Middle Years") only been obliquely hinted at.

If the popular success of *The Turn of the Screw* is thus easily to be accounted for, the reasons for its *aesthetic* success are by no means so immediately obvious, yet nothing can be plainer than the fact that the story is eminently successful in this sense also. Had its success been merely of one kind, critics would have let it go at that; they have not, however, been content to do so, and there are now almost as many interpretations of the story as there have been critics willing to venture them. On one point alone are they all (with the very prominent exception of Mr. T. S. Eliot, who does not definitely commit himself) in substantial agreement, and that is that *The Turn of the Screw* is one of James's finest novels. The disagreement, in other words, does not concern the fact, but the reason therefor.

SOURCE: *Partisan Review,* XVI (February, 1949), 175–187. Reprinted by permission of the editors and the author.

I have little hope, in the face of so much distinguished discord, of settling once and for all a problem so delicate and so complex. I should like, however, to contribute to the general controversy by suggesting an interpretation which (all miraculously) has thus far, to my knowledge, never been put forth. And there is one thing which, before doing this, I *should* like to settle once and for all, and that is the question of the reality of the apparitions in the story.

It is commonly supposed that Miss Edna Kenton was the first to consider the possibility that the ghosts of Peter Quint and Miss Jessel do not really appear to the governess who tells the story, but are instead mere hallucinations, the creatures of her own disordered imagination. As a matter of fact, this possibility appears to have occurred previously to several readers, none of whom, however, was willing to entertain it very seriously or for very long. Only a few weeks after the book was published *The Critic* observed that "the heroine had nothing in the least substantial upon which to base her deep and startling cognitions. She perceives what is beyond all perception, and the reader who begins by questioning whether she is supposed to be sane ends by accepting her conditions and thrilling over the horrors they involve."

So far as I know, however, Miss Kenton was the first to go on record as *not* accepting the governess's conditions, and to state positively that the ghosts are nothing more than "exquisite dramatizations of her little personal mystery, figures for the ebb and flow of troubled thought within her mind." In her opinion James quite deliberately planned the story as a test of that attentiveness which he felt every author had a right to expect of his readers, and she offers in support of this theory James's reference to the story (in the definitive edition preface) as "a piece of ingenuity pure and simple, of cold, artistic calculation, an *amusette* to catch those not easily caught." She also stresses the fact that James nowhere *states* that the ghosts appear to anyone but the governess. On the strength, chiefly, of these two pieces of "evidence," she rather largely concludes: "Just a little wariness will suffice to disprove, with a single survey of the ground, the traditional, we might almost call it a *lazy* version of the tale. Not the children, but the little governess was hounded by the ghosts." It will be seen that, thus viewed, *The Turn of the Screw* becomes a sort of elaborate hoax, a trap for readers lazier and less wary than Miss Kenton.

This ingenious interpretation, which, as I shall later attempt to show, does so little justice to James's intention in writing the story and so narrowly delimits the reader's appreciation of it, attracted almost no attention when, in 1924, it appeared in *Arts* accompanied by an interesting set of illustrations by Charles Demuth. But ten years later Mr. Edmund Wilson published in *Hound and Horn* his now famous essay. "The Ambiguity of Henry James" (included with some additions in *The Triple Thinkers,* 1938), in which he popularized and expanded this theory. In his opinion *The Turn of the Screw* is "simply a variation on one of James's familiar themes: the frustrated Anglo-Saxon spinster." He professes to discover specific Freudian meanings in the facts that the male ghost first appears on a tower, the female beside a lake; and that, on the occasion of the latter visitation, the child Flora is carrying (I quote from the story) "a small flat piece of wood, which happened to have in it a little hole that had evidently suggested to her the idea of sticking in another fragment that might figure as a mast and make the thing a boat."

Beyond pointing out such circumstances as these, Mr. Wilson did not really add substantially to Miss Kenton's interpretation. The Kenton-Wilson theory, at any rate, is now familiar to most Jamesians, and although it has elicited considerable random disapproval, I have nowhere seen it attacked point by point. An exception is Philip Rahv, but even he concedes, "Of course there is no doubt that the story may be read that way."

II

Both Miss Kenton and Mr. Wilson have conveniently ignored the letters, in which James made it perfectly clear that in *The Turn of the Screw* he was writing a tale of the *supernatural.* Its origin, as he declared in a letter to A. C. Benson (March 11, 1898) was a "small and gruesome *spectral* story" (italics mine) related to him by Archbishop Benson, grandfather of the educator. A few months later James wrote to Dr. Louis Waldstein that it was merely a "wanton little Tale" unworthy of such praise as the doctor had apparently given it. He added, however, that "the poet is always justified when he is not a humbug; always grateful to the justifying commentator," and continued: "My *bogey-tale* [italics mine] dealt with things so hideous that I felt that to save it at all I needed some infusion of beauty or prettiness, and the beauty of the pathetic was the only attainable—was indeed inevitable. But ah, the exposure indeed, the helpless plasticity of childhood that isn't dear or sacred to *somebody!* That *was* my little tragedy!" That was, indeed, the tragedy: the corruption of the two children by the living servants, and the possession (in the supernatural sense) of them afterwards by the ghosts of those same servants. In the light of this avowal, what happens to the "tragedy" if we think of the story simply as a careful trap, or as a mere case history of a governess subject to hallucinations?

In a letter to H. G. Wells (December 9, 1898), who had apparently objected that the governess's character did not receive sufficient delineation, James defended himself as follows:

> Of course I had, about my young woman, to take a very sharp line. The grotesque business I had to make her trace and present were, for me at least, a very difficult job, in which absolute lucidity and logic, a singleness of effect, were imperative. Therefore I had to rule out subjective complications of her own—play of tone, etc., and keep her impersonal save for the most obvious and indispensable little note of neatness, firmness and courage—without which she wouldn't have had her data.

Witness the phrase, "I had to rule out subjective complications of her own," and observe how incompatible it is with the notion that she is merely exposing her private neurosis in the story. Witness, too, how little this picture of the governess coincides with Wilson's conception of her as a pronounced hysteric.

Writing to F. W. H. Myers (December 19, 1898) he is even more specific:

> The thing that, as I recall it, I most wanted not to fail of doing, under penalty of extreme platitude, was to give the impression of the communication to the children of the most infernal imaginable evil and danger—the condition, on their part, of being as *exposed* as we can humanly conceive children to be. This was my artistic knot to untie, to put any sense or logic into the thing, and if I had known any way of producing *more* the image of their contact and condition I should have been proportionately eager to resort to it.

Here James specifically states his conscious ambition, and I hope I do not need to point out that without the apparitions there is no evil, no danger, and no *exposure*. Finally there is the letter to his French translator, Auguste Monod (July 17, 1907). If James's intention had been as devious as the hoaxists and the nonapparitionists (if I may term them this) would have us believe, surely he would have hinted as much to his translator; instead, he unambiguously refers to his book as a "*fantaisie absolue dans le genre de recherche du frisson.*"

There is some evidence that James's opinion of the merits of *The Turn of the Screw* altered between the date of its first publication in 1898 and its appearance ten years later in the definitive edition: thus, in the above-mentioned letter to F. W. H. Myers, he refers to it as "a very mechanical matter, I honestly think—an inferior, a merely *pictorial* subject and rather a shameless potboiler," but in the preface, as Philip Rahv has commented, he gives it serious and lengthy treatment. It is possible, of course, that James was merely being overmodest in the Myers letter (the tone of many of his letters is self-deprecatory in this way, betraying their author's concern for "good taste"), but again it is possible that he did not immediately realize how consummately successful he had been in his attempt to communicate to the reader a sense of "most infernal imaginable evil and danger"—the poet, as he himself so well put it, being always grateful to the justifying commentator. Neither explanation supports the Kenton-Wilson view: as we have seen, there is no evil or danger without the apparitions; and if James had intended to conceal the point of the narrative as carefully as they claim—if, in other words, it was to be the subtlest of his stories in this sense—he would scarcely have referred to it as a potboiler.

The changes which James made for the definitive edition were of a purely verbal character and do not affect the plot in any way. However, the preface which he composed for the new edition is invaluable for the light which it throws on his intentions. Miss Kenton has not ignored this preface; she has done what is far worse: she has lifted one of its sentences out of its context, interpreted it in a very special kind of way, and then, claiming it as "evidence," has proceeded to construct upon it her very largest argument. In the case of a writer such as James, where context is almost all-important, this is particularly reprehensible. The sentence in question reads as follows: "I need scarcely add after this that it [*The Turn of the Screw*] is a piece of ingenuity pure and simple, of cold artistic calculation, an *amusette* to catch those not easily caught (the fun of the capture of the merely witless being ever but small), the jaded, the disillusioned, the fastidious." Miss Kenton focuses on the first part of this sentence—very shrewdly for her purpose, for the adjectives "jaded," "disillusioned," and "fastidious" support a context she has deliberately chosen not to recognize. James has been speaking of the many difficulties which beset the writer of the fantastic, of how unsuccessful, in this age of sophistication, modern ghost stories have been in their attempt to "rouse the dear old sacred terror." The meaning of the sentence is simply that in *The Turn of the Screw* James believed he had hit upon the perfect formula for rousing this type of terror—rousing it, moreover, in those the least susceptible, "the jaded, the disillusioned, the fastidious." What this formula is we shall see in a moment.

Mr. Wilson is guilty of much the same sort of thing. He interprets James's statement in the preface, that "She [the governess] has 'authority,' which is a good deal to have given her," as meaning that the governess, by reason of her "neurosis," was a dubious person to exert authority over children. But James is not using "authority" in this sense at all; he does not mean that the governess has authority where the *children* are concerned, but where the *reader* is, as will be obvious when one views the statement in its context. James has been defending himself against the accusation that the governess is insufficiently characterized (H. G. Wells, as we have noted, made the same charge) and concludes: "It constitutes no little of a character indeed, in such conditions, for a young person, as she says, 'privately bred,' that she is able to make her particular credible [*sic*] statement of such strange matters. She has 'authority,' which is a deal to have given her, and I couldn't have arrived at so much had I clumsily tried for more." This last sentence, which we have seen the nonapparitionists quote (without benefit of context) to their own purpose, really offers the most convincing proof that they are mistaken; in it James is simply saying that we are to accept as authoritative the governess's account of what happens in *The Turn of the Screw.*

James goes on to tell exactly what his motives were in writing his "bogey-tale": "Good ghosts, speaking by book, make poor subjects, and it was clear that from the first my hovering prowling blighting presences, my pair of abnormal agents, would have to depart altogether from the rules. They would be agents in fact; there would be laid in them the dire duty of causing the situation to reek with the air of Evil." Finally he defines his formula for making the situation reek to capacity with the "air of Evil." Alive, the servants had performed sufficient *specific* harm in corrupting their little charges; what additional outrage could they now perform that would not be anticlimactic? The problem, as James was perfectly aware, was a difficult one; he solved it, and solved it successfully, by deliberate refuge to the general, the nonspecific—solved it, in other words, by simple *omission:* "Only make the reader's general vision of evil intense enough, I said to myself . . . and his own experience, his own sympathy (with the children) and horror (of their false friends) will supply him quite sufficiently with all the particulars. Make him *think* the evil, make him think it for himself, and you are released from weak specifications." One may well wonder how it is possible to read all this and believe that James intended the ghosts to be nothing more than mere hallucinations.

The prologue is equally unambiguous. A group of house guests are gathered about a fire on Christmas Eve. Someone has just told a story in which a small child is visited by an apparition. One of the guests, Douglas, then remarks that he knows of a similar case involving *two* children; "Nobody but me, till now, has ever heard. It's quite too horrible. It's beyond everything. Nothing at all that I know touches it." The others are naturally curious, and he tells them he will send at once to London for the story, which it appears has already been written down by the governess of the haunted children, who was an actual witness.

Observe that Douglas himself never implies for a moment that he doubts the governess's account. On the contrary, one of James's motives in writing the prologue is to provide her with a "character reference" so that we may listen to her with respect. Douglas, who knew her intimately, certainly did not think that she was emotionally unstable: " 'She was my sister's governess,' he quietly said. 'She was the most agreeable woman I've ever known in her position; she would have been worthy of any whatever.' " Had James's intention been to characterize her as an irresponsible neurotic, what could have been his motive in having *the only person who knew her,* and was therefore able to vouch for her character, speak in this fashion?

I come now to the story itself. Miss Kenton and Mr. Wilson make much of the fact that, in the second scene by the lake, Miss Jessel's ghost is visible to the governess but not to the housekeeper. This power (of appearing only to certain individuals) has been the privilege of ghosts throughout all literature; it is, indeed, one of their most traditional attributes. And James has his own reasons for making use of it in *The Turn of the Screw:* it constitutes a definite victory for the ghosts, thus sharpening the conflict between them and the governess for the "possession" of the children; and it adds an almost unbearable tension to the story. One could not, incidentally, wish for stronger evidence of the stability of the governess's personality than the fact that, although the housekeeper herself has seen nothing, she does not doubt that her friend has—a point which James, who certainly sees the necessity for it, drives home again and again.

The nonapparitionists have never satisfactorily explained the coincidence between the governess's description of the ghosts and the impression which the housekeeper has retained of the living servants; and they have been forced to account for the death of little Miles at the end by saying that the governess herself, in attempting to make him see what is not there, simply scares the life out of him—this in spite of James's last sentence, "We were alone with the quiet day, and his little heart, *dispossessed* [italics mine], had stopped."

They also have not accounted for the fact that the housekeeper testifies toward the end that little Flora is, indeed, bewitched. For not only does Mrs. Grose believe that the governess has seen what she herself was unable to see, but her subsequent session with the little girl convinces her that the latter is definitely possessed. Referring to the last dreadful scene by the lake, Mrs. Grose observes: "It has made her, every inch of her, quite old." (Previously the governess has told the housekeeper, "At such times she's not a child: she's an old, old woman.") I reproduce the following conversation between the two servants:

> "You mean that, since yesterday, you *have* seen—?"
> She shook her head with dignity. "I've *heard*—!"
> "Heard?"
> "From that child—horrors! There!" she sighed with tragic relief. "On my honour, Miss, she says things—!" But at this evocation she broke down; she dropped, with a sudden sob, upon my sofa and, as I had seen her do before, gave way to all the grief of it.
> It was in quite another manner that I, for my part, let myself go. "Oh, thank God!"
> She sprang up at this, drying her eyes with a groan. "Thank God?"
> "It so justifies me!"
> "It does that, Miss."

Mrs. Grose then goes on to say that the child has been abusing the governess in language which she "can't think wherever she must have picked up." But immediately she adds, "Well, perhaps I ought to also—since I've heard some of it before." She has heard it "before," of course, from Miss Jessel herself. Finally the governess asks her:

> "Then, in spite of yesterday, you *believe?*"
> "In such doings?" Her simple description of them required, in the light of her expression, to be carried no further, and she gave me the whole thing as she had never done:
> "I believe."

Should there, after all this, remain any doubt in the reader's mind as to the reality of the apparitions, let him now glance back at the beginning of the story, *before* Peter Quint's ghost first appears. The governess has just arrived at Bly, knowing nothing of her unhappy predecessors. Immediately she senses that Mrs. Grose is strangely glad to see her: "I perceived within half an hour that she was so glad—stout, simple, plain, clean, wholesome woman—as to be positively on her guard against showing it too much. I wondered even then a little why she should not wish to show it . . ." It is several times hinted, at the first of the story, that the housekeeper is uneasy, that she is trying to conceal a suspicion that everything is not as it should be—a suspicion which she could only have arrived at independently, since the governess has barely arrived.

The governess, who has not even met the children yet, spends a rather uneasy first night: "There had been moments when I believed I recognized, faint and far, the cry of a child; there had been another when I found myself just consciously starting as at the passage, before the door, of a light footstep." From the very beginning James spares no pains in informing us that supernatural forces are at work within the house: the housekeeper is already aware of them, and the governess becomes aware long before she could have any reason to invent them.

III

I hope I have not overlabored my point here. I thought the risk worth running, at any rate, since I am convinced that it is impossible to fully appreciate *The Turn of the Screw* unless one accepts the reality of the apparitions.

Mr. Wilson remarks that *The Turn of the Screw,* on any other hypothesis than the one he proposes, would be "the only thing James ever wrote which did not have some more or less serious point." But to view the novel as an implied case history, a mere clinical record, is to deprive the reader of the peculiar sense of horror which it was James's ambition to arouse in him. Take, for example, the scene where little Miles, exerting all his charms, distracts the governess with his precocity at the piano, while his sister steals off to consort with Miss Jessel's evil shade. Suddenly the governess remembers: "Where, all this time, was little Flora? When I put the question to Miles he played on a minute without answering, and then could only say, 'Why, my dear, how do *I* know?'—breaking moreover into a happy laugh which, immediately after, as if it were a vocal accompaniment, he prolonged into incoherent, extravagant song." The whole infernal effectiveness of this scene (and it is immensely effective) resides in the fact that the little concert has been nothing more than a careful ruse on the children's part to lure the governess into temporarily forgetting her responsibility and relaxing her vigilance.

Or take the eerie scene just before this, in which the governess is pleading with Miles to confess his domination by the evil ghost of

Peter Quint: " 'Dear little Miles, I just want you to help me to save you!' But I knew in a moment after this that I had gone too far. The answer to my appeal was instantaneous, but it came in the form of an extraordinary blast and chill, a gust of frozen air and a shake of the room as great as if, in the wild wind, the casement had crashed in." The child shrieks ("a note either of jubilation or of terror") and the candle goes out:

> "Why, the candle's out!" I cried.
> "It was I who blew it, dear!" said little Miles.

Observe how immeasurably the effect of horror here is heightened by our conviction that the child is in league with those supernatural forces which, momentarily, and doubtless of his own volition, have become translated into natural ones.

I tend to agree with the late Ford Madox Ford when he says: "If you will take *The Turn of the Screw,* with its apparent digressions, its speculations, its twists and its turns, you will see that the real interest centres round the proposition: 'Is the narrator right or wrong in thinking that if the little boy can only disburden himself of a full confession, he will be saved for ever from the evil ascendency of Peter Quint?' " By "real" interest Ford here means narrative interest, and on the subject of James's narrative technique Ford was particularly well informed. Without the possession theme, which necessitates the reality of the ghosts, there is simply no conflict, no drama, no *story.* That James was thoroughly conscious of this is proved by the artistry with which he focuses on those details which sharpen the conflict and thus intensify the drama of the situation. Take for example the above-mentioned bedroom scene, and note how skillfully it is suggested to the reader (always through the medium of the governess, to whom the impressions occur in appropriate images) that little Miles is *sick,* spiritually sick: "His clear, listening face, framed in its smooth whiteness, made him for the moment as appealing as some wistful patient in a children's hospital; and I would have given, as the resemblance came to me, all I possessed on earth to be the nurse or the sister of charity who might have helped to cure him."

I agree also with Mr. Philip Rahv in his opinion that the sense of *evil* which James sought to communicate is to be conceived of largely in sexual terms. The horror of the situation is heightened, moreover, by the fact that the boy has been corrupted by the male servant; the girl, by the female. Peter Quint's abnormality is hinted at ("There had been matters in his life . . . secret disorders, vices more than half suspected"), and Mrs. Grose says in so many words that he had been "much too free" with little Miles, who had "gone off with the fellow, and spent hours with him." Then there is the unambiguous dialogue between the governess and Mrs. Grose:

> "At all events, while he was with the man—"
> "Miss Flora was with the woman. It suited them all!"

Neither Ford's interpretation nor Mr. Rahv's is sufficient, however, to account for the really uncanny effectiveness of *The Turn of the Screw.* I feel that both are valid, and that they perhaps sufficiently explain the book's contemporary popularity; but it seems to me that these two elements (supernatural possession and sexual impropriety) are really secondary reasons, surface involvements of a theme at once more comprehensive, more fundamental, and more profound: the theme, that is, of appearance versus reality.

This theme, apparently not sufficiently serious for Mr. Wilson, is as old as philosophy itself. An extension of it, on the ethical plane, is the theme of good versus evil, and in fact some of the more perceptive contemporary reviewers of the book discovered this meaning in it. But in James the ethical conflict is not presented in a straightforward manner, as it is, say, in Blake (where a child is always a child, a lamb always a lamb, and both are always innocent), but with complication and irony. In *The Turn of the Screw,* with devastating effect, the lambs are not lambs at all, but tigers; the children are not really children, but, as Mrs. Grose perceives in the end, are as old as evil itself.

The problem of appearance versus reality, which to my mind constitutes the primary theme of the story, James logically expresses in the form of a paradox. Whether consciously or intuitively, he realized the artistic importance of selecting a situation wherein the *apparent* should be innocuous, and the *real* overwhelming in its horror. The horror of the real would, indeed, be in exact proportion to the charm of the apparent—which is why James makes his children the very personification of youthful beauty and innocence, and provides for them such an idyllic setting. Hawthorne was preoccupied with the same paradox; Wilde expressed it, though with infinitely less ingenuity than James, in *The Picture of Dorian Gray;* and it was to become almost an obsession with Pirandello. James himself had treated it earlier, and much less grimly, in "The Liar"; and it is interesting to note that in the definitive edition he included *The Turn of the Screw,* not in the same volume with *Covering End* (as these two had first been issued under the title of *The Two Magics*) or "The Jolly Corner" (another "ghost" story), but with "The Liar."

If one accepts this interpretation of the story, it is interesting to observe how skillfully James goes about the process of constructing his paradox. Again and again it is emphasized to the reader that the beauty of these children (like that of Dorian Gray) is a *lie*. At the very beginning it is suggested that Miles's appearance belies the suspicion which the governess (who has not yet seen him) is beginning to form concerning the reasons for his expulsion from school. "See him, Miss, first," Mrs. Grose tells her. "*Then* believe it!" When the governess does see him, it is "in the great glow of freshness, the same positive fragrance of purity, in which I had, from the first moment, seen his little sister." She is struck, not only by his beauty, but by something else too: "something divine that I have never found to the same degree in any child—his indescribable little air of knowing nothing in the world but love." This initial impression, terrible in its irony, is confirmed and reinforced by many later ones. And somehow the "rose flush of his innocence" is never so intense as when he is most actively engaged in positive evil.

I have no illusions that this interpretation of *The Turn of the Screw* exhausts the story's meanings. It does not exclude other interpretations; it has the virtue of extreme inclusiveness, though I fear there is no room in it for either Miss Kenton or Mr. Wilson. I think it does better justice to James's intention than certain narrower notions and that it permits a wider and deeper appreciation of the novel than any of these. As Mr. Rahv says, in James we are always justified in assuming a maximum of intention: the task of the "justifying commentator," in the case of a book like *The Turn of the Screw*, is indeed endless.

Innocence and Evil in James's *The Turn of the Screw*

Charles G. Hoffmann

James usually treats evil as a social aspect of moral human conduct. Thus, infidelity (*Portrait of a Lady, The Golden Bowl*), betrayal of a trust (*Wings of the Dove*), lack of taste (*The Spoils of Poynton*) are the social evils which James is largely concerned with. Pitted against these evils is the principle of right conduct—doing the unselfish, right thing whether it means renouncing immediate happiness or being above selfish revenge. However, in *The Turn of the Screw* the problem of innocence and evil is the central conflict and theme of the story rather than an aspect of social conduct.

The theme of innocence-and-evil recurs again and again in James's fiction from the early *nouvelle, Daisy Miller,* to the late fragment, *The Ivory Tower.* In James innocence is hardly ever a virtue in itself. Though innocence is usually linked with moral good by James, the innocent are also usually ignorant of evil and thus are prey to those who would betray them; thus, the innocent, like Isabel Archer and Milly Theale, are easily betrayed by those who take advantage of their innocence, and the innocent like Daisy Miller betray themselves because they are incautious in their innocence when placed in an evil environment. Sometimes innocence is largely a matter of not being initiated into a particular society or environment rather than of good versus evil; thus Maisie and Nanda are initiated into an adult world, but in so doing lose their innocence because the process of initiation is also the process of growing up (the loss of the innocence of youth). However, in *The Turn of the Screw* innocence and evil coexist as evil-in-good.

SOURCE: *The University of Kansas City Review,* XX (Winter, 1953), 97–105. Reprinted by permission of the editors and the author.

It is significant that James chose children as the central actors in this drama of moral evil. From the cynical pessimism of Morgan in "The Pupil" to the growing adult awareness of Maisie and Nanda, James in this middle period of his writing had experimented with the problem of youthful innocence in relation to an adult world and with the problem of point of view in revealing the gulf between a child's world and an adult's world. *The Awkward Age* treats of a young girl who is at that awkward age when she is not quite old enough to be initiated into the complexities of an adult social circle and yet too old to be ignored as a mere child by the adults. The novel is a *tour de force* in dramatic technique, consisting almost entirely of dramatic dialogue without the usual Jamesian "sign-posts" of narrative technique by which the reader is guided toward a central point of view (the central observer, the confidant, irony) and even without much of conventional expository and descriptive narration. The gulf between the innocence of youth and the adult code of social conduct is revealed from ten different points of view (ten "lamps" or illuminators for the occasion, as James himself explains the technique in his preface) rather than from one central point of view.

The technique of point of view in *What Maisie Knew* is the obverse of that in *The Turn of the Screw:* to portray an adult world through the eyes of a child. From the point of view of Maisie, a sensitive and acute child, we share her innocent wonder at the complicated rules of behavior that govern the lives of adults who love and hate in a context that Maisie at first cannot understand but gradually comes to know, a development from innocence to knowledge, from youth to maturity. But it is in the earlier short story, "The Pupil" (1891), that we find a situation similar to *The Turn of the Screw.* What we find in the beginning is the "innocent eye" of the narrator (Pemberton, the tutor) from whose point of view we see the world of evil (the Moreens); the pupil (Morgan) reveals the evil quite early in the story, but the cynicism of the youth is at first discredited by the manipulations of the Moreens and by the disbelief of the narrator who only gradually discovers the evil of the Moreens. No ghosts appear; the evil is human in form.

In *The Turn of the Screw* the choice of children as the central characters intensifies the vision of evil James sought to achieve because of the discrepancy between the traditional Christian myth of the innocence of children (to say nothing of modern sentimental values attached to childhood) and their corruption as gradually revealed in the novel. The very language used in describing Miles and Flora sanctifies them: they are incredibly beautiful and most lovable and good; they are both extraordinarily charming and perfect; they are, in fact, angels. Their beauty and their goodness make their corruption all the more intense and horrible.

This vision of evil is gradually revealed to us in all its intensity and horror entirely from the point of view of the governess who is the narrator throughout. The establishment of the point of view is therefore all-important to an understanding of what that vision of evil is. The purpose of the introductory "frame" to the novel itself, besides providing the "occasion" for the story and revealing the existence of the manuscript which is the record of the events narrated, is to establish that point of view. It is a conventional device (though James strips it of any Gothic implications), and ordinarily one would quickly pass on from it to the narrative proper without a thought to possible ambiguities. However, more than any other work by James, *The Turn of the Screw* has been the center of a critical controversy, and the central issue of that controversy is the point of view. Again, ordinarily one would quickly pass on from the controversy to the story itself, but the problem of the point of view is central to an interpretation and understanding of the vision of evil revealed in the story.

Edmund Wilson, in an essay in the *Hound and Horn* (1934), accepts the theory first suggested by Miss Edna Kenton that the governess is sexually repressed and that the ghosts are not real but only hallucinations of the governess. This Freudian interpretation has been denied by other critics, especially by Professor Heilman.[1] The basis for the Freudian interpretation is the information in the introductory frame that the governess fell in love with her employer, the uncle and guardian of the children. But nowhere is her love described as or suggested to be abnormal. On the contrary, being the youngest daughter of a poor country parson, she would naturally be impressed by and infatuated with the handsome, wealthy gentleman, her employer:

> . . . such a figure as had never risen, save in a dream or an old novel, before a fluttered, anxious girl out of a Hampshire vicarage . . . He was handsome and bold and pleasant, off-hand and gay and kind. He struck her, inevitably, as gallant and splendid, but what took her most of all and gave her the courage she afterwards showed was that he put

[1] Cf. Edmund Wilson, "The Ambiguity of Henry James," in F. W. Dupee, *The Question of Henry James* (New York, 1945). Wilson revised the original article for Dupee's book. Cf. also Robert B. Heilman, " 'The Turn of the Screw' as Poem," *University of Kansas City Review,* XIV (Summer, 1948).

the whole thing to her as a kind of favour, an obligation he would gratefully incur.[2]

A Jane Austen character of romantic sensibility she might be; a Freudian personality of repressed sexuality she could hardly be.

Further, she is described by Douglas, the owner of her manuscript, as "a most charming person . . . the most agreeable woman I've ever known in her position; she would have been worthy of any whatever."[3] Douglas had been in love with her some time after the events related (she was his sister's governess); but though she liked him, she was ten years older than he, it is emphasized.

II

The narrative proper (exclusive of the frame) begins quietly and objectively. The beginning is realistic; descriptive details and impressions are presented in a realistic tone. No detail is wasted, no impression is without significance, if not for itself then in terms of later developments. What the first pages achieve is the impression for the reader that the governess as narrator is *normal* in her attitudes and impressions. The picture we see of her is that of a nervous excitable young woman alternating between confidence and doubt about her new position. This reaction is normal in one who (we know from the introduction) being of poor parents would be overwhelmed by the splendor of a gentleman's estate. The quickness and intensity of her perceptions and impressions have, beyond the measure of her nervousness and excitability, the quality of sensitivity characteristic of the fine intelligences James often used as central observers.

In the beginning the atmosphere is normal, devoid of sinister suggestion. The governess seems even somewhat disappointed:

> . . . I had the view of a castle of romance inhabited by a rosy sprite, such a place as would somehow, for diversion of the young idea, take all colour out of story-books and fairy-tales. Wasn't it just a story-book over which I had fallen a-doze and a-dream? No; it was a big, ugly, antique, but convenient house . . .[4]

And even the uneasiness which she sometimes feels is to be attributed to her nervousness about the new position, and not to any premonition of evil.

[2] Henry James, "The Turn of the Screw" in *The Novels and Tales of Henry James*, XII (New York, 1908), 153.
[3] *Ibid.*, p. 149.
[4] *Ibid.*, p. 163.

This appearance of normality provides a deliberate contrast to the intense atmosphere of evil that is gradually built up. The first suggestion of anything "wrong" occurs in the second chapter when it is learned that Miles has been dismissed from school. This in itself is by no means sinister (and were it a different kind of novel, it might be called normal), but the tone of the letter from the headmaster raises doubts as yet unfocused. No particular reason is given for the dismissal, other than "he's an injury to the others," suggesting that something unmentionable or abnormal on Miles' part might be the real reason for his dismissal. However, this is only the barest suggestion that there might be something wrong with Miles; after all, the headmaster is described as "an awful bore," suggesting he does not understand sensitive children like Miles, or, for that matter, it could be taken merely as James's reluctance to be specific about some details (as for example, Milly's fatal "disease" in *The Wings of the Dove*). The matter is dismissed by Mrs. Grose, the housekeeper, and the governess as being a natural and even healthy form of "naughtiness" in a boy.

The same ambiguity exists surrounding the circumstances of the governess's predecessor who like the present governess was young. She left the house at the end of the year for a holiday, " 'but our young lady never came back, and at the very moment I was expecting her I heard from the master that she was dead.' "[5] And again no reason is given. There is no direct suggestion of evil in her death—" 'she was not taken ill, so far as appeared, in this house' "—and yet the unexplained reason for her death creates doubt and foreshadows the atmosphere of evil and corruption; it hints at mystery without any definite basis for it, but which is all too well borne out by later developments.

It is in chapter three that we are suddenly and directly thrust into the presence of evil. "It may be, of course, above all, that what suddenly broke into this gives the previous time a charm of stillness —that hush in which something gathers or crouches. The change was actually like the spring of a beast."[6] The first appearance of Quint's ghost is seen by the governess. It happens, not in the middle of a thunder storm at midnight, but at the end of the afternoon in the twilight. The apparition presented no overt act of evil, no threat of violence, no sense of horror. The governess's reaction was one of shock and surprise, doubting her own vision at first and yet knowing the apparition was not of her own imagination.

As revealed in the fourth chapter, the governess is not certain

[5] *Ibid.*, p. 170.
[6] *Ibid.*, p. 174.

that it was a ghost, but that it might be "an insane, an unmentionable relative kept in unsuspected confinement,"[7] or even that the servants might be playing a trick on her. But with the second appearance of the ghost any such simple explanation seems doubtful. The apparition does not speak, but intuitively the governess understands something of his purpose from watching him: "on the spot there came to me the added shock of a certitude that it was not for me he had come there. He had come for someone else."[8] Though this knowledge gives her a moment of courage, its effect is to intensify the growing atmosphere of evil.

The role of Mrs. Grose, though minor, is an important one. The charming housekeeper is portrayed in these early chapters as a sane, common-sensical, down-to-earth sort of person; she is not, however, a superstitious person as one might associate with fictional characters of her type. She presents a realistic point of view that remains in contact with the everyday world in contrast to the intense awarenesses of the governess, who becomes more and more entangled in the world of evil. Because of her realistic viewpoint, her belief in the existence of the ghosts is important corroborative evidence for both the governess and the reader. Though she never sees the apparitions, she comes to believe in them.

Thus, in chapter four, James twists the situation around so that the governess, standing exactly where the ghost had stood a moment before looking into the room, is seen by Mrs. Grose in precisely the same way the governess had seen the ghost. And Mrs. Grose reacts *as if she had seen a ghost:*

> . . . she pulled up short as I had done; I gave her something of the shock I had received. She turned white, and this made me ask myself if I had blanched as much. She stared, in short, and retreated on just *my* lines, and I knew she had then passed out and come round to me and that I should presently meet her. I remained where I was, and while I waited I thought of more things than one. I wondered why *she* should be scared.[9]

And the reader wonders too.

The identity of the apparition is soon revealed (chapter five). From the governess's description, Mrs. Grose identifies him as Peter Quint, the master's valet, who is dead. By implication this information, though negative evidence, corroborates the governess's belief in the real existence of the apparition, for it is significant that Mrs. Grose does not at all question the validity of what the governess

[7] *Ibid.*, p. 179.
[8] *Ibid.*, p. 184.
[9] *Ibid.*, pp. 185–186.

saw, knowing as she did that Quint is dead and what the governess saw must therefore be a ghost. Unless we are to believe that the governess as narrator is a false center of revelation and that whatever she reports is suspect (even to imagining this conversation with Mrs. Grose), we can safely assume that James's intention is to present supporting evidence without giving the whole thing away.

James's notebooks contain specific references to ghosts and to the children's corruption:

> . . . the story of the young children (indefinite number and age) left to the care of servants in an old-country-house, through the death, presumably of parents. The servants, wicked and depraved, corrupt and deprave the children; the children are bad, full of evil, to a sinister degree. The servants *die* . . . and their apparitions, figures, return to haunt the house *and* the children, to whom they seem to beckon, whom they invite and solicit, from across dangerous places, the deep ditch of a sunk fence, etc.—so that the children may destroy themselves, lose themselves, by responding, by getting into their power. So long as the children are kept from them, they are not lost; but they try and try, these evil presences, to get hold of them.[10]

It is clear from this passage (the only passage in the notebooks concerned with *The Turn of the Screw*) that there is no ambiguity involved: the ghosts are real, and the children are corrupt and evil. The above passage, however, cannot be taken as the author's interpretation of the completed novel; since it was written before the novel was begun, we can conclude only that James *started* with that interpretation in mind.

The preface to *The Turn of the Screw* gives us a definite clue as to whether the ghosts were real or not: "Recorded and attested 'ghosts' are in other words as little expressive, as little dramatic, above all as little continuous and conscious and responsive, as is consistent with their taking the trouble . . . to appear at all."[11] That is to say,

> good ghosts, speaking by book, make poor subjects, and it was clear that from the first my hovering prowling blighting presences, my pair of abnormal agents, would have to depart altogether from the rules. They would be agents in fact; there would be laid on them the dire duty of causing the situation to reek with the air of Evil . . . The essence of the matter was the villainy of motive in the evoked predatory creatures; so that the result would be ignoble—by which I mean would be trivial—were this element of evil but feebly or inanely suggested.[12]

[10] Henry James, *The Notebooks of Henry James,* ed. by F. O. Matthiessen and Kenneth Murdock (New York, 1947), p. 178.

[11] James, "The Turn of the Screw," preface, p. xx.

[12] *Ibid.*

In other words, Peter Quint and Miss Jessel are not "stage" ghosts who clank chains and whirl across the stage in white sheets in order to frighten a character and thrill an audience. They are agents who create an atmosphere of evil. It is their evil *effect,* not their appearance, that is important. It is worthy of note to remember that at the time of conception of *The Turn of the Screw,* James was using a similar technique in writing *The Spoils of Poynton.* The central light was placed not on The Things themselves, but on their *effect* on the lives of the characters. By concentrating on the effect of the beauty of the possessions on the characters, he avoided the pitfall of weak or misplaced specification and yet achieved the desired effect. Similarly, in *The Turn of the Screw,* James created an intense atmosphere of evil and corruption by concentrating on the effect the ghosts had on the characters, an effect felt by the reader through the sensibilities of the narrator. As James tells us in his preface, his problem was to

> make the reader's general vision of evil intense enough . . . and his own experience, his own imagination, his own sympathy (with the children) and horror (of their false friends) will supply him quite sufficiently with all the particulars. Make him *think* the evil, make him think it for himself, and you are released from weak specifications.[13]

And this James achieves with remarkable success.

III

In the early chapters, the children have remained mostly in the background; but with the realization by the governess that the ghosts of Peter Quint and Miss Jessel have come for the children, Flora and Miles become the focus of attention. They are the key to the problem of evil in the novel. To what extent they have been corrupted or not, to what extent they are corrupt in themselves or innocent is the crux of the problem. The clue to their innocence or evilness is to be found in the imagistic language James uses.[14]

The beauty and light of innocence are allegorically contrasted with the ugliness and darkness of evil in recurrent images. In the Christian allegorical tradition two-valued contrasts between good and evil are represented by the contrast between the beauty of perfection (sinlessness) and the ugliness of imperfection (sinfulness), and the contrast between light (God as the creator of light) and

[13] *Ibid.,* p. xxi.

[14] Cf. Heilman, " 'The Turn of the Screw' as Poem" for detailed analysis of the imagistic and symbolic language.

darkness (the devil as the prince of darkness). Through the years these allegorical contrasts have lost their direct religious denotations but retained their good versus evil connotations. Thus, James in *The Spoils of Poynton,* written shortly before *The Turn of the Screw*, could identify beauty with the good life lived with a sense of taste, and identify ugliness with a lack of taste, an aesthetic "evil." In *The Turn of the Screw* James's intent in using these allegorical contrasts is to suggest evil-in-good. For example, Miles is described as:

. . . gentleness itself, and while I wagged my head at him he stood there more than ever a little fairy prince. It was his *brightness* indeed that gave me a respite . . . He fairly *glittered in the gloom* . . . He literally *bloomed* so from this exploit that he could afford *radiantly* to assent. "How otherwise should I have been bad enough?" he asked. (Italics mine).[15]

Here the intensity of Miles's beauty and brilliance is in contrast to the gloom of the dusk which suggests the evil surrounding him. But Miles's question gives us another turn on the screw: it presents an ironic ambiguity between outward appearance and inward intention; the allegorical values of light and darkness become twisted around so that the brightness suggests a false veneer, a surface glitter, and the gloom and its connotation of evil ironically suggests the evil underneath, suggests evil-in-good.

More directly the change in Flora is drastic: "'. . . at such times she's not a child: she's an old, old woman.'"[16] And again: ". . . she was literally, she was hideously, hard; she had turned common and almost ugly."[17] Allegorically, evil or guilt is evident in physical manifestations as a kind of corruption of original purity. But beyond this level, the change also represents, from the governess's viewpoint, the psychological shock of seeing Flora's personality and behavior change so suddenly and drastically.

The final appearance of Miss Jessel brings about this change in Flora. Both Miles and Flora have denied seeing the ghosts, but the governess is convinced they are lying. In the scene at the lake (chapters nineteen and twenty), surpassed in dramatic intensity only by the final scene of the novel, the governess sees Miss Jessel standing on the opposite bank of the lake. Though Mrs. Grose does not see Miss Jessel and therefore cannot corroborate the governess's vision, it is a well-established tradition in ghost-lore that a ghost has the power to appear to one person and not to others. Shaken—she

[15] James, "The Turn of the Screw," pp. 233–235.
[16] *Ibid.*, p. 279.
[17] *Ibid.*, p. 281.

had counted on Mrs. Grose seeing Miss Jessel—the governess realizes how Miss Jessel has triumphed. But prepared as she is for Mrs. Grose's reaction, she is not prepared for Miss Jessel's complete triumph. Flora takes up the cue from Mrs. Grose and turns on the governess, denying seeing Miss Jessel and pleading to be taken away from the governess.

If Flora is lost, Miles can yet be saved. He must confess if he is to be saved; and if he is saved, then the governess is saved too. In the light of later developments, Miles's dismissal from school, revealed early in the novel, can be taken as the first outward sign of his inner corruption. Quint, a year before his death, had charge of the children, especially of Miles. From the governess's and Mrs. Grose's point of view Quint was the corrupter, the instigator of evil. But it must be remembered that both the governess and Mrs. Grose are at this point concerned with defending the innocence and goodness of the children, even to the point of taking refuge in the nostalgia of childhood that after all "boys will be boys" and "naughtiness" is a good sign of natural spirits in a boy.

Quint and Miss Jessel, however, are the agents rather than the personification of evil. As agents of evil, they merely draw out, not originate, the propensity for evil that is potential in human nature. The children have within themselves the seeds of evil (as well as good); Quint and Miss Jessel return from the dead to claim Miles and Flora as of their own kind. One of the basic ironies of the novel is that the governess, in the role of protectress, causes evil to come out in the open; it is to her that the ghosts first appear, and it is her overdeveloped sense of duty that is the very means by which the children's corruption is revealed. She is not evil in herself, but her high sense of duty leads her, like Oedipus, to seek the truth, a course that can only lead to destruction; for moral good, which values truth as a virtue, can be destroyed by knowledge of the truth. Flora is lost to Miss Jessel because the governess precipitates the crisis that leads to Flora's moral destruction and then is powerless to save Flora. Miles's death is caused by the governess's insistence on his confession; the confession is wrested from him, but he dies from the shock.

The confession begins with Miles admitting he stole the letter. The governess, now in the role of confessor, does not accuse; she encourages, urges Miles to confess all. And "as if to blight his confession and stay his answer," [18] Peter Quint appears. Miles acknowledges his presence: the governess has triumphed; Miles is saved, Peter Quint has lost. But the experience—the fright, the horror, the

[18] *Ibid.*, p. 308.

recognition of evil—is too much for Miles. He utters an anguished cry of horror and dies in the governess's arms.

The novel ends with this revelation. To have gone beyond that point would have destroyed the dramatic unity and intensity of the novel. The whole effect of horror is concentrated in that final paragraph. Like Kurtz in Conrad's *The Heart of Darkness,* Miles is taken to the edge of the abyss. Like Kurtz's cry—" 'The horror! The horror!' "—Miles's cry is a glimpse of naked horror and evil. Like Kurtz, Miles cannot survive the frightful intensity of that experience. Like Kurtz, he dies with a cry of anguish on his lips, the anguish of the damned, who at the last moment wrest from fate a particle of salvation by recognizing the horror of evil.

The ultimate problem, whether evil really and absolutely exists outside of human experience, is left unanswered. But within the realm of human experience (and the *effect* of the ghosts, if not the ghosts themselves, is within the realm of human experience) evil is a real quality. As a real quality of human experience, evil is not separate from innocence but coexists with it. For dramatic and allegorical purposes innocence and evil are presented in conflict as a duality, but the total effect of James's treatment of the theme in *The Turn of the Screw* is the ironic ambiguity that innocence and evil are reverse sides of the same coin. The discrepancy between appearance and reality is not merely the false appearance of beauty and brightness hiding the inner reality of ugliness and darkness underneath, but also the lack of knowledge of what is underneath. As with many of James's novels of this period, *The Turn of the Screw* presents innocence as a lack of knowledge of evil. Here, however, the corruption exists already; the lack of knowledge is the governess's. Miles and Flora first appear wholly perfect and beautiful, wholly innocent and good, but change as the governess learns more of the truth. The final truth, which remains ambiguous until the final scene, is revealed by Miles admitting the existence of Peter Quint.

Henry James as Freudian Pioneer

Oscar Cargill

The tenderest of men, Henry James could hardly have used the illness of his sister Alice as the basis of a story while she lived, or later, without elaborately disguising it—particularly since that illness, though not concealed, was only guardedly revealed as mental. But a decade before he employed *The Turn of the Screw* as a story title, perhaps when he first used the phrase in *The Reverberator*, he saw its aptness as applied to some climactic episode in the career of a hysteric. Delicacy, propriety, affection instantly inhibited the development of so rich a "germ," but it remained planted in James's ingenious and subtle mind until he could bring it forth so altered that his closest intimates would not suspect its source or connections. The product was one of the greatest horror stories of all time.

Until Edmund Wilson designated *The Turn of the Screw* a study in psychopathology, only three persons had had the temerity to guess that it was something more than a ghost story. The three attracted no attention, but Wilson stirred up an indignant and vociferous opposition which literally "threw the book at him"—the book, however, being James's own comments on his story which seemed largely to lead away from Wilson's interpretation. It apparently did not occur to any of Wilson's critics that James might have an adequate motive for disguising his purpose in the tale; neither they nor Wilson referred to Alice James, though her tragic story provides an explanation for the "ambiguity" of both the commentary and the tale itself. James's "strategy" consisted in overlaying his real story with another which might, with complete plausibility, be read as a

SOURCE: *Chicago Review*, X (Summer, 1956), 13–29. Reprinted by permission of the editors and the author.

ghost story. The limitations of that "strategy," however, are that it confounds the acute and perceptive, and, like life, rewards the obtuse and conventional. Thanks to it, *The Turn of the Screw* continues to be misread as "a pure ghost story."

For a proper reading some of the difficulties that James himself interposed must be skirted or eliminated. The chief of these seems to be James's indication that the primary source of his inspiration was the fragment of a ghost story given him by a friend. At least Wilson's opponents have taken this to be the primary source, though James himself designated it the "private source": A circle of friends, one winter afternoon, round the hall fire of an old country house, lamenting the disappearance of the old-fashioned ghost story, were comforted by their host with "one of the scantest fragments of this form at its best," got from a lady when he was young.

> The story would have been thrilling could she have found herself in better possession of it, dealing as it did with a couple of small children in an out-of-the-way place, to whom the spirits of certain bad servants, dead in the employ of the house, were believed to have appeared with the design of "getting hold" of them. This was all, but there had been more, which my old friend's converser had lost the thread of: she could only assure him of the wonder of the allegations as she had anciently heard them made.

When James's *Letters* were published in 1920, the novelist's recollection of this "germ" for his tale was apparently supported by a letter to Arthur Christopher Benson, dated March 11, 1898, after the story had begun to appear in America in *Collier's Weekly*, in which the host is stated to have been the latter's distinguished father, the Archbishop, and the time and place "one of those two memorable—never to be obliterated—winter nights that I spent at the sweet Addington . . . in the drawing room by the fire." The "essence" of the anecdote struck James and he went home and made a note of it "of the most scrappy kind." With the publication of James's *Notebooks* (1947) his "scrappy" memorandum came to light:

> *Saturday, January 12th, 1895.* Note here the ghost-story told me at Addington (evening of Thursday 10th), by the Archbishop of Canterbury: the mere vague, undetailed faint sketch of it—being all he had been told (very badly and imperfectly), by a lady who had no art of relation, and no clearness: the story of the young children (indefinite number and age) left to the care of servants in an old countryhouse, through the death presumably of the parents. The servants, wicked and

depraved, corrupt and deprave the children; the children are bad, full of evil, to a sinister degree. The servants *die* (the story vague about the way of it) and their apparitions, figures, return to haunt the house *and* children, to whom they seem to beckon, whom they invite and solicit, from across dangerous places, the deep ditch of a sunk fence, etc.—so that the children may destroy themselves, by responding, by getting into their power. So long as the children are kept from them, they are not lost; but they try and try and try, these evil presences, to get hold of them. It is a question of the children "coming over to where they are." It is all obscure and imperfect, the picture, the story, but there is a suggestion of a strangely gruesome effect in it. The story to be told—tolerably obviously—by an outside spectator, observer.

Yet this double verification of James's recollection of the "private source" of his tale is undermined as absolute by the complete double failure of A. C. Benson and his brother to recall that their father ever told such a story. In fact, they are unusually emphatic in their separate denials that the tale was in their father's repertoire.

This contradiction is extraordinary, but it is still more extraordinary that James tries immediately, in fact, almost insistently, to establish his indebtedness to the Archbishop, for it was not his habit thus to acknowledge his sources. Did he not have a special reason for it in this instance?

Leaving this question unanswered for the moment and temporarily admitting the Archbishop's anecdote to have been *a* source, let us concentrate our attention on the most important element that the anecdote leaves out—the narrator of the tale. James's memorandum merely indicates that he once felt that the narrator should be "an outside spectator," an objective observer. He has totally abandoned this idea and given the story *two* narrators, the second emotionally involved with the first, and the first the principal actor in the tale—the inexperienced, provincial, and newly-hired governess of the young children. The first narrator is a man named Douglas who promises a group of friends a tale which "for sheer terror" surpasses everything; but he has to send up to London for it, since it is contained in an autobiographical document entrusted to him some twenty years ago by his younger sister's governess, who allegedly had written it out. Even before it arrives we are led to infer that Douglas was in love with the original narrator and we learn that she had begun her adventure as protectress of the children by falling in love herself in the single interview over her charges-to-be that she had with her future employer.

It is James's own emphasis on the governess and her facility for involvement that has led a few critics to inquire into her role and into the meaning of her narrative. The first to do this was the anonymous reviewer in *The Critic,* who, shortly after the story appeared in book form, observed,

the heroine . . . has nothing in the least substantial upon which to base her deep and startling cognitions. She perceives what is beyond perception, and the reader who begins by questioning whether she is supposed to be sane ends by accepting her conclusions and thrilling over the horrors they involve.

In 1919 Professor Henry A. Beers casually observed in an essay on Hawthorne: "Recall the ghosts in Henry James's *The Turn of the Screw*—just a suspicion of evil presences. The true interpretation of that story I have sometimes thought to be, that the woman who saw the phantoms was mad."

Five years later, Miss Edna Kenton, noting sharply that James had described the tale as "a piece of ingenuity, pure and simple, of cold artistic calculation, an *amusette* to catch those not easily caught," indicated that she thought *The Turn of the Screw* to be a kind of hoax story to test the attentiveness of his readers, the lazy apprehending it only as a ghost story, the more attentive getting a deeper richness. It is the Kenton thesis that the ghosts *and the children,* the pictorial isolation, are "only the exquisite dramatizations of her [the governess'] little personal mystery, figures for the ebb and flow of the troubled thought within her mind, acting out her story."

Tacitly avoiding Miss Kenton's hoax thesis but fully acknowledging the generic power of her suggestion in regard to the character of the governess, Edmund Wilson in a now famous and always challenging article, "The Ambiguity of Henry James," in the Henry James Issue of *Hound & Horn,* contended that the key to *The Turn of the Screw* lies in the fact that "the governess who is made to tell the story is a neurotic case of sex repression, and that the ghosts are not real ghosts but hallucinations of the governess." In 1938 and again in 1948 Wilson, as a result of his own rereading and reflection, revised his case, but stuck with conviction to his major premise, the neuroticism of the governess. She is still the fluttered, anxious girl out of a Hampshire vicarage who in her first interview becomes infatuated with her employer, and after confused thinking about him at Bly, discovers her first apparition, the figure of a man on a tower. With her help the figure, after a second appearance, is identified by the housekeeper, Mrs. Grose, as that of the master's handsome valet Peter Quint, (now dead), who had appropriated the master's clothes and used "to play with the little boy [Miles] . . . to spoil him." By the shore of a lake where she is watching the little girl,

Flora, at play the governess sees another apparition which she concludes is that of her young deceased predecessor, Miss Jessel, who allegedly had an affair with the valet. Suspecting the children as privy to this relationship, she is confirmed in her notion that they have been previously corrupted by these evil servants who have come back to get them. The game of protection which she plays is, however, according to Wilson's further analysis, one in which she transfers her own terror, and *more*, to the children, thwarts the boy's desire to re-enter school or to write his uncle, fixes upon him an unnatural fervid affection, and finally alienates the housekeeper before she literally frightens her young male charge to death.

Like Miss Kenton, Wilson insists that nobody but the governess sees the ghosts. "She believes that the children see them, but there is never any proof that they do. The housekeeper insists that she does not see them; it is apparently the governess who frightens her." At only one point was Wilson's interpretation labored; he could not adequately explain how Mrs. Grose was able to identify the male apparition as that of Peter Quint from the minute description given by the governess (who had never met the deceased valet) after her second encounter. The critics of the Wilson thesis—and they are an insistent score—bore down so heavily on this weakness that in 1948 Wilson capitulated, adding a separate note of retraction to his essay: "it is quite plain that James's conscious intention . . . was to write a *bona fide* ghost story; . . . not merely is the governess self-deceived, but James is self-deceived about her."

That James could be so completely deceived about the motivation of any one of his characters is a thesis very hard to accept in view of his marvelous understanding of human psychology; hence a reasonable doubt bids us review the whole difficulty again. The identification of Peter Quint by the housekeeper is at present the seemingly insurmountable thing, and here we must note that the governess herself indicates to Mrs. Grose, when the latter wavers in accepting the young woman's version of extraordinary later events, that *it is unimpeachable proof* that she has not invented the apparitions:

> To hold her [Mrs. Grose] perfectly, . . . I found I had only to ask her how, if I had "made it up," I came to be able to give, of each of the persons appearing to me, a picture disclosing, to the last detail, their special marks—a portrait on exhibition of which she had instantly recognized and named them.

If we persist in thinking this a crushing demonstration that the apparitions are supernatural, we are more gullible even than Mrs. Grose who at least became suspicious enough, toward the end of the tale, to separate little Flora from the governess and thus save her life.

Mrs. Grose and we are the victims of a palpable deception, the trick of a demonstrable pathological liar, a pitiful but dangerous person, with an unhinged fancy. We cannot examine all of the minute details of the governess' tendency (to the close reader they are multitudinous), but we can glance at one or two of the larger demonstrations of her complete unreliability. At the climax of the tale the governess promises to write a letter to her employer telling the state of things at Bly; this letter is stolen by little Miles who opens it to discover, as he confesses and as she reiterates, that it contains "nothing." Again, in the sixteenth chapter, the governess reports to Mrs. Grose a conversation which she asserts she has just had with the "ghost" of Miss Jessel in which the latter admitted she is "of the lost" and "of the damned" and that "she wants Flora." But we have just witnessed the whole of that encounter, and the only words uttered were by the governess—" 'You terrible, miserable woman!' . . . *There was nothing in the room the next minute but the sunshine.* [Italics ours.] . . ." And finally, let us look at the first appearance of the apparition of Miss Jessel, the former governess. The present governess is seated before a little lake and Flora is at play in front of her; she suddenly becomes aware "without direct vision" of "the presence, at a distance, of a third person." Lifting her eyes from her sewing, the governess perceives a specter across the lake, but little Flora, busy at fitting one piece of wood into another to form a boat, is "*back to* the water [Italics ours.] and obviously does not see the visitant. Yet when the governess reports the episode to Mrs. Grose, she states a flat untruth, "Flora *saw!*" When the housekeeper expresses some doubt about the episode, the governess breaks out with, " 'Then ask Flora—she's sure!' " But she instantly apprehends the danger from this and adds, in consternation, " 'No, for God's sake, *don't!* . . . she'll lie!' " Throughout, the governess covers her own mendacity by attributing lies or dissembling to the children in her keeping. If this is a ghost story, the governess' lies are inexplicable. We *must* believe her completely to accept the presences as ghosts and not hallucinations. We must also dismiss as frivolous the warning of James's amanuensis, Miss Bosanquet, that the chief obstacle to understanding his stories is failure to perceive that so many of his characters are liars.

With some knowledge now of the governess' character, we may look at the mystery of the identification of Peter Quint. After her *second* encounter with the male apparition, the governess produces some minute details about his appearance: he was hatless, wore smart clothes (not his own), had curly red hair and little whiskers. He might have been an actor, but he was never a gentleman. Mrs. Grose (who, the governess sees, has already recognized the man) asks if he were handsome. "*I saw the way to help her.* 'Remarkably!' . . . She faltered but a second. 'Quint!' she cried . . . 'Peter Quint, his valet, when he was here!'" Mrs. Grose has come out with the identification that the governess *expected.*

When the governess came to Bly she knew only of her predecessor, Miss Jessel, who, on the word of her employer, "was a most respectable person." On her second day at Bly she is conducted about the place by little Flora, who shows it to her "room by room, *secret by secret,* [Italics ours]" displaying a "disposition to tell me so many more things than she asked." (This innocent trait in little Flora has been utterly ignored.) Two days later the governess picks up from the housekeeper the fact that there had been a man around who had an eye for "young and pretty" women, like Miss Jessel and the present governess. After young Miles has come home from school, the governess has her *first* hallucination: she has been thinking of her handsome young employer; suddenly she perceives his actual presence—on a tower to which little Flora had formerly conducted her; a second glance assures her it is not her employer but another person. Yet she notes at this time only his straight bold stare—a thing singularly oppressive (at least in fiction) to a diseased mind. But if the apparition were close enough in appearance to the master to be taken for him, he cannot be quite the same figure as appears in the second encounter. The details that the governess supplied the housekeeper after the second occasion must have come from another source—from the prattle of her youngest charge and from her own seemingly artless prompting to the children. She has morbidly dwelt on them in the interval and they are a part of the second vision.

It is important to note also that the governess possesses a mind singularly open to evil suggestion. The letter informing her that Miles has been dismissed from his school states no reason; it is she who conjectures, "'he's an injury to others.'" A little later, on no new evidence, she thinks of "the little, horrid, unclean school-world" that Miles had left. Similarly, there is absolutely no reason for supposing the former governess and valet corrupt; the master gives Miss Jessel a good character and Quint had been his personal manservant. It is Mrs. Grose, out of the petty jealousy common to domestic servants, who at the prompting of the governess, embroiders the tale about a relation between the pair; it is the governess who gobbles every morsel of this and invents the theme of their evil designs upon the children. That she carries her insinuations to the children themselves (despite what she says to the contrary) is indicated by Mrs. Grose's declaration, after she had taken over Flora, that she has heard "horrors" from the child. Miles also betrays that the governess has implied an evil relationship between him and Quint, for when in the last scene she calls his direct attention to her specter (Miles "glaring vainly over the place and missing wholly"), the boy guesses at what she means him to see and names her a fiend: " 'Peter Quint—you devil!' "

Fiend she is, but a sick young woman, too. It is a triumph of James's art that he can give so much pathological information about the governess without damaging her credibility for many readers. He shows her apprehensive about going to Bly, yet her susceptibility to masculine charm is such that she pushes aside her fears to go as a result of her effortless conquest by the master; to the end of the tale her sudden infatuation is the mainspring of her action—she seeks to wring an admission from the tortured boy in order to clear herself with his uncle. She sequesters the children's letters because "they were too beautiful to be posted; I kept them myself; I have them all to this hour." She will not write herself about events at Bly because she fears that the master will look upon it as a device "to attract his attention to my slighted charms." From the beginning to the end she reiterates that she is highly disturbed, excited, and in a nervous state. She is, in addition, "in receipt these days of disturbing letters from home, where things are not going well." There is a broad hint that her trouble is hereditary—she speaks of "the eccentric nature of my father." She exults in her superiority to Mrs. Grose and in the way she can influence that ignorant woman:

> I had made her a receptacle of lurid things, but there was an odd recognition of my superiority. . . . She offered her mind to my disclosures as, had I wished to mix a witch's broth and proposed it with assurance, she would have held out a large clean saucepan.

With disarming candor, the governess summarizes herself, "I was queer company enough—quite as queer as the company I received" —meaning the spectral visitors. James, with marvelous symbolic irony, perhaps the best example in his fiction, has the mad young woman run around the house to a window where she has just seen a visitant and peer in herself—to frighten Mrs. Grose half out of her wits; then the novelist caps it with the governess' observation, "I wondered why *she* should be scared."

One thing is clear, if James got his anecdote from Archbishop Benson, he did not mean us to take it as the *only* source of his story.

He specifically labels it, as we have seen, the "private source." Might there not have been public sources, *i.e.*, things in print, available to everyone? Has it been remarked at all that James confesses to many "intellectual echoes" in recalling the creation of the tale? He adds further, "To knead the subject of my young friend's, the suppositious narrator's mystification thick . . . I seem to see draw behind it today a train of associations . . . so numerous I can but pick among them for reference." Not all of these possibilities can be investigated here, but one of them can hardly be neglected—the direct influence of Sigmund Freud.

Wilson's provocative paper should have led the author or others to the writings of Freud for a source for *The Turn of the Screw.* While most critics would concede that an author of genius could in his characterizations anticipate a later scientific elucidation of behavior, none has held that James in his study of the governess combined the perceptions of genius with actual technical knowledge. The date of the story, 1898, seems too early, save for the remote possibility that there might be something relevant in that early joint publication of Doctors Breuer and Freud—*Studien über Hysterie*—in 1895. But indeed here is included a case of the greatest relevancy, one which supplies more important elements than Archbishop Benson's anecdote, "The Case of Miss Lucy R."

A victim of "chronic purulent rhinitis," Lucy R. came to Freud late in 1891 for a treatment that lasted nine weeks and resulted in a complete cure. Lucy R. was the governess of two children, the daughters of a factory superintendent living in the suburbs of Vienna. She was "an English lady of rather delicate constitution" who was suffering from "depression and lassitude" as well as being "tormented by subjective sensations of smell," especially the smell of burned pastry. Freud's inquiry led to the discovery that this odor was associated with an actual culinary disaster which had occurred two days prior to her birthday when the governess was teaching her charges to cook in the schoolroom. A letter had arrived from her mother in Glasgow which the children had seized and kept from her (to retain for her birthday) and during the friendly scuffle the cooking had been forgotten. Struck by the fact that the governess' illness was produced by so small an event, Freud pressed further to discover that she was thinking of returning to her mother, who, he developed, stood in no need of her. The governess then confessed that the house had become "unbearable" to her. "The housekeeper, the cook, and the French maid seemed to be under the impression that I was too proud for my position. They united in intriguing against me and told the grandfather of the children all sorts of things about me." She complained to the grandfather and the father; not receiving, however, quite the support she expected, she offered her resignation, but was persuaded by the father to remain. It was in this period of crisis that the schoolroom accident occurred.

Though Freud had now an adequate "analysis of the subjective sensation of smell," he still was not satisfied and made a bold suggestion to the governess in order to study its effect:

> I told her that I did not believe all these things [exceptional "attachment for the children and sensitiveness towards other persons of the household"] were simply due to her affection for the children, but that I thought she was rather in love with the master, perhaps unwittingly, that she really nurtured the hope of taking the place of the [dead] mother, and it was for that reason that she became so sensitive towards the servants. . . . She feared lest they would notice something of her hope and scoff at her. She answered in her laconic manner: "Yes, I believe it is so."—"But if you knew that you were in love with the master, why did you not tell me so?"—"But I did not know it, or rather I did not wish to know it. I wished to crowd it out of my mind, never to think of it, and of late I have been successful."

The governess was not ashamed because she loved the man, she told Freud; she was chagrined because she thought that she would be ridiculed if her feelings were discovered since he was rich, of a prominent family, and her employer. After this admission she readily gave a complete account of her infatuation: Her love had sprung out of *a single intimate interview with the master:* "He became milder and much more cordial than usual, he told her how much he counted on her in the bringing up of his children, and looked at her rather peculiarly. It was this moment that she began to love him, and gladly occupied herself with the pleasing hopes she conceived during that conversation. However, this was not followed by anything else, and despite her waiting and persevering no other heart-to-heart talk following, she decided to crowd it out of her mind."

The governess' confession had led to a strange symbolic substitution in her subjective sense of smell, that of the aroma of a cigar for the burned pastry; Freud determined by analysis to remove this new memory symbol and thus get at the real root of the neurosis. A visitor, an elderly accountant, after dinner when the men were smoking, had kissed the children and thrown the father into a rage. This recalled an earlier scene in which a lady visitor had also kissed both children on the lips; the father had barely controlled himself until she was gone and then had berated the unfortunate governess.

He said that he held her responsible for this kissing, . . . that if it ever happened again, he would entrust the education of his children to someone else. This occurred while she believed herself loved and waited for a repetition of that serious and friendly talk. This episode shattered all her hopes.

Miss Lucy R. having thus completely disburdened her memory, her neurosis and rhinitis were cured and her sense of smell was restored.

There is one over-all resemblance between "The Case of Miss Lucy R." and the story of the governess of Bly: they are both presented as reports or case histories, for unlike most of James's stories, *The Turn of the Screw* is a tale with an elaborate portico. As we have seen, a man named Douglas produces a document which is the governess' story. It is Douglas who tells us that the governess began her adventure by falling in love in the single interview that she had with her future employer—as did Lucy R. This instant infatuation, decidedly not typical of James's stories, must be taken as a sign of susceptibility or abnormality. The employer is rich and handsome and of an old Essex family; he is the uncle of orphaned children—not two girls, but a niece and a nephew—whom he has neither the experience nor the patience to minister to personally. Like Miss Lucy's master, this new master gives the governess an unusual sense of commission and trust in the interview, a factor in her infatuation.

And as for the governess' "case"—the story within the story of *The Turn of the Screw*—that has special points of resemblance also with "The Case of Miss Lucy R." The valet and the former governess may be seen as trying to possess little Miles and Flora in their protectress' fancy as did the kissing male and female visitors the children of the Vienna manufacturer—hint enough for James to differentiate the sexless "bad servants" of Archbishop Benson's anecdote. In the episode of the children's retaining Miss Lucy's letter at a crucial time is the germ of the whole elaborate business with letters in *The Turn of the Screw:* the governess retains a letter from Miles's school saying that his return is not desired, she prevents Mrs. Grose from engaging to get a letter written to the master describing conditions at Bly, and the empty letter which she herself writes is allegedly stolen and destroyed by Miles.

In Miss Lucy's fear that others would discern her feelings is the governess' dread that Miles will reveal them to his uncle and a hint of the suspicion with which the other servants at Bly regard her after Mrs. Grose departs with the ill little Flora for London—thereby saving the child's mind, if not her life. On the other hand, the governess early reveals her love for the master to Mrs. Grose with the same candor that surprised Freud in Lucy R. Whether James was unconsciously influenced by Freud's analysis of Lucy's difficulties with her sense of smell or not, the governess has a peculiarly keen organ—she notes the smell of lately-baked bread in the housekeeper's room, the "fragrance of purity about the children," and even the talk of little Miles, just before his death, comes to her "like a waft of fragrance." The impatience of the children's uncle (which the governess seems to dread throughout her adventure) derives from the impetuosity of the Vienna manufacturer as certainly as the governess' characterization as a rural parson's daughter comes from the Glasgow mother of Miss Lucy, a suggestion redolent of Presbyterianism. But perhaps the most interesting revelation that James thought of the governess' story as a psychoneurotic case history is the fact (to which the governess constantly refers and which James surely meant the acute reader to note) that her all-important interview took place in "Harley Street"—the conventional "physicians' row" of fiction dealing with London. In this connection we should recall James's preference in the use of existing names as the "only ones that carry weight." "Harley Street" is surely such a name.

One of the most difficult evaluations of the governess to accept is that supplied by Douglas, who produces her case and who reports that later, when he knew her, "She was the most agreeable woman I've ever known in her position; she would have been worthy of any whatever." There is no implication in this that the governess is at all marked by any sorrow for young Miles who had died while in her charge—whatever the cause of his death. Does James mean to imply that, by telling her story to as sympathetic a listener as Douglas the governess underwent the kind of pathological purgation, as did Lucy R., which led to health and sanity? Allowing for the possible charity and understanding which might have modified Douglas' estimate twenty years after the woman's death, one is still persuaded that the outcome of the fiction was influenced by the outcome of the genuine case history so far as the governess is concerned.

Despite as many resemblances as are ever found in a literary source, despite the fact that none of these things is found in Benson's anecdote, some may claim that, though "The Case of Miss Lucy R." was available, it would hardly have come to James's knowledge. This brings us next to the tragic story of Alice James, as revealed in her *Journal* (1934). This woman, of whom the novelist was so fond, lucid and brilliant most of the time, was subject to "violent turns of hysteria," the first attacks occurring in 1867 or 1868 (or earlier), when she was nearing twenty. She writes of her struggle to conquer these "turns":

> As I used to sit immovable, reading in the library, with waves of violent inclination suddenly invading my muscles, taking some one of their varied forms, such as throwing myself out the window or knocking off the head of the benignant Pater, as he sat, with his silver locks, writing at his table; it used to seem to me that the only difference between me and the insane was that I had all the horrors and suffering of insanity, but the duties of doctor, nurse, and strait jacket imposed on me too.

One of her worst attacks came in the "hideous summer of 1876 when I went down to the deep sea and its waters closed over me and I knew neither hope nor peace." "Her malady is a kind of which little is known," her mother reports sadly, and from family letters we learn that "Alice is in New York undergoing motorpathy with Dr. Taylor" or "is being treated electrically by Dr. Neftel." The Monro treatment is tried and abandoned. After the death of her mother ("Alice is unaccountably upheld after this blow," her brother Robertson writes) and that of her father, she went to England to be where her brother Henry could care for her. London came to be regarded as too taxing, and she was located with a companion, Kate Loring, in Bournemouth, and then, when she was "much less well," in Leamington. During her English illnesses she was attended by various distinguished alienists; but in December, 1891, she was subjected, at the suggestion of William James, to the "therapeutic possibilities" of hypnotism as a device to relieve "all hideous nervous distresses," which morphine could not.

This treatment of hysteria had been utilized by the great French Doctor J. M. Charcot. In 1882 William James had studied with Charcot, and the following year Alphonse Daudet, Henry's friend, had dedicated *L'Évangeliste* to Charcot. Henry had used the novel for suggestions for *The Bostonians,* and his neurotic Olive Chancellor appears derived from Daudet's neurotic Mme. Autheman, and both in turn from the studies of Charcot. Hence there is no reason to suppose that Henry James was not as well acquainted with Charcot's therapy as was his brother William. And is it not reasonable to suppose that, when the methods of the Frenchman were superseded by those of Breuer and Freud, Henry James became acquainted with those as well? If he did not come to read *Studien über Hysterie* because of his continuing interest in his sister's case (she had died on March 6, 1892), it is possible that his friend, F. W. H. Myers, who had written the first notice of the book in English (*Proceedings*, Society for Psychical Research, IX, 12–15), may have brought it to his attention. Or Doctor Hack Tuke, of Bethlehem Hospital for the Insane, his sister's alienist, whom she fondly called "Tuckey" and who had taught Kate Loring the simple methods of hypnosis that were used with her.

But prior to any knowledge of *Studien über Hysterie* was James's personal acquaintance, of course, with the illness of his sister and with the delusions and fantasies of that illness. After her death he must have read her *Journal* with these things in mind. He noted her lively curiosity for sexual anecdotes, such as the premarriage chastity of her previous doctor, Sir Andrew Clark, and the vices of the Eton boys. When she sets down as fact Kate Loring's experience of *always* coming, at a turn of the stairs, upon a waiter and a chambermaid, in osculatory relaxations, Henry could regard that as a shared fantasy, but it may have suggested to him the relations of Quint and Miss Jessel, as imagined by the governess. When Douglas of *The Turn of the Screw* fails to reveal the name of the governess, that may be regarded as the protection a lover might offer, but the failure of Mrs. Grose ever to call the governess by name can only be looked upon as an unconscious revelation of how deeply fixed was James's caution to avoid the suspicion that his narrative had its source in Alice's illness.

James's dependence upon his personal knowledge of hysteria and on "The Case of Miss Lucy R." makes it clear that Wilson was profoundly right about the characterization of the governess: strictly, there are no "ghosts" in the story—the phantoms are creations of a hysterical mind, they are hallucinations. Just how much of the governess' narrative James meant as fantasy is hard to say: Wilson accepts the children as real and the death of little Miles as a fact; Miss Kenton suggests that even the children—"what they are and what they do—are only exquisite dramatizations of her [the governess'] little personal mystery, figures for the ebb and flow of troubled thought within her mind, acting out her story. . . ." If Miss Kenton is right, there is no tragedy in *The Turn of the Screw.* There is only ill-health. But this interpretation is not consistent with James's declaration to Doctor Louis Waldstein, "But, ah, the exposure, indeed, the helpless plasticity that isn't dear or sacred to *some*body! That was my little tragedy, . . ." or his confession to F. W. H. Myers, "The thing . . . I most wanted not to fail of doing . . . was to give the impression of the communication to the children of the most infernal imaginable evil and danger—the condition, on their part, of being as *exposed* as we can humanly conceive children to be." The children are *real*, and if the governess was the source of their terror, they were for the time being hardly dear to anybody. No evil is surely more "infernal" than that originating with an assigned protectress, and Flora was made ill and Miles was killed by her terrorizing them. If the governess is "the suppositious narrator," however, does James imply that someone must have written out her story as Freud did Miss Lucy's? Was either Douglas or the governess' employer of Harley Street a doctor?

But whoever set down the governess' story or whatever his profession, one of Miss Kenton's facts we cannot get away from—at some time the story proceeded wholly from the governess' lips and at no time is it to be wholly relied on for its facts. In the light of her unreliability, especially, how are we to view her monstrous insinuations in regard to the conduct of young Miles with Quint and the boy's dismissal from school—insinuations we now know to be taken from the note on the "vices" of the Eton boys in Alice's *Journal*? Lyon Richardson, who takes them as having substance (and one *has to* if one believes this a ghost story), writes: "The ghosts of Peter Quint and Miss Jessel hover over the lives of Miles and his sister as evil incarnate, permeating *The Turn of the Screw* with a terrible sense of eroticism." He proceeds to point out resemblances between Miles and young Morgan Moreen of *The Pupil* (1892), between whom and his tutor as Clifton Fadiman has indicated, a "perfectly unconscious homosexual love exists." Richardson goes still further: "Surrounded by some strange miasma of evil, it is the fate of Morgan to die in the arms of his tutor, even as Miles dies in the arms of the governess."

Before Richardson, Professor William Lyon Phelps had taken the same view of Miles's positive corruption, but had added a note that helps to explain further the evasiveness and ambiguity of all James's remarks upon *The Turn of the Screw*. Phelps wrote, "The connoting strength of its author's reticence was never displayed to better advantage; *had he spoken plainly the book might have been barred the mails. . . .*" Certainly, if the governess' insinuations had been plainly written out in the twilight of the Victorian age, or if they had been pointed to and discussed when the scandal and punishment of Oscar Wilde was still fresh memory, Henry James would have had his difficulties with the law—or with scandal, which he might have feared worse. He was already suspect for having associated himself briefly with the *Yellow Book* crowd. It would have availed him nothing to protest that the inferences drawn were not his meaning—the story might plausibly be read as Phelps and Richardson have read it; James had to "cover up" as best he could. Posterity could point out that little Miles's crime at school was only the pathetic one of stealing his young friends' letters (as the governess lets slip); the future could demonstrate that James never drew wicked children, but only children sinned against, as in *What Masie Knew;* James had to protect himself from a very present danger. It would be fantastic to suppose that he invented and "planted" in his own *Notebooks* Archbishop Benson's anecdote knowing that the latter was dead and could not deny it, but it is possible that solely to "cover up" he appealed to the family of the deceased Archbishop to substantiate his claim that the anecdote was the primary source of *The Turn of the Screw* when it may have been only a supplementary source. What better avoucher for one's morality than the Primate of the Church of England? Could a foul story have originated in so pure a source?

If there are things in the Preface to the volume containing *The Turn of the Screw* that are ambiguous or mystifying, they are justifiably so: Henry James had the duty of shielding Alice's memory and the necessity of setting up a legal shield, which he did in such seemingly artless phrases as "my bogey-tale," my "irresponsible little fiction," my "fairy tale pure and simple," behind which he could hide. The wonder is that James did not more positively emphasize the possibilities of reading the tale as a ghost story, did not lead the reader further astray save that there must have been a faint hope lodged in his heart that the central *motif* in his story, the horror of children betrayed by their protectress, a mad woman, might in time emerge and his transcendent skill as an artist be understood.

A Note on the Freudian Reading of "The Turn of the Screw"

John Silver

If the ghosts of "The Turn of the Screw" are not real, certainly the controversy over them is. Ever since Edna Kenton [1] and Edmund Wilson [2] entered the field, James's ghosts have been subjected to searching and repeated analysis. The so-called "Freudian" interpretation, as best set forth by Edmund Wilson, sees the ghosts as figments of the sexually repressed governess's imagination. On the other hand, the "conventional" critics claim that the governess is psychologically sound, that the ghosts are perfectly "real," as ghosts go, and that the children are, somehow, in contact with supernatural evil. Perhaps this interpretation's chief exponent is Robert B. Heilman.[3] This essay proposes to lend support to Mr. Wilson's interpretation by dissipating, substantially if not entirely, the major objection to it.

In general, the conventional viewpoint makes too little of the fact that James specifically (though not, as is his custom, repeatedly) points out that the tale is the governess's *story as told by*

SOURCE: *American Literature,* XXIX (May, 1957), 207–211. Reprinted by permission of the Duke University Press.

[1] "Henry James to the Ruminant Reader," *The Arts,* VI, 245–255 (Nov., 1924).

[2] "The Ambiguity of Henry James," *The Triple Thinkers* (New York, 1948).

[3] "The Freudian Reading of *The Turn of the Screw,*" *Modern Language Notes,* LXII, 433–445 (Nov., 1947). Other anti-Freudian essays are: Oliver Evans, "James's Air of Evil: 'The Turn of the Screw,'" *Partisan Review,* XVI, 175–187 (Feb., 1949); Glenn Reed, "Another Turn on James's 'The Turn of the Screw,'" *American Literature,* XX, 413–423 (Jan., 1949); E. E. Stoll, "Symbolism in Coleridge," *PMLA,* LXIII, 214–233 (March, 1938); Robert Liddell, *A Treatise on the Novel* (London, 1947), pp. 138–145.

the governess.[4] It is only human nature in such a situation for a person to paint her own picture as flatteringly as she convincingly can; the intense interest of the story is provided by the fact that the governess possesses a generous and deucedly clever amount of human nature. From the governess's point of view, her whole story is an *apologia,* a justification (note how often that word is on her lips) of her behavior at Bly. The title can best be understood as descriptive of the progressive accumulation of obstacles which the governess places in her own path. The object of her whole attempt is to make her final triumph (another concept always in her mind) so resounding that the master could not help noticing her—indeed, he would in all likelihood splendidly reward her by marrying her, just as in the story-book romances in whose terms the master is first described.[5]

The governess seems hardly the ideal "tutorial type" Mr. Heilman, for example, would make her out to be. Even from the conventional viewpoint, she clearly risks the lives of the children by trying to go it alone against the ghosts; indeed, little Miles pays with his life for her poor judgment in this matter. Furthermore, she grossly neglects the obviously important subjects of the cause for Miles's dismissal from school and the question of a new school next fall. Certainly these are the proper and primary concerns for a governess.

Nor can we, with really good sense, use Mrs. Grose as a kind of touchstone character and conclude that since she believes in the governess, we should also. In the first place, the reader should be more intelligent and discerning than the good but simple housekeeper. Secondly, Mrs. Grose could hardly side "against" the governess and tell her superior that she had ghosts in her belfry. As it is, the governess has a difficult time bringing Mrs. Grose to her point of view. And even then, at the showdown near the end of the book, relying on the intense dictates of her own good sense and momentarily free from the cajolery of the governess, Mrs. Grose rebels. When the governess confronts the runaway Flora with the figure of Miss Jessel, Mrs. Grose spoils the governess's "triumph" by comforting Flora with, "She isn't there, little lady, and nobody's there. . . . It's all a mere mistake and a worry and a joke—and we'll go home as fast as we can!" [6]

[4] Glenn Reed, for instance, describes the governess as "a character who is at the same time in the place of the action . . . *yet not involved too personally in the action*" (italics mine) (*op. cit.,* p. 419).

[5] ". . . such a figure as had never risen, save in a dream or an old novel, before a fluttered, anxious girl out of a Hampshire vicarage" (Modern Library ed., p. 6: all references are to this edition).

[6] P. 110.

The governess is skillful, *convincing*, and likable; Mrs. Grose is simple, trusting, untutored—and certainly devoted to protecting the children (which is just how the governess puts the case). The relationship which develops between the two women is beautifully rendered by James on the morning following the night the governess discovered Miles on the lawn. Mrs. Grose and the governess are sitting on the terrace watching the children: "They moved slowly, in unison, below us, over the lawn, the boy, as they went, reading aloud from a story-book and passing his arm round his sister to keep her quite in touch. Mrs. Grose watched them with positive placidity; then I caught the suppressed intellectual creak with which she conscientiously turned to take from me a view of the back of the tapestry." [7] The back of the tapestry is the side from which we can analyze the pretty picture on the front, the side where we see the "real threads" of the picture, and also—whether we like it or not—likely to be the dirty side. Without the governess, Mrs. Grose would have always watched them "with positive placidity."

But we have yet to face the anti-Freudians' strongest and most legitimate objection. How, they say, can the ghosts be figments of the governess's imagination when Mrs. Grose is able to identify *as Peter Quint* her description of a male apparition at a time when she had no knowledge of Quint? Both in his original essay and in his appended note of 1948, this is the only circumstance with which Mr. Wilson has trouble. Thus, Mr. A. J. A. Waldock, for example, holds Wilson's theory untenable for two reasons: "(1) The identification is absolute. . . . (2) Up to this moment the governess has never heard of Peter Quint. Here are two stubborn facts of the story, and *they must be accounted for*." [8] Well, let us see if we can account for them, and in so doing it may be enlightening to look at the housekeeper's identifications of both Miss Jessel and Peter Quint from the governess's descriptions of the figures she has seen.

In Chapter VIII we are told that the governess and Mrs. Grose have had a talk in which Mrs. Grose, not yet fully cowed into belief in the ghosts,[9] asks the governess *how she can be sure* that what she has seen were not, in effect, hallucinations. The governess's reply is typical of the half-truths she uses to bend Mrs. Grose to her will: "I found I had only to ask her how, if I had 'made it up,' I came to be able to give, for each of the persons appearing to me, a

[7] P. 68.

[8] "Mr. Edmund Wilson and *The Turn of the Screw*," *Modern Language Notes*, LXII, 332 (May, 1947).

[9] For an excellent exposition of the governess's technique of persuasion, see pp. 106–109 of Marius Bewley, "Appearance and Reality in Henry James," *Scrutiny*, XVII, 90–114 (Summer, 1950). The last section of this essay (pp. 102–114) is generally illuminating on "The Turn of the Screw."

picture disclosing, to the last detail, their special marks—a portrait on the exhibition of which she instantly recognized and named them."

If we turn first to the female apparition, even a cursory glance at Chapter VII shows that Mrs. Grose had *not* "instantly recognized and named" Miss Jessel. At this point the governess is telling Mrs. Grose of the "portentous" incident and appearance which she had just witnessed at the lake. Mrs. Grose asks:

> "Was it someone you've never seen?"
>
> "Yes. But someone the child has. Someone you have." Then, to show how I had thought it all out: "My predecessor—the one who died."
>
> "Miss Jessel?"
>
> "Miss Jessel. You don't believe me?" I pressed.
>
> She turned right and left in her distress. "*How can you be sure?*" [Last italics mine.]

And the governess's only answer to this well-put question is the evasive, "Then ask Flora—*she's sure!*" If, then, it is clear that Mrs. Grose does *not* identify Miss Jessel but has the name thrust upon her, we have only to show that it was possible for the governess to have found out about the existence of Peter Quint, prior to her description of him, in order to discredit fully the governess's rejoinder to Mrs. Grose's suggestion that she had "made it up."

It is true, as the governess maintains, that when she described to Mrs. Grose the male apparition, which she had by then seen twice, Mrs. Grose identified the figure as the dead valet; the governess's description was a good one. It can be shown, however, that James has carefully dropped four hints which, to say the least, allow the possibility that the governess has already learned about Peter Quint before her seemingly amazing description of the dead man.

First (and this is the only reference which Mr. Wilson notes; hence his apprehension about the hallucination hypothesis), there is in Chapter II an ambiguous reference to a man who liked the children's governess to be "young and pretty." It is left unclear whether this man is the master on Harley Street or someone else. This ambiguity may, as Mr. Wilson suggests, have started the governess wondering about a mysterious and unknown person on the premises, for the governess comments on the vague reference.

The next three hints combine to establish the possibility that the governess learned about Quint from people she met or overheard in the village. First, in Chapter IV, we learn that the village "through the park and by the good road" is only twenty minutes away, thus allowing convenient intercourse between Bly and the village. Second, in Chapter V, when the governess is telling Mrs. Grose about the apparition's first appearance, on the tower, the governess lets drop that she has actually *been to the village to check.* Mrs. Grose asks:

> "Was he a gentleman?"
> I found I had no need to think. "No." . . .
> "Then nobody about the place? *Nobody from the village?*"
> "Nobody—nobody. *I didn't tell you, but I made sure.*" [Italics mine.]

And finally, in Chapter VI, we get *from the governess* the whole story of Peter Quint's death—"the icy slope, the turn mistaken at night and in liquor"—when we have never witnessed Mrs. Grose telling the governess any of these details. How, then, could the governess have known except from some outside source? In view of James's technique throughout the story, it seems extremely unlikely that he would suppress any scene in which Mrs. Grose gives the governess information. The governess is the one who suppresses things. Furthermore we do not know whether or not Mrs. Grose herself knows the details of Quint's death.

In his original essay Mr. Wilson couched his reservation in these terms: "There seems to be only a single circumstance which does not fit into the hypothesis that the ghosts are mere fancies of the governess: the fact that her description of the masculine ghost at a time when she knows nothing of the valet should be identifiable as the valet by the housekeeper." [10] It seems reasonable, then, to say that the above considerations make it a distinct possibility that the governess, at the times of her descriptions of both apparitions, knew a good deal about both Quint and Jessel and that James has her skilfully cloak her knowledge in order to maneuver Mrs. Grose (and, more importantly, the reader) into believing in the reality of her ghosts.

[10] *The Triple Thinkers,* p. 90.

A Pre-Freudian Reading of *The Turn of the Screw*

Harold C. Goddard

Prefatory Note by Leon Edel

The following essay on Henry James's *The Turn of the Screw* was discovered among the posthumous papers of the late Harold C. Goddard, professor of English and former head of the department at Swarthmore College. According to Professor Goddard's daughter, Eleanor Goddard Worthen, he read this essay to generations of students, but made no attempt to have it published. It was written, she says, "about 1920 or before," and this is evident from the critics he mentions, no one later than William Lyon Phelps. The manuscript was communicated by her to Edmund Wilson, whose 1934 essay on "The Ambiguity of Henry James" first propounded the hallucination theory of *The Turn of the Screw* with a bow in the direction of an earlier essay by the late Edna Kenton. Mr. Wilson, in turn, sent the Goddard paper to me and we both agreed that even at this late date, when the ink flows so freely around the Jamesian ghostly tale, it should be made available to scholars and critics.

To Professor Goddard must now go the credit of being the first to expound, if not to publish, a hallucination theory of the story. Indeed he went much farther than Mr. Wilson was to go after him —and without the aid of Sigmund Freud. Goddard's essay is a singularly valuable example of textual study. He relied wholly on what James had written, and he gave the tale that attentive reading which the novelist invited when he called his work a "trap for the unwary." Professor Goddard does not seem to have been aware, when he read the tale, that there was a "trap" in it. He is the only

SOURCE: Reprinted from *Nineteenth-Century Fiction,* XII, No. 1 (June, 1957), 1–36; published by the University of California Press. Used by permission of the Regents of the University of California.

reader of *The Turn of the Screw* I have found who not only sought to understand the psychology of the governess but examined that heroine from the viewpoint of the children entrusted to her. No other critic has paid attention to the governess' account of the wild look in her own eyes, the terror in her face. Above all, however, we must be grateful to Professor Goddard's scrupulous analysis of the "identification" scene—the scene in which Mrs. Grose is led, step by step, to pronounce the name of Peter Quint. Even the most confirmed hallucinationists have never done sufficient justice to the ambiguity of this scene.

Before the discovery of this essay, Edna Kenton's "Henry James to the Ruminant Reader" published in *The Arts* in November, 1924, stood as the first to attract attention to the importance of the point of view in the tale: the fact that the story is told entirely through the governess' eyes. Miss Kenton did not suggest in her published essay the idea attributed to her by Edmund Wilson that the governess represented a "neurotic case of sex repression." This idea was wholly Mr. Wilson's, and earlier seems to have been Ezra Pound's who called the tale "a Freudian affair." Miss Kenton's article is patently innocent of any such theory, and those critics who have spoken of the "Kenton-Wilson" theory of *The Turn of the Screw* quite obviously had read only Wilson, not Kenton.

With the studies of Goddard, Kenton and Wilson before us, I would suggest that three points are now clearly established: (1) that Henry James wrote a ghost story, a psychological thriller, intended to arouse a maximum of horror in the minds of his reader; (2) that a critical reading of the story to see how James achieved his horror reveals that he maneuvered the reader into the position of believing the governess' story even though her account contains serious contradictions and a purely speculative theory of her own as to the nature and purpose of the apparitions, which she alone sees; (3) that anyone wishing to treat the governess as a psychological "case" is offered sufficient data to permit the diagnosis that she is mentally disturbed. It is indeed valid to speculate that James, in speaking of a "trap," was alluding not only to the question of the governess' credibility as a witness, but to her actual madness.

There is one particular aspect of Professor Goddard's paper which we must not neglect. I refer to the fact that he was able to relate the story to his own memory of a governess he had when he was a boy. I think this important because it represents the use of the reader's personal experience for which James made so large an allowance—as he confided to his doctor, Sir James Mackenzie, who questioned him about the story, and also as he explained in his preface: that is James's refusal to specify the "horrors" so that the reader might fill them in for himself. Goddard's experience happened to be particularly close to the very elements in the story. There was thus a happy conjunction of personal fact with his "factual" reading.

Professor Goddard's other works, also published posthumously, include *The Meaning of Shakespeare, Atomic Peace, Blake's Fourfold Vision,* and an article published in *College English* proposing that Hamlet's love letter was a forgery by Polonius.

•

A good many years ago I came upon *The Turn of the Screw* for the first time. I supposed I already knew what it was to be gripped by a powerful tale. But before I had read twenty pages I realized I had never encountered anything of this sort before. From the first, one of the things that chiefly struck me about James's tale was the way in which it united the thrills one is entitled to expect from a ghost story with the quality of being entirely credible, even by daylight. True, it evoked plenty of mystery, propounded plenty of enigmas, along the way. But the main idea of the thing was perfectly plain. So at any rate I thought. For it never occurred to me that there could be two opinions about that. What was my surprise, then, on taking it up with a group of students, to discover that not one of them interpreted it as I did. My faith in what seemed to me the obvious way of taking the story would have been shaken, had I not, on explaining it, found the majority of my fellow readers ready to prefer it to their own. And this experience was repeated with later groups. Yet, even after several years, it had not occurred to me that what seemed the natural interpretation of the narrative was not the generally accepted one among critics, however little it might be among students. And then one day I ran on a comment of Mr. Chesterton's on the story. He took it precisely as my students had. I began watching out in my reading for allusions to the story. I looked up several references to it. They all agreed. Evidently my view was utterly heretical. Naturally I asked myself more sharply than ever why I should take the tale as a matter of course in a way that did not seem to occur to other readers. Was it perversity on my part, or profundity? And then one day it dawned over me that perhaps it was neither. Perhaps it was the result rather of a remarkable parallelism between a strange passage in my own early experience (of which I will tell at the proper time) and what I conceived to be the situation in *The Turn of the Screw*. However that may be, at every rereading of the story I found myself adhering more firmly than ever to my original idea, and I continued to find that it met with hospitable reception among others. Not that there were no skeptics. Or now and then a strenuous objector.

It was not until long afterward that I happened to read James's own comment on *The Turn of the Screw* in the introduction to the collected edition of his works. A man with an hypothesis runs the risk of finding confirmation for it everywhere. Still, I set down for what it is worth the fact that in this introduction I thought I detected a very clear, but very covert, corroboration of the interpretation I favored, and later still, I got a similar impression, on the publication of James's letters, from passages referring to the story.

I

From the point of view of early critics of the tale [Chesterton, Rebecca West, Carl Van Doren, Stuart P. Sherman, William Lyon Phelps, and others], the story may be summarized, in bare outline, as follows:

An English gentleman, by the death of his brother in India, becomes guardian of a small niece and nephew whom he places in charge of a governess at his country home, Bly. On his departure from Bly, he leaves behind him his valet, a certain Peter Quint, with whom the governess, Miss Jessel, soon grows intimate. The valet is thus thrown in close contact with the children, with the boy in particular, who goes about with him as if he were his tutor. Quint and Miss Jessel are a depraved pair and the children do not escape exposure to their evil. As to the details of the contamination they suffer the author leaves us mercifully in the dark. But it is easy enough to guess its general nature. A point at any rate that is certain is the character of the language that the children pick up from their two protectors: language the use of which, later, was the cause of the boy's mysterious expulsion from school. Prior to this, however, Peter Quint, while drunk, slips on the ice and is killed, and Miss Jessel, whose reason for leaving Bly is broadly hinted, goes away—to die.

The world seems well rid of such a pair. But it turns out otherwise. For it is precisely at this point that the full horror of the situation develops and the infernal character of the tale emerges. Such, it transpires, was the passion of Quint and Miss Jessel to possess the souls of the innocent children that they return to their old haunts *after death*, appearing to their helpless victims and infecting them still further with their evil. Meanwhile, however, a new governess has been procured, who, fortunately for the children, is herself susceptible to visitation from the world beyond, and who, accordingly, does not long remain in the dark as to what is going on. Moved by a love for her little charges and a pity for them as deep as were the opposite emotions of their former companions, she attempts to throw herself as a screen between them and the discarnate fiends who pursue them, hoping that by accepting, as it were, the first shock of the impact she may shield and ultimately save the innocent children. In her protracted and lonely struggle with the agents of evil, she succeeds, but at a fearful price. The children are indeed dispossessed. But the little girl is driven in the process into a delirium which threatens the impairment of her intellect, while the boy expires at the very moment when he is snatched back from the brink of the abyss down which he is slipping.

So taken, the story is susceptible equally of two interpretations. It may be conceived, literally, as an embodiment of the author's belief in survival after death and in the power of spirits, in this case of evil spirits, to visit the living upon earth. Or, if one prefers, it may be taken as an allegory, in manner not unlike *Dr. Jekyll and Mr. Hyde:* the concrete representation of the truth that the evil that men do lives after them, infecting life long after they themselves are gone. Either way, except for the heroism of the second governess, the story is one of almost unmitigated horror. One can understand Mr. Chesterton's doubt as to whether the thing ought ever to have been published.

II

It is possible, however, to question the fidelity of either of these versions to the facts of the story and to ask whether another interpretation is not possible which will redeem the narrative from the charge of ugliness and render even its horror subordinate to its beauty.

Consider the second governess for a moment and the situation in which she finds herself. She is a young woman, only twenty, the daughter of a country parson, who, from his daughter's one allusion to him in her story, is of a psychically unbalanced nature; he may, indeed, even have been insane. We are given a number of oblique glimpses into the young woman's home and early environment. They all point to its stifling narrowness. From the confinement of her provincial home this young and inexperienced woman comes up to London to answer an advertisement for a governess. That in itself constitutes a sufficient crisis in the life of one who, after one glimpse, we do not need to be told is an excessively nervous and emotional person. But to add to the intensity of the situation the young woman falls instantly and passionately in love with the man who has inserted the advertisement. She scarcely admits it even to herself, for in her heart she knows that her love is hopeless, the object of her affection being one socially out of her sphere, a gentleman who can never regard her as anything other than a governess. But even this is not all. In her overwrought condition, the unexplained death of the former governess, her predecessor, was enough to suggest some mysterious danger connected with the position offered, especially in view of the master's strange stipulation: that the incumbent should assume *all* responsibility, even to the point of cutting off all communication with him—never writing, never reporting. Something extraordinary, she was convinced, lurked in the background. She would never have accepted the place if it had not been for her newborn passion; she could not bring herself to disappoint him when he seemed to beg compliance of her as a favor—to say nothing of severing her only link with the man who had so powerfully attracted her.

So she goes down to Bly, this slip of a girl, and finds herself no longer a poor parson's daughter but, quite literally, the head of a considerable country establishment. As if to impart the last ingredient to the witch's broth of her emotions, she is carried away almost to the point of ecstasy by the beauty of the two children, Miles and Flora, who have been confided to her care. All this could supply the material for a nervous breakdown in a girl of no worldly experience and of unstable psychical background. At any rate she instantly becomes the victim of insomnia. The very first night she fancies that she hears a light footstep outside her door and in the far distance the cry of a child. And more serious symptoms soon appear.

But before considering these, think what would be bound to happen even to a more normal mentality in such a situation. When a young person, especially a young woman, falls in love and circumstances forbid the normal growth and confession of the passion, the emotion, dammed up, overflows in a psychical experience, a daydream, or internal drama which the mind creates in lieu of the thwarted realization in the objective world. In romantic natures this takes the form of imagined deeds of extraordinary heroism or self-sacrifice done in behalf of the beloved object. The governess' is precisely such a nature and the fact that she knows her love is futile intensifies the tendency. Her whole being tingles with the craving to perform some act of unexampled courage. To carry out her duties as governess is not enough. They are too humdrum. If only the house would take fire by night, and both children be in peril! Or if one of them would fall into the water! But no such crudely melodramatic opportunities occur. What does occur is something far more indefinite, far more provocative to the imaginative than to the active faculties: the boy, Miles, is dismissed from school for no assigned or assignable reason. Once more, the hint of something evil and extraordinary behind the scenes! It is just the touch of objectivity needed to set off the subconsciousness of the governess into an orgy of myth-making. Another woman of a more practical and common sense turn would have made inquiries, would have followed the thing up, would have been insistent. But it is precisely complication and not explanation that this woman wants —though of course she does not know it. The vague feeling of fear with which the place is invested for her is fertile soil for imaginative invention and an inadvertent hint about Peter Quint dropped by the housekeeper, Mrs. Grose, is just the seed that that soil requires. There is no more significant bit of dialogue in the story. Yet the reader, unless he is alert, is likely to pass it by unmarked. The governess and the housekeeper are exchanging confidences. The former asks:

"What was the lady who was here before?"

"The last governess? She was also young and pretty—almost as young and almost as pretty, Miss, even as you."

"Ah then I hope her youth and her beauty helped her!" I recollect throwing off. "He seems to like us young and pretty!"

"Oh he *did,*" Mrs. Grose assented: "it was the way he liked everyone!" She had no sooner spoken indeed than she caught herself up. "I mean that's *his* way—the master's."

I was struck. "But of whom did you speak first?"

She looked blank, but she coloured. "Why, of *him.*"

"Of the master?"

"Of who else?"

There was so obviously no one else that the next moment I had lost my impression of her having accidentally said more than she meant.

The consciousness of the governess may have lost its impression, but we do not need to be students of psychology to know that that inveterate playwright and stage manager, the subconscious, would never permit so valuable a hint to go unutilized.

Mrs. Grose, as her coloring shows and as the governess discerns, is thinking of some one other than the master. Of what man would she naturally think, on the mention of Miss Jessel, if not of Miss

Jessel's running mate and partner in evil, Peter Quint? It is a momentary slip, but it is none the less fatal. It supplies the one character missing in the heroic drama that the governess' repressed desire is bent on staging: namely, the villain. The hero of that drama is behind the scenes: the master in Harley Street. The heroine, of course, is the governess herself. The villain, as we have said, is this unknown man who "liked them young and pretty." The first complication in the plot is the mysterious dismissal of the boy from school, suggestive of some dim power of evil shadowing the child. The plot itself remains to be worked out, but it will inevitably turn on some act of heroism or self-sacrifice—both by preference—on the part of the heroine for the benefit of the hero and to the discomfiture of the villain. It is a foregone conclusion, too, that the villain will be in some way connected with the boy's predicament at school. (That he really was is a coincidence.) All this is not conjecture. It is elemental human psychology.

Such is the material and plan upon which the dreaming consciousness of the governess sets to work. But how dream when one is the victim of insomnia? Daydream, then? But ordinary daydreams are not enough for the passionate nature of the governess. So she proceeds to act her drama out, quite after the fashion of a highly imaginative child at play. And the first scene of her dramatic creation is compressed into the few moments when she sees the stranger on the tower of Bly by twilight.

Whence does that apparition come? *Out of the governess's unconfessed love and unformulated fear.* It is clearly her love that first evokes him, for, as she tells us, she was thinking, as she strolled about the grounds that afternoon, how charming it would be suddenly to meet "some one," to have "someone" appear at the turn of a path and stand before her and smile and approve, when suddenly, with the face she longed to see still vividly present to her mind, she stopped short. "What arrested me on the spot," she says, "—and with a shock much greater than any vision had allowed for —was the sense that my imagination had, in a flash, turned real. He did stand there!—but high up, beyond the lawn and at the very top of the tower. . . ." Instantly, however, she perceives her mistake. It is not he. In her heart she knows it cannot be. But if her love is too good to be true, her fears, unfortunately, are only too true. And forthwith those fears seize and transform this creation of her imagination. "It produced in me," the governess declares, "this figure, in the clear twilight, I remember, two distinct gasps of emotion, which were, sharply, the shock of my first and that of my second surprise. My second was a violent perception of the mistake of my first: the man who met my eyes was not the person I had precipitately supposed. There came to me thus a bewilderment of vision of which, after these years, there is no living view that I can hope to give." What has happened? The hint that the housekeeper dropped of an unnamed man in the neighborhood has done its work. Around that hint the imagination of the governess precipitates the specter who is to dominate the rest of the tale. And because he is an object of dread he is no sooner evoked than he becomes the raw material of heroism. It only remains to link him with the children and the "play" will be under way with a rush.

This linking takes place on the Sunday afternoon when the governess, just as she is about to go out to church, becomes suddenly aware of a man gazing in at the dining room window. Instantly there comes over her, as she puts it, the "shock of a certitude that it was not for me he had come. He had come for someone else." "The flash of this knowledge," she continues, "—for it was knowledge in the midst of dread—produced in me the most extraordinary effect, starting, as I stood there, a sudden vibration of duty and courage." The governess feels her sudden vibration of duty and courage as the effect of the apparition, but it would be closer to the truth to call it its cause. Why has the stranger come for the children rather than for her? Because she must not merely be brave; she must be brave for someone's sake. The hero must be brought into the drama. She must save the beings whom he has commissioned her to protect. And that she may have the opportunity to save them they must be menaced: they must have enemies. That is the creative logic of her hallucination.

"Hallucination!" a dozen objectors will cry, unable to hold in any longer. "Why! the very word shows that you have missed the whole point of the story. The creature at the window is no hallucination. It is he himself, Peter Quint, returned from the dead. If not, how was Mrs. Grose able to recognize him—and later Miss Jessel—from the governess's description?"

The objection seems well taken. The point, indeed, is a capital one with the governess herself, who clings to it as unshakable proof that she is not mad; for Mrs. Grose, it appears, though she seems to accept her companion's account of her strange experiences, has moments of backsliding, of toying with the hypothesis that the ghosts are mere creatures of the governess' fancy. Whereupon, says the latter, "I had only to ask her how, if I had 'made it up,' I came to be able to give, of each of the persons appearing to me, a picture disclosing, to the last detail, their special marks—a portrait on the exhibition of which she had instantly recognized and named them."

This retort floors Mrs. Grose completely, and she wishes "to sink the whole subject."

But Mrs. Grose is a trustful soul, too easily floored perhaps. If we will look into the matter a bit further than she did, we will perceive that it simply is not true that the governess gave such detailed descriptions of Peter Quint and Miss Jessel that Mrs. Grose instantly recognized their portraits. In the case of Miss Jessel, indeed, such a statement is the very reverse of the truth. The "detailed" description consisted, beyond the colorless fact that the ghost was pale, precisely of the two items that the woman who appeared was extremely beautiful and was dressed in black. But Mrs. Grose had already told the governess explicitly, long before any ghost was thought of, that Miss Jessel was beautiful. Whether she had been accustomed to dress in black we never learn. But that makes little difference, for the fact is that it is *the governess herself and not Mrs. Grose at all who does the identifying:*

> "Was she someone you've never seen?" asked Mrs. Grose.
>
> "Never," the governess replies. "But some one the child has. Some one *you* have." Then to show how I had thought it all out: "My predecessor—the one who died."
>
> "Miss Jessel?"
>
> "Miss Jessel," the governess confirms. "You don't believe me?"

And the ensuing conversation makes it abundantly plain that Mrs. Grose is still far from convinced. This seems a trifle odd in view of the fact that Peter Quint is known to be haunting the place. After having believed in one ghost, it ought not to be hard for Mrs. Grose to believe in another, especially when the human counterparts of the two were as inseparable in life as were the valet and the former governess. Which makes it look as if the housekeeper were perhaps not so certain after all in the case of Quint. Why, then, we ask, did she "identify him"? To which the answer is that she identified him because the suggestion for the identification, just as in the case of Miss Jessel, though much more subtly, come from the governess herself. The skill with which James manages to throw the reader off the scent in this scene is consummate.

In the first place, the housekeeper herself, as we have had several occasions to remark, has already dropped an unintentional hint of someone in the neighborhood who preys on young and pretty governesses. This man, to be sure, is dead, but the new governess, who did not pay strict enough attention to Mrs. Grose's tenses, does not know it. We have already noted the part that the fear of him played in creating the figure in the tower. When now that the figure comes closer and appears at the window, it would be strange indeed if, in turning over in her head all the possibilities, the idea of the unknown man to whom the housekeeper had so vaguely referred did not cross at least the fringe of the governess' consciousness. That it actually did is indicated by her prompt assumption that Mrs. Grose can identify their extraordinary visitor. "But now that you've guessed," are her words.

"Ah I haven't guessed," Mrs. Grose replies. And we are quite willing to agree that at this point she hasn't. But notice what follows:

The governess has assured Mrs. Grose that the intruder is not a gentleman.

"But if he isn't a gentleman—" the housekeeper begins.

"What *is* he?" asks the governess, completing the question and supplying the answer:

"He's a horror."
"A horror?"
"He's— God help me if I know *what* he is!"
Mrs. Grose looked round once more; she fixed her eyes on the duskier distance and then, pulling herself together, turned to me with full inconsequence. "It's time we should be at church."

What was the thought which was seeking entrance to Mrs. Grose's mind as she gazed at the duskier distance and which was sufficiently unwelcome to make her throw it off with her gesture and quick digression? Was it something that the word "horror" had suggested, something vaguely hinted in the governess's "He's—God help me if I know *what* he is!"—as if their visitant were a creature not altogether mortal? We cannot be sure. But when, immediately afterward, the governess refuses to go to church on the ground that the stranger is a menace to the *children,* there is no longer any question as to the thought that dawns over the housekeeper. *A horror in human form that is a menace to the children!* Is there anything, or anyone, in Mrs. Grose's experience that answers that description? A thousand times yes! Peter Quint. Can there be a shadow of doubt that it is Quint of whom she is thinking when, to use the author's words, her

large face showed me, at this, for the first time, the far-away faint glimmer of a consciousness more acute: I somehow made out in it the delayed dawn of an idea I myself had not given her and that was as yet quite obscure to me. It comes back to me that I thought instantly of this as something I could get from her; and I felt it to be connected with the desire she presently showed to know more.

So do the governess' fears and repressed desires and the housekeeper's memories and anxieties unconsciously collaborate.

The conversation is resumed and the governess gives, in the most vivid detail, a picture of the man she has seen at the window. Following which, from the governess's challenge, "You *do* know him?" the housekeeper holds back for a second, only to admit, a moment later, that it is Peter Quint and to stagger her companion, in the next breath, by her calm declaration that Quint is dead.

Now with regard to all this the critical question is: Granted that Mrs. Grose's mind was already toying with the idea of Quint, how could she have identified him unless the governess' description tallied with the man? For, unlike Miss Jessel's, she has received no advance hint with regard to Quint's personal appearance, and the description, instead of being brief and generalized, is lengthy and concrete. The objection seems fatal to the view that the apparitions were mere creatures of the governess' imagination. But upon examination this line of argument will be found, I think, to prove too much.

Suppose a missing criminal is described as follows: "A squat, ruddy-cheeked man about thirty years old, weighing nearly two hundred pounds; thick lips and pockmarked face, one front tooth missing, two others with heavy gold fillings; big scar above left cheek bone. Wears shell glasses; had on, when last seen, brown suit, gray hat, pink shirt and tan shoes." Then suppose a man flushed with excitement, were to rush into police headquarters exclaiming that he had found the murderer. "How do you know?" the chief detective asks. "Why! I saw a man about thirty years old with shell glasses and tan shoes!"

Well, it is only a slight exaggeration to say that Mrs. Grose's "identification" of Peter Quint, in the face of the governess' description, is of exactly this sort. The picture the latter draws of the face at the window, with its red curling hair and peculiar whiskers, is so vivid and striking that Mrs. Grose, if she was listening and if it was indeed a description of Quint, ought not to have hesitated a second. But she did hesitate. It may of course be said that she hesitated not because the description did not fit but because Quint was dead. But if so, why, when she does identify him, does she pick out the least characteristic points in the description? Why, when she does "piece it all together" (what irony in that "all"!), does her identification rest not at all on the red whiskers or the thin mouth, but, of all things, on the two facts that the stranger wore no hat and that his clothes looked as if they belonged to someone else? As if good ghosts always wore hats and bad ones carried their terrestrial pilferings into eternity! That touch about "the missing waistcoats" is precisely at Mrs. Grose's intellectual level, the level, as anyone who has ever had the curiosity to attend one knows, of a fifth-rate spiritualistic seance.

The thing is really so absurd that we actually wonder whether Mrs. Grose was listening. Recall the beginning of the dialogue:

> "What's he like?" [asks Mrs. Grose]
>
> "I've been dying to tell you. But he's like nobody."
>
> "Nobody?" she echoed.
>
> "He has no hat." Then seeing in her face that she already, in this, with a deeper dismay, found a touch of picture, I quickly added stroke to stroke.

We see what we expect to see. That Mrs. Grose should so instantaneously find a touch of picture in the colorless item that "he had no hat" is a measure of the high degree of her suggestibility, as good proof as one could want that an image is already hovering in the background of her mind waiting to rush into the foreground at the faintest summons. That, as we have seen, is exactly what the image of Peter Quint is doing. And so, is it at all unlikely that in completing the picture of which the mention of the hat has supplied the first touch, Mrs. Grose pays scant attention to the other, verbal picture that the governess is drawing? The point need not be urged, but at any rate she gives no evidence of having heard, and at the governess' concluding sentence, "He gives me a sort of sense of looking like an actor," her echoed "An actor!" sounds almost as if it were at that point that her wandering attention were called back. That of course is only conjecture. But what is not conjecture, and significant enough, is the fact that the two shaky pegs on which Mrs. Grose hangs her identification come, one at the very beginning, the other at the very end, of a long description the intervening portions of which would have supplied her, any one of them, with solid support. When a man crosses a stream on a rotten wooden bridge in spite of the fact that there is a solid one of stone a rod or two away, you naturally wonder whether he has noticed it.

III

"But why waste so much breath," it will be said, "over what is after all such a purely preliminary part of the story and over such an incidental character as Mrs. Grose. Come to the main events, and to the central characters, the children. What *then* becomes of your theory that Quint and Miss Jessel are just hallucinations? How can they be that, when Miles and Flora see them?"

Before coming to this certainly pertinent objection, I wonder if I may interject the personal experience mentioned at the beginning. It may be that this experience subconsciously accounts for my reading of *The Turn of the Screw.* If its influence is justified, it is worth recounting. If it is unjustified, it should be narrated that the reader may properly discount its effect on my interpretation of the tale. It may be that for me this memory turns into realism what for even the author was only romance.

When I was a boy of seven or eight, and my sister a few years older, we had a servant in the family—a Canadian woman, I think she was—who, I now see on looking back (though no one then suspected it), was insane. Some years later her delusions became marked, her insanity was generally recognized, and she was for a time at least confined in an asylum. Now it happened that this woman, who was of an affectionate nature and loved children, used to tell us stories. I do not know whether they were all of one kind, but I do know that the only ones my memory retained were of dead people who came to visit her in the night. I remember with extraordinary vividness her account of a woman in white who came and stood silent at the foot of her bed. I can still see the strange smile—the insane smile, as I now recognize it to have been—that came over the face of the narrator as she told of this visitant. This woman did not long remain a servant in our family. But suppose she had! Suppose our parents had died, or, for some other reason, we had been placed exclusively in her care. (She was a woman of unimpeachable character and kindliest impulses.) What might have happened to us? What might not! Especially if she had conceived the notion that some of her spiritual visitants were of an infernal character and had come to gain possession of us, the children for whom she was responsible. I tremble to think. And yet no greater alteration than this would have been called for in an instance within the range of my own experience to have duplicated essentially what I conceive to be the situation in *The Turn of the Screw.*

Now the unlikelihood of this situation's occurring is precisely the fact that in real life someone would recognize the insanity and interfere to save the children. This was the difficulty that confronted the author of *The Turn of the Screw,* if we may assume for the moment that I have stated his problem correctly. The extraordinary skill and thoroughness with which he has met it are themselves the proof, it seems to me, that he had that difficulty very consciously in his mind. He overcomes it by fashioning the characters of the master and the housekeeper expressly to fit the situation. The children's uncle, from the first, wishes to wash his hands entirely of their upbringing, to put them unreservedly in the hands of their governess, who is *never*, in any conceivable way, to put up her problems or questions to him in person or by letter. The insistence on this on this from beginning to end seems needlessly emphatic unless it serves some such purpose as the one indicated. The physical isolation of the little household in the big estate at Bly is also complete. The governess is in supreme authority; only she and the housekeeper have anything to do with the children—and Mrs. Grose's character is shaped to fit the plot. If she is the incarnation of practical household sense and homely affection, she is utterly devoid of worldly experience and imagination. And she is as superstitious as such a person is likely to be. She can neither read nor write, the latter fact, which is a capital one, being especially insisted on. She knows her place and has a correspondingly exalted opinion of persons of higher rank or education. Hence her willingness, even when she cannot understand, to accept as truth whatever the governess tells her. She loves the children deeply and has suffered terribly for them during the reign of Quint and Miss Jessel. (Her relief on the arrival of Miss Jessel's successor, which the latter notices and misinterprets, is natural.) Here is a character, then, and a situation, ideally fitted to allow of the development of the governess' mania unnoticed. James speaks of the original suggestion for *The Turn of the Screw* as "the vividest little note for sinister romance that I had ever jotted down," expressing wonder at the same time "why so fine a germ, gleaming there in the wayside dust of life, had never been deftly picked up." His note, he says in one of his letters, was "of a most scrappy kind." The form which the idea assumed in his mind as it developed we can only conjecture. My own guess would be that it might, in content at least, have run something like this: *Two children, under circumstances where there is no one to realize the situation, are put, for bringing up, in the care of an insane governess.*

IV

With this hypothesis as a clue, we can trace the art with which James hypnotizes us into forgetting that it is the governess' version of the story to which we are listening, and lures us, as the governess unconsciously lured Mrs. Grose, into accepting her coloring of the facts for the facts themselves.

It is solely on the governess' say-so that we agree to the notion that the two specters have returned in search of the *children.* Again it is on her unsupported word that we accept for fact her statement that, on the occasion in the garden when Miss Jessel first appeared, Flora *saw*. The scene itself, after Miss Jessel's advent, is not presented. (Time enough to present his scenes when James has "suggested" to his readers what they shall see.) What happened is narrated by the governess, who simply announces flatly to Mrs. Grose that, "Two hours ago, in the garden, Flora *saw*." And when Mrs. Grose naturally enough demands, ". . . how do you know?" her only answer is, "I was there—I saw with my eyes," an answer valuable or worthless in direct proportion to the governess' power to see things as they are.

In the case of Miles the method is the same except that James, feeling that he now has a grip on the reader, proceeds more boldly. The scene is not narrated this time; it is presented—but only indirectly. The governess, looking down from a window, catches Miles out at midnight on the lawn. He gazes up, as nearly as she can figure, to a point on the building over her head. Whereupon she promptly draws the inference: "There was clearly another person above me. There was a person on the tower." This, when we stop to think, is even "thinner" than in the case of Flora and Miss Jessel, for this time even the governess does not see, she merely infers. The boy gazes up. "Clearly" there was a man upon the tower. That "clearly" lets the cat out of the bag. It shows, as every tyro in psychology should know, that "clear" is precisely what the thing is not.

These two instances are typical of the governess' mania. She seizes the flimsiest pretexts for finding confirmation of her suspicions. Her theories swell to such immense dimensions that when the poor little facts emerge they are immediately swallowed up. She half admits this herself at the very beginning of the story. "It seems to me indeed, in raking it all over," she says of the night following the appearance of Quint at the dining room window, "that by the time the morrow's sun was high I had restlessly read into the facts before us almost all the meaning they were to receive from subsequent and more cruel occurrences." Scarcely ever was the essence of mania better compressed into a sentence than in her statement: "The more I go over it the more I see in it, and the more I see in it the more I fear. I don't know what I *don't* see, what I *don't* fear!" Or again, where in speaking of the children's lessons and her conversations with them she says:

> All roads lead to Rome, and there were times when it might have struck us that almost every branch of study or subject of conversation skirted

forbidden ground. Forbidden ground was the question of the return of the dead in general and of whatever, in especial, might survive, for memory, of the friends little children had lost. There were days when I could have sworn that one of them had, with a small invisible nudge, said to the other: "She thinks she'll do it this time—but she won't!" To "do it" would have been to indulge for instance—and for once in a way —in some direct reference to the lady who had prepared them for my discipline.

And from this she goes on to the conviction that the children have fallen into the habit of entertaining Quint and Miss Jessel unknown to her.

"There were times of our being together when I would have been ready to swear that, literally, in my presence, but with my direct sense of it closed, they had visitors who were known and were welcome. Then it was that, had I not been deterred by the very chance that such an injury might prove greater than the injury to be averted, my exaltation would have broken out. "They're here, they're here, you little wretches," I would have cried, "and you can't deny it now!"

Her proof in these cases, it will be noted, is the fact that she "could have sworn" that it was so.

How completely innocent and natural the children really were through all these earlier passages of the drama anyone will see who will divest himself of the suggestion that the governess has planted in his mind. The pranks they play are utterly harmless, and when she questions the perpetrators, because they are perfectly truthful, they have the readiest and most convincing answers at hand. Why did little Miles get up in the middle of the night and parade out on the lawn? Just as he said, in order that, for once, she might think him *bad*. Why did Flora rise from her bed at the same hour? By agreement with Miles. Why did she gaze out the window? To disturb her governess and make her look too. These answers, true every one, ought to have disarmed the children's inquisitor. But she has her satanic hypothesis, so that the very readiness of their replies convicts instead of acquitting them in her eyes. They are inspired answers, she holds, splendidly but diabolically inspired. They scintillate with a mental power beyond the children's years. "Their more than earthly beauty, their absolutely unnatural goodness. It's a game," she cries, "it's a policy and a fraud!"

And the same is true of the children's conversation as of their conduct. Always their remarks are direct and ingenuous; always she reads into them an infernal meaning—until, when she says of Miles, ". . . horrible as it was his lies made up my truth," we see that the exact reverse of this is the case: that in reality his truth, and Flora's, made up her lies. If Miles asks about "this queer business of ours," meaning the queer way his education is being attended to, she takes it as referring to the boy's queer intercourse with Quint. If, when she remarks to Miles that they are alone, the latter replies that they still have "the others," obviously referring to the servants, the governess is not content to take his words at their face value but must interpret "the others" as referring to the specters. So candid, so unsophisticated, so prompt are the children's answers that even the governess' insane conviction at times seems shaken. But always—so James contrives it—some convenient bit of *objective* evidence comes in to reassure her: the fearful language that Flora uses in her delirium, the boy's lie about the letter, the clear evidence at the end that he has something on his mind that he longs to confess.

As these last examples suggest, it is necessary to qualify the idea that Miles and Flora are just happy natural children. They are that during the earlier passages of the story. But they do not continue to be. And the change is brought about by no one but the governess herself. Herein lies one of the subtlest aspects of the story.

Fear is like faith: it ultimately creates what at first it only imagined. The governess, at the beginning, imagines that the actions and words of the children are strange and unnatural. In the end they become strange and unnatural for the good and sufficient reason that the children gradually become conscious of the strangeness and unnaturalness of her own attitude toward them. They cannot put it into words: they have never heard of nervousness, still less of insanity. But they sense it and grow afraid, and she accepts the abnormal condition into which their fear of *her* has thrown them as proof of their intercourse with the two specters. Thus do her mania and their fear feed and augment each other, until the situation culminates—in a preliminary way—in two scenes of shuddering terror.

The first of these is the occasion when the governess comes at night to Miles's bedside and tries, without mentioning the dreaded name of Quint, to wring from the child a confession of the infernal intercourse which, she is convinced, he is guilty of holding. Forget, for the moment, the governess' version of the occurrence and think of it as it must have appeared in the child. A little boy of ten, who has for some time felt something creepy and uncanny in the woman who has been placed in charge of him and his sister, lies awake in the dark thinking of her and of the strangeness of it all. He hears steps outside his door. At his call the door opens, and there, candle in hand, is this very woman. She enters and sits beside him on the edge of the bed. For a moment or two she talks naturally, asking him why he is not asleep. He tells her. And then, quite suddenly, he notices in her voice the queer tone he has felt before, and the something in her manner, excited but suppressed, that he does not like. As they go on talking, this excitement grows and grows, until in a final outburst she falls on her knees before him and begs him to let her *save* him! Visualize the scene: the hapless child utterly at a loss to know what the dreadful "something" is from which she would "save" him; the insane woman on her knees almost clasping him in her hysterical embrace. Is it any wonder that the interview terminates in a shriek that bursts from the lips of the terror-stricken boy? Nothing could be more natural. Yet, characteristically, the governess interprets the boy's fright and outcry as convincing proof of the presence of the creature she is seeking to exorcise. Utterly unconscious of the child's fear of *her,* she attributes his agitation to the only other adequate cause she can conceive.

The corresponding scene in the case of Flora occurs the next day by the lake. Once more, think of it from the angle of the child. A little girl, too closely watched and confined by her governess, seizes an opportunity for freedom that presents itself and wanders off for half an hour in the grounds of the estate where she lives. A little later, the governess and the housekeeper, out of breath with searching, come upon her. A half-dozen words have hardly been exchanged when the governess, a tremor in her voice, turns suddenly on the child and demands to know where her former governess is—a woman whom the little girl knows perfectly well is dead and buried. The child's face blanches, the housekeeper utters a cry, in answer to which the governess, pointing across the lake and into vacancy cries out: "She's there, she's there!" The child stares at the demented woman in consternation. The latter repeats: "She's there, you little unhappy thing—there, there, *there,* and you know it as well as you know me!" The little girl holding fast to the housekeeper, is frozen in a convulsion of fear. She recovers herself sufficiently to cry out, "I don't know what you mean. I see nobody. I see nothing. I never *have,*" and then, hiding her head in the housekeeper's skirts, she breaks out in a wail, "Take me away, take me away—oh take me away from *her!*"

"From *me?*" the governess cries, as if thunderstruck that it is not from the specter that she asks to be delivered.

"From you—from you!" the child confirms.

Again, is not the scene, when innocently taken, perfectly natural? Yet again the governess is incapable of perceiving that the child is stricken with terror not at all at the apparition but at *her* and the effect the apparition has had upon her.

V

"All of which is very clever and might be very convincing," it will be promptly objected, "if it did not calmly leave out of account the paramount fact of the whole narrative, that in the end Miles *does* see and identifies Quint by name. It was this "supreme surrender of the name" that justified and redeemed the governess' devotion. Never, never—it was a point of honor—had the name of Quint crossed her lips in Miles's presence. When, then, it crossed his lips in her presence, it was the long sought proof that from the first he had been holding communication with the spirit of the dead man. That is the very point and climax of the story."

If you think so, you have failed to trace the chain of causation down which the name of Peter Quint vibrates from the brain of the governess to the lips of little Miles.[1] True, it was a point of honor with her not to breathe the name of Quint in the children's presence. But how about the name of Quint's companion? Ought not silence with regard to Miss Jessel's to have been equally sacred? It surely should have been. But there, it will be remembered, the governess' self-control failed her. On that day, by the lake, when, as we have seen, she blurted out to Flora her fatal, "Where, my pet, is Miss Jessel?" only to answer her own question a second later by gazing into what to the two others was vacancy and shrieking, "She's there, she's there!" she fixed forever in the child's mind a bond between her own (that is, the governess') strange "possession" and the name of Miss Jessel.

Flora, as we have remarked, is driven half out of her senses with fright, and while she has never "seen" Miss Jessel previously, nothing is more probable than that she "sees" her now. At the very least, memories of her and of the time the child was in her care figure prominently in the delirium that follows the shock of witnessing the governess' strange affliction. Whatever Flora's feelings toward her former governess originally were, from now on they will be linked inextricably with her fear of her present one. The two are merged in a single complex. How do we know? Because the child, in her delirium, uses shocking language or ideas which she has picked up in the days when Miss Jessel consorted with Peter Quint. To poor Mrs. Grose this is, at last, final proof that the governess is right in suspecting the little girl of diabolical intercourse. To the reader it ought to be proof of nothing of the sort. Nearly everyone remembers the case of the ignorant maidservant of the Hebrew scholar who, on being hypnotized, would overflow in a

[1] For I do not think we are entitled to infer that Miles learned anything from the stolen letter.

torrent of extraordinary fluent Hebrew. This gift came very far from proving her learned in Hebrew. Quite as little did the "horrors," to use Mrs. Grose's word, to which Flora gives utterance in her fever prove her a depraved or vicious child. An interesting parallel and variant of the same motive is found in the innocent profanity of Hareton Earnshaw in *Wuthering Heights,* verbally shocking language from the lips of a rarely beautiful character.

The next link in the chain is the fact that Miles sees Flora between the time she is taken ill and the scene of his final interview with the governess. The very brevity of the author's reference to this fact suggests his expectation that the breathless or unwary reader will read right over it without getting its significance. (If it has no significance, why mention it at all?) The governess, fearing that Flora, who has now turned against her, will influence Miles to do the same, warns Mrs. Grose against giving her the opportunity to do so.

"There's one thing, of course" [she says]: "they mustn't, before she goes, see each other for three seconds." Then it came over me that, in spite of Flora's presumable sequestration from the instant of her return from the pool, it might already be too late. "Do you mean," I anxiously asked, "that they *have* met?"

At this she quite flushed. "Ah, Miss, I'm not such a fool as that! If I've been obliged to leave her three or four times, it has been each time with one of the maids, and at present, though she's alone, she's locked in safe. And yet—and yet!" There were too many things.

"And yet what?"

Mrs. Grose never really answers this "And yet what?" which, together with her flushing when the governess asks her if the children have met, more than intimates that they already have, especially in view of the assumed complete trustworthiness of "the maids." That they do meet later, at any rate, we know from half a sentence thrown in with seeming inadvertence in the next chapter. Vague as the matter is left, it is clear that the boy had an opportunity to fix in his mind a connection between his sister's illness, her dread of their present governess, and—Miss Jessel. It was an uncomprehended connection to be sure, but its effect on the boy's mind must have been all the more powerful on that account—and the more so at this particular moment because under the stress of the governess' attempt to extort a confession from him his mind was already magnifying his venial fault about the letter into a mortal sin.

When, then, at the end, the governess in the presence of her hallucination shrieks to Peter Quint that he shall possess her boy "No more, no more, no more!" and the child, panting in her insane embrace, realizes that she sees someone at the window, how natural, how inevitable, that he should ask if "she" is "*here*," and to the echoed question of the governess, who this "she" is, should reply, "Miss Jessel, Miss Jessel!" Bear in mind that, all through, it is Miss Jessel, according to the governess, who has been visiting Flora, while it is Quint who has been holding communication with Miles. Why, if the boy has been in the habit of consorting with the spirit of Quint and if he senses now the nearness of a ghostly visitant, why, I say, does he not ask if *he* is here? Surely, then, his "Is *she* here?" is the best possible proof that the idea of a spiritual presence has been suggested not at all by past experiences of a similar sort but precisely by something he has overheard from Flora, or about her, plus what he gets at the moment from the governess.

"I seized, stupified, his supposition," she says, at his utterance of Miss Jessel's name, "—some sequel to what we had done to Flora, but this made me only want to show him that it was better still than that." (In one flash that "better" lays bare the governess' possession!) "It's not Miss Jessel!" she goes on. "But it's at the window —straight before us. It's *there,* the coward horror, there for the last time!"

If we could hear her voice when she cries, "It's not Miss Jessel!" I suspect that her intonation of the last two words would show how completely, if unconsciously, she conveyed *to* the boy's mind the very name which her whole justification depended on receiving *from* him. The child's next question, "It's *he?*" is but an ellipsis for "If, then, it is not *she,* you mean it must be the other one of the two who were always together?" But the governess, determined not to be the first to mention the unmentionable name, demands, "Whom do you mean by 'he'?"

"Peter Quint—you devil!" is the child's reply in words that duplicate, more briefly and even more tragically, the psychology of the "horrors" uttered by his sister in her delirium. But even now he does not see, though he accepts the governess' assurance that Peter Quint is there. "Where?" he cries. And that last word his lips ever utter, as his eye roams helplessly about the room in a vain endeavor to *see,* gives the ultimate lie to the notion that he does see now or has ever seen. But the governess, deluded to the end, takes it as meaning that at last the horror is exorcised and the child himself dispossessed.

VI

If on your first reading of *The Turn of the Screw* the hypothesis did not occur to you that the governess is insane, run through the story again and you will hardly know which to admire more, James's daring in introducing the cruder physical as distinguished from the subtler psychological symptoms of insanity or his skill in covering them up and seeming to explain them away. The insane woman is telling her own story. She cannot see her own insanity—she can only see its reflection, as it were, in the faces, trace its effect on the acts, of others. And because "the others" are in her case children and an ignorant and superstitious woman, these reflections and effects are to be found in the sphere of their emotions rather than in that of their understandings. They see and feel her insanity, but they cannot comprehend or name it.

The most frequent mark of her disease is her insane *look* which is mirrored for us in the countenances and eyes of the others.

Mrs. Grose first sees this look in something like its fullness when the governess gazes through the window of the dining room after she has seen Peter Quint. So terrible is the sight of her face that Mrs. Grose draws back blanched and stunned, quite as if it were a ghost that she had seen. "Did I look very queer?" the governess asks a moment later when the housekeeper has joined her. "Through this window?" Mrs. Grose returns. "Dreadful!"

There are a dozen other passages that strike the same note:

"I was conscious as I spoke that I looked prodigious things," says the governess, "for I got the slow reflection of them in my companion's face."

"Ah with such awful eyes!" she exclaims in another passage, referring to the way Miss Jessel fixed her gaze on Flora. Whereupon, she continues, Mrs. Grose "stared at mine as if they might really have resembled them." And a moment later: "Mrs. Grose—her eyes just lingering on mine—gave a shudder and walked to the window."

In a later conversation between the same two: "I don't wonder you looked queer," says the governess, "when I mentioned to you the letter from his school!" "I doubt if I looked as queer as you!" the housekeeper retorts.

"I remember that, to gain time, I tried to laugh," the governess writes of her walk to church with Miles, "and I seemed to see in the beautiful face with which he watched me how ugly and queer I looked."

To which should be added the passage, too long to quote, in which Flora recognizes for the first time the full "queerness" of her governess, the passage that culminates in her agonized cry: "Take me away, take me away—oh take me away from *her!*"

The governess' insane laugh, as well as her insane look, is frequently alluded to. Of this we have just mentioned one example.

Of references to her maniacal cries there are several: "I had to smother a kind of howl," she says when Mrs. Grose tells her of Quint's relations with the children. Or again, when she catches Miss Jessel sitting at her table: "I heard myself break into a sound that, by the open door, rang through the long passage and the empty house." What do we say of persons who shriek in empty houses—or who frighten children into similar outbreaks? "The boy gave a loud high shriek which, lost in the rest of the shock of sound, might have seemed, indistinctly, though I was so close to him, a note either of jubilation or of terror."

The wonder is not that the children cried out, but that they did not cry out sooner or oftener. "I must have gripped my little girl with a spasm that, wonderfully, she submitted to without a cry or a sign of fright." The implications of that sentence prepare us for the scene in Miles's bedchamber where the governess falls on her knees before the boy and for the final scene where she locks him in her insane embrace.

But the psychological symptoms are more interesting than the more obviously physical ones.

The consciousness of the governess that she is skirting the brink of the abyss is especially significant. It reminds us of Lear's: "That way madness lies." Only in her case we have to take her word for it that she never goes over the edge.

"We were to keep our heads," she says, "if we should keep nothing else—difficult indeed as that might be. . . ."

"I began to watch them in a stifled suspense," she remarks of the children, "a disguised tension, that might well, had it continued too long, have turned to something like madness. What saved me, as I now see, was that it turned to another matter altogether." Of the truth of this last assertion the governess presents precisely nothing but her own word as proof. Or, to put it from her own angle, she presents—the apparitions. "She was there," she says of Miss Jessel's appearance by the lake, "so I was justified; she was there, so I was neither cruel nor mad." The irony of summoning a specter as witness that one is not mad is evident enough.

Indeed this style of reasoning does not quite satisfy the governess herself in her more normal intervals. There are moments throughout the tale when a lurking doubt of her own sanity comes to the surface. When, for instance, Mrs. Grose begs her to write to the master and explain their predicament, she turns on her with the question whether she can write him that his little niece and nephew are mad. "But if they *are,* Miss?" says Mrs. Grose. "And if I am myself, you mean?" the governess retorts. And when she is questioning Miles, on the very edge of the final catastrophe, the same paralyzing thought floats for a second into her consciousness: ". . . if he *were* innocent what then on earth was I?" That she never succeeded in utterly banishing this terrible hypothesis is shown by the view of the case she takes long after the events are over and she is writing her account of them: "It was not," she sets it down, "I am as sure to-day as I was sure then, my mere infernal imagination." Clear proof that she was sure at neither time.

There are a dozen other passages, if there were only space to quote them, that show how penetratingly, if unconsciously, the sane remnant of the governess' nature can diagnose her own case and comprehend the character of the two apparitions. "What arrested me on the spot," she says of the figure on the tower, ". . . was the sense that my imagination had, in a flash, turned real." "There were shrubberies and big trees," she says when she is hunting for Quint on the lawn, "but I remember the clear assurance I felt that none of them concealed him. He was there or was not there: not there if I didn't see him." The account of the first appearance of Miss Jessel, too, if read attentively, reveals clearly the psychological origin of the apparition, as does the governess' account of the experience, later, to Mrs. Grose:

"I was there with the child—quiet for the hour; and in the midst of it she came."

"Came how—from where?"

"From where they come from! She just appeared and stood there—but not so near."

"And without coming nearer?"

"Oh for the effect and the feeling she might have been as close as you!"

But perhaps the most interesting and convincing point in this whole connection is the fact that the appearance of the ghosts is timed to correspond not at all with some appropriate or receptive moment in the children's experience but very nicely with some mental crisis in the governess'. In the end their emergence is a signal, as it were, of a further loss of self-control on her part, and advance in her mania. "Where, my pet, is Miss Jessel?" she asks Flora, committing the tragic indiscretion of mentioning the interdicted name. And presto! Miss Jessel appears. "Tell me," she says, pressing Miles cruelly to the wall in their last interview, "if, yesterday afternoon, from the table in the hall, you took, you know, my letter." And instantly Peter Quint comes into view "like a sentinel before a prison." But the last instance of all is the most revealing. With the ruthlessness of an inquisitor she has extorted from Miles the confession that he "said things" at school. It is not enough that he tells her to whom he said them. She must follow it up to the bitter end. "What *were* these things?" she demands unpardonably. Whereupon, "again, against the glass, as if to blight his confession and stay his answer, was the hideous author of our woe—the white face of damnation." If perfect synchronization is any criterion, surely, with these instances before us, the inference is inescapable that if Peter Quint has come out of the grave to infect or capture anyone, it is the governess and not the child.

VII

There will doubtless be those who can quite agree with all I have said about *The Turn of the Screw* who will nevertheless not thank me for saying it. "Here was the one ghost story left," they will protest, "that carried a genuine mystery in it. And you proceed to rationalize it ruthlessly, to turn it, in James's own words, into a 'mere modern "psychical" case, washed clean of all queerness as by exposure to a flowing laboratory tap.' What a pity!"

But do I rationalize it, ruthlessly or otherwise? Is insanity something easier to probe and get to the bottom of than a crude spiritualism? Are Peter Quint and Miss Jessel a whit less mysterious or less appalling because they are evoked by the governess's imagination? Are they a whit less real? Surely the human brain is as solid a fact as the terrestrial globe, and inhabitants of the former have just as authentic an existence as inhabitants of the latter. Nor do I mean by that to imply, as to some I will seem to have implied all through, that Peter Quint and Miss Jessel exist *only* in the brain of the governess. Perhaps they do and perhaps they don't. Like Hawthorne in similar situations—but with an art that makes even Hawthorne look clumsy—James is wise enough and intellectually humble enough to leave that question open. Nobody knows enough about insanity yet to be dogmatic on such a matter. Whether the insane man creates his hallucinations or whether insanity is precisely the power to perceive objective existences of another order, whether higher or lower, than humanity, no open-minded person can possibly pretend to say, however preponderating in the one direction or the other present evidence may seem to him to be. Whoever prefers to, then, is free to believe that the governess sees the actual spirits of Peter Quint and Miss Jessel. Nothing in the tale, I have tried to show, demands that hypothesis. But nothing, on the other hand, absolutely contradicts it. Indeed, there is room between these extremes for a third possibility. Perhaps the governess' brain caught a true image of Peter Quint straight from Mrs. Grose's memory via the ether or some subtler medium of thought transference. The tale in these respects is susceptible of various readings. But for one theory it offers, I hold, not an inch of standing ground: for the idea, namely, that the children *saw.*

This is the crucial point. Everything else is incidental. Believe that the children saw, and the tale is one thing. Believe that they did not see, and it is another—as different as light from darkness. Either way the story is one of the most powerful ever written. But in the former event it is merely dreadful. In the latter it is dreadful, but also beautiful. One way, it is a tale of corrupted childhood. The other, it is a tale of incorruptible childhood. Of the two, can it be doubted which it is? Miles and Flora are touched, it is true, by the evil of Peter Quint and Miss Jessel, but they are not tainted. That evil leaves its mark, if you will, but no trace of stain or smirch. The children remain what they were—incarnations of loveliness and charm. Innocence is armor plate: that is what the story seems to say. And does not life bear out that belief? Otherwise, in what but infamy would the younger generation ever end? Miles and Flora, to be sure, are withered at last in the flame of the governess' passion. But corrupted—never! And the withering of them in the flame is rendered tragic rather than merely horrible by the heroism that they display. The things that children suffer in silence! Because, as here, their heroism generally takes the form of endurance rather than of daring, rarely, if ever, in literature or in life, is justice done to the incredible, the appalling courage of childhood. This story does do justice to it.

But in stressing the courage of the children, we must not pass over the same quality in the governess. That is clear enough however we read the tale. But her courage gets an added value, if we accept her mental condition as abnormal, from the fact of its showing the shallowness of the prevailing notion that insanity inevitably betokens a general breakdown of the higher faculties. It may mean that. But it may not. No small part of the horror and tragedy of our treatment of the insane flows from our failure to realize that mental aberration may go hand in hand with strength and beauty of character. It does in this case. The governess is deluded, but she rises to the sublime in her delusion.

The tale clarifies certain of the causes of insanity also. The hereditary seed of the disease in this instance is hinted at in the one reference to the young woman's father. And her environment was precisely the right one for its germination. The reaction upon a sensitive and romantic nature of the narrowness of English middle class life in the last century: that, from the social angle, is the theme of the story. The sudden change of scene, the sudden immense responsibility placed on unaccustomed shoulders, the shock of sudden unrequited affection—all these together—were too much. The brain gives way. And what follows is a masterly tracing of the effects of repressed love and thwarted maternal affection. The whole story might be reviewed with profit under this psycho-analytic aspect. But when it was done, less would probably have been conveyed than James packs into a single simile. He throws it out, with seeming nonchalance, during the governess's last interview, after Flora's delirium, with little Miles:

> Our meal was of the briefest—mine a vain pretence, and I had the things immediately removed. While this was done Miles stood again with his hands in his little pockets and his back to me—stood and looked out of the wide window through which, that other day, I had seen what pulled me up. We continued silent while the maid was with us—as silent, it whimsically occurred to me, as some young couple who, on their wedding-journey, at the inn, feel shy in the presence of the waiter.

The simile strikes the governess as whimsical. Whimsical in reality is precisely what it is not, guiding us, as it does, straight into her soul and plucking out the mystery of her lacerated heart.

VIII

If anyone will take the trouble to read, in the letters of Henry James, all the passages referring to *The Turn of the Screw*, I shall be surprised if he does not come away with the impression—which at any rate is emphatically mine—of a very charming and good-humored, but a nonetheless very unmistakable, side-stepping of questions or comments which had evidently been flung at him, touching his "bogey-tale," as he calls it, by H. G. Wells, F. W. H. Myers, and at least one other correspondent—a side-stepping to the effectiveness of which, without risk or offense to its victims, James's peculiar style was not less than gloriously adapted. He consistently deprecates his tale as a "very mechanical matter . . . an inferior, a merely *pictorial*, subject, and rather a shameless pot-boiler." The element of truth in this is obvious. We need not question James's sincerity. But in the face of the long list of notable critics and readers, who, with different turns of phrase, have characterized *The Turn of the Screw* as one of the most powerful things ever written, it will not do to dismiss it as a mere exercise in literary ingenuity. It is easier to believe either that the author had a reason for belittling it or that his genius builded better than he knew. And indeed when we read his comment on the tale in the preface to the twelfth volume of his collected works, we see that he had come, partly perhaps under the pressure of its reception, which clearly exceeded his "liveliest hope," to put a somewhat higher estimate on his quondam "pot-boiler." He still speaks of it as a piece of "cold artistic calculation" deliberately planned "to catch those not easily caught (the 'fun' of the capture of the merely witless being ever but small), the jaded, the disillusioned, the fastidious." But in the restrospect he does not disguise his satisfaction with the tale or his sense of having struggled successfully with its technical difficulties and dangers. "Droll enough," he confesses, referring to letters received after its publication, was some of the testimony to that success. He tells of one reader in particular "capable evidently, for the time, of some attention, but not quite capable of enough," who complained that he hadn't sufficiently " 'characterized' " the governess. What wonder that the author's "ironic heart," as he puts it, "shook for the instant almost to breaking," under the reproach of not having sufficiently characterized a figure to the penetrating and detailed setting forth of whose mental condition every sentence of the story (barring part of the brief introductory chapter), from the first one to the last, is dedicated! "We have surely as much of her own nature as we can swallow," he writes in answer to this critic, "in watching it reflect her anxieties and inductions." He speaks of the necessity of having the governess keep "crystalline her record of so many intense anomalies and obscurities," and then adds, "—by which I don't of course mean her explanation of them, a different matter."

Now whether these various references to catching "those not easily caught," to the "droll" evidence of the success of his "ingenuity," to his "ironic heart" that "shook for the instant almost to breaking" under the reproaches of readers incapable of quite enough attention, whether all of these things, coupled with the clear, if casual, warning that the governess's "explanation" of her experiences is a "different matter" from a clear record of them, have any separate or cumulative significance, I will not pretend to say. In even hinting at anything of the sort, I may be guilty of twisting perfectly innocent statements to fit a hypothesis. They do appear to fit with curiously little stretching. But I do not press the point. It is not vital. It in no way affects the main argument. For in these matters it is always the work itself and not the author that is the ultimate authority.

The Governess Turns the Screws

John Lydenberg

The interpretation of *The Turn of the Screw* made by Edmund Wilson in the thirties is today a dead horse, oft beaten. Every reader of the exegeses of Henry James's most famous ghost story must by now be convinced that James did not intend it as an account of the hallucinations of a frustrated, sex-starved governess.

At present it is the fashion to read the story not as a Freudian analysis but as Christian myth, suggestive of "archetypal" religious experiences. Robert W. Heilman has given the fullest exposition of this symbolic interpretation in "*The Turn of the Screw* as Poem,"[1] an essay as typical of late forties' criticism as the Wilson interpretation, now dubbed "overrationalistic," was typical of criticism in the thirties. Heilman demonstrates most convincingly how James has laced his story with an intricate network of words and symbols carrying general religious connotations and specifically suggesting the Judeo-Christian myths of Eden, the Fall, and the Redeemer. The drama is played against a backdrop of the gardens of Bly, a sum-

SOURCE: Reprinted from *Nineteenth-Century Fiction,* XII, No. 1 (June, 1957), 37–58; published by the University of California Press. Used by permission of the Regents of the University of California.

[1] *Forms of Modern Fiction,* ed. William Van O'Connor (Minneapolis, 1948), pp. 211–228. The Edmund Wilson piece appeared in *The Triple Thinkers* (New York, 1938) as part of "The Ambiguity of Henry James," pp. 122–164. In a 1948 edition of *The Triple Thinkers* he added a postscript. In this he concedes that he "tried to force a point"; but he does not change his basic thesis—except to agree that James did not *intend* his governess to be seen as Wilson sees her ("not merely is the governess self-deceived, but . . . James is self-deceived about her"). There are, of course, many more discussions of this tale. Since I am not interested here in criticizing the critics, I make no attempt to mention or list them.

mery Eden transformed by the cold, rainy blasts that bring the fall of the year. The children are essentially angelic creatures, bright, fresh, innocent, adorable, divine—and foredoomed. They have already been corrupted by Quint, with his red hair and fixed, snake-like eyes, and by Miss Jessel in her black garb, and they change as Bly changes, the angels becoming fiends, the divine, infernal. With selfless devotion, the governess dedicates herself as sister of charity, confessor, savior to the hopeless task of saving the souls of the blameless innocents from the anti-Christs who have risen that the children may *not* have life. In his attempt to achieve the purest distillation of horror, James inevitably drew upon our common religious heritage for words and images that would evoke the most intense feeling of evil. The story continues to live and to horrify new generations of readers because it recalls the archetypal religious experiences, and specifically because it suggests, subtly and delicately, our particular religious myth.

James's own comments on *The Turn of the Screw,* in letters, notebooks, and his Preface to the New York edition, make it reasonably clear that he intended neither a psychological study of the governess nor a religious parable. He was simply writing a story of horror for horror's sake. He refers to it as "a piece of ingenuity pure and simple, of cold artistic calculation," and discusses the devices he used to "give the impression of the communication to the children of the most infernal imaginable evil and danger. . . ." Most important of these devices was the negative one of refusing to specify the nature of the evil lest specification lessen the horror for any particular reader. "My values," he says, "are positively all blanks." Thus he tempts each reader to fill in the blanks with his own notion of the greatest evil. Though we can scarcely claim that "James meant so-and-so," we are as good as invited to go on beyond his intent and interpret the story in whatever way our ingenuity permits.

Just as James left the evil undefined, so he tried to leave the governess' personality undefined. He claims that his sole interest in her was to make her a credible reporter of Bly's horrors. To do that, he says, "I had to rule out subjective complications of her own —play of tone etc.; and keep her impersonal save for the most obvious and indispensable little note of neatness, firmness and courage. . . ." Though Edna Kenton and then Wilson in effect denied that James meant what he said about her, many critics have not only granted that he intended the governess to be merely an objective recorder but even insisted that he achieved his intent. Representative of this familiar view is Pelham Edgar's assertion about the governess: "save for courage and devotion she has no discussable characteristics." But this is nonsense. Whatever James may have intended to do—or not do—he has made the governess a character with eminently discussable characteristics.

She is of course the narrator, and as such she is never seen from the outside (except briefly in the prologue). Neither author nor other characters give us ready-made characterizations of the governess; she alone provides the information from which we can deduce the essential facts about her personality. Here it is certainly true that, as Spinoza said, "What Paul says about Peter tells us more about Paul than about Peter." The more we examine the governess' account, the more we feel that she is very much, and very tragically, a person with will and passion of her own. The richness—and the confusion and ambiguity of the tale—lie just here: we can know the children and the apparitions only through the governess, and we can know the governess only through her own words: her observations and actions and conclusions. To understand the events we must evaluate the governess' evaluations, and to do this we must evaluate the governess herself.

Heilman is fully aware of this. He sees that the governess is no blank automaton but an actor with characteristics that go beyond mere "firmness and courage." And he considers her central to the religious interpretation of the story. The words applied to her, he says, "suggest that James is attaching to her the quality of savior, not only in a general sense, but with certain Christian associations." It is at this point that his otherwise admirable analysis slips a crucial notch. These words are not simply words that James attaches to her; they are words that James has *her* attach to *herself*. And the words suggesting that the children are angelic creatures corrupted by infernal agents are *her* words, words that give us her vision—or version—of the fall of the house of Bly. Heilman is quite right in holding that "the center of horror is not the apparitions themselves . . . but . . . the children, and our sense of what is happening to them." But when he says, "What is happening to them is Quint and Jessel," he oversimplifies. What is happening to the children is what the governess says is happening, and more than that, what is happening to them is, clearly and terribly, the governess herself.

Our sense of horror is indeed aroused by the plight of the children. But what exactly do we sense their plight to be? We feel an undertone of sexual perversity—but to build an interpretation of the whole story upon that, as in essence Wilson did, is to give an explanation that is too rationalistic, too specific to accord with the full depth of the conveyed horror. We recognize that the children are symbols of the tortured state of mankind, and that the horror of their corruption is heightened by the fact that they are essentially such angelic children. But this Heilman interpretation is, if not too rationalistic, at least too abstract; it provides a symbolic interpretation that we can grasp intellectually but that we do not truly feel.

So it is for me, at least. Heilman's conception makes sense intellectually but not emotionally. I do not truly feel the corruption of the children or the horror of their putative relations with Quint and Jessel. What I feel is the governess ever tightening the screws. I respond—intensely as James wants us to respond—to the plight of two children, potentially angelic but human like all of us, harried to distraction and death by an overprotective governess. The character and outcome of the struggle, as I feel it, is determined not by the infernal ghosts but by the character of the protecting governess: she is anxious, fearful, possessive, domineering, hysterical and compulsive. The children are pawns which she must protect and can use, but for which she has no real concern; she is concerned primarily with herself. After seeing what she does with and to them I would say, paraphrasing Emerson, "If they are the Devil's children, let them live then with the Devil." Salvation by such as the governess doesn't save. And if it *had* saved the children for the governess' continued ministrations, that I fear would have been the greater of the two evils.

If then we are to see her as a would-be savior—and I agree with Heilman that we must—we see her as a false savior. And I rather think, though I certainly cannot be sure, that James unconsciously saw her so too. In theological terms, she embodies the sin of pride in daring to take upon herself, unaided, the task of saving the children. In other terms, she is a compulsive neurotic who with her martyr complex and her need to dominate finally drives to destruction the children she wishes to possess. Thus the Christian myth becomes twisted: the religious interpretation gives us a story which is, in some manner at least, antireligious. Or maybe, admitting as I do the essential ambiguity of almost everything in the story, I should more cautiously suggest that any religious significance we find here is necessarily double-edged. To me the governess is central; and although I grant that she puts up a heroic fight for the souls of her charges, I find myself basically suspicious of her, not of her good will and certainly not of her "firmness," but of her coolness, her judgment, her wisdom, and above all her ability to cope with human beings who as human beings are inevitably a mixture of good and evil.

Let us now listen to the governess in some detail. One particular paragraph merits careful reading.

> I scarce know how to put my story into words that shall be a credible picture of my state of mind; but I was in these days literally able to find a joy in the extraordinary flight of heroism the occasion demanded of me. I now saw that I had been asked for a service admirable and difficult; and there would be a greatness in letting it be seen—oh, in the right quarter!—that I could succeed where many another girl might have failed. It was an immense help to me—I confess I rather applaud myself as I look back!—that I saw my services so strongly and so simply. I was there to protect and defend the little creatures in the world the most bereaved and the most lovable, the appeal of whose helplessness had suddenly become only too explicit, a deep constant ache of one's own committed heart. We were cut off, really, together; we were united in our danger. They had nothing but me, and I—well, I had *them.* It was, in short, a magnificent chance. This chance presented itself to me in an image richly material. I was a screen—I was to stand before them. The more I saw, the less they would. I began to watch them in stifled suspense, a disguised excitement that might well, had it continued too long, have turned to something like madness. What saved me, as I now see, was that it turned to something else altogether. It didn't last as suspense—it was superseded by horrible proofs. Proofs, I say, yes—from the moment I really took hold.

I would almost be willing to rest my case on this one paragraph alone, which exhibits in concentrated form all the major traits of the governess, traits that go far beyond James's simple qualities of "firmness and courage." It is her "state of mind" that she, and thus we, are first of all concerned with, and she recognizes that her audience will not easily find it "credible." She sees herself as "committed" to a "service admirable and difficult" and is determined not to miss this "magnificent chance" to display her dedication so that it will be recognized "in the right quarter"—that of the master. She and the children are isolated, "cut off" and "united"; if she has lost herself in them, she has also found herself by *having them,* to "protect and defend" and indeed to possess. Thus, for her relations with the children, the servants are at the same time a threat and a necessity. Though she talks of stifling her suspense and disguising her excitement, she can in no wise do so, for she has worked herself into such a state of mind that, as she admits, it is essential to her sanity and salvation for proofs of the rightness of her imaginings to be forthcoming. So she eagerly offers herself as a screen. She will receive the images of the evil past, cut them off from the children —but the images will be there on that screen, and we might suggest that were the screen not there to bring them out, they would never become visible or effective.

Thus she "takes hold," with a compulsive "joy" in her heroism, a determination that the children shall submit not to the dark apparitions but to her. And she appears as an almost classic case of what Erich Fromm calls the authoritarian character: masochistic in that she delights in receiving the tortures as an "expiatory victim," a phrase she later applies to herself, and at the same time sadistic in her insistence on dominating the children and Mrs. Grose.

This statement of her compulsive dedication and the need that is almost a desire for the proofs to materialize is made after Quint's first visitation. But even before she had been challenged by ghosts, before she had found any outlet for her nervous tension, she had already revealed something of her character. Her first words, describing her feelings as she drives from London to Bly, present us with a person doubtful of herself, highstrung, swinging from one extreme to another without apparent cause:

> I remember the whole beginning as a succession of flights and drops, a little see-saw of the right throbs and the wrong. After rising, in town, to meet his appeal, I had at all events a couple of very bad days—found myself doubtful again, felt indeed sure I had made a mistake. In this state of mind I spent the long hours of bumping, swinging coach that carried me to the stopping-place at which I was to be met by a vehicle from the house. This convenience, I was told, had been ordered, and I found, toward the close of the June afternoon, a commodious fly in waiting for me. Driving at that hour, on a lovely day, through a country to which the summer sweetness seemed to offer me a friendly welcome, my fortitude mounted afresh and, as we turned into the avenue, encountered a reprieve that was probably but proof of the point to which it had sunk. I suppose I had expected, or had dreaded, something so melancholy that what greeted me was a good surprise.

Once arrived, she remains "uneasy," unwilling to take things for what they seem, finding Flora's very charm and beauty cause for wonderment and Mrs. Grose's friendliness cause for suspicion. No wonder she slept restlessly that night. She hears mysterious night noises, but aware of her hypertension puts them down to an overwrought fancy. When we learn later that Bly is really haunted, we know that these sounds were actually there to be heard. But this early in the story we construe them much as the governess does—as the result of her imagination—and they accentuate the impression, left by her first two pages of narration, that we have here a very tense and excitable young lady.

Whatever aspects of the story are ambiguous, there is no doubt that unrelaxed nervous anxiety is an essential trait of the governess. Casual comments after the opening paragraphs add steadily to the impression that this quality is not merely the result of the nerve-racking situation into which she is thrown: it is part of her normal character. She says she was "in receipt in these days of disturbing letters from home, where things were not going well." She refers to her previous life as "my small, smothered life." She lacks self-confidence: Miles "was too clever for a bad governess, a parson's daughter to spoil. . . ." "I'm rather easily carried away," she says to Mrs. Grose very early in the story; "I was carried away in London!" After the apparitions have started she comments: "I was queer company enough." Reasonable all right for her to be queer by then; but one feels that she was not exactly relaxing company to begin with, that she would have been queer even without the other, ghostly company to aggravate matters.

Indeed James so effectively sets the mood for the horrible doings, through the governess' initial doubts and worries, that we come to feel the visitations serve her as a blessing in evil disguise. The apparitions satisfy a deep-lying need; they permit her to objectify her fears, to project her uncertainties onto something external; they give her a chance to be applauded for her heroic devotion. Quint's first appearance is preceded by two pages of troubled introspection. She is self-satisfied, almost smug, and at the same time a bundle of tensions straining for release. "I dare say I fancied myself, in short, a remarkable young woman and took comfort in the faith that this would more publicly appear."

Though it takes her awhile to realize, or decide, that the evil figure on the tower is threatening the children, once decided she moves unflinchingly to save her charges. Her concern, she would insist, is only for them. But to the reader it often seems that her real concern is with herself. She paces the sunny paths and the dark halls of Bly as if always holding a mirror before her, in which to observe with care and admiration her displays of heroism, and in which to catch in the shadowy background the lurking figures visible only to someone with her preternatural acuity. We quite agree with her when she says, "The shock I had suffered must have sharpened all my senses." Possessed by what she calls her "endless obsession," and her "dreadful liability to impressions of the order so vividly exemplified" by the apparitions, she stalks her prey; but we are often uncertain whether the prey is Quint and Jessel, as she thinks, or Miles and Flora, as it finally seems, or even, in some perverse fashion, herself.

James meant the ghosts to be real. But what they are we can never quite decide. Sometimes indeed it almost seems as though they are creatures of what she calls her "mere infernal imagination," as though she makes them or thinks she does. "There were shrubberies and big trees, but I remember the clear assurance I felt that none of them concealed him. He was there or was not there; not there if I didn't see him." Though that seems reasonable enough at first, on second thought one wonders why the evil one could not secrete himself, why his existence, or at least his presence, should be contingent on the governess' recognition of him? Is her dread of the figures actually a disguised desire to see them? "There was many a corner round which I expected to come upon Quint, and many a situation that, in a merely sinister way, would have favored the appearance of Miss Jessel." Or—horrible thought!—could it be that they are not evil? Once when she saw Jessel at the desk: "I had the extraordinary chill of a feeling that it was I who was the intruder." "I" who was the evil intruding on Bly to destroy the children by possessing them?

Just as her words suggest that somehow she calls up the ghosts, and with them the evil, so they suggest that she imposes the meaning upon the events. Her long verbal struggles with Mrs. Grose are ostensibly attempts to make that woman of little understanding appreciate the true horror that surrounds and penetrates the children, but they appear equally as attempts to darken the light of the housekeeper's common sense with the fearful suspicions of the governess. Her supersensitivity to the presence of the apparitions is complemented by her marvelous understanding of their intentions and of the pattern of the future. "It seems to me indeed, in retrospect, that by the time the morrow's sun was high I had restlessly read into the facts before us almost all the meaning they were to receive from subsequent and more cruel occurrences." All ambivalently, she makes her grisly interpretations and then tries to persuade herself that she has not done so. The "strangest if not the brightest thread in the pensive embroidery I just spoke of was the impression I might have got, if I had dared to work it out. . . ." "It suited me too, I felt, only too well; by which I mean that it suited exactly the particularly deadly view I was in the very act of forbidding myself to entertain." Her conscious mind recoils in horror from the horrors that it discovers and that her subconscious wishes to evoke.

Such reluctance to foretell the worst is not usual with her. More often she sees through the deceptions of the children and the dullness of Mrs. Grose to the truth beneath—to *her* truth, welcomed with exaltation.

> "He was looking for little Miles." A portentous clearness now possessed me. "*That's* whom he was looking for."
>
> "But how do you know?"
>
> "I know, I know, I know!" My exaltation grew. "And *you* know, my dear!"
>
> She didn't deny this, but required, I felt, not even so much telling as that.

She stalks the halls through the dark night, straining to discern the prowlers—and reasonably enough occasionally seeing them. She listens at doors and stands behind curtains to watch the children whom she suspects of slipping out onto moonlit lawns—and happily catches them at it once or twice. Then she can explain it to the obtuse housekeeper; it was worse than she had dared to expect.

> "Lord, you do change!" cried my friend.
>
> "I don't change—I simply make it out. The four, depend upon it, perpetually meet. If on either of these nights you had been with either child, you would clearly have understood."

"Clearly!" Could any word be more inappropriate as description of the understanding possible to anyone except this omniscient, determined governess? The most dramatic example of her marvelously clear prevision is the long dialogue with Mrs. Grose before the second trip to the lake to find Flora and Miss Jessel. Like a magician beguiling an expectant audience, the governess explains what the children and their tempters are up to and drags the housekeeper to the site at which she expects the new visitation.

By its ghostly nature the relation of the governess to the apparitions is inevitably hard to define. Much clearer, and essentially indisputable, is the iron control she increasingly exercises over the children. She is not the progressive teacher providing them with opportunities to develop according to their needs and to solve their own problems. She is not the firm disciplinarian teaching them to develop according to accepted standards. She is the authoritarian ruler denying any rights to her subjects, the Puritan certain that depravity inheres in everyone and that she alone is elected to fight it. The shock of the first apparition fortunately permits her to translate her diffuse nervousness into a stern dedication. "I have my duty," she says to Mrs. Grose, shortly thereafter. And from then on the sense of rigorous duty increasingly pervades the story as she constantly tightens the screws, bearing down with a "rigid control" and a "rigid will." She freely admits that the children, beleaguered by the ghosts, are prisoners of hers:

> Something or other had brought nearer home to me that I had all but pinned the boy to my shawl and that, in the way our companions were marshalled before me, I might have appeared to provide against some danger of rebellion. I was like a jailer with an eye to possible surprises and escapes.

Never would she leave them alone: "I was careful almost never to be out of" their company. And she says that the final occasion on which Flora escapes to Miss Jessel and the lake "was the very first time I had allowed the little girl out of my sight without some special provision."

Oppressive as this unrelenting surveillance would have seemed to the children, her love for them must have been an even heavier burden. The governess thinks she is enchanted and charmed by her little charges, imagines herself passionately devoted to them, and well-nigh smothers them in demonstrations of this love.

> There were moments when, by an irresistible impulse, I found myself catching them up and pressing them to my heart.
>
> . . . .
>
> I needed nothing more than this to feel the full force of Mrs. Grose's comparison, and, catching my pupil in my arms, covered her with kisses in which there was a sob of atonement.

These caresses are not expressions of a spontaneous, relaxed affection. With their accompaniment of sobs of atonement and their nervous pressure, they must seem to the children compulsive and indeed frightening.

> I was, of course, thoroughly kind and merciful; never, never yet had I placed on his little shoulders hands of such tenderness as those with which, while I rested against the bed, I held him there well under fire.
>
> . . . .
>
> One of these [ideas of how to interpret the children's actions], for a moment, tempted me with such a singular intensity that, to withstand it, I must have gripped my little girl with a spasm that, wonderfully, she submitted to without a cry or a sign of fright.

We *can* see the children as little devils who submit to these extravagant blandishments as the price they have to pay for their freedom to consort with their unearthly visitors. But I find myself more inclined to pity them as objects of a hysterical, possessive love that they accept, with remarkable imperturbability, as part of the strange world of strange governesses into which they had been born.

I threw myself upon him and in the tenderness of my pity I embraced him. "Dear little Miles, dear little Miles!"

My face was close to his, and he let me kiss him, simply taking it with indulgent good humor. "Well, old lady?"

The governess comments pridefully on the tenderness they show toward her, little realizing that under the enforced demonstrations of a conventional love smolders a resentment and hatred that will burst out all the more violently because so long suppressed.

Beneath the governess' displays of love and care lies her determination not merely to protect and control but fully to possess her charges. The idea of their having been "familiar" with Quint and Jessel is insupportable. "Too free with *my* boy?" she exclaims in horror and determination. Sharing is impossible; the children must be either hers or theirs. "They haven't been good—they've only been absent. It has been easy to live with them, because they're simply leading a life of their own. They're not mine—they're not ours. They're his and they're hers!" When Flora is irretrievably lost to her, she is almost happy because it means she will be left alone with Miles; it is Miles for whom her possessive passion is most acute, Miles whom she most fears and whom she most damages. "Won't, if he has any chance turn on me? Yes, I venture still to think it. At all events, I want to try. Get off with his sister as soon as possible and leave me with him alone." On any level the story is a struggle for the possession of the children, and once we begin to doubt the governess' interpretation of events, once we see her as an agent with positive effects upon the children, it is difficult to avoid the conclusion that what she is striving for is complete authority, complete dominance, complete possession of the children, whose innocence may have already been besmirched by Quint and Jessel but who at least had a life and existence of their own before the arrival of their governess with her duty and her love.

Her complete possession of the children is contingent upon the continuation of the threat. I have already cited some of the passages that leave us feeling that she actually wants the apparitions to be there, wants the children to succumb, almost, to the pressures of their tempters. Always we see her waiting for new developments, consciously fearing the worst, but unconsciously fearing that the worst might *not* develop, that the threat might evaporate.

"Surely you don't accuse *him*—"

"Of carrying on an intercourse that he conceals from me? Ah, remember that, until further evidence, I now accuse nobody." Then, before shutting her out to go, by another passage, to her own place, "I must just wait," I wound up.

Note particularly the following sentence, which can be read as merely another example of Jamesian ambiguity or can be construed as clear Jamesian revelation of the governess' ambivalence:

Say that, by the dark prodigy I knew, the imagination of all evil *had* been opened up to him; all the justice within me ached for the proof that it could ever have flowered into an act.

In actuality, though she may think she is saying something else, she wants the worst to come true. As she worries the strange happenings over and over with Mrs. Grose, proclaiming always that it "was a pity" they had to talk about them and insisting on their "duty of resistance to extravagant fancies," she makes us feel that her disclaimers are gauze-thin veils for her fears that her fancies were unfounded. As she says, "It would distress me much more to lose my power than to keep it." For her power to sense presences that no one else senses is her power to coerce the children and to drag Mrs. Grose along with her in her fine perceptions. Power she must continue to exert, and she can do so only if her antagonists continue their aggressions. Without ever sharper pieces of evidence, her case, her power, her sanity will collapse.

Thus the struggles with Mrs. Grose, who cannot safely be allowed to remain an innocent and uncommitted bystander, are as crucial as those with the children. The most puzzling passages in the book, masterpieces of Jamesian ambiguity, are the dialogues between the governess and this good, simple woman, whom we can interpret as representative either of gross insensibility to the forces of evil or of common-sense acceptance of the human mixture of good and bad. Whatever is ambiguous in these dialogues, however, there is no doubt that the governess forces Mrs. Grose into submission, "dragged her at my heels," as she puts it. She presses and presses—those are her words—probing for additional bits that can be forced into her predetermined pattern, often seeming to tell Mrs. Grose what to say, explaining the true, dark meanings that Mrs. Grose has failed to appreciate, ever fearful lest she lose Mrs. Grose as an ally. The apparent innocence of the children is a continual threat to Mrs. Grose's allegiance.

Flights of fancy gave place, in her mind, to a steady fireside glow, and I had already begun to perceive how, with the development of the conviction that—as time went on without a public accident—our young things could, after all, look out for themselves, she addressed her greatest solicitude to the sad case presented by their instructress.

The case must always be made to concern the "others," and the governess' imagination must always find ways to redirect Mrs. Grose's suspicions when they threaten to swerve toward the governess instead of the children.

Mrs. Grose watched them [being particularly manageable and angelic on the lawn] with positive placidity; then I caught the suppressed intellectual creak with which she conscientiously turned to take from me a view of the back of the tapestry. I had made her a receptacle of lurid things, but there was an odd recognition of my superiority—my accomplishments and my function—in her patience under my pain. She offered her mind to my disclosures as, had I wished to mix a witch's broth and proposed it with assurance, she would have held out a large clean sauce pan.

So, hounding and loving the children, pressing ever harder on Mrs. Grose, she controls all her inferiors rigidly, until unable to bend, they break in the climactic scenes: the scene of Jessel's second lake appearance, to which Mrs. Grose is dragged along, passively submitting to the governess' authority until she finally wrenches herself free to comfort the sobbing, broken Flora with the assurance that no one was there after all; and the final scene of Miles gripped tight by the governess as she keeps demanding explanations and confessions and complete submission until finally he collapses dead in her arms—"his little heart, dispossessed" of the demons which kept her from possessing it herself, completely, until now she has it in death.

Along with the governess' determination to make others submit goes a desire on her own part to relax in submission to something else. On her first night at Bly, she says: "I had the fancy of our being almost as lost as a handful of passengers in a great drifting ship. Well, I was strangely, at the helm!" These are her feelings before any apparitions had appeared, even before the first breath of suspicion falls on Miles with the word of his dismissal from school. She is at the helm, she will steer, she will determine the course, and take her passengers where she wills. That she assumes authority and exercises it with implacable firmness we have seen. But the determination, so noticeable as the story progresses, to steer her passengers along her course is not the dominant aspect of this image. She is not only the helmsman; she is one of the passengers, lost with them, drifting.

Here we have the other face of the authoritarian character: the masochism that often accompanies sadism. Lacking any true direction or personality of her own, she tries to find and make her life, partly by bending others to her will, partly by submitting and in effect giving herself over to Quint and Jessel. Quint and Jessel permit her to escape from the freedom she showed herself fearful of in the opening paragraphs. They give her the necessary excuse to dominate the children and the housekeeper, and they give her a way to lose herself in what she disguises, for herself as well as for Mrs. Grose, as dedication to a cause. If she feels herself at the helm, she also feels the ship drifting; and as we have seen in another image, she wishes to serve as a screen, to receive onto herself the evil ministrations of the apparitions, for whom she readily admits, nay insists, that she is searching.

This submissive aspect of the governess' character appears more in the overtones of her narrative than in specific statements and is thus much harder to demonstrate by particular quotations than is her desire to dominate. There are two passages that make her desire for self-immolation reasonably explicit.

> I had an absolute certainty that I could see again what I had already seen, but something within me said that by offering myself bravely as the sole subject of such experience, by accepting, by inviting, by surmounting it all, I should serve as an expiatory victim and guard the tranquility of my companions.
>
> Whether the children really saw or not—since, that is, it was not yet definitely proved—I greatly preferred, as a safeguard, the fulness of my own exposure. I was ready to know the very worst that was to be known.

We have seen that she seems really to want things to happen, wants her worst previsions to come true. Trouble and danger come as a welcome "relief." They are a relief in part because they allow her to tighten the screws further each time, and also because they take her out of herself, making action automatic, something she does, not as herself but as an instrument. And when action fails, when she is unable to keep control, she responds with hysterical submission herself.

> Of what first happened when I was left alone [after the second appearance of Jessel at the lake] I had no subsequent memory. I only knew that at the end of it, I suppose, a quarter of an hour, an odorous dampness and roughness, chilling and piercing my trouble, had made me understand that I must have thrown myself, on my face, on the ground and given way to a wildness of grief. I must have lain there long and cried and sobbed, for when I raised my head the day was almost done.

Beneath her overt firmness and her stern exertion of authority lies a realization that what she is doing is dangerous, even evil. She is caught in a trap of her own making.

> [Miles] couldn't play any longer at innocence; so how the deuce would he get out of it? There beat in me indeed, with the passionate throb of this question, an equal dumb appeal as to how the deuce I should.
>
> "By writing to him [the master] that his house is poisoned and his little nephew and niece mad" [she queries in answer to a suggestion of Mrs. Grose]?
>
> "But if they *are,* Miss?"
>
> "And if I am myself you mean?"
>
> Within a minute there had come to me out of my very pity the appalling alarm of his being perhaps innocent. It was for the instant confounding and bottomless, for if he *were* innocent, what then on earth was *I?*

Thus she throws herself weeping into Mrs. Grose's sheltering arms or she lies sobbing on the ground, and gains as much satisfaction by such self-abasement as she does by controlling her companions. For she lives in a world of extremes, a world composed only of masters and slaves, and if she fails to demonstrate the objective existence of those she claims have enslaved the children, she is left helplessly dangling, alone in a normal world of normal people, a world in which she cannot operate.

The children, however, cannot live in this hysterical world which she has to create. They want to escape her. But their first indications of this she construes as a desire to leave her kindly surveillance that they may be with the evil others; and even the reader finds that he *can* go along with her construction.

> "I thought you wanted to go on as you are" [she says to Miles]. . . .
>
> "I don't—I don't. I want to get away."

But finally it is obvious that it is the hounding rather than the haunting that they must get away from.

> "Take me away, take me away—oh, take me away from *her!*"
>
> "From *me?*" I panted.
>
> "From you—from you!" she cried.
>
> . . . . .
>
> Flora was so markedly feverish that an illness was perhaps at hand; she had passed a night of extreme unrest, a night agitated above all by fears that had for their subject not in the least her former, but wholly her present governess. It was not against the possible re-entrance of Miss Jessel on the scene that she protested—it was conspicuously and passionately against mine.

The governess cannot fail to admit now that they fear and hate her. But she cannot admit that she is the cause; they hate only because they are completely corrupted, completely enslaved by evil. So when Mrs. Grose reports that she has heard from Flora "horrors" about the governess, the governess engages in one of her most nimble bits of interpretation.

> It was in quite another manner that I, for my part, let myself go. "Oh, thank God!" She sprang up again at this, drying her eyes with a groan, " 'Thank God'?"
>
> "It so justifies me!"
>
> "It does that, Miss!"
>
> I couldn't have desired more emphasis, but I just hesitated, "She's so horrible?"

Recall again the last long scene of Miles' death—or murder. She will make him confess, by whatever third-degree methods prove necessary; she will find a way to demonstrate that all actions, all explanations prove his guilt. He will not escape like Flora. She will hold him tight and keep him all for herself, even though she can possess him as she wishes only in death.

In conclusion let me return to the point from which I started. I am convinced that James was not intending to write an allegory, or a story with a moral—James seldom if ever did anything as simple as that. Nor was he writing a nouvelle of his usual sort: "realistic," in the sense that it was designed to convey the feeling of recognizable experience in all its complex density. He was trying to write a horror story, to communicate by all the mechanisms he could devise a sense of pure evil rather than real life. But his genius was such that he could not create something that, like an inferior Gothic novel or modern whodunit, would give the impression of merely mechanical contrivance. Hence the feeling of life crept in, and critics are properly compelled to attempt explications and definitions of this life, and of the nature of this horror.

The greatest difficulty arises when we try to discuss the "reality" of the ghosts, and here my interpretation is in most danger of coming a cropper. As long as I do not hold that the ghosts are mere hallucinations of the governess, I have to grant them some sort of reality. And if they are real and evil, neither the governess nor I have any right to treat them lightly. Once grant that the evil spirits have really returned to haunt the children and it would be preposterous to ask the governess to remain calm, collected, and normal; instead her heroic self-dedication should be deemed wholly admirable and proper.

But this question of the ghosts' reality is a thorny one. If we conceive of them as real, it is hard to find rational grounds on which to judge how she should have faced such a ghastly and impossible situation. Presumably her realistic reaction to real invaders would have been promptly to wire the master, the police, maybe also a priest, or better a witch doctor. But then there would have been no story. Indeed, such a view of the intruders makes any interpretation superfluous. We could take the story only as sheer horror, mere contrivance, and enjoy it on that level.

The reality we impute to the ghosts must instead be somehow symbolic. Then we have to ask what they symbolize. But we have seen that James denied that they were allegorical figures, insisted that he carefully refrain from assigning them specific symbolic meaning. The meaning we ascribe to them will depend, as James meant it to, upon our own reading of the story and our feeling of its drama, which in turn depends upon our view of human life and its attendant evils.

I do not feel that Quint and Jessel represent pure evil: James does not say so, nor does his presentation of the struggle make me feel it dramatically. The governess may indistinctly consider the ghosts as the essence of evil, and, as Heilman points out, she certainly chooses words which identify them with Satan and herself with the Savior. But our vantage point is different from the governess': we see her as one of the combatants, and as the story progresses we become ever more uncertain who is fighting whom. We have to grant that she really sees Quint on the tower. But from then on the confrontations are increasingly subject to other interpretations; we feel more and more that Quint and Jessel are creatures haunting her, desired by her, almost controlled by her.

This is not to deny that evil is present; it is undoubtedly there somehow. It seems to me that the ghosts symbolize not so much some particular evil attacking the children as a more generalized evil that is part of man, of the governess as well as the children, an evil we must all continually fight. The nature of this evil is not something given; it is developing and malleable. The way it is treated or combated determines the way it actually affects people. And it is the governess who determines and carries out the treatment. Though she neither imagines nor creates the evil, she seems to exacerbate it. She makes active, effective, dominant what might have remained quiescent; she forces issues which—for all we can see in the story—need not have been forced. The story is drama as well as fable,—and more than poem. As drama it presents not so much perverted innocents as a frightened, frightening governess struggling with her wards. We don't really know or feel what Quint and Jessel are doing to Miles and Flora. But we know and feel that the governess is hounding them, pressing them and Mrs. Grose, helping (at the very least) to create such an atmosphere of tension and suspicion that finally they hate and fear her and want only to be left alone. This is not a study of the governess' unstable psyche —it is not a *study* of anything. It is a story in which a hysterical woman turns a quiet summer into a fall of dark hatred and tragedy.

I have attempted to demonstrate that the governess is an authoritarian character: hysterical, compulsive, sado-masochistic. Some readers may, however, prefer to use the terms she chooses in describing her actions: duty, service, expiatory victim, torment, atonement, savior. They may insist that the actions and attitudes I have characterized as authoritarian are simply those of the true Christian. They may hold that her incessant vigilance, unrelenting pressure, selfless submission, and refusal to compromise in any manner with evil are entirely proper and necessary in the unremitting struggle against the forces of evil. This would be to adopt what we loosely call the Puritan view of Christianity, and to say that the governess is essentially a Puritan. She would indeed have been worthy coadjutor of Paul or Augustine or Luther (though she is too blind to the possibilities of there being sin in *her* to have been wholly approved by them). If we accept this view of her, the important thing to note is that James pictured her battle as futile and fatal. If he approved her methods, he certainly did not deem them effective; if he approved her self-dedication as savior, he did not think that she could save.

Readers who do not have a predilection for this variant of Christianity will almost certainly see the governess differently, and believe that James saw her differently. Through her insistence on recognizing only the extreme whites of Edenlike innocence and the extreme blacks of Quint and Jessel, and her refusal to accept the shaded grays that are necessary for any true *human* understanding and sympathy, she alienates the children so completely that they have no alternative but to go to the devil. She looks upon them first as angelic then as infernal, never as something in between. Unable to offer them the positive, sympathetic love which might have helped them develop as humans and accommodate themselves to the evil with which all men must by their nature live, she can only strive to recast them in her rigid authoritarian mold. She turns the screws of Puritan discipline and suspicion until the children fatally crack under the strain. Whatever the multitude of ambiguities in this story, one thing is not ambiguous: once one fills the blanks with Christian values, one must see the story as a covert, if unconscious, attack on one strain of Christianity, a New England strain with which James was most familiar.

Inadequacy in Eden: Knowledge and *The Turn of the Screw*

Joseph J. Firebaugh

Putting aside the question of whether the governess at Bly is subject to illusion, and whether her creator wished her visions to be taken as "real," we may perhaps approach James's intention more closely by examining another matter. Since the whole tale is illusion in the pure sense, and since in any provable sense ghosts are always illusions, this much-argued point is no question at all. The sense in which it is a question, whether James was writing a mere thriller or a serious story with some moral point, may be solved not by looking first at technique, but by looking squarely at the moral point, which has a great deal to do with personal freedom, and hence with educational questions, and hence with problems of knowledge.

In other fiction written during this same period, James was much concerned with the question of how knowledge replaces innocence, and with the results of that transition, the results for the individual who is moving from one state to the other. *The Awkward Age* (1899) deals with little else; so too, *The Ambassadors* (1903). Nanda Brookenham and Lambert Strether have this in common: that they are made sound through knowledge: that they are better people with knowledge than without it: and that their world, not being equipped to understand the fact, rejects them and makes their lives a sacrifice rather than a fulfillment. The same pattern, with interesting variations, occurs in the lives of Miles and Flora.

SOURCE: *Modern Fiction Studies,* III (Spring, 1957), 57–63. Reprinted by permission of the Purdue Research Foundation and the author.

This paper has been written from notes for a lecture presented to the students of Rhodes University, Grahamstown, June 4, 1956, and to the Friends of the South African Public Library, Cape Town, August 24, 1956.

They are children; though very young, they have already been "exposed." Nanda is a grown girl when we meet her, and her exposure, one gathers, has not been lifelong. Strether, for his part, was innocent, by any standard of real sophistication, for most of his adult life.

In *The Turn of the Screw* (1898), the problem is taken up as it concerns the early years of immaturity: the years which are most vulnerable to exposure—hence, the years which need to be most responsibly dealt with. Yet, in the situation as it presents itself, we meet a solid wall of irresponsibility or inadequacy on the part of everyone who has any concern with the children. The adults in the story could not have been more irresponsible or less adequate if they had deliberately conspired against the children. They did not do so, but *someone* did: the author of the story, whose aesthetic and moral purposes were alike served by adult incompetents. James gave all who had anything to do with the children motives of corruption, indifference, selfishness or downright ignorance. He did so because he wished to give the children's situation the final turn of the screw: to show very young children of ineffable charm and intelligence completely under the control of persons whose venality, or innocence, or even illiteracy, make them simply incompetent to deal with children, and especially with children of real substance. He wished to make them completely helpless in the hands of absolutely incompetent persons. James wished to do this, I suggest, not only because he wished to give an artistic sense of the full horror of such entrapment, but also because he wanted to imply a parallel with the education, the advance toward personal fulfillment, of every superior person: an advance that is handicapped by guardians, by teachers, by authorities who only half perceive what they are dealing with: whose lack of ability leads them to mistake perceptiveness and loving-kindness for evasion of duty and corruption. James wished also, I think, to imply the whole growth of man from ignorance to knowledge, handicapped as he is by ancient identifications of knowledge with sin. Professor Heilman is surely right in seeing something "primal and universal" in the children, as he is in seeing Bly as another Eden; there is something of pristine glory about little Miles and Flora, something which the devil himself—Quint—and his female counterpart—Miss Jessel—cannot do nearly as much to destroy as can the well-meaning but bungling governess. Having so little learning herself, the governess instinctively identifies knowledge imparted by others with evil. Like many a teacher, she abhors what earlier teachers have taught her students and would teach them all over again, on absolutely new principles.

Thus she would "save" them: but since what she would save them from is knowledge, even if a knowledge of corruption, she would save them by denying the truth inherent even in corruption. She would deny what is in the world, to impose on her pupils a new version of that world. Innocent, she requires innocence of others: innocent, her horror of these children is a horror of their knowledge, of their knowing more than she does. No doubt, like many guardians of the young, she would argue about knowledge "suitable to their years"—thus ignoring the practical truth that knowledge suitable to years is the knowledge that is grasped so as to be used—whatever the year.

Before dealing further with the governess and with her inadequacies, let us look at the inadequacies of others. First, there is the irresponsible Harley Street uncle. Although he assures the governess that he wishes only what is best for his orphaned nephew and niece, he clearly wishes this best to occur with a minimum of trouble to himself. He has a bachelor life of his own which he has no intention of modifying. To protect this life, he lays down absolute rules that permit *no* exception, rules which seem to anticipate *no* contingency which may urgently require his attention—or else, anticipating such contingencies, help him to evade their demands. Having provided Bly and its staff, a new Eden, he withdraws to his worldly pursuits as completely as the Old Testament God withdraws to heaven, leaving behind him a state of being which seems to him satisfactory for anyone in a condition of innocence, and rules which make him inaccessible to any attention but the most distant and awestricken worship. He does not provide for the fact that probable change in the state of innocence will require his assistance, yet he does provide the agents—Quint and Miss Jessel—even as the Old Testament God provided the snake—which will assure the fall from innocence. That fall occurs, and when it does, he turns his back, providing, not a new moral code based upon an assumption of knowledge, but the governess, a priestess of an old moral code, based on an assumption of innocence and its desirability, in a state where innocence no longer exists. After Quint and Miss Jessel, the only code which the governess can apply—that devoted to preserved innocence—is absurdly inapplicable to the children's state. Unlike many of his priests, God recognized the inadequacy of Eden to a state of knowledge, but the Harley Street uncle does not. He employs as governess a woman competent only to preserve an innocence that no longer exists, just as many priests who have served in the name of God have sought to preserve an innocence which could survive only in an Eden without a serpent. Just as the serpents of Bly, Quint and Miss Jessel, are out of key with Miles and Flora in their prelapsarian state, so is the governess absurdly misplaced in their new state. Her authority no longer applies, but it is nevertheless imposed from above: her power is an anachronism with children whose knowledge now has prepared them to ask questions and to seek answers for themselves. The governess is the agent of denial: she denies Miles and Flora the power to carry out their inquiries, to exercise their perceptiveness in a new world of knowledge. The Harley Street uncle, content with his own state of knowledge, appoints a governess/priestess who worships him from afar and assists him in denying his knowledge to others.

Denial of knowledge is in fact a major theme in the story. The headmaster, in expelling Miles, offers no explanation, and thereby makes possible any amount of speculation—a privilege of which the governess swiftly avails herself. The headmaster has refrained from offering the least explanation. In acting so finally, without offering the interview which would have clarified the matter for better or for worse, he is not only withholding knowledge—surely a major sin for any teacher—but he is evading the responsibility of discussing the matter. A wise governess would of course have insisted on an interview and a full explanation; but this governess wishes not only to preserve others from knowledge, she wishes to preserve herself—and this last for apparently the worst of motives—so that she can speculate as to Miles' nameless evil, and can believe things about the child without running the risk of having her beliefs either shattered or confirmed by evidence.

Denial of knowledge, however, is not the method of Quint and Miss Jessel. Neither is the evasion of authority. Quint in fact is in the habit of assuming the mantle of his employer's authority by taking his clothing. The symbolic significance is clear: if authority is not exercised by those who possess it, it will be assumed by others; if knowledge is not communicated by the Harley Street uncle—or by God—it will be communicated by others. The others may in fact be corrupt, but they offer something which can fill the vacuum of innocence.

Nor is it necessary to assume that a corrupt source of knowledge means that innocence will be corrupted. The results of knowledge are the only means of judging it. What use have the innocents made of it? That is the chief question. Even assuming the worst, what are the results for the children? They are both delightful; Miles has "an indescribable little air of knowing nothing in the world but love." To be sure, he has been expelled from school; and we learn that he has been expelled because of something he has told the others—not all the others, but only those he liked. The hint of boyish homosexuality can scarcely be ignored. But we need not be put off by this, unless we are as naive as the governess. If that is the nameless crime, it is still knowledge—a highly useful knowledge in the world as it is unfortunately constituted—and it is moreover the knowledge the child has been able to get from his limited sources. He gives this knowledge to his schoolmates, moreover, in love rather than in malice. Of knowledge communicated to him in corrupt purpose, he has made, in his young innocence, something which expresses love. Neither the governess nor the headmaster is able to accept love in any specific non-generalized form, though the governess does see that Miles knows nothing but love. The governess, who knows no middle ground, has to believe Miles either guilty or innocent: she cannot conceive that he might be both: possessed of knowledge, and utterly innocent in his use of it. Neither, presumably, can his headmaster; for confiding in his schoolmates, in the spirit of love, the boy is expelled. Had he been corrupt, he might well have escaped expulsion, through secrecy; he is expelled, not because he is corrupt, but because he is *not* corrupt. Thus he suggests comparison with the highest martyrs, who suffered for like causes; they were put to death not for their evil, but for their goodness. This is what happens to Miles.

It might be said, indeed, that Miles dies because he knows more than his governess. There is no doubt that he knows more. In the course of the story, his knowledge outstrips hers so far that she is herself aware of the fact. Her lack of learning is not the greatest of her inadequacies. Once she realizes that she does not know enough to teach the boy, it occurs to her to seek out a school for him. But she does not do so. This would be to put him "on his own," it would thwart her determination to return him to a state of innocence—or, as she puts it, to "save" him from knowledge superior to her own. Miles asks to be sent to school; he desires to be, as he puts it, with his own kind; he frankly tells the governess (Chapter XIV) that he wants to see more life; in other words, to be free to seek knowledge through experience, to find a fulfillment he cannot find in the enforced innocence of Bly under the rule of his governess.

Her youth and limited education are by no means the governess's only disqualifications. In accepting her position, she accepts conditions no experienced governess would have accepted—she foregoes the right ever to communicate with her employer. An experienced woman would have anticipated difficulties that could make such conditions impossible to accept. Professor Edel, in his *The Psychological Novel*, has remarked upon her jumping to conclusions. We may resume some of her eager assumptions: Mrs. Grose's relief at meeting her; her conviction, upon receiving the headmaster's letter, that it "can have but one meaning"—when, as a matter of fact, it might have one of several meanings; her refraining from asking Mrs. Grose about the first appearance of Quint; her "knowledge," not through evidence, but through intuition—"the shock of a certitude," "the flash of this knowledge," "with certitude and yet without direct vision."

Her lack of respect for evidence (despite her claim at the end of Chapter VIII) is proportionate to her lack of learning. Most appalling is the fact that although she is employed to teach the children, she actually withholds knowledge from them. She keeps Miles out of school. She does not discuss with him the reasons for his expulsion. Her belated vague question, "What happened?" (Chapter XVII) may well be meaningless to him. She does not ask him and Flora directly about the "visits" she suspects them of receiving from the spirits of Quint and Miss Jessel—"visits" which symbolize surely their continued concern with such knowledge of life as, without their present governess, they have been able to get. She does not ask them until, in the climactic scenes of the story, she is ready to force the children to see Quint and Miss Jessel as images of evil, to impose those images on them with all the force of her own personality, to make them feel her own fear of guilt; a fear they have not previously possessed. She keeps the children's letters to their uncle and is then indignant when Miles informs himself of the contents of her letter to the guardian. Cut off from all information, Miles will seek any means of getting it. At every point, the governess imposes herself between the children and information. She will not let the children out of her sight: this too in order to "save" them; she describes her society as "inexorable" and "perpetual." All that she does, she does for their own best good; this is usually true of everyone who stands between the would-be knower and the knowledge he seeks. To the extent that the children would desert their governess, to that extent she ties them unmercifully to her. Every means of communication is cut off! Mrs. Grose, being illiterate, cannot write to the Harley Street uncle; the children's letters are not sent. And the governess becomes nearly frantic when the children themselves are briefly out of her sight.

Subject to a teacher who has no knowledge to give, and who would cut them off from other sources of knowledge, the children are trapped. They seek ways of asserting the independence they have been denied. Failing, they find imposed on them the governess's visions of sin—Quint and Miss Jessel. They can no longer see themselves as free spirits in a world where experience and information can be acquired because it is good to fulfill oneself. Rather they must accept the governess's view of their sinful nature and of the essential sinfulness of knowledge. Small wonder that Flora cries out against this restrictiveness. Small wonder that she uses foul language—such words are the only ones she has that are adequate to express her hatred of a being who would so restrict her young life. Small wonder that Miles dies; he has been forced to see the only source of knowledge he has known in his brief life, Quint, as an embodiment of evil, and himself as a victim of Original Sin. What sort of life remains for one who has been forced to see as wholly sinful the chief positive experiences of his life? Flora lapses into hysteria, Miles into death, because their young efforts to know have been forced into the pattern of Original Sin.

We need not concern ourselves overmuch with whether the governess is neurotic, or whether she sees visions, if we will concentrate on her incompetence, shown in numerous ways. She may well have been as *good* a person as James's narrator makes her out to be. But a good person may often do evil in the name of good—may do so through an inadequate theory of knowledge and a questionable view of human nature. The high value the governess places on intuition as opposed to evidence, shown in her ready acceptance of things she does not see, and in her refraining from putting inquiries; her conviction, despite all the external evidence of their characters, that the children are corrupt, the victims of Sin, through knowing what everyone must know—these facts show that the governess's theory of knowledge is inadequate, and her theory of human nature at least as doubtful as the dogma of Original Sin.

The Governess, then, is the inadequate priestess of an irresponsible deity—the Harley Street uncle, whose apparent inaccessbility, as well as his ultimate responsibility for the state of the children, is not unlike the situation of the Creator. As His priestess, the governess would impose upon innocent children her conviction that knowledge is sin, and that lack of knowledge, or innocence, is the only salvation. She destroys the children by imposing on them images of evil formed in her conviction of the essential sinfulness of mankind. Her imposition of Original Sin on innocent children, standing here for the human race, assures not their salvation, but their destruction.

Point of View in *The Turn of the Screw*

Alexander E. Jones

Although Henry James described *The Turn of the Screw* as "rather a shameless potboiler," subsequent criticism has treated the work with more respect. As Robert Heilman has pointed out, the tale has inspired a surprising amount of discussion and speculation. Indeed, Heilman feels that James must have "hit upon some fundamental truth of experience that no generation can ignore and that each generation wishes to restate in its own terms."

Identifying that "fundamental truth" has, however, proved most difficult. Some critics classify *The Turn of the Screw* as a ghost story—"the thriller of thrillers, the last word in creeping horror stories." Others have described it as a sophisticated hoax, an allegory of good and evil in the manner of Hawthorne, a dramatic poem employing Christian symbolism to depict the twofold nature of man (a "morality play in modern dress"), an attack upon authoritarianism, a rejection of New England Puritanism, an account of hallucination due to terror, a case study of neurosis or even of psychopathology, an exercise in Freudian symbolism—or even as a projection of the doubts and obsessions of James's own "haunted mind." Such differences of opinion only serve to add a note of irony to James's remark to Lady Gosford, who complained that she had read the story with excitement and a growing sense of terror—but without really understanding what was happening: "My dear Mildred, no more do I. The story was told me by Archbishop Benson. I have caught the impression his mystery made on me and I have passed it on to you—but as to understanding it, it is just gleams and glooms."

SOURCE: *PMLA*, LXXIV (March, 1959), 112–122. Reprinted by permission of the Modern Language Association and the author.

The rather spectacular lack of agreement among the critics seems largely to stem from dissimilar interpretations of the governess, from whose point of view the story proper is narrated. Indeed, the whole question of James's handling of the technical problems of point of view is central to a proper understanding and appreciation of the work. It is, of course, a truism that no piece of fiction would have been the same had the author chosen some other angle from which to project his tale. In *The Turn of the Screw,* however, point of view takes on added significance, and it would therefore seem profitable to scrutinize the governess carefully. For only after one has analyzed her personality and behavior can he determine the meaning of the work as a whole.

Of course, *The Turn of the Screw* does not begin either with the governess herself or with those events which are to be the chief concern of the narrative. Instead, James opens with a sort of prologue in which he introduces the reader to a character, Douglas, who in turn presents the story proper by reading from an old manuscript which the governess has presented to him years before. This parenthetical device, or "frame," is at least as old as the writings of ancient Egypt; and writers as dissimilar as Chaucer, Hawthorne, and P. G. Wodehouse have all employed the technique of the story within a story. But the device seems peculiarly useful to writers dealing with the supernatural and may be found in the works of Poe, Bierce, Kipling, Onions, Blackwood, and Lovecraft. Ghost stories were originally oral tales, whispered before a winter fire while the wind howled outside and darkness crowded in upon the little circle of firelight; and writers who propose to deal with the supernatural are obliged to recreate imaginatively this atmosphere of superstitious but pleasing shudders. For only then will the reader suspend his broad-daylight, common-sense disbelief and enter into the mood of the story. James has elsewhere referred to this process as the production of "conscious and cultivated credulity," and the establishment of such a mood certainly seems to be one of his main reasons for employing the frame in *The Turn of the Screw.* The little circle of friends around the fire are "breathless," and the previous tales have been "gruesome." Moreover, the next tale is to be the ultimate in terror, dreadfulness, "general uncanny ugliness and horror and pain." Little cryptic hints are given, and Douglas appears unnerved by what he is to relate. Thus James uses his prologue to set the mood at the proper emotional pitch.

Closely related to this evoking of mood is James's use of the frame to establish an illusion of reality. By placing himself within the confines of the story as "I," the narrator, James makes himself one of the characters rather than an omniscient author. No one is left on the "outside" of the story, and the reader is made to feel that he and James are members of the circle around the fire; James called this getting "down into the arena." Moreover, as Leon Edel has pointed out, by making himself a character in the story—a member of Douglas' audience—James has disassociated himself from the events recorded by the governess: "The skeptic may scoff at the ghosts, the haunting, the sorcery: but James answers—here is the 'document.'" In this way the tale achieves an air of authenticity. Finally, James is able to present a great deal of expository material in the prologue without shattering the illusion of reality. Douglas, rather than James, can prepare the reader for what is to follow. He can explain what sort of person the governess was, why she went to Bly, what that household was like, and similar matters. After this the stage is set, and the reader can settle back comfortably while Douglas opens the faded red cover of a "thin old-fashioned gilt-edged album" and reads aloud the narrative inscribed in "old, faded ink, and in a most beautiful hand." [1]

That is, theoretically the reader can settle back comfortably. In actual practice, critical controversy begins at precisely this point. In her narrative the governess has told of going to Bly, of encountering the ghosts of Peter Quint and Miss Jessel, and of struggling desperately to shield little Miles and Flora from their evil influence. But what sort of person *was* the fluttered, anxious girl, fresh from a Hampshire vicarage? Douglas goes out of his way to testify in her behalf. She was "charming," "the most agreeable woman I've ever known in her position . . . worthy of any whatever," "clever and nice." Many readers accept these remarks at their face value; for them, the governess is a reliable recorder of the events at Bly, and *The Turn of the Screw* is therefore a ghost story. But to other readers the governess seems hysterical or even deranged; for them, the "ghosts" are merely the creations of her disturbed mind, and James's tale achieves horror by encompassing the abnormal rather than the supernatural.

Well, then, are the ghosts "real" or not? While editing *The Ghostly Tales of Henry James* (New Brunswick, N.J., 1948), Leon Edel implied that such a question was irrelevant—a "confusion" arising from failure to see that *The Turn of the Screw* has several levels of meaning which must not be scrambled. The "horrified little governess," said Edel, "has fantasies which may or may not be founded on reality." More recently, Joseph J. Firebaugh has advo-

[1] All quotations of the text of James's story are from the Modern Library ed. (New York, 1930).

cated "putting aside the question of whether the governess at Bly is subject to illusion"; he feels that "this much-argued point is no question at all." [2] Nevertheless, such ambiguity seems undesirable; for, granted that the story may have various levels of meaning, it would appear on the whole unwise to have them mutually contradictory. Recognizing this fact, Edel has taken a more definite stand. In *The Psychological Novel: 1900–1950* (New York, 1955) he stated: "The ghosts, of course, are there: they belong to the experience of the governess," for whom fantasy "seems to be reality." More recently, he has summarized his views: (1) "Henry James wrote a ghost story"; (2) the governess' story "contains serious contradictions and a purely speculative theory of her own as to the nature and purpose of the apparitions, which she alone sees"; (3) "anyone wishing to treat the governess as a psychological 'case' is offered sufficient data to permit the diagnosis that she is mentally disturbed." [3]

In other words, Edel accepts the ghosts as more than mere hallucinations; and he is therefore in essential agreement with the many critics who have asserted that the ghosts *are* real: Joseph Warren Beach, Carl Van Doren, F. O. Matthiessen, Kenneth Murdock, Elmer Stoll, Philip Rahv, Robert Heilman, Oliver Evans, Glenn Reed, Robert Liddell, Edward Wagenknecht, Mark Van Doren, Katherine Anne Porter, and Allen Tate. Critical opinion, however, has been far from unanimous. Some scholars continue to dissent both vigorously and persistently, and no serious study of *The Turn of the Screw* can afford to ignore their conclusions.

Although earlier critics had contented themselves with "reservations" concerning the validity of the governess' testimony, Henry A. Beers remarked in 1919 that he had sometimes thought "the woman who saw the phantoms was mad." Expanding this suggestion, Edna Kenton argued in 1924 that the whole sequence of events was merely a flight of the governess' disordered fancy. James himself had described *The Turn of the Screw* as "a piece of ingenuity pure and simple, of cold artistic calculation, an *amusette* to catch those not easily caught"; and so Miss Kenton interpreted the whole tale as a sort of hoax based on hallucination:

> the reader, persistently baffled, but persistently wondering, comes face to face at last with the little governess, and realizes, with a conscious thrill greater than that of merely automatic nerve shudders before

[2] "Inadequacy in Eden: Knowledge and 'The Turn of the Screw,'" *Modern Fiction Stud.,* III (Spring 1957), 57–63.

[3] Prefatory note to Harold C. Goddard, "A Pre-Freudian Reading of *The Turn of the Screw,*" *NCF,* XII (June 1957), 2.

"horror," that the guarding ghosts and children—what they are and what they do—are only exquisite dramatizations of her little personal mystery, figures for the ebb and flow of troubled thought within her mind, acting out her story.

Miss Kenton's theory attracted considerable attention, and in 1934 Edmund Wilson invoked Freudian psychology to develop it further. According to Wilson, *The Turn of the Screw* should be read as "a neurotic case of sex repression," in which "the ghosts are not real ghosts but the hallucinations of the governess." Accordingly, toy boats and towers become phallic symbols, and the story is primarily a characterization of a woman in love with her employer: "her somber and guilty visions and the way she behaves about them seem to present . . . an accurate and distressing picture of the poor country parson's daughter, with her English middle-class class-consciousness, her inability to admit to herself her natural sexual impulses." Wilson's essay, as might be expected, proved highly controversial. Critics pointed out a passage in James's notebooks, published after Wilson's essay was already in print, which seemed to indicate that *The Turn of the Screw* was intended as a ghost story; they argued that Wilson had ignored certain incidents in the narrative which his theory could not explain adequately; they pointed out that Freud had not yet evolved his theory of dream symbolism when James composed his tale. Indeed, the bombardment was so heavy that in 1948 Wilson beat a strategic retreat. It had become quite clear to him, he said, "that James's conscious intention, in *The Turn of the Screw*, was to write a *bona fide* ghost story." Nevertheless, he did indulge in a little rear-guard skirmishing, implying that James's conscious and subconscious intentions were quite different: "One is led to conclude that, in *The Turn of the Screw*, not merely is the governess self-deceived, but that James is self-deceived about her." At best, however, this was but a delaying action. It was generally agreed that Wilson had surrendered, and in 1952 Edward Wagenknecht felt able to dismiss the whole matter in a footnote. The theory that the ghosts were "creatures of the governess's sex-starved imagination" had, he said, "about as much critical standing as the aberrations of the Baconians."

Nevertheless, several new Freudian interpretations of James's story have been published recently. Perhaps the most provocative is Oscar Cargill's "Henry James as a Freudian Pioneer." [4] According to Cargill, the governess' experiences are based upon the case history of "Miss Lucy R." in Freud's *Studien über Hysterie;* but James

[4] *Chicago Rev.*, X (Summer 1956), 13–29.

was deliberately ambiguous in order to shield the memory of his sister Alice, herself the victim of severe recurrent hysteria.

Miss Lucy R. was an English governess. One of Freud's patients, she suffered from complete loss of smell but was subject to olfactory hallucinations, especially the imaginary odor of burnt pudding. Freud decided that these were "chronic hysterical symptoms"; and, having learned that she had actually burned a pudding two months previously, he attempted to discover some traumatic experience which the smell would symbolize in memory. After extended questioning, Miss Lucy reluctantly admitted that she had been in love with her widowed employer but had finally concluded that he had no romantic interest in her. Soon after this confession the imaginary smell of pudding was replaced by a new hallucination—the odor of cigar smoke; and Freud realized that he had not yet uncovered the cause of her trauma. Finally, at his insistence she remembered that her employer had become angry at a guest who had tried to kiss the children goodbye; and since the guest had been smoking, the smell of cigar smoke had stuck in Miss Lucy's memory. Moreover, under Freud's prodding, she remembered a similar incident—a departing lady guest had kissed the children, and the infuriated employer had threatened to discharge Miss Lucy if it happened again. This outburst crushed her hopes, for she realized that he would not have made such threats over a trivial matter if he had loved her. According to Freud, the traumatic moment had been that of her employer's outburst. Its effects were not immediately apparent; but after the first reinforcing "auxiliary moment" involving the male guest, conversion took place, producing the cigar-smoke hallucination. A second auxiliary moment masked the first symptom of cigar smoke with that of burnt pudding "so that the first was not clearly perceived until the second had been cleared out of the way." Eventually, after nine weeks of treatment, Freud was able to cure his patient completely.

Such, in essence, is the case of Miss Lucy R., which Cargill has linked closely with *The Turn of the Screw.* In fact, he asserts that Freud's account exhibits "as many resemblances as are ever found in a literary source." Among the parallels which he cites are the following: each story presents the case history of a governess who takes care of two orphaned children, feels an "unusual sense of commission and trust," and is in love with her employer; Peter Quint and Miss Jessel "may be seen as trying to possess little Miles and Flora in their protectress' fancy as did the kissing male and female visitors"; each case history includes a stolen or appropriated letter; James's governess has an unusually keen sense of smell, whereas

Miss Lucy suffers from complete loss of smell coupled with vivid olfactory hallucinations; and "by telling her story to as sympathetic a listener as Douglas," the governess may have undergone "the kind of pathological purgation, as did Lucy R., which led to health and sanity."

Although Cargill's theory sounds plausible, it contains serious weaknesses. In the first place, he has overlooked certain differences between James's tale and Freud's case history. James's governess saw her employer only twice and knew he had no romantic interest in her; Miss Lucy saw her employer daily and allowed herself to hope that he loved her. James's governess believed the ghosts were corrupting Miles and Flora; but it was the employer, not Miss Lucy, who felt the guests might harm the children by kissing them. Finally, James's governess was an inexperienced girl trying to protect her charges, while Miss Lucy was a mature woman primarily concerned with her own welfare. Although not decisive, these differences at least indicate that the two narratives are not parallel in every respect.

There is also a more serious objection to Cargill's theory. If we assume that James had read Freud's *Studien über Hysterie,* we must also assume that he understood what he read. Miss Lucy R. was the victim of conversion hysteria; and Freud believed in 1895 that this neurosis developed, in a person predisposed to the condition, when a painful memory or idea was repressed into the subconscious. There it would take "its revenge . . . by becoming pathogenic," producing constant irritation like a thorn in the flesh; and this revenge might result in various hysterical phenomena, including hallucination. Freud stressed, in other words, two conditions necessary to the development of conversion hysteria: first, a memory too painful to be retained in the consciousness; second, an actual traumatic moment, "at which the incompatibility forces itself upon the ego and at which the latter decides upon the repudiation of the incompatible idea" by repressing it into the subconscious. These conditions are, of course, met in the case of Lucy R.; but in *The Turn of the Screw* there is neither a repressed incompatible idea nor a traumatic moment. James's governess had no painful memory of her employer; to the contrary, she thought him charming. Moreover, she made no attempt to repress her infatuation but poured out her feelings freely to Mrs. Grose. Finally, she thoroughly enjoyed her life at Bly until her encounters with Peter Quint and Miss Jessel. Lest it be thought that these encounters might qualify as traumatic moments, let us remember that traumatic moments must *precede* any related hallucinations; the latter are symptoms or effects—they cannot be their own causes. Since Freud explained his theory clearly and fully, it seems unlikely that James would compose a study of hysteria in which none of the basic requirements for hysteria are present. Therefore, despite certain resemblances, the accounts of Lucy R. and James's governess are not really parallel; and Cargill's theory seems to be untenable.

Apparently, then, there is no close bond between *The Turn of the Screw* and Freud's history of Lucy R. That fact, however, does not in itself prove James's tale a ghost story, and it is still necessary to determine the governess' reliability as a narrator of the events at Bly. Several recent articles specifically seek to discredit her testimony. Such an attempt is made by John Silver in "A Note on the Freudian Reading of 'The Turn of the Screw.' "[5] In particular, Silver tries to demolish the two chief objections to the hallucination theory: that the governess gives a detailed description of Peter Quint, and that she has never previously heard of him. First, he cites the governess' remark concerning the stranger on the tower—how she had "made sure" he was "nobody from the village." Silver considers this evidence that she has been asking questions in the village, and thereby presumably learning about Quint. Actually, it probably means that she has been making inquiries among the other servants at Bly. And, incidentally, if one wishes to assume that the governess has learned about Quint prior to supposedly seeing him on the tower, why send her on a trip to the village? She could learn the necessary details from the other servants at Bly. Second, Silver considers it significant that the governess can discuss Quint's death although we never witness Mrs. Grose supplying her with these facts; he feels James would not "suppress" a scene of such importance. But that is absurd—Mrs. Grose undoubtedly held many "off-stage" talks with the governess, and Quint's death may well have been discussed during the conversation mentioned at the beginning of Chapter vi. Moreover, although Silver suggests that Mrs. Grose might not have known the facts of Quint's death, such ignorance is almost inconceivable under the circumstances. Therefore, we can only conclude that he has neither proven his case against the governess nor demonstrated that the ghosts are unreal.

Another attempt to prove the governess unreliable is contained in Harold Goddard's posthumous article (n. 3, above). Written "about 1920 or before," this study is important as the earliest known presentation of the hallucination theory. On the other hand, it is seriously weakened by a tendency to stack the cards against the governess. Some of the evidence is merely irrelevant: for example,

[5] *American Lit.*, XXIX (May 1957), 207–211.

the author has cited his own boyhood experiences with an insane servant who believed that ghosts "came to visit her at night." More serious are the distortions and strained interpretations of James's story: for example, in order to show a "hereditary seed" of mental disease, Goddard describes the governess' father as "psychically unbalanced" and possibly "even . . . insane," whereas James merely calls him "eccentric." It would be possible to point out many similar distortions; but there is one which is more serious than the rest: Goddard's attempt to discount the governess' description of Quint. He begins with a false analogy:

Suppose a missing criminal is described as follows: "A squat, ruddy-cheeked man about thirty years old, weighing nearly two hundred pounds; thick lips and pockmarked face; one front tooth missing, two others with heavy gold fillings; big scar above left cheek bone. Wears shell glasses; had on, when last seen, brown suit, gray hat, pink shirt and tan shoes. Then suppose a man, flushed with excitement, were to rush into police headquarters exclaiming that he had found the murderer. "How do you know?" the chief detective asks. "Why! I saw a man about thirty years old with shell glasses and tan shoes!" (p. 15)

This is obviously not comparable with the governess' account of the mysterious intruder. Goddard himself admits that his analogy is "a slight exaggeration," but it is more than that. The governess is able to describe Quint's height, carriage, general appearance, complexion, hair, whiskers, eyebrows, eyes, mouth and lips, and clothing. Perhaps the best proof that her description is adequate lies in Mrs. Grose's ability to identify Quint. Goddard considers it significant that Mrs. Grose hesitates before doing so; but inasmuch as Quint is dead, that is hardlly surprising. He also asks why the governess should stress "the least characteristic points in the description"—namely, that the man was bareheaded and dressed in borrowed clothing. Yet, if the governess had a normal amount of feminine "clothes sense" it would be quite natural for her to detect a lack of harmony between the intruder's apparel and his general personality; and she would consider his being bareheaded worthy of mention since men of that period customarily wore hats while outdoors. At any rate, both of these details are meaningful, for Mrs. Grose announces that Quint "never" wore his hat but did appropriate his master's waistcoats. Goddard suggests that Mrs. Grose seizes upon these two details and "pays scant attention" to the rest. But does he mean to imply that Quint does *not* have curly red hair and all the other characteristics ascribed to him? Surely the reader must assume that the governess' description is substantially correct, and is accepted as such by Mrs. Grose. Goddard's logic seems rather strained, and he must have been aware of that fact; for he has shifted the grounds of his argument from his original position to one that is more easily defensible. At the beginning of his article, he specifically calls the governess "insane" and the ghosts "hallucinations"; before he concludes, he concedes that the specters may actually exist: "Perhaps they do and perhaps they don't." Indeed, he adds that nothing in the tale "absolutely demands" or "absolutely contradicts" the theory that the ghosts are real. All this, he says, is "incidental"; the crucial point is that the children are uncorrupted —"incarnations of loveliness and charm." But this is not his original position; and one can only conclude that he has beat a strategic retreat.

It would seem, then, that a Freudian reading of *The Turn of the Screw* is not justified, and that its advocates are inclined to present only those facts which support their thesis, ignoring any which conflict with it. Some Freudians influenced by the New Criticism even argue that one should use his "utmost ingenuity" in interpreting the story to suit himself. This is hardly objective analysis. But if it *is* permissible to expend unbridled ingenuity upon a set of carefully selected facts, why are Freudian critics content to depict the governess as hysterical? Using their present methods, one could "prove" that she is afflicted with pedophilia erotica and is therefore attempting to seduce little Miles.

Actually, there is an impressive amount of evidence to reinforce this interpretation—provided, of course, that it is considered *out of context*. The governess obviously prefers Miles to Flora; in fact, she admits that she "throws" herself upon him. Driven by the hope of "possessing" him, she is constantly kissing him, folding him in her arms, or hugging him tightly "to . . . [her] breast." She encourages him to address her as "my dear" and tells him that she is remaining at Bly primarily for the pleasure of "his company." She admits that his "secret precocity" makes him seem like an adult—"as accessible as an older person"—and she persuades Mrs. Grose to take Flora away so that she will be left alone with the boy. Having succeeded in this design, the governess reflects that she and Miles resemble a shy "young couple . . . on their wedding-journey"; and she asks him if he does not recall the night when she sat on his bed and told him that "there was nothing in the world" she would not do for him. To the reader she confesses that Miles had been for her "a revelation of the possibilities of beautiful intercourse"—a phrase loaded with Freudian ambiguity.

Does it seem unlikely that the governess could be sexually aroused by a boy ten years younger than herself? Let us not forget that eight years after the tragic events at Bly she manages to make Douglas fall in love with her; and is it mere coincidence that he, too, is ten years her junior? Also, since Goddard has cited the insane servant woman from his own childhood while attempting to establish the governess' insanity, perhaps it would be permissible to mention other examples of pedophilia erotica. There is, for instance, the governess named "Miss Lilian" who seduced young Kirk Allen in Robert Lindner's case history, "The Jet-Propelled Couch." Or, if that comparison seems too remote, there is the "pious" Scottish girl mentioned by Leslie A. Marchand in *Byron: A Biography*—a young woman employed in the Byron household who used to "come to bed" to Byron when he was only nine years old and "play tricks with his person." This last example is especially interesting, since the James notebooks suggest that Henry James was familiar with it. He had waded through the "masses of ancient indecency" in the Byron papers—in 1895, only a few months before writing *The Turn of the Screw.*

The above evidence is as solid as much of the data presented by Wilson, Cargill, Silver, and Goddard. Yet it does not constitute unassailable proof; rather, it demonstrates the shortcomings of excessive ingenuity. The odds are astronomical that James was *not* writing a tale of sexual abnormality. What, then, was he attempting to do? Goddard has asserted that James's conscious intention is unimportant: "it is always the work itself and not the author that is the ultimate authority." Nevertheless, before we examine the tale, it is interesting to note James's own comments. According to him, the story is a "bogey-tale," a "little firm fantasy," a "fantastic fiction," a "fairy-tale pure and simple," and a work "grossly and merely apparitional." In 1898 he informed Arthur C. Benson that the source of *The Turn of the Screw* was a "small and gruesome spectral story" about children and dead servants which had been related to him by Benson's father, the Archbishop of Canterbury. Moreover, three years earlier James had recorded this spectral story in his notebook: After corrupting the young children entrusted to their care, wicked servants had died. Their ghosts had then returned to haunt the house and the children, whom they attempted to destroy. "So long as the children are kept from them, they are not lost; but they try and try, these evil presences, to get hold of them. It is a question of the children 'coming over to where they are.' It is all obscure and imperfect, the picture, the story, but there is a suggestion of strangely gruesome effect in it. The story to be told—tolerably obviously—by an outside spectator, observer." [6]

[6] *The Notebooks of Henry James,* ed. F. O. Matthiessen and Kenneth B. Murdock (New York, 1947), pp. 178–179.

Ordinarily, such a statement would be looked upon as decisive evidence of James's intentions. Moreover, he explained to Frederick W. H. Meyers, one of the most active members of the Society for Psychical Research, that his whole intention had been to "give the impression of the communication to the children of the most infernal imaginable evil and danger." Why, then, does anyone hesitate to accept James's story as a tale of the supernatural? Among the most important reasons for this reluctance must surely be the ambiguous remarks which he included in his preface to the New York edition. He spoke of "our young woman's keeping crystalline her record of so many intense anomalies and obscurities—by which I don't of course mean her explanation of them, a different matter"; he described the tale as "a piece of ingenuity pure and simple, of cold artistic calculation, an *amusette* to catch those not easily caught."[7] Some critics have viewed these statements as a veiled confession that *The Turn of the Screw* is a "trick" designed to make the reader mistake hallucinations for hobgoblins. But such a view is an obvious misinterpretation of James's remarks. James was attempting to tell a story which would be the ultimate in "general uncanny ugliness and horror and pain." Knowing the dullness of most modern psychical investigation—prosaic, authenticated tabulations of knocks and raps and levitated tables—he was determined that his ghosts would not be in the tradition of contemporary psychical phenomena; instead, they would be "goblins, elves, imps, demons . . . [or] fairies of the legendary order, wooing their victims forth" (*Art of the Novel,* p. 175). In other words, they were to be the traditional haunters of the dark. But James was also aware that it is easier to promise an ultimate than to deliver it, for a reader's expectations are likely to exceed the author's powers of invention. James's solution was to create an atmosphere of evil, a tone of "suspected and felt trouble," but to allow each reader to imagine the details for himself. Through a process of adumbration he would create a mood of portentous evil, and the reader would do the rest: "Only make the reader's general vision of evil intense enough, I said to myself . . . and his own experience, his own imagination, his own sympathy (with the children) and horror (of their false friends) will supply him quite sufficiently with all the particulars. Make him *think* the evil, make him think it for himself, and you are released from weak specifications. This ingenuity I took pains . . . to apply" (ibid., p. 176). This, then, was the *amusette:* to terrify each reader with the fruits of his own imagination. And in this way James proposed to catch and hold the interest of sophisticated readers who

[7] "Preface to 'The Aspern Papers,'" *The Art of the Novel: Critical Prefaces by Henry James,* ed. Richard P. Blackmur (New York, 1934), pp. 172, 173.

would find ordinary ghost stories boring. His trap was set for "the jaded, the disillusioned, the fastidious."

An examination of *The Turn of the Screw* reinforces this view of James's intentions. By allowing the little governess to relate her own experiences, James gives the tale added interest. For the first-person point of view contributes more than the vividness of an eye-witness report: in addition, it produces suspense. As she gradually pieces together the sinister facts, the governess is increasingly horrified by what they suggest; also, she realizes in despair that she cannot be in two places at once—with the result that one of her little charges can serve as decoy while the other slips off to some infernal rendezvous: " 'The trick's played,' I went on; 'they've successfully worked their little plan. He found the most divine little way to keep me quiet while she went off.' " Unlike the third-person omniscient narrator who knows exactly what is happening and is therefore obligated to furnish "specifications," the governess can only guess and hope and fear. The children are inscrutable, and Peter Quint and Miss Jessel appear and disappear without warning. Moreover, the absence of the ghosts is even more disturbing than their intermittent materializations; for they are apparently still at work undetected, weaving their subtle web around Miles and Flora. Thus the story is fundamentally a study in tone—"the tone of suspected and felt trouble . . . of tragic, yet of exquisite, mystification." This, then, is the "turn of the screw"—the agonizing and steadily increasing pressure of uncertainty, helplessness, and terror.

In most stories, first-person point of view also produces a sense of credibility; after all, an eye-witness account of an incident is usually the most authentic report possible. In *The Turn of the Screw* that customary effect is not produced automatically; it is first necessary to establish the reliability of the governess' observations. Of course, the Freudian critics would insist that we cannot trust her version of the events at Bly. Since they consider her a victim of hallucinations, a pathological liar, or both, it is only natural that they should view her unsympathetically. But two scholars have recently published studies which concede the existence of the ghosts, and it is interesting to note that they are as unsympathetic as the Freudians.

As we have already seen, Joseph Firebaugh is not really interested in whether or not the ghosts are real. His article, "Inadequacy in Eden: Knowledge and 'The Turn of the Screw' " (n. 2, above), is an allegorical interpretation of James's story; and he feels that "denial of knowledge" is the major theme. The "delightful" children represent the human race. Peter Quint and Miss Jessel perform the function of the serpent. The uncle symbolizes the "irresponsible" deity of the Old Testament. And the governess is his "inadequate priestess"—a personification of incompetent authority, an ignorant person who fears knowledge, an "agent of denial." Believing that knowledge is sin, she struggles to preserve the children's innocence but eventually destroys them by imposing original sin upon them. Firebaugh's main point is somewhat obscured by his contention that there is a hint of "boyish homosexuality" in Miles's misdeeds at school, but that this is "highly useful knowledge in the world as it is unfortunately constituted." Nevertheless, it is quite clear that he has no sympathy for the governess, or for her effort to stand "between the would-be knower and the knowledge he seeks." The kindest thing he can say about her is that she may be a "good" person who, through ignorance, does evil "in the name of good." In other words, he accepts the ghosts as symbols, but he rejects the governess' interpretation of every incident in the story. As the very embodiment of ignorance, she cannot give reliable testimony.

John Lydenberg has reached a similar conclusion in "The Governess Turns the Screws." [8] Clearly recognizing that James did not intend his story to deal with "the hallucinations of a frustrated, sex-starved governess," Lydenberg accepts the ghosts as real. Yet he finds the question of their reality "a thorny one"; for he wishes to show that the "two children, potentially angelic but human like all of us, [are] harried to distraction and death by an overprotective governess." Certainly, he paints a most unflattering portrait of her. She is hysterical, compulsive, overly possessive, tense, excitable, nervous, lacking in wisdom, and prone to make faulty judgments. A Puritan, she appears an "almost classic case" of the authoritarian character, alternately masochistic and sadistic. The "sin of pride" leads her to take upon herself, unaided, the task of saving the children, who are mere "pawns which she must protect and can use, but for which she has no real concern"—she wishes to attract attention to herself through an "extraordinary flight of heroism," and the ghosts present her with a "magnificent chance." The apparitions satisfy a "deep-lying need" to "objectify her fears, to project her uncertainties onto something external." She even welcomes them, since her possession of the children is contingent upon the continued threat of supernatural evil; subconsciously "she wants the worst to come true." In other words, Lydenberg believes that what is happening to Miles and Flora "is, clearly and terribly, the governess herself." She "turns the screws of Puritan discipline and suspicion until the children fatally crack under the strain."

[8] *NCF,* XII (June 1957), 37–58.

At this point, however, a critical problem arises: "Once grant that the evil spirits have really returned to haunt the children and it would be preposterous to ask the governess to remain calm, collected, and normal; instead her heroic self-dedication should be deemed wholly admirable and proper." Having admitted the existence of the ghosts, but not wishing to view the governess as "admirable," Lydenberg attempts to minimize the importance of Quint and Miss Jessel. First, he asserts that their reality is "somehow symbolic"—that they do not represent "pure evil" and are symbolic "not so much [of] some particular evil attacking the children as [of] a more generalized evil that is part of man, of the governess as well as the children." Second, although conceding that the governess does see Quint atop the tower, he feels that subsequent confrontations are increasingly ambiguous, and that we feel "more and more that Quint and Jessel are creatures haunting her, desired by her, almost controlled by her." Third, he criticizes the governess for continuing to "exacerbate" the evil, for making "active, effective, dominant what might have remained quiescent." Finally, he suggests that her influence is more injurious than that of the ghosts: "We don't really know or feel what Quint and Jessel are doing to Miles and Flora. But we know and feel that the governess is hounding them." To Lydenberg *The Turn of the Screw* is a story "in which a hysterical woman turns a quiet summer into a fall of dark hatred and tragedy."

As Lydenberg points out, James has made the governess "a character with eminently discussable characteristics." Furthermore, although they disagree concerning some of the particulars, Cargill, Silver, Goddard, Firebaugh, and Lydenberg are all firmly united in the conviction that she is an unreliable recorder of the events at Bly. Yet such was not James's intention. He himself referred to her "particular credible statement of such strange matters" and said she had "authority." Indeed, he explained to H. G. Wells that he had deliberately kept her an "impersonal" observer save for "the most obvious and indispensable little note of neatness, firmness and courage"—he had attempted to "rule out subjective complications of her own."

But despite these avowed intentions, James was too interested in subtle shades of character to keep the governess impersonal. In addition to the neatness, firmness, and courage, he endowed her with many other qualities. Some of them are admirable: the governess possesses a keen intelligence, remarkable devotion to duty, and another characteristic which can only be described as acute sensibility—a highly developed trait of awareness of discernment that is in marked contrast to the stolidity of Mrs. Grose. On the other hand, her personality is certainly not free from undesirable traits. She is often impulsive—for example, in her decision not to investigate Miles's expulsion from school. She tends to employ hyperbole rather than exact language ("What *is* he? He's a horror.") She is nervous, sometimes fearful for her own sanity, and given to unusual mannerisms ("I had to smother a kind of howl") and eccentric flights of fancy ("we continued . . . as silent . . . as some young couple on their wedding-journey"). She has odd "scruples" against mentioning the ghosts in the presence of the children; and her verbal fencing, her circling around "forbidden ground," and her preoccupation with "instinctive delicacy" strike the reader as peculiar—as does the fact that Miles's evasions and subterfuges seem "charming" and shake her "with admiration." She occasionally displays a tendency toward self-dramatization that is half egotism and half irony ("I was wonderful"; "I confess I rather applaud myself as I look back"). She is quick to give up Flora as lost, abandoning her as "hideously hard" and a "vulgar, pert little girl" at the very time when the child presumably needs help most; and she expresses her anger rather vulgarly ("Ah, she's 'respectable,' the chit!"). Also, it is not very charitable of her to say, "Oh, thank God!" when she learns of Flora's appalling language, or to feel alarm that Miles might be innocent ("for if he *were* innocent, what then on earth was *I*?").

Obviously, the governess falls short of perfection. But her recording of these flaws only makes her seem more honest. A pathological liar would have related the events at Bly much more smoothly and plausibly. Moreover, the governess need not have written the manuscript at all, or have shown it to Douglas. Silver asserts that she has written her apologia. If so, she has been remarkably unsuccessful in hiding her defects. Instead, she has displayed ironic detachment in giving a full account of her youthful shortcomings—her vanities, confusions, and terrors; and that ironic detachment is of considerable significance to any interpretation of the story. Looking back across the years from the vantage point of middle age, the governess has seen her former self as slightly ridiculous; and, far from portraying that former self as a magnificent heroine or as a savior, she has been consistently self-deprecatory. As the result of modesty, reticence, or some other scruple, she has perhaps failed to do herself justice. At any rate, she has presented her defects with unflinching candor. And while the resulting record clearly indicates human frailty, it does not reveal hysteria. As Lydenberg has said, if evil spirits *are* haunting the children, "it would be preposterous to ask the governess to remain calm, collected and normal."

The governess has, however, another trait which some readers find disturbing. She tends to jump to conclusions, and then to report her deductions as though she were stating facts rather than interpretations. For example, when Miss Jessel appears at the lake, the governess assumes on rather slender evidence that Flora is deliberately pretending not to see the apparition; and she later tells Mrs. Grose, "Flora *saw!*" Although some scholars feel that she is either lying or else speaking irrationally, her actual meaning is as follows: "It is my belief that Flora saw." We can be sure of her intention, for she informs the reader that she has "made it out to her [Mrs. Grose], made it out perhaps only now with full coherency even to myself." In other words, she has pondered the incident at the lake and then expressed her considered opinion. Unfortunately, she tends to employ overly emphatic, and overly dramatic, language; but this is a trait which is not uncommon among Jamesian characters—for instance, Lambert Strether and Maria Gostrey are sometimes equally dogmatic in *The Ambassadors* when speculating about Chad. Similarly, when the governess observes Miles on the lawn at night, staring at something which is "apparently" above her, she deduces that there is "clearly" a person on the tower; and she states the possibility as though it were a certainty. Yet the result is obvious exaggeration, not calculated deception—she is employing overstatement to achieve added emphasis. In other words, she *feels* quite strongly that there must be someone on the tower. Had she been a pathological liar, the governess would have flatly stated that she *saw* the ghost.

This same tendency can be observed after she catches sight of Miss Jessel in the schoolroom and later allows Mrs. Grose to believe that there has been an actual conversation. Of course, she does not flatly state that Miss Jessel has talked to her; rather, she says, "It came to that"—that is, the encounter has been *equivalent* to a conversation since Miss Jessel's facial expression has spoken volumes. But as might be expected, Mrs. Grose misunderstands the governess' remark—and so does Cargill, who confuses overstatement with deliberate falsehood. Yet the governess is truthfully relating her *impression* of the encounter. It is interesting to note that her earlier account of the incident contains the same conversation-equivalent which she mentions while talking with Mrs. Grose:

> She rose, not as if she had heard me, but with an indescribable grand melancholy of indifference and detachment, and, within a dozen feet of me, stood there as my vile predecessor. Dishonoured and tragic, she was all before me; but even as I fixed and, for memory, secured it, the awful image passed away. Dark as midnight in her black dress, her haggard beauty and her unutterable woe, *she had looked at me long enough to*

> *appear to say that her right to sit at my table was as good as mine to sit at hers* [my italics]. While these instants lasted indeed I had the extraordinary chill of a feeling that it was I who was the intruder. It was as a wild protest against it that, actually addressing her—"You terrible, miserable woman!"—I heard myself break into a sound that, by the open door, rang through the long passage and the empty house. She looked at me as if she had heard me, but I had recovered myself and cleared the air. There was nothing in the room the next minute but the sunshine and a sense that I must stay (pp. 89–90).

When the governess later mentions the above scene to Mrs. Grose, the latter asks, "Do you mean she spoke?" And the governess replies, "It came to that," by which she means, "It amounted to that." Where is the deception? At most, the governess can be charged only with ambiguity. It is true that she often presents interpretations rather than raw facts. As Edel has pointed out, James made many changes in the text of *The Turn of the Screw* while preparing it for the New York edition; and the net result was "to put the story into the realm of the governess's feelings. Where he had her say originally 'I saw' or 'I believed' he often substituted 'I felt.'" But when the governess says "I felt," she clearly labels the ensuing statement as a personal impression; neither a pathological liar nor a hysterical victim of hallucination would make such a distinction.

It would seem, then, that the governess' testimony is generally reliable. When she says that she saw Peter Quint and Miss Jessel, or that she felt a gust of icy air in a sealed room, there is no reason to suppose her hysterical. Certainly the fact that Mrs. Grose is consistently unable to see the specters does not prove them unreal; rather, it indicates that the governess somehow possesses a psychic power that the stolid housekeeper lacks. This convention, incidentally, is quite common in tales dealing with the supernatural: only Macbeth can see Banquo's ghost, only Jack Pansay can see Mrs. Keith-Wessington in Kipling's "The Phantom 'Rickshaw," and only Topper can see the madcap Kirbies in Thorne Smith's comic fantasies. Moreover, there are many incidents in James's story which cannot be dismissed as subjective sensory impressions. Of these, three are especially significant.

First, after her initial encounter with Peter Quint the governess is able to describe his appearance in such minute detail that Mrs. Grose identifies him immediately. Cargill assumes that the governess has previously acquired the necessary information from Flora, but the governess states specifically that the children have not mentioned Quint. Silver suggests that she has been asking questions in the village; but, as we have seen, there is no real evidence to support this hypothesis. Therefore, the governess' description of Quint seems proof that she has actually seen his ghost.

Second, although Mrs. Grose is consistently unable to see the spirits, she becomes convinced of their corrupting power after little Flora's outburst: "From that child—horrors! . . . On my honour, Miss, she says things——!" Furthermore, they are "shocking" things, "beyond everything, for a young lady," and they convince Mrs. Grose that the ghosts are real. "I believe," she states flatly. Goddard has tried to discount this bit of evidence by comparing Flora's appalling language with the "innocent profanity" of Hareton Earnshaw in *Wuthering Heights,* but the two cases are not parallel. For Hareton openly and frequently uses the shocking language he has heard, while Flora cleverly sustains the illusion of angelic innocence throughout most of the story.

Third, although the governess is careful never to mention Peter Quint to the children, Miles is at last goaded into a "surrender" of his name. It is true, of course, that the governess has accused Flora of meeting Miss Jessel at the lake. But the children have been kept apart, except for one breakfast under the watchful eye of Mrs. Grose; and it is therefore unlikely that there would have been any talk of Miss Jessel. But even if Miles somehow knew about the scene at the lake, an innocent child would not necessarily sense the connection between Miss Jessel and Peter Quint. Moreover, during the last scene of the story, the governess gives no hint that the "white face of damnation" outside the window belongs to Quint. She carefully refers to the ghost as "it" and "coward horror"; it is Miles who asks, "It's *he?*" "Whom do you mean by 'he'?" demands the governess. And Miles, frustrated and enraged, hurls back at her the fateful name "Peter Quint—you devil!"

These three incidents prove that the ghosts are real; for there is no other way satisfactorily to explain the governess' knowledge of Quint's appearance, Flora's shocking language, or Miles's final "surrender of the name." Or, more accurately, there is but one other way—to assume that the governess is a pathological liar offering deliberately falsified evidence. Cargill does make that assumption. To him, the reader is the victim of "palpable deception, the trick of a demonstrable pathological liar, a pitiful but dangerous person, with an unhinged fancy." But if the governess were indeed a liar, her "authority" would be gone; and the reader would be obliged to disbelieve the tale *in toto.* For in any story employing the first-person point of view, the narrator must, on the whole, be trustworthy. Of course, the narrator need not be infallible. He may be immature like Huck Finn, mentally defective like William Faulkner's Benjy, inclined toward obvious exaggeration like Mark Twain in *Roughing It,* or somewhat muddleheaded like Conan Doyle's Dr. Watson. Indeed, like Dr. Sheppard in Agatha Christie's *The Murder of Roger Ackroyd,* he may even deliberately withhold information from the reader—provided that fact is eventually revealed. But he may not deceive the reader *permanently;* for the basic convention of first-person fiction is necessarily a confidence in the narrator. Otherwise, how would we know whether Huck Finn really drifted down the Mississippi on a raft? After all, we have only the word of that inveterate liar himself. And how could we be sure that Captain Ahab really pursued his white whale around the globe? For if we do not accept the authority of Ishmael, there is always the possibility that *Moby Dick* is merely a wild sea story—a hoax played upon gullible landlubber readers. Or, to cite *The Turn of the Screw* itself, how can we be positive that Douglas is not the liar, forging a manuscript to entertain his little circle of friends? Indeed, what assurance have we that the "I" narrator at the beginning of the story is not deceiving the reader by fabricating both the tale of an imaginary governess and also the opening "frame" device, with its storytellers around a Christmas fire in an old house? Once an erosion of authority begins, who can say where it must stop?

Therefore, unless James has violated the basic rules of his craft, the governess cannot be a pathological liar. To the contrary, he has gone to great pains to give her authority, and there is no reason to consider her less reliable than Huck or Ishmael. As James commented later, "To knead the subject of my young friend's, the suppositious narrator's, mystification thick, and yet strain the expression of it so clear and fine that beauty would result: no side of the matter so revives for me as that endeavour."

It would seem, then, that the conventional interpretation of *The Turn of the Screw* is probably correct. The evil spirits do appear; the children are corrupted; and the governess does struggle to save them. Unless we accept the story as a fantasy, Miles's death is absurd—in real life, children do not drop dead merely because someone insists a ghost is peering in the window. Clearly, James did not intend to portray the governess as a sex-starved spinster, a hysterical personality subject to hallucinations, a deliberate liar, or an embodiment of ignorance and repression; on the other hand, he did not mean her to stand as a "Christ-symbol," a "Good Angel," or a paragon of all the virtues. Rather, she is a little Hampshire parson's daughter—inexperienced, bewildered, frightened—who battles the powers of darkness. Superficially, hers may seem a Pyrrhic victory. "Salvation by such as the governess doesn't save," says

Lydenberg. Nevertheless, according to the conventions of the classical ghost story, she *does* save the children. For she is engaged in immortal—rather than mortal—combat; and the prize is nothing less than the souls of her young pupils. Before she makes her appearance, the ghosts are comfortably entrenched, casting their evil spell unhindered. By the end of the story, Flora has been removed from the corrupting atmosphere of Bly; and, although Miles is dead, his heart has been "dispossessed." Granted, the governess is not perfect; but her all-too-human frailty should not blind the reader to her great accomplishment. Standing resolutely at her own little Armageddon, she has routed the forces of evil.

Bibliography

The interested reader will find more or less complete bibliographical references to Henry James in the following works:

PHILLIPS, LEROY. *A Bibliography of the Writings of Henry James.* Revised Edition. New York: Coward-McCann, 1930.

RICHARDSON, LYON N. *Henry James: Representative Selections.* New York: American Book Company, 1941.

SPILLER, ROBERT E., *et. al. Literary History of the United States.* New York: The Macmillan Company, 1948. III, 584–590.

BEEBE, MAURICE, AND WILLIAM T. STAFFORD. "Criticism of Henry James: A Selected Checklist with an Index to Studies of Separate Works." *Modern Fiction Studies,* Henry James Special Number, III (Spring, 1957), 73–96.

EDEL, LEON, AND DAN H. LAURENCE. *A Bibliography of Henry James.* London: Rupert Davis, 1957.

The works listed on the following pages are highly and arbitrarily selective. They include only those items which are thought to be most readily available or most helpful to students desiring to further their acquaintance with Henry James. Works containing material on "The Turn of the Screw" are starred.

Secondary Sources

Articles

AUDEN, W. H. "Henry James and the Artist in America." *Harper's,* CXCVII (July, 1948), 36–40.

BEACH, JOSEPH WARREN. "The Witness of the Notebooks." *Forms of*

Modern Fiction. William Van O'Connor, ed. Minneapolis: University of Minnesota Press, 1948. Pp. 46–60.

BELL, MILLICENT. "A James 'Gift' to Edith Wharton." *Modern Language Notes,* LXXII (March, 1957), 182–185.

BERLAND, ALWYN. "Henry James." *University of Kansas City Review,* XVIII (Winter, 1950), 94–108.

BETHURUM, DOROTHY. "Morality and Henry James." *Sewanee Review,* XXXI (July, 1923), 324–330.

BEWLEY, MARIUS. "Henry James and 'Life.'" *Hudson Review,* (Spring, 1958), 167–185.

*COLLINS, CARVEL. "James's 'The Turn of the Screw.'" *Explicator,* XIII (June, 1955), item 48.

*EDEL, LEON. "Hugh Walpole and Henry James: The Fantasy of the Killer and the Slain." *American Imago,* VIII (December, 1951), 3–21.

———. "The Literary Convictions of Henry James." *Modern Fiction Studies,* III (Spring, 1957), 3–10.

GALE, ROBERT L. "A Note on Henry James's First Short Story." *Modern Language Notes,* LXXII (February, 1957), 103–107.

———. "Freudian Imagery in James's Fiction." *American Imago,* XI (Summer, 1954), 181–190.

*HEILMAN, ROBERT B. "The Freudian Reading of 'The Turn of the Screw.'" *Modern Language Notes,* LXIII (November, 1947), 433–445.

*LEVY, LEO B. "*The Turn of the Screw* as Retaliation." *College English,* XVII (February, 1956), 286–288.

LIND, ILSE D. "The Inadequate Vulgarity of Henry James." *PMLA,* LXVI (December, 1951), 886–910.

*MINER, EARL R. "Henry James's Metaphysical Romances." *Nineteenth-Century Fiction,* IX (June, 1954), 1–21.

ROSENZWEIG, SAUL. "The Ghost of Henry James: A Study in Thematic Apperception." *Partisan Review,* XI (Fall, 1944), 435–455.

*STOLL, E. E. "Symbolism in Coleridge." *PMLA,* LXIII (March, 1948), 229–233.

VIVAS, ELISEO. "Henry and William." *Kenyon Review,* V (Autumn, 1943), 580–594.

VOLPE, EDMUND L. "James's Theory of Sex in Fiction." *Nineteenth-Century Fiction,* XIII (January, 1958), 36–47.

*WOLFE, ROBERT. "The Genesis of 'The Turn of the Screw.'" *American Literature,* XIII (March, 1941), 1–8.

Books

ANDERSON, QUENTIN. *The American Henry James.* New Brunswick, N.J.: Rutgers University Press, 1957.

*BEACH, JOSEPH WARREN. *The Method of Henry James.* Revised edition. Philadelphia: Albert Saifer, 1954.

*BEWLEY, MARIUS. *The Complex Fate.* London: Chatto and Windus, 1952.

CREWS, FREDERICK C. *The Tragedy of Manners: Moral Drama in the Later Novels of Henry James.* New Haven: Yale University Press, 1957.

*DUPEE, F. W. *Henry James.* New York: William Sloane Associates, 1951.

———, ed. *The Question of Henry James.* New York: Henry Holt & Co., 1945.

EDEL, LEON. *Henry James: The Untried Years, 1843–1870.* New York: J. B. Lippincott & Co., 1953.

*———. *The Psychological Novel, 1900–1950.* New York: J. B. Lippincott & Co., 1955.

GRATTAN, C. HARTLEY. *The Three Jameses, A Family of Minds.* New York: Longmans, Green and Co., 1932.

HOFFMAN, FREDERICK J. *The Modern Novel in America.* Chicago: Henry Regnery Co., 1951.

LEARY, LEWIS. *Articles on American Literature.* Durham, N.C.: Duke University Press, 1954.

*LEVY, LEO B. *Versions of Melodrama: A Study of the Fiction and Drama of Henry James, 1865–1897.* Berkeley: University of California Press, 1957.

*LIDDELL, ROBERT. *A Treatise on the Novel.* London: Jonathan Cape, 1947.

MC CARTHY, HAROLD T. *Henry James: the Creative Process.* New York: Thomas Yoseloff, 1958.

MATTHIESSEN, F. O. *Henry James: the Major Phase.* New York: Oxford University Press, 1944.

———. *The James Family.* New York: Alfred A. Knopf, Inc., 1947.

NOWELL-SMITH, SIMON. *The Legend of the Master.* New York: Charles Scribner's Sons, 1948.

*WINTERS, YVOR. *In Defense of Reason.* Denver, Col.: University of Denver Press, 1947.

Primary Sources

(Works by Henry James)

NOTE: The best-known edition of Henry James's works is the New York Edition. Its full title is *The Novels and Tales of Henry James: New York Edition,* New York: Charles Scribner's Sons, 1907–1917; 26 vols. A later, and more complete, edition is *The Novels and Stories of Henry James: New and Complete Edition,* London: Macmillan, 1921–1923; 35 vols.

Listed below are works that are, for the most part, easily obtainable. Many of them are paper-bound editions.

The Ambassadors. New York: Anchor Books, 1958.
The American. New York: Rinehart Editions, 1955.
The American Novels and Stories of Henry James. New York: Alfred A. Knopf, Inc., 1947.
The Art of the Novel: Critical Prefaces by Henry James. R. P. Blackmur, ed. New York: Charles Scribner's Sons, 1934.
The Aspern Papers and *The Spoils of Poynton.* New York: Dell, 1959.
Autobiography of Henry James. F. W. Dupee, ed. New York: Criterion, 1956.
The Awkward Age. New York: Anchor Books, 1958.
Four Selected Novels of Henry James. New York: Universal Library, 1958.
**The Ghostly Tales of Henry James.* New Brunswick, N.J.: Rutgers University Press, 1948.
The Golden Bowl. New York: Evergreen Books, 1959.
**The Great Short Novels of Henry James.* New York: Dial Press, 1944.
In the Cage and Other Tales. New York: Anchor Books, 1958.
**The Letters of Henry James.* Percy Lubbock, ed. New York: Charles Scribner's Sons, 1920. 2 vols.
**The Notebooks of Henry James.* F. O. Matthiessen and Kenneth Murdock, eds. New York: Oxford University Press, 1947.
Parisian Sketches: Letters to the New York Tribune. Leon Edel and Ilse D. Lind, eds. New York: New York University Press, 1957.
The Portable Henry James. New York: Viking Press, 1951.
The Portrait of a Lady. Boston: Riverside Editions, 1956.
The Reverberator. New York: Evergreen Books, 1957.
The Sacred Fount. New York: Evergreen Books, 1955.
Selected Short Stories of Henry James. New York: Rinehart Editions, 1957.
Stories of Writers and Artists. New York: New Directions, 1944.
Washington Square and *The Europeans.* New York: Dell, 1959.
What Maisie Knew. New York: Anchor Books, 1954.
The Wings of the Dove. New York: Dell, 1958.

Exercises

I. Arrange the items in this book in proper bibliographical order.

II. The following exercise is designed to acquaint you with bibliographical problems encountered in original, as opposed to controlled, research. Your assignment is to work up a series of bibliography cards for one of the following topics. *The topics in exercise B have been included in order not to overload the facilities of your library.*

A. Henry James
1. Henry James's Early Education
2. Henry James and Edith Wharton
3. Henry James in England
4. The Literary Friendships of Henry James
5. Henry James as a Dramatist
6. Alice and Henry James
7. William and Henry James
8. The Nature of Henry James's Injury

B. Authors Other Than Henry James
1. Joseph Conrad's Career as a Seaman
2. Edgar Allan Poe's Marriage
3. Walt Whitman in the Civil War
4. Theodore Dreiser as a Magazine Editor
5. George Bernard Shaw, Dramatic Critic
6. Alexander Pope and His Enemies
7. John Dryden's Religious Conversion
8. Jonathan Swift's Attitude toward Women
9. Byron's Exile from England
10. D. H. Lawrence and the Social Conventions

11. John Keats and Fanny Brawne
12. Matthew Arnold in America
13. A. E. Housman as a Professor
14. Katherine Mansfield's Marriages
15. Percy Bysshe Shelley's Elopement
16. William Wordsworth and His Sister
17. Sir Francis Bacon in Parliament
18. Robert Browning's Courtship
19. William Butler Yeats and the Abbey Theatre
20. Herman Melville in the U.S. Navy
21. Shakespeare's Marriage
22. John Milton's Blindness
23. Andrew Marvell in Politics
24. Samuel T. Coleridge and Opium Addiction
25. Dr. Samuel Johnson's Social Life
26. Edmund Waller and Charles II
27. James Joyce, Irishman

Theme Topics

1. In a theme of approximately 500 words, write an analysis of one of the following characters in "The Turn of the Screw": Miles, Flora, or Mrs. Grose.

2. In a theme of approximately 400 words, state what you think is Douglas's interest in Bly.

3. Write a theme of approximately 500 words in which you explore the significance of the ghosts in "The Turn of the Screw."

4. In a theme of approximately 700 words, defend the interpretation of "The Turn of the Screw" that, in your opinion, is the most reasonable of those presented in this book.

5. In a theme of the same length, attack the interpretation that, in your opinion, is the least valid.

6. Write an original interpretation, length to be left to your discretion, of "The Turn of the Screw."

Long Research Paper Topics

1. Without taking sides, write a paper, length to be determined by your instructor, in which you summarize the various critical positions taken toward "The Turn of the Screw" in this book.

2. In a theme of approximately 2500 words, write a critical appraisal of "The Turn of the Screw." In your essay, you are to take a position based on your reading of the story, which you are to support

through references to the critical essays contained in this book. In order to take into account the arguments of the opposition, you may also (and this is good strategy) refer to the essays with which you disagree.

3. In a theme of approximately 2500 words, attack or support the Freudian interpretation of "The Turn of the Screw." You are to bring into your theme the various arguments set forth by the authors in this book. While your attack (or defense) may be original, your use of the authorities should help you to make your point.

4. Write a theme of approximately 2000 words in which you appraise the critical strengths and weaknesses of what you take to be the five most significant essays in this book. If you begin your theme with a strong thesis statement, you will be giving purpose and direction to your writing, and you will avoid the working up of a mere catalogue.